REVOLT
OF THE
HAVES

**TAX REBELLIONS
AND
HARD TIMES**

Robert Kuttner

SIMON AND SCHUSTER • NEW YORK

COPYRIGHT © 1980 BY ROBERT KUTTNER
ALL RIGHTS RESERVED
INCLUDING THE RIGHT OF REPRODUCTION
IN WHOLE OR IN PART IN ANY FORM
PUBLISHED BY SIMON AND SCHUSTER
A DIVISION OF GULF & WESTERN CORPORATION
SIMON & SCHUSTER BUILDING
ROCKEFELLER CENTER
1230 AVENUE OF THE AMERICAS
NEW YORK, NEW YORK 10020
SIMON AND SCHUSTER AND COLOPHON ARE TRADEMARKS OF SIMON &
SCHUSTER
DESIGNED BY EVE METZ

MANUFACTURED IN THE UNITED STATES OF AMERICA

1   2   3   4   5   6   7   8   9   10

LIBRARY OF CONGRESS CATALOGING IN PUBLICATION DATA

KUTTNER, ROBERT.
  REVOLT OF THE HAVES.

  INCLUDES BIBLIOGRAPHICAL REFERENCES.
  1. TAXATION—UNITED STATES.   2. LOCAL TAXATION—
UNITED STATES.   3. TAXATION, STATE.   4. REAL PROPERTY
TAX—CALIFORNIA.   I. TITLE.
HJ2381.K87   336.2'00973   80-36882
ISBN 0-671-25099-X

  The quotation on page 122 is from Diane Paul, *The Politics of the Property Tax*,
Lexington, Mass.: D. C. Heath, copyright 1975.
  The quotation on page 228 is from Henry J. Aaron, *Inflation and the Income
Tax*, Washington, D.C.: Brookings Institution, copyright 1976.

IN MEMORY OF MY FATHER

Preface

This is a book about the great taxpayer revolt of the late 1970s, a mass political event whose meaning is still widely debated. Was it an ideological sea-change? A cynical revolt of the rich against the poor? A populist spasm against bloated bureaucracy? A misplaced reaction to pocketbook frustrations? A protest against high taxes? Or all of these?

Whatever its origins, the national tax revolt sparked by California's Proposition 13 has assumed the status of political watershed, conveniently separating the New Deal–Great Society era from a newer, leaner period that finds the public far stingier with tax dollars and increasingly skeptical about government's basic competence to solve problems.

I have approached this topic as a reporter, by boning up on the subject and then getting out of the office to find the story. Despite its initial exaggeration by the press, the tax revolt is probably the biggest domestic story of the late seventies that occurred (mercifully) outside Washington. It was a thoroughly authentic, far-flung event that didn't happen quite the same way in any two places. I traveled, interviewed, and delved into cases a good deal more than I had intended.

The political significance of the tax revolt defies easy classification. It was not, as many commentators first concluded, a simple turning to the right by the electorate. Nor, despite my title, was it simply a crass revolt by the well-off against sharing their bounty with the poor. The most valid tax grievances, which fueled Proposition 13 and its imitations, resulted from excessive and often erratic tax burdens on Americans of quite mod-

erate means. Unfortunately, Proposition 13 and most of the other remedies gave the bulk of the tax relief to those who needed it least. The cuts
in public services (though mild so far) typically reduced programs that
serve the needy. And when far more ordinary conservatives than Howard
Jarvis seized the momentum of his tax protest to assure that the biggest
tax cuts went to the well-off, then the tax revolt truly became a revolt of
the haves.

Much of the commentary has painted the tax revolt as something far
simpler than it was. Reams of academic studies by economists and political scientists have viewed tax protest deterministically, as a direct reaction to the growth of government outlays. This line of inquiry misses the
fact that most of the growth of government came during the fifties and
sixties; it overlooks the shifting distribution of the tax load, and the
broader economic frustrations that fueled voter anger. It misses the rich
political dimension of the tax revolt.

By the same token, much of the *political* commentary and the polemical
literature has mistaken the tax revolt for an ideological shift. And this
view ignores the maddening tax inequities that were quite sufficient by
themselves to infuriate taxpayers who nonetheless still look to government to broker decisions, redress wrongs, and offer services.

I am convinced that voter anger in most states was directed against
unfair tax burdens first, general pocketbook frustrations second, and
"government" only a distant third. But the failure of many orthodox
liberals to take tax grievances seriously, and their reflexive concern with
defending the level of government outlays rather than their quality, drove
many working-class constituents into an odd alliance with right-wing populists of the Jarvis stripe and later with business conservatives.

I am also convinced that the tax revolt must be understood in the
particular. It was no accident that Proposition 13 broke out in California,
and that it was directed against the property tax, because California's
property tax had gone quite berserk. New York, with higher overall tax
levels, had no mass tax protest until the courts began tinkering with
assessments. And Idaho, with very low taxes, had a more extreme revolt
than California. In Massachusetts the first wave of tax revolt was articulated by the Left.

All these disparate events, puzzling and difficult to summarize, become
intelligible if one looks at the particulars—fiscal, economic, and political.
And the particulars turn out to be quite fascinating. For want of two votes
in the state senate, California liberals failed to pass a tax reform bill that
almost surely would have headed off Proposition 13. In several states, a

series of relatively esoteric court decisions caused property taxes to shift massively from business property onto homeowners. Where pocketbook grievances were addressed by legislatures, tax revolt fizzled.

Though a seemingly technical and forbidding topic, *Revolt of the Haves* has provided me the intellectual pleasure of unexpected discovery. Turning over innocent-looking rocks, one can view the teeming antique world of tax assessors, unchanged in its essentials from the last century; one encounters a remarkable tax abatement bar, made up of hundreds of high-priced attorneys who do nothing but contest property valuations; one stumbles onto a largely ignored shift in property tax burdens from commercial property onto homeowners, and a long, boisterous legacy of popular and scholarly protest against the property tax.

For a journalist wrestling with a fairly esoteric topic, the best surprise of all is that the tax revolt turns out to be a good story.

Taxation is a tricky, technical subject, but it isn't unduly complicated in the concrete. Tax protest has a wonderfully American amateur tradition, as old as the Boston Tea Party. For better than a century, ordinary people very much like Howard Jarvis, without formal expertise in public finance, have haunted county courthouses, bitching about unfair assessments, and generally raising hell. Whenever tax abuses boiled over, they attracted followers. The little people who rallied behind Jarvis in 1978 might not have grasped the finer points of incidence theory, but they surely understood that something in the tax system was giving them a good screwing. The result was a genuine political upheaval, in which an authentic popular grievance was badly fumbled by the mainstream politicians and carried by the Right, setting in motion ideological tides that have developed their own rhythm.

In more normal times, tax legislation remains politically marginal. Usually, it is the province of gray public finance administrators, the product of inside pulling and hauling between different levels of government; it rarely results in an equitable distribution of the tax load. It is the special domain of obscure corporate lobbies with disarmingly civic names like the American Council for Capital Formation, the California Taxpayers Association, or the Tax Foundation. These groups are part of the permanent landscape; they quietly exercise enormous legislative influence, year in and year out, to assure that taxes on the well-to-do are kept at about the same level as taxes on ordinary people, and to slow down public expenditures.

The corporate tax lobby was distinctly uncomfortable with the crude, unreined populism of a Howard Jarvis and his remarkably similar counterparts in other states: Jim Whittenburg, the leader of Oregon's tax revolt, a convicted bad-check artist; Idaho's Don Chance, a retired insurance-salesman; Bob Tisch, a rural Michigan drain commissioner; and Don Feder of Massachusetts, who contended that the only proper function of the State is to assure the public safety. These were not people whose counsel one sought for legislative strategy, or whom one invited to dinner.

In its early phase, the tax revolt at its core enlisted that class of people the French call Poujadiste: little people with a tenuous hold in the middle class, vulnerable to economic reverses from events beyond their control. They were the same people who made up much of the 1968 George Wallace constituency, and they were authentically mad as hell.

Movements like Jarvis' seldom display much staying power, and it is rare in America for economic grievances to be so acute or the political center so deaf that leadership is thrust upon consummate outsiders like Jarvis. Nor is the ballot initiative a good vehicle for lasting influence. It is a great way to get the legislature's attention, but a poor mechanism for refining tax law. Not surprisingly, the virulent and crudely populist phase of tax revolt in California burned itself out almost as soon as the property tax was cut down to tolerable size, leaving the field to the regulars.

Still, the melody lingers on. The inheritors of Jarvis' momentum, unfortunately, are mostly Fortune 500 corporations, nimble trade associations, and well-off investors—not the sort of people being driven from their very homes by property tax excesses. If anybody can afford to pay the bill for a decent society, they can. Yet business conservatives have effectively channeled the raucous popular energy of the tax revolt into an orderly drive for systematic limitations on the welfare state and reductions in taxes on the well-to-do. And popular frustration is still high.

One final thought: I believe that American society still has stubborn inequities that will not be cured by a reversion to market economics. There are still 25 million people officially classified as poor. The warmed-over free-market theories under the new label "supply-side economics" are oblivious to the lessons of the 1920s and 1930s and even more ignorant of how Western Europe manages to have a more humane political economy than our own, by marrying capitalist enterprise with democratic planning and effective public services.

But my tour of the tax revolt leaves me with the conviction that the era of steady government expansion in the United States is quite finished, and that may not be such a bad outcome. The numbing failure of bureaucratic programs to cure social ills is surely the dirty little secret of American liberals. The taxpayers are on to the secret, and the money is no longer there to squander. Today, you can't put together a majority coalition around the idea that inequities should be addressed by bigger and more costly federal programs. But neither will cutbacks in social programs solve the inequities of the tax system.

Despite the dose of opportunism in the tax revolt and the widespread desire to brake government expansion, there is still a reservoir of popular support in the United States for basic social justice, and remarkably little enthusiasm for repealing the New Deal. Political progressives have only to think up something better than more bureaucracy as a way to advance social progress.

If they do not, economic policy is likely to be left to the mercies of corporate trickle-down; the political center will continue to drift rightward; and government itself will be increasingly discredited—not just as a dispensary of largesse, but in its more ancient and fundamental role as democratic adjudicator.

Acknowledgments

Countless people contributed to *Revolt of the Haves,* by exchanging insights, granting unhurried interviews, and providing general encouragement.

The concept and the title were first suggested by Bill Alexander. John Brockman helped me refine the idea. The John F. Kennedy Institute of Politics at Harvard offered a timely fellowship, which afforded a year of reflection and study. Jonathan Moore, the Institute's Director, and his staff were generous with their time and provided every conceivable logistical support. Many in Boston's rich academic community helped me think through ideas. Professor Oliver Oldman of the Harvard Law School deserves special thanks for deepening my understanding of public finance and tax law, making both subjects quite fascinating. Ray Torto, Mayor Kevin White's tax advisor, helped explain Massachusetts fiscal rituals. Lester Thurow of M.I.T. provided a keen reality check within the economics profession. My fellow Institute Fellows, especially Ned Pattison, Evelyn Murphy, and Bruce Adams, provided intellectual camaraderie.

In my forays into California I relied heavily on Tom DeVries to help interpret that state's baffling political culture, and on Dean Tipps to initiate me to California's tax politics. From the tax reform side, Bob Brandon, Jonathan Rowe, Ira Arlook, Barry Margolin, and Bob McIntyre, among others, took time to share insights and sources. In the tax revolt camp, I had equally generous guides in Jim Davidson, Yvonne Chicione, Maureen Fitzgerald, Kirk West, Lew Uhler, and Harvey Englander.

Howard Jarvis greeted me at home in his pajamas for a lengthy and memorable interview. Danice Bordett helped unearth details of the Wolden trial.

Numerous friends offered enriching conversation as the book progressed, notably Lee Webb, Carol Greenwald, Michael Lipsky, Paul Starr, Ralph Whitehead, Ron Grzywinski, Frank Levy, Dave Smith, Ken McLean, and Bill Whiteside. Sam Sanchez, Richard Pomp, Helen Ladd, and Jim Wetzler were especially helpful as tax mentors.

David Kelston of the Harvard Law School assisted in documenting the tax shift, with the support of a summer research grant from the Youth Project. Margaret Doner efficiently typed the manuscript, changing typewriters and locations without complaint. My children graciously let their father work at home.

Several people at Simon and Schuster deserve special thanks: Alberta Harbutt, James Daly, and my editor, Alice Mayhew, who offered just the right measure of enthusiasm when I was close to vanishing into the fiscal mire. My constant editor and friend, Sharland Trotter Kuttner, deserves much of the credit if this prose has won the battle with its subject matter.

CONTENTS

INTRODUCTION

On June 6, 1978, California voters, by a margin of almost 2 to 1, ratified the Jarvis-Gann initiative, cutting property taxes by more than $6 billion. For a school system, a city government, a county, or a park district, the passage of Proposition 13 seemed to mean the loss of a quarter to a half of its total budget. But California voters were willing to take the chance that government would somehow soldier on; and government did. For these voters, the more pressing need was to keep the property tax from confiscating their homes.

The urgency and the desperation of the California tax revolt were virtually without modern parallel. As a purely economic protest, it recalled the mass movements of the Depression years, in which armies of the hungry descended on Washington demanding veterans' bonuses, or flocked to the banner of eccentric share-the-wealth populists like Francis Townsend or Huey Long. Yet Jarvis' legions were well fed, well off, mostly middle-class rebels.

Proposition 13 created instant shock-waves nationally. As much as any other event, it seemed to signal an abrupt end to the era that had begun in 1933, in which the voters looked to government to remedy ills, and government consumed a bit more of the national income each year. Proposition 13 seemed to signal legislators that government had to live within limits. It ushered in a new public sector austerity, where liberals outdid conservatives to seem parsimonious; few new programs could be launched by any level of government, and existing ones did well to keep their appropriations adjusted for inflation. It set back plans for new social legislation like national health insurance. It helped derail President Carter's bold campaign for tax reform, aimed at the three-martini lunch and other loopholes. In its place, Congress enacted a regressive program of tax relief for the well-off. A decade earlier, the voters seemed angry that some taxpayers were overburdened while others failed to pay their fair share. But after Jarvis-Gann, that distinction was lost.

Proposition 13 sent politicians a message that the voters were genuinely mad as hell. It put the entire Keynesian economic establishment on the defensive. It seemed to symbolize a conservative resurgence, in which the new economic ideas were fresh twists on Adam Smith, and the electorate was newly wary of all government intervention.

And yet . . . .

The story of the great tax revolt is filled with one "and yet" after another: And yet the polls consistently showed that the public, by margins of well over 80 percent, continued to look to government to provide more—not fewer—services. And yet the bulk of the tax relief in California went, not to the small homeowners whose property tax burden led to Proposition 13, but to big businesses and landlords. And yet California Governor Jerry Brown, who had opposed Proposition 13, managed to ride it to a stunning reelection victory. And yet Howard Jarvis, the Jeremiah of California, failed utterly in his attempt to go national. And yet the California public, which could support a "conservative" tax protest, could turn around in city after city and approve "liberal" rent control initiatives, opposed by the same real estate groups that had sponsored Proposition 13. And yet the public finance system in California two years after Proposition 13 looked far more like something that liberals might have designed: less reliance on the regressive property tax; less local authority; more control of programs and setting of standards by Sacramento and more state aid to localities; and wider sharing of the property tax revenues. And yet despite the supposed new conservatism, most states did not adopt imitations of Proposition 13. The drive for a U.S. Constitutional Amendment to require a balanced budget was stalemated; Congress did not roll back taxes.

If the great tax revolt was a watershed event, the waters have not yet cleared.

I will argue that the taxpayer revolt of the late seventies was not primarily a protest against the rising cost and size of government. Government outlays had already reached approximately their present share of gross national product by the late sixties, fully ten years before Proposition 13. Rather, the tax revolt was a quite valid reaction against inequities in the tax systems, exacerbated by broader economic distress. It was essentially a pocketbook protest, which nonetheless produced a sort of ideological windfall for conservatives and created a severe setback for mainstream liberalism. In its aftermath government would have to make do with what it had.

Howard Jarvis' Proposition 13 was that rarest of political events, an authentic mass protest brought on by economic grievances. Quite simply, property taxes for ordinary California homeowners had gone entirely out of control, yoked as they were to the dizzying rise in the prices of California homes. This mechanical result was an unfortunate side effect of a 1967 reform, in which the California legislature had required all property to be reassessed periodically, at a uniform fraction of its market value. This reform prevented local assessors from following the time-honored custom of assessing homes at preferential rates.

As a consequence, homes came to assume an ever greater share of the property tax load during the seventies, creating the entirely erroneous impression that local government was rolling in revenue and wasting the money. At the same time, the California state government, with its highly progressive income tax system, was indeed reaping more tax dollars every year, because inflation was pushing taxpayers into ever higher brackets. And as consumer prices rose, sales tax receipts soared, too.

In a stunning default, the state legislature failed to redress either grievance. The extra income-tax revenues piled up in state accounts. And instead of using this windfall to buy bigger and better public services, or to relieve local property taxes, Governor Brown and the legislature built up a $4 billion state surplus, setting the stage for the "unreasonable" remedy, Proposition 13.

That is the long and short of how Proposition 13 originated. The full story is told in Part I of this book. Ballot initiatives to limit the property tax had been circulated in California almost annually since 1968. But not until the property tax went haywire did the issue catch on.

As the tax revolt brewed, the mainstream politicians in California, beginning with Governor Jerry Brown, issued increasingly unbelievable warnings that Proposition 13 would destroy government and plunge the state's economy into recession. In fact, it did neither, thanks to the huge state budget surplus. Liberated by Proposition 13, the billions of idle dollars in state reserves both bailed out local government and were put back to work in the state's private economy.

Both of these outcomes made Jarvis look like a true prophet, and gave his brand of tax revolt broader credibility. A year after Proposition 13, the public opinion polls in every state reflected wide voter support for steep tax cuts modeled on Proposition 13. Thanks to the hidden state revenue surplus, California voters could enjoy a temporary free lunch although a prepaid one. Taxes were cut sharply, and public services were only slightly reduced. Most economists expect that California's day of reckoning, when voters will have to choose between restoring taxes and losing services, will not come for another few years. In the meantime, Proposition 13 enjoys understandably wide support.

Two years after Proposition 13, the same commentators who had proclaimed that Jarvis-Gann equaled a revolt against government expressed surprise that the fickle electorate in June 1980 suddenly turned against Jarvis by voting down his latest initiative to cut the state income tax in half. Now, it seemed, the fickle electorate had decided that government was necessary after all. But if Proposition 13 is kept in proper perspective, there is no contradiction. The 1978 voters were voting against a burdensome injustice in the way the property taxes were apportioned, which was doublingly insulting given the state surplus. There was no such popular outrage against California's progressive income tax, and by 1980 the state surplus was almost depleted. Only those who mistakenly interpreted Proposition 13 as an ideological protest against government should be puzzled.

The distributional consequences of Proposition 13 mark it as a striking bonanza for the haves. The $6.15 billion tax relief allocated under Howard Jarvis' formula rewarded business and corporate property owners first, wealthy individual homeowners second, small householders last, and tenants not at all. The revenues lost to government—though the loss was far less catastrophic than first predicted, thanks to Governor Brown's expanding surplus—also hurt the needy disproportionately, through lost job opportunities in local and state government and through program cuts and higher fees in social services, public health, and formerly free recreation programs.

The bout of national tax revolt fever set off by Proposition 13 was another matter. Most states had no surplus like California's to cushion the impact of deep tax cuts; no other state could get away with a drastic reduction in taxes without a corresponding cut in public services. And few states experienced the acute sort of tax panic that the property tax spiral engendered in California homeowners.

Nonetheless, the squeeze in personal finances caused by inflation and the slowdown in real economic growth was national. So was the residue of bad feeling about government left over from Vietnam and Watergate. And throughout the country, there were long-standing inequities in the way Americans were taxed, which were compounded during the seventies by stagflation, demographic changes, and shifts in the tax load. Although federal taxes consume more dollars, state and local taxes tend to operate in the more arbitrary and unjust manner. State and local taxes are also more vulnerable to local public protest.

While the federal income tax is mildly progressive, most state and local taxation is severely regressive; that is, the highest rate of tax is paid by people of lowest income. According to a landmark study by economist Steven Lile, a family of four in the mid-seventies paid a higher state and local tax rate at $10,000 a year than at $25,000 a year in all but five or six states. Another recent study, by Professor Donald Phares of the University of Missouri at St. Louis, found that the total state and local tax burden was highly regressive in every state, with the lowest-income class paying a far higher rate than the highest.

For ordinary voters, the property tax is the most unfair tax of all. Though it once supplied the bulk of state revenues, the property tax today is a local tax. The base of taxable property is limited by the total wealth of a community. As a consequence, towns and cities with large numbers of poor people who most need public services tend to have the least available property wealth to tax. Thus in order to produce the same revenues, their tax rate must be higher than in wealthier communities. In addition, poor neighborhoods within poor cities tend to be assessed at higher ratios than rich neighborhoods, where assessments typically lag behind rising property values. So poor people in poor neighborhoods in poor cities often pay the highest effective rates of all. This applies to tenants, whose rents often reflect the landlord's tax bill, as well as to working-class homeowners.

In addition, the property tax is notoriously oblivious to one's ability to pay. Income can drop, hardship can be incurred; the tax is due just the same. Until recently, locally elected tax assessors in many parts of the country were willing to adjust assessments to fit circumstances, but the modernization of the property tax, pioneered ironically by California, put an end to that tradition.

Thus, even in "normal" times, there is a standing legacy of entirely valid resentment against the property tax. (That story is told in Part II.) The resentment is especially pronounced on the part of people vulnerable to other economic reverses, such as the moderate-income and elderly homeowners who rallied to Proposition 13.

The long-term problems with the property tax are exaggerated during a period of wider economic distress, for reasons that have little if anything to do with the size, or the rate of growth, of that old Devil government. The number one villain is inflation. Like so much else in the economy, the tax system is not designed for a prolonged period of inflation. Not only does inflation frustrate real economic growth, leaving people with more dollars but often less real money with which to pay all their bills including their taxes; more insidiously, inflation combines explosively with both the income tax and the property tax. It pushes wage earners into ever higher tax brackets, and it raises property taxes in lockstep with purely paper increases in the market value of one's house. Because commercial property values have not risen nearly as fast as housing prices, and because assessment methods shield commercial property from inflation, the property tax burden has been shifted onto homeowners.

Beyond the pocketbook frustrations of the seventies, demographic changes that again had little to do with the total size of government also incited taxpayers. Many commentators have painted the tax revolt as a revolt of the haves, in the sense that the middle-class finally got tired of shelling out to pay benefits for the poor. In fact, the plight of the poor improved only slightly as a result of the antipoverty programs and tax reforms of the late sixties and early seventies. But it is true that the redistribution that did occur was mainly a transfer from the middle class to the poor. The wealthy quite successfully resisted efforts to increase significantly their real rate of taxation. Taxes did go up during this period on all income groups except the very poor; however, the steepest increase was on the middle class.

But fewer of the tax dollars, it seemed, were going to services you could see: garbage collection, mail deliveries, good schools, attractive streets. Where *were* all those tax dollars going? Admittedly, more of them were going to the invisible poor; some of them indeed went to fatten bureaucracies that could be self-serving and unresponsive. But the biggest chunk of them—better than $115 billion a year by 1979—was being efficiently channeled to a largely invisible dependent class that everybody supported in theory: our own retired parents.

The steepest tax hike of all, the eightfold increase in social security taxes since 1964, resulted from the aging of the population, the falling birth rate, the ability of the enlarged millions of pensioners to lobby successfully for more benefits, and the early failure of the social security system to build up sufficient reserves to pay benefits out of earnings from past premiums. But this tax increase was certainly not the result of government "waste" or excessive solicitude for the hard-core poor. Social security is essentially an intergenerational transfer, not an interclass transfer.

Because of the growing elderly population and other demographic changes, ordinary working taxpayers found themselves increasingly taxed to pay for services they couldn't see and didn't use. The local political center—the League of Women Voters, the PTA stalwarts, even the more conservative Rotarians and Junior Leaguers, all longtime fighters for school levies and sewer bonds in the name of basic civic virtue—suddenly eroded around the edges. And the local political center seldom could claim more than 55 or 60 percent of the voters to begin with.

With fewer school-age children in the late seventies, the constituency for public education, the biggest consumer of property tax dollars, had to shrink. In the late seventies for the first time, less than 50 percent of California households had family members in public schools. By 1980, at least one governor, Lee Dreyfus of Wisconsin, was openly proposing to exempt retired people from the public school tax, on the ground that they didn't consume the service.

The efforts to reform public school finance by courts and legislatures also undercut the constituency for local taxation. Before the series of decisions that began with California's *Serrano* case, which required substantially equal per-pupil expenditure regardless of the property wealth of the school district, affluent school districts happily taxed themselves heavily to finance what were, in everything but name, elite private schools.

With the drive toward greater equality of school finance expenditure, and more assumption of financing by the state, there was less direct payoff in agreeing to very high local property taxes. And by the late seventies, although young professional whites were flocking back to the cities, big city school systems remained heavily minority and poor. Fewer voters wanted to pay exorbitant property taxes on behalf of other people's children.

All these shifts helped created a climate in which the voters increasingly felt they were not receiving enough value for their tax dollars. These economic frustrations are explored in Part III.

The political turmoil that bubbled in the wake of Proposition 13 confused three very compelling and entirely distinct questions: *How big a government do we Americans want? What do we want it to do?* And, *How shall we pay for it?*

The tax revolt managed to blur these three issues into a single reaction against high taxes and big government. Logically, this made little sense, since even the most rabid of the tax protesters recognized the need for public services that somebody had to pay for. Much of the rancor in California exploded precisely because the tax bills fell too heavily on people who couldn't afford them, not because of the total tax burden to society. But mass movements are seldom entirely logical; virtually all the public debate in the tax revolt focused on the size of government and almost none on the distribution of taxes.

When the dust settled, the more perceptive of the small homeowners who enlisted in the tax revolt realized, dimly, that their pocket had been picked again. Although the distribution of the tax load was not squarely framed as a public issue (with a few notable exceptions), most of the tax relief provided by Proposition 13, its imitations in other states, and by the federal tax legislation of 1978, went to the well-to-do.

The stunning success of the corporate lobby in translating popular tax revolt fever into effective tax relief for big businesses and their investors is also discussed in Part III.

How big a government do we Americans want? The public's answer to that first question, as expressed in dozens of referenda and legislative actions in the two years following Jarvis-Gann, has been remarkably uniform—but not quite what Proposition 13 first seemed to signal. We want a government about as big as the one we have now, the voters declared, and no bigger. But not really smaller, either. We want public services increased, not reduced. And most of all, we want government to become more efficient.

Even as the public was rebelling against "government waste," it was eager for government to do more. In 1978, the year of the great revolt and a year of declining economic confidence, 82 percent of Americans polled thought the federal government was "spending too much"—as an abstraction—but by majorities of 5 and 6 to 1, Americans also thought that the government should spend more to protect the environment, improve the nation's health, aid cities, enhance education, and even assist minorities. Every major poll reported only one exception to the widespread popular support for more public services—welfare. Most respondents thought welfare outlays should be reduced. But at the same time, 74 percent of Americans queried by a *New York Times*–CBS poll thought that the government should guarantee that everybody who wants to work should have a job. Two out of three Americans queried in a *Washington Post* poll said they would prefer to pay their present level of taxes and get improved services, rather than take cuts in both taxes and services.

The same sorts of contradictions are evident in the public's attitude toward another popular scapegoat—regulation. Commentators widely viewed the tax revolt, in part, as a backlash against government red tape as well as government spending. And indeed, polls showed the same generalized opposition to regulation as to spending. But once again, in the particular, respondents felt by margins of 3 to 1 that consumer and environmental regulation was worth the cost. And while healthy majorities thought that the overall burden of regulation was excessive, the public supported by even larger majorities *more* regulation of every single major industry.

Finally, the polls showed public confidence in every major institution in society slipping as the economic gloom deepened. In the late seventies for the first time since the major polling organizations began to ask such questions, huge majorities said they agreed with propositions like "The government wastes a lot of tax dollars," and "The government is run for a few big interests." But at the same time, the favorable ratings also plummeted for big business, trade unions, the medical profession, higher education, the press, and other big, distant institutions. Small-scale institutions close to home enjoyed the greatest confidence.

Most of all, the public believed by overwhelming majorities that government suffers from massive inefficiency. And as a corollary, the voters hoped that taxes could be cut without proportional cuts in public services. Poll after poll showed that the public believed that government contained massive amounts of "fat," like the glistening gristle around the edge of a sirloin, which could be trimmed away without affecting the quality of public services.

But the "fat" metaphor really misses the point. Fat suggests an extraneous waste product, which nobody wants. As Massachusetts State Representative Barney Frank has observed, the fat in government is no waste product. It is there precisely because it is very much wanted. Reform-minded legislators who go after pork barrel legislation and redundant agencies soon come to understand that one man's fat is another's meat. Legislators get reelected by delivering money for their districts, not by championing ideological crusades against the fat in other members' districts. In Representative Frank's superb extension of the metaphor, fat in government is *marbelized,* finely strewn through the body politic in ways that tenaciously resist excision.

President Carter naively spent untold amounts of his early political capital in a hapless attempt to reorganize the federal bureaucracy. He failed utterly. Most of the fat was where it was for very good reasons. And while there was great political support for the idea of cutting away fat as a desirable abstraction, there was almost no support to be gained for removing particular globets, which invariably turned out to be somebody's pet project. After a Herculean struggle, Carter actually managed to shut down a handful of superannuated federal agencies—most notably the U.S. Travel Service, a totally redundant office that had been established to promote European tourism in the U.S. in the days before the play-money dollar of camera-laden foreign hordes was spontaneously attracted to America's bargain-basement shores. Even as these puny agencies expired, several big new ones proliferated, including a cabinet-level Department of Education.

In Massachusetts, Governor Michael Dukakis fell victim to the same forces. A liberal but also a serious partisan of efficiency in government, Dukakis fatally alienated his liberal constituency when he trimmed back social programs. He was decisively beaten in the 1978 Democratic primary when an ultraconservative, Edward King, courted the Jarvis constituency while many of Dukakis' embittered liberal supporters sat on their hands. One of King's first political moves was to overturn efforts by Dukakis' Administration to introduce management efficiencies into the Massachusetts Bay Transit Authority which had been resisted by leaders of the MBTA's unions, who had backed King in the election.

Thus, after a year of King's Administration, the voters of Massachusetts who assumed they were voting for fiscal conservatism and austerity were hit with deeper public subsidies and threatened fare increases to keep their transit system operating. The wasteful labor practices, requiring that management bargain with twenty-eight separate unions and tolerate chronic absenteeism, were a drain on the public trough which would put the sassiest welfare mother to shame. Yet the blue-collar workers on the "T" and their families overwhelmingly backed Governor Ed King, that champion of fiscal austerity, and they were politically untouchable. Such are the strange products of tax revolt.

The voters in most states must have had an intuitive sense about the way fat in government really worked, because they rejected almost every opportunity to enact extremist antitax measures. (Remember that even Proposition 13 was extremist only in form, thanks to the safety net of the $4 billion state surplus.)

California's great revolt sputtered out June 3, 1980, when voters decisively rejected Jarvis' Proposition 9, the initiative to cut the state income tax in half. But this apparent caprice on the part of the voters should puzzle only those who insist on seeing in Proposition 13 the "antigovernment" revolt that it never was. Unlike Jarvis' ill-conceived income tax amendment, Proposition 13 at least spoke to a real, deeply felt grievance—the gross maldistribution of the property tax load. And unlike the pre-Jarvis property tax, California's steeply progressive state income tax is widely accepted as fair.

Even with the far deeper economic malaise two years after Proposition 13, Californians in mid-1980 bore no deep-seated desire to punish government; there was no ideological ground swell against the income tax, and even Howard Jarvis failed to manufacture one. Proposition 13, fueled by a true voter panic, was qualified for the ballot by thousands of little people volunteering their time; it cost Jarvis about a nickel a signature. There was no populist revolt in the campaign for Proposition 9. Jarvis *bought* the signatures—at an average of $2.53 each.

The radical antitax movement that was supposed to emulate Proposition 13 never quite materialized nationally. Instead, with only one exception (Idaho), voters and legislatures in state after state approved narrowly drawn measures, "capping" government expenditures at roughly their current share of total personal income. In virtually every case where the voters were offered more radical measures to slash taxes and presumably cut deeply into public services, these measures were rejected. Nationally, the more radical ideas of requiring a balanced budget by Constitutional amendment, or steeply ratcheting back federal outlays, were also rejected. This is explored in Part IV.

Yet the "cap" movement, though it is far tamer than Jarvis' crusade, should not be underrated. The idea that government cannot resist pandering to this or that special interest group has merit. The movement to place Constitutional limits on government's total outlays is probably the most durable and consistent contribution of contemporary American conservatism. It has its theoretical roots, of course, in the checks and balances of the original Constitution. Limits, however, affect the supply of government outlays, not the demand for them. And caps may simply intensify special interest lobbying and not make government more efficient.

Though there is little support for repealing the welfare state, the tax revolt unmistakably drew on a dormant, deeply American impulse—the profound distrust of government. The modern view of government as friend of the common man and engine of economic well-being is barely fifty years old. The older view of government as restrained tyrant (and taxation as the instrument of that tyranny) was the essence of our national revolt against the British Crown.

By invoking this tradition, conservatives were able to sound oddly populist, as they mobilized popular grievances against tax inequity. For liberals, the most distressing thing about Proposition 13 was precisely its populism—the spectacle of Jarvis and Gann, two spokesmen, after all, for real estate interests, rallying the masses. And not just masses of suburban stockbrokers, either, but blue-collar homeowners with FHA mortgages and pensioners on social security, two mainstays of the New Deal coalition. And to what end? Why, to shackle that beneficent instrument of social and economic justice, the government.

The tax revolt signals a new political era after all. We may not repeal the New Deal, but it will be a very long time before government in the United States grows significantly bigger. In many respects, Proposition 13 and its progeny marked the public recognition of that fact, not the origin. Even before Proposition 13, the New Deal coalition was in serious disarray, privately despairing that more federal programs could actually accomplish very much; divided between the rather elite social liberalism of new life-styles and environmentalism and the older economic liberalism of organized labor, minorities, and the poor; defensive about its bureaucratic albatross; and largely out of fresh ideas.

By June 1978, when Jarvis scored his triumph, it had been a full decade since the waning days of Lyndon Johnson's Great Society. By June 1978, at least a dozen states had already slapped limits on the growth of local expenditures or taxes. By 1978 we were four years into a new federal budget control process that had effectively frozen federal outlays as a percentage of national income, forcing public expenditures to compete with one another; we were midway through the term of the most conservative Democrat to occupy the White House since Grover Cleveland, who was nonetheless to the left of Congress. And the old liberal coalition was already fighting a largely futile budgetary battle, under the limp rallying cry of "Cut less!"

This transformation of the political context had been happening under our noses for a decade. It took Proposition 13 to make it a recognized movement.

PART I

Mr. Jarvis and His Revolt

1

THE CROOKED ASSESSOR

"Bring Back the Crooked Assessor"
—San Francisco bumper sticker, 1967

THE CROOKED ASSESSOR was a well-loved municipal rogue named Russell L. Wolden, in his day one of the most popular officeholders in San Francisco county. Wolden had held the job since 1938, succeeding his late father, who had first been elected San Francisco assessor in the twenties. Under the Woldens, the County Assessor's office was run like a family business.

At fifty-five, Russ Wolden was a dapper dresser who liked to speak in confidential tones and let a knowing smile substitute for the details of a deal. His office in San Francisco's ornate city hall had the prettiest secretaries and the best-stocked liquor cabinet; it was the place where the little people of San Francisco political life gathered election night to hoist a few drinks and celebrate the returns.

In the best tradition of grafting urban benefactors, Russell Wolden was a sly Robin Hood who mixed altruism with opportunity. Like most elected county assessors since colonial days, Wolden had a simple formula for winning hearts and reelections. He kept assessments on homes very, very low, especially in those wards that tended to vote. The real estate market could rise, you could paint the place and add a sunporch, and the assessment rarely moved. Homeowners were pleased, and Wolden's political fortunes prospered.

This, however, was not where the real corruption lay. With the voters securely charmed by the bargain assessments, Wolden could turn his appetite to San Francisco's overassessed business community. These assessments could be reduced too, but for a price. On the side, the assessor ran a tax consulting firm to "advise" clients how to shave their assessments. In time, as the business grew, he discreetly relied on other tax consultants to launder his kickbacks. By the sixties, when Wolden was finally caught, he had reduced it all to a precise formula: To obtain a tax reduction worth $10,000, a business paid a fee of $5,000, which would be split evenly between the tax consultant and the assessor.

Through his wide contacts in the assessors' professional associations, Russ Wolden could even arrange reduced assessments on property that his clients owned in other cities. He nearly got into trouble in the late forties, when he tried to pay a Detroit assessor to lower assessments on a Michigan property owned by one of Wolden's San Francisco cronies. Investigative bodies repeatedly went after Wolden, but to no result. A grand jury report in 1955 carped about his tax consulting business, but took no action. Wolden's colleagues from those years remember him as a veritable Milo Minderbinder of assessors, leaving no angle unplayed. For better than a decade, Wolden quietly blocked repeal of the anachronistic property tax on personal furniture—so he could continue to assess San Francisco households at a token $50, winning their undying gratitude.

But in the summer of 1965, Wolden's empire collapsed, sending the assessor to prison and helping to fuse a time bomb—a very slow one—that exploded thirteen years later as Proposition 13.

Wolden was undone by an opportunistic and somewhat erratic accountant named Norman Phillips, whose own motives remained unclear. Phillips was working for one of Wolden's tax consultants, James Tooke. In Tooke's files, Phillips encountered detailed evidence of Wolden's kickback scheme, which would titillate readers of the San Francisco papers all that summer. Like the careful accountant he was, Tooke had kept meticulous records of the clients' fees, the bribes to Wolden, the before-and-after assessments, and even photostats of the canceled checks.

These documents became public when Phillips botched an apparent attempt at reform or at blackmail. On the Fourth of July, 1965, Phillips drove down to Tooke's closed office in suburban Castro Valley, piled five filing boxes into a rented trailer, and sought to negotiate for the return of the incriminating documents.

When Tooke wouldn't play ball, it dawned on Phillips that he might end up in the bottom of the Bay. A week later, as a kind of life insurance policy, he slipped the documents to a reporter.

Except for this fiasco, the corruption might have remained hidden, since most of the reduced assessments were on business plant and equipment, whose assessments were not a matter of public record. But once Phillips spilled Tooke's files, investigators had an easy time unraveling the whole racket, which involved several other assessors as well.

Wolden's scheme, fully laid out during a lengthy trial, proved wondrously brazen. Besides the kickbacks, there were campaign contributions traded for lowered assessments, as well as special courtesies to local notables.

A grateful business community flocked to Wolden's defense, holding support rallies even while the grand jury was still deliberating whether to indict. The well-known hotelier and Democratic party fund-raiser Ben Swig ran an impromptu telephone tree, quickly raising $11,000 for the Russell Wolden Defense Fund. Swig later testified for the defense, insisting that his Fairmont Hotel, if anything, was overassessed.

Wolden admitted taking a gift from another prominent hotel owner, a $38,000 co-op apartment in a building owned by Louis Lurie, proprietor of the famed Mark Hopkins; Wolden denied there was any *quid pro quo*. But according to sworn testimony from one of Wolden's auditors, the auditor had recommended that the Mark's personal property assessment be increased by $150,000, yet Wolden had still insisted on a reduction of $210,000. Pressed to justify the reduction, the defense pointed to outdated hotel stationery and stocks of worthless canasta cards.*

At a break in the trial, reporters inquired how Wolden, on a modest civil service salary, could afford to run the elegant San Francisco co-op apartment as well as his fully staffed suburban estate on the Peninsula.

"You forget," Wolden replied, breaking up the courtroom, "my father was assessor before me."

Ultimately, Wolden went to prison. So did Donald Feragen, the assessor of Alameda County across the Bay, and several subordinates. In San Diego, assessor Donald McQuilken committed suicide, and his chief deputy died in jail. Other assessors narrowly escaped prosecution. Los Angeles County assessor Philip Watson, of whom more later, was indicted for taking contributions but found not guilty.

It was, of course, not sufficient to send the malefactors to jail. Here was a corrupt system, crying out for reform.

In theory, California's State Board of Equalization carefully supervised the county assessors and kept assessments within proper limits. The California constitution requires all property to be assessed at "full cash-

---

* This was the one count on which the jury deadlocked.

value." But the board had become a passive instrument that kept statistics and periodically met to rubber-stamp what the county assessors did.

With their power to determine taxes, the county assessors, through their trade association, wielded immense influence in Sacramento. "The legislative committees would bow and scrape before the assessors," recalls the chief civil servant at the Equalization Board during those years. "They treated them as highly proficient experts in their field. Mainly, they were expert at getting reelected."

Throughout the fifties, commissions and committees and the board's own surveys repeatedly found that assessments widely diverged from actual values, but the State Equalization Board, though it had the legal power to act, lacked the political juice.

In 1956, after some futile attempts to get assessors to equalize assessments, board officials had come hat in hand to the assessors' annual convention at Monterey and concluded what amounted to a treaty with a sovereign power, promising not to intrude as long as each county's assessment ratios, on average, kept within a "zone of tolerance."

The averages, however, concealed a crazy quilt of variations among properties, some corrupt, some benign, and others merely inept.

When the Wolden scandal broke, therefore, the pent-up frustration of the State Equalization bureaucracy combined with indignant public opinion to ignite a reform whose logic and ultimate consequences were not even dimly perceived by its sponsors.

The reform was a bill, Assembly Bill 80, entitled the "assessment Reform Act of 1966." It was sponsored by two Bay Area liberals, Nicholas Petris of Oakland and John Knox of Richmond, who chaired two powerful assembly committees. The bill required all property to be uniformly assessed at 25 percent of actual market value, required periodic, systematic reassessment, and took away the local assessors' discretion.

Every good-government group in the state strongly backed the reform, as did Governor Edmund G. (Pat) Brown, Sr., and the powerful assembly speaker, Jesse Unruh.

It was widely assumed that homeowner taxes were paying for Wolden's corruption, and that once the favored businesses were made to pay their fair share, homeowners' taxes would drop. The state attorney general estimated that $200 million a year in business taxes were being avoided because of underassessments, and the League of California Cities placed the figure at $480 million.

But the reality was exactly the reverse. Wolden was indeed a Robin

Hood, if a selective one. The few businesses that paid bribes enjoyed cut-rate assessments, but the vast majority of businesses were assessed at a substantially higher level than homeowners. Though this practice of assessing income-producing property at higher levels was not sanctioned in California law, it was the custom there and in most other states.

Therefore, when AB 80 caused all property to be assessed at the same 25 percent of actual value, it set in motion a massive tax shift. Most San Francisco businesses, it turned out, were being assessed, not at 25 percent, but at close to 50 percent. Under AB 80, this was cut in half. Homes, in contrast, had been assessed at something like 9 percent. By 1970 this had risen to 19 percent. Something like half a billion dollars of assessed valuation shifted from businesses to homes.

When the first tax notices went out in 1967 under the AB 80 rules, all hell broke loose. The press had clamored for reform, leading homeowners to expect a tax *reduction*. Homeowner groups who lobbied for the bill felt utterly betrayed. Hence the bumper sticker. From his cell at Vacaville the crooked assessor remained far more popular than the well-meaning reformers who helped send him there.

Yet these were minor explosions compared with what was to come. San Francisco was almost unique because Wolden had kept homeowner assessments so very low. The rest of the state experienced a relatively mild tax shift, which was mitigated in 1968 and again in 1972 when the state legislature responded to voter pressure by passing increasingly generous homestead exemptions reducing effective assessment levels on homes. Statewide, the share of property taxes paid by homeowners rose only about one percent in 1967–68, and then dropped 2 percent after the first homestead exemption took effect in 1969.

Not until the mid-seventies, when inflation fueled an unprecedented rise in California housing prices, did the real tax shift materialize and the real voter anger build. Under other circumstances, two fail-safe mechanisms should have prevented a mass taxpayer revolt. The legislature might have stepped in, as it did in 1968 and again in 1972, to make sure that taxes on homes did not follow housing values out of sight. But California had two consecutive governors bent on improving the state's business climate and far more solicitous of business taxes, and a legislature that couldn't agree on the precise form of a tax cut. After 1972 no significant homeowner relief was forthcoming from Sacramento.

Failing legislative action, however, the local assessor, knowing his electorate, would have played his traditional role, making sure that assessments did not slavishly follow inflation. But by the mid-seventies when the inflation struck, California's assessment machinery would be a national model of efficient uniformity. In each county every home would be periodically reassessed, usually on a three-year cycle. The rising assessments would faithfully reflect the soaring prices.

Thanks to AB 80, the State Equalization bureaucracy would be in charge, the disgraced local assessors would be stripped of their discretion, and most of the process would be automated, with sophisticated formulas determining the value of each home.

And as housing prices doubled and then doubled again, the local assessor could only feed the inflating values into his computer and stand by helplessly like a sorcerer's apprentice.

MR. WATSON

The growing taxpayer resentment would prompt one man long acquainted with Los Angeles assessment politics to propose a constitutional limitation on property taxes, restricting the tax to one percent of value. The legislature in Sacramento did not take him seriously, so the man went directly to the voters and collected enough signatures to place his revolutionary proposition directly on the ballot.

The state establishment united against him, claiming that the draconian initiative would cut services and misdirect tax relief. The new governor, a fiscal conservative, challenged his arithmetic. Tax experts ridiculed his logic.

The man's name was not Howard Jarvis.

The year was 1968, not 1978, and the initiative, designated "Proposition 9" on the ballot, was sponsored by the Los Angeles tax assessor himself, Philip Watson. The Watson initiative failed in 1968, and a repeat attempt failed in 1972.

Why would the tax assessor, of all people, sponsor an initiative to limit taxes? For the same reason that Russ Wolden up in San Francisco went easy on homeowners. Though assessors calculate property *values*, not property *taxes*, the voters tend to confuse the two. Assessors often take the heat for rising taxes.

In 1968 one of those angry taxpayers nipping at Watson's heels was an obscure crank named Jarvis, who had emerged as a spokesman for the little homeowner associations that dotted the San Fernando Valley.

For a decade, Watson and Jarvis competed for leadership of the tax protest in Los Angeles. They were an odd duo. Watson was highly suspect to the hard-core tax resisters, because he was, after all, the assessor. Jarvis was suspect elsewhere because he was such a perennial nut.

Politically well connected and looking to statewide office, Watson spent his stormy fourteen years as assessor devising one gimmick after another to convince homeowners that he was not to blame for rising taxes. In his office hung a prominent sign: "We Don't Make Values. We Follow Them." That was true. If the county supervisors failed to drop the tax rate and took a free ride on the rising assessments, that was their doing, not Watson's.

Early into his first term of office in 1963, Watson made headlines when he refused to let the county board see his new tax rolls, insisting that the higher property values would only whet the politicians' appetite to squander money. "Expenditures will rise to meet income available," he declared, quoting C. Northcote Parkinson. "Budget-making should be separate and apart from assessing."

Eventually, the county board persuaded the legislature in Sacramento to pass a law forcing Watson to disclose his rolls in time for budget season. But the ploy was great politics for Watson. The mail supporting his stand ran better than 100 to 1. Unlike Jarvis, Watson was not an adamant foe of government spending, though he believed, with some justification, that the property tax was overburdened. "People-related services," he argued, such as welfare and education, should be financed by more general taxes, while the property tax should be reserved for such "property-related services" as police and fire protection, streets, sidewalks, sanitation, and community amenities. Years later, Proposition 13 would accomplish just that.

Watson remained the establishment figure of the two. While Jarvis collected his signatures from a determined following of tax protest groups in the San Fernando Valley, Watson gathered petitions in the more usual California manner: he bought them. In 1968, when Watson collected his 745,000 signatures to qualify Proposition 9, they were procured by a San Francisco firm that charged fifteen cents a signature up front and an additional quarter for each one that proved valid.

In that year, Jarvis was promoting a more radical initiative to abolish the property tax altogether. It failed dismally, collecting only 55,000 signatures, and Jarvis reluctantly supported Watson's Proposition 9.

The Los Angeles tax protest in the mid-sixties foreshadowed the statewide revolt a decade later. The cause was very much the same—a shift in tax burdens.

Watson had good reason to fear the wrath of homeowners. When he had taken office in 1963, he had inherited a hundred million dollars' worth of lawsuits, by businesses claiming overassessment. The California constitution required all property to be assessed at market value, but Los Angeles homeowners enjoyed the same sorts of breaks provided by Wolden in San Francisco.

Faced with the lawsuits, Watson initially bluffed, threatening to audit any business that pursued a suit. But the county counsel would not defend. Businesses were indeed overassessed in comparison with homes, in the time-honored tradition, if not by the law. Knowing the howls it would provoke, Watson reluctantly devised a reform that later became the model for AB 80 after the Wolden scandal: uniform valuation of all property at 25 percent and periodic reassessment.

Like AB 80, this reform produced a miniature tax revolt.

When taxes on business dropped, homeowner taxes took up the slack. Little pockets of tax protest gathered force. It was 1964; Southern California was in a period of furious expansion; the baby boom was swamping the public schools; times were good and demands for public services high. As fringe suburbs incorporated, new property taxes were levied and roundly resented by the longtime population of retired people. The tax shift produced when Watson agreed to equalize assessments only spiced the broth.

In the San Fernando Valley, tax protest was also growing. As greater Los Angeles sprawled, the land adjoining new subdivisions increased in value. Out-of-the-way chicken farms were suddenly reassessed as prime development land. Stories appeared in the papers about retired couples on an acre or two who were taxed out of their homes.

The small-time real estate investors and retirees hit by rising taxes in the mid-sixties would become Howard Jarvis' unlikely shock troops a decade later. Typical of the early tax protest was a retired Van Nuys couple named Harry and Doris Crown. The Crowns had invested in several older houses that happened to be on land zoned for commercial use. As subdivisions sprouted nearby, they watched the taxes quadruple on their properties, which could not command higher market rents.

The Crowns began haunting Watson's files, complaining that they were being harassed into selling out so that Watson cronies could buy their land. They charged that shopping centers enjoyed lower assessments. In a memorable media stunt, the Crowns posted a sign in front of one of their houses, on Gresham Street: WATSON'S WASTELAND. They posed their tenants, an elderly couple, in front of the frame house, which was taxed at $3,600 (largely for its two-acre plot). This American Gothic snapshot was paired with a photo of Philip Watson's own home in Mar Vista, then taxed at $1,100. A flyer featuring the two houses and their taxes was circulated by the tax protest groups in the 1966 campaign for county assessor.

Doris Crown remembers Jarvis from the media tours of Watson's Wasteland. "I knew who he was," she recalls. "Howard was leading the campaign to keep Dorothy Healey off the ballot for assessor because she was an admitted Communist. That was good enough for us."

MR. JARVIS

Howard Jarvis was a robust sixty-two, tireless and cantankerous. He had sold his home-appliance factory and had plenty of time to dabble in fringe politics. He would later reminisce about those years, insisting that his other escapades had been intended only to publicize his resistance to taxes, but in fact he was involved in a wide array of right-wing causes. He badly lost a 1962 challenge in the Republican primary to Senator Thomas Kuchel, and founded his own, short-lived maverick Conservative party. As Conservative party chairman, he unsuccessfully sued to keep Communist party members such as Mrs. Healey off the ballot.

One Los Angeles civil liberties activist concluded a memo about Jarvis' lawsuit: "Nobody here takes Jarvis seriously. He hasn't even succeeded in getting acceptance among the right-wing organizations."

If that was true, it wasn't for lack of effort. Besides his Conservative party, Jarvis founded a local anti-union right-to-work committee, and served on the national board of the Liberty Amendment Committee, a group promoting repeal of the federal income tax. In 1964, Jarvis and two friends fell afoul of the postal inspectors when they raised money for an unauthorized campaign committee for Barry Goldwater. Of the $115,000 raised by Jarvis' "Businessmen for Goldwater," postal inspectors found, $88,000 was retained by Jarvis and his associates as fees, and the remainder went for telephone and office expenses. None of the money went to Goldwater, who eventually filed suit to stop Jarvis from raising money in his name.

Jarvis and William Morrison, one of the partners in the 1964 Goldwater episode, pulled the same caper a decade later, when they took in more than $57,000 in the name of "Friends for Hayakawa," none of which found its way to the Hayakawa Senate campaign. Again, the candidate sued.

After his 1962 defeat, Jarvis organized his first taxpayer group. They met at the home of a widow named Leona Magidson, on West Fifth Street in West L.A. "He was the first human being I came across politically who I thought cared," Mrs. Magidson remarked years later.

By the mid-sixties Los Angeles was dotted with at least thirty little tax protest groups, dominated by retired people and small real estate investors. These Jarvis helped fuse into a chaotic United Organization of Taxpayers, which could count on a few hundred stalwarts. "Loser-types," Watson called them. Jarvis was perpetually in motion, traversing the canyons and ridges of Los Angeles to address meetings of half a dozen homeowners. He led fights to defeat school board tax-override elections. He was a perennial spectator at the cavernous Los Angeles civic auditorium, where he would harangue the board of supervisors until they turned off his microphone.

Jarvis' own life story sounds something like a page of Horatio Alger, with an assist from Mel Brooks' Two-Thousand-Year-Old Man. Born in 1903, the eldest of Judge John Ransom Jarvis' four sons, he grew up on a hardscrabble farm near Magna, Utah, where his chores included shooting the hogs with a .22 and chopping the necks off the chickens. From a rough-and-tumble boyhood, Jarvis graduated in the very first class of the town's first high school, Cypress High, in 1921. He put himself through college working nights in the tubing section of the Magna Copper Mill, and earned money summers at nearby coal and silver mines.

Young Jarvis was wiry and athletic. He played semi-pro baseball and fought twenty-one professional fights as a boxer, sparring with Jack Dempsey in two exhibitions. After college, Jarvis borrowed $15,000 to acquire a failing local weekly newspaper, the Magna *Times*. This he turned into a regional eleven-paper chain of nearly identical weeklies, "You just change the headline, change a couple of slugs, and there you go—you've got another paper," Jarvis recalled. He proved to be a shrewd entrepreneur. With a chain, he could acquire national advertising and big-name columnists. Before he was thirty, according to his autobiography, Jarvis was "making $30,000 or $40,000 a year, which was a lot of money in those days."

In 1931, he left Utah for California, on the advice (Jarvis swears) of an obscure Republican D.A. named Earl Warren. He gravitated to Republican politics, briefly running press operations on Herbert Hoover's 1932 campaign train; he ghosted a biography of J. Paul Getty and invented an array of purely American devices that Sinclair Lewis would not have dared attribute to a Jarvis-like character—the first pushbutton radio tuner, a process to demagnetize Liberty ships to foil U-boats, the Jarvis gas heater (it didn't smell), and even a prototype garbage disposal.

"I should have held on to that garbage disposal," Jarvis said years later. "I didn't realize how big it was going to become."

He lived the life of an all-American tinkerer, dabbling in real estate and politics, opening and closing manufacturing plants, making good money.

When World War II broke out, Jarvis had a brush with bureaucracy that he still recounts with bitterness. His manufacturing plant was producing insulation padding, for which a key ingredient was latex. After Pearl Harbor, the government confiscated his stocks of imported latex as a strategic war material. Not long afterward, synthetic rubber was invented, but Jarvis was out of business. Toward the end of the war, Jarvis insists, he found his old latex drums, spoiled but unused, in a War Production Board warehouse. It took four years for the government to compensate him for the loss.

After the war, Jarvis opened a home appliance factory, which he continued to operate until 1962. His interest in politics deepened. He was a member of the local Republican nominating committee in 1946 that launched Richard Nixon's career as a young congressman, after a bitter campaign against liberal Democrat Jerry Voorhis.

With several hundred thousand dollars from the sale of his factory in 1962, Jarvis retired and turned to politics full time. In the middle seventies, he also took on a part-time paid job as the director of the Los Angeles Apartment Owners Association. His association with his Proposition 13 partner, Paul Gann, did not begin until 1977. Gann, a very different sort of traditional conservative, ran a small citizens' group called the People's Advocate, based in Sacramento, and never became a close ally of Jarvis. Later, in 1979, Gann split with Jarvis and promoted his own successful initiative to cap government spending.

In the sixties, however, as local taxpayer protest gathered momentum, the person most closely associated with tax revolt was neither Jarvis nor Gann, but the Los Angeles County assessor, Philip Watson. As Jarvis tried to organize the small homeowner groups around Los Angeles, he found himself constantly overshadowed by the better-financed and better-known Watson.

Watson was one of those indicted in the statewide probe of assessment practices that followed the Wolden scandals. Like Wolden, he was accused of cutting business assessments in exchange for contributions. The most damning charge was that he dropped an audit on a company that subsequently paid a campaign contribution. But Watson successfully argued that the audit was merely part of the bargaining that preceded the change in assessment formulas, and the judge directed a verdict of not guilty. Looking for popular vindication, Watson began planning his one percent initiative almost as soon as his trial was over.

The year 1968, when both Watson and Jarvis unsuccessfully promoted tax limitation initiatives, should have been a good year for tax protest. The Bay Area counties were first feeling the sting of AB 80; the Los Angeles tax grievances had been festering for several years. But in 1968, unlike 1978, the authorities in Sacramento stole the thunder with their own, more moderate plan. Governor Reagan and the Democratically controlled legislature, this being an election year, exempted the first $750 of homeowners' assessed value, which restored the old balance between business and homeowner property taxes. To mollify business, the legislature also exempted 15 percent of business inventories from taxation.

Politically, the homeowner's exemption was presented quite plausibly as a more responsible alternative to Watson's Proposition 9. Since Watson did not specify how the revenue would be made up, opponents could argue that the initiative would lead to increases in other taxes, or cuts in services. And unlike in 1978, there was no ballooning state surplus to redistribute. Most importantly, times were good and tax grievances scattered. In the November election, the voters rejected the Watson initiative better than 2 to 1.

During the next decade, Jarvis and Watson competed for the leadership of the tax protest movement. Watson remained the more respectable and better financed, leaving Jarvis to play the screwball. Jarvis managed to win the Republican nomination for a seat on the State Board of Equalization in 1970, only to lose the election. Jarvis' second initiative drive, in that year, again failed to qualify for the ballot for lack of signatures.

Watson came back in 1972 with a second tax limitation initiative, to limit property taxes to 1½ percent and shift costs to the state. Mindful of the loss of his earlier initiative, Watson this time specified increases in the corporate income tax and the sales tax, as well as higher "sin taxes" on alcohol and tobacco. This plan did slightly better than the first Watson initiative, losing by 66 percent to 34 percent. Again, Governor Reagan and the legislature came forward with their own tax relief plan, increasing the homeowner's exemption to $1,750 and the business inventory exemption to 50 percent revising the school aid formula, slapping a revenue limit on school finance, and limiting the tax rate local governments could set.

The rate limit, of course, would prove useless in the housing inflation of the late seventies, when taxes were soaring because of higher property values and nominal rates were actually dropping.

Again in 1972, Howard Jarvis and his irregulars weighed in with a petition drive, which again failed to qualify for the ballot. During this period, one more tax limitation initiative nearly succeeded, and it was sponsored by Governor Reagan.

To cap government revenues, Reagan had appointed a task force on tax reduction headed by his economic opportunity director, a John Birch Society leader named Lewis Uhler, who would reemerge as chairman of the National Tax Limitation Committee. Uhler's task force devised a very complicated formula to reduce total taxation as a percentage of personal income over a fifteen-year period at the rate of one-tenth of a percent a year.

Unlike the Watson initiatives, Reagan's Proposition 1 in 1973 was aimed at the size of government, not the distribution of taxes. But the tax relief would come slowly, and the formula of the 5,700-word proposition was so Byzantine that even Governor Reagan confessed he didn't understand all the technicalities, leading the opposition to point out that if the sponsor didn't understand his own proposal, a prudent vote was no. In the November election, Proposition 1 failed, but it gathered 44 percent of the vote.

Howard Jarvis would remember the complexity and the 5,700 words, and Proposition 13 would be brief and to the point; the tax relief would be massive and immediate. No further tax limitation initiative would qualify for the ballot until Proposition 13, although in 1976, Watson tried one last time and failed to get enough signatures. His heart condition was worsening and his old enemies on the County Board of Supervisors were determined to hound him from office. Since Watson had no taxpayers' association to draw on, his initiative drives were financed by contributions, in many cases from companies that had business with the assessor's office. Some yacht owners who contributed to Watson were found to be underassessed. He and several staff members vacationed at the expense of a Las Vegas billboard company holding extensive taxable California property. Watson's nemesis, county supervisor Baxter Ward, and the DA's office brought in Carmine Bellino, who had once been Bobby Kennedy's chief investigator, to draw up a dossier on the assessor.

Finally, in August 1977, with his health failing and the pressure mounting, Watson agreed to resign. Bellino produced more smoke than fire, but once again the odor of corruption hung over the assessor's office, and reform was indicated. To succeed Watson, the supervisors turned to a soft-spoken civic leader with the literary name of Alexander Pope and a scholarly temperament to match. Pope's political innocence, which seemed an ideal qualification, would later be exploited brilliantly by Howard Jarvis. The era of the corrupt assessors was over. In its place was a clean, efficient, and uncontrollable taxing machine.

2

HAM AND EGGS

HOWARD JARVIS is one in a long line of California pseudopopulists who appear periodically to tap the unease that lingers in this precarious Eden. The California good life is nothing if not fragile. The lush harvests are coaxed from temperamental, irrigated soil; the hillside palaces straddle geological faults. The imagery of earthquakes, canyon fires, cults, and droughts suggests an elemental vulnerability that can be easily exaggerated, but that leaves its mark on politics.

The California political culture is a mass culture, without the highly refined local institutions operating at a personal scale that broker political life in the more settled areas of the United States. Instead, the language of California mass politics is articulated through mass media, and through symbols, not through living-room coffees and local political clubhouses. The relative absence of pluralist institutions may be one price California voters pay for the state's compulsive mobility and transience.

Mobility is a double-edged sword. The dominant California ethic of frantic novelty and impermanence conceals a deeper human need for certitude and order. The migrant who settles at the far edge of the continent will not willingly be evicted. Transience is disconcerting enough when it is voluntary; it is quite another matter when one is evicted by the pressure of external forces—say, floods, or forest fires, or property taxes.

California's uneasy, fluid brand of politics makes for apparent ideological lurches, which turn out to have scant basis in ideology. The voters who elected such decent and reasoned progressives as Earl Warren and

Pat Brown could also seek consolation in outright political primitives like the fundamentalist state school superintendent, Max Rafferty; the diminutive bookish S. I. Hayakawa, who won cheers for bashing the Jacobins at San Francisco State; and the crudely demagogic mayor of Los Angeles, Sam Yorty.

These men, like Jarvis, did not represent the careful, ideological conservatism of seasoned money fearing the passions of the mob, but the frightened, know-nothing clamoring of the mob itself. The very extremism of the popular fevers excited by Jarvis sent business scuttling into the opposition camp, even though Proposition 13 bestowed $3.5 billion on business. With such anger thrashing about, business might easily be the next target, as landlords discovered when the inchoate passions turned against rising rents.

California's political greenhouse freely germinates political movements —sudden, tropical profusions with shallow roots and short, intense lives. It produces hybrids that often defy attempts at easy classification. How could Jarvis, whose paid job was director of a landlords' association, emerge as a champion of hard-pressed homeowners? Was Jerry Brown the first hippie governor—or a symbol-stealing stooge for business?

California hothouse politics of course thrive on the great progressive era contribution to direct democracy—the initiative. By putting propositions before the voters, the initiative translates waves of popular sentiment directly into law, without the delaying filters of local voluntary institutions and intermediary legislative refinement so revered by Madison, Tocqueville, and the great theorists of liberal restraint.

Though other states allow direct initiative, California has raised it to an art form. With only 8 percent of the electorate required to sign petitions and the use of paid solicitors permitted, the California initiative has served as a convenient vehicle for varied political zealotry. Its existence helps make the political culture one of extremes, with the polarized, issue-oriented politics that uninitiated eastern liberals find so appealing. The prospect of short-circuiting the legislature and the need to collect half a million signatures create a perfect organizing tool. The media attention attracted by the initiative campaign draws in further recruits in a manner that conventional lobbies can't touch.

The progressive reformers who invented the initiative saw it as a means for the people to blast open legislatures controlled by special interests when Madisonian restraint froze into elitist deadlock. It is no small irony that the initiative, brought to California by the great trust-busting Governor Hiram Johnson, became the indispensable tool of a campaign to produce a massive tax windfall for business. Yet even though his remedy misdirected much of the tax relief, Jarvis succeeded precisely because the legislature stalemated, just as the early progressives foresaw.

Howard Jarvis was not the first political eccentric to popularize an unorthodox idea via the California initiative. He was merely the first to prevail. Before Jarvis, the initiative had produced a number of establishment-backed reforms, several more extreme near-misses, but only a very infrequent controversial policy change, like the coastal zone initiative that voters approved in 1972 to regulate private development along the Pacific coast. Usually, mainstream groups rose up either to defeat or to co-opt the more radical remedies to popular grievances. And the initiative remained the reformist tool intended by its progressive-era inventors.

Like Proposition 13, fiscal initiatives have been a favorite topic. During the Depression, when local governments were hard pressed to provide essential services, California voters successfully initiated a state income tax and later a sales tax to take pressure off local taxes on property. Later, during World War II, they turned down initiatives to repeal both. On several occasions, they rejected a "single tax" on the unearned appreciation of land, promoted by followers of the populist economist Henry George. The initiative was also used to broaden state aid to education. Over the years, Californians voted down measures to prohibit everything from vaccinations to vivisections, as well as more serious antisubversive and right-to-work measures.

The best known of the also-ran ideas was a Depression pension scheme based on the ideas of Dr. Francis Townsend, which went under a variety of names including "Ham and Eggs" and "$25 Every Wednesday." With unemployment high, Townsend's idea was to induce people over sixty to retire on pensions to be financed by a sales tax. In 1938 the Ham and Eggs proposition qualified for the ballot with 789,000 signatures and only narrowly failed to win approval. With slight variation, Ham and Eggs petitions were circulated throughout the next decade. $25 Every Wednesday became $30 Every Thursday and eventually inflated to Sixty Dollars at Sixty. All failed.

In 1948 the Ham and Eggers gave it one last try with a monstrous 21,000-word proposition that sought to build a grand coalition of such diverse issues as pensions, taxes, Indian rights, gambling, and reapportionment, prompting the legislature to write a procedural amendment limiting future initiatives to a single subject.

The first attempts by Jarvis and assessor Watson to promote a tax limitation initiative did little more than provide an organizing vehicle that would later prove quite useful. In 1968 the timing was wrong. Tax grievances, though present, were not pervasive. But when housing prices went into orbit in the mid-seventies and the legislature failed to produce, the little pockets of tax protest groups would still be there, and the dry runs would serve Jarvis well.

TAXES AND PATCHWORK GOVERNMENT

Much that was modern and progressive about California's political system seemed almost perversely fated to give birth to a know-nothing tax revolt. A progressive era invention, the initiative, provided the vehicle. A typically Californian "good-government" assessment reform unknowingly seeded the grievance. Generous social programs seemed an extravagance when the economy soured. The state constitution, with its admirable home rule provisions, gave local government ample power to tax and spend, while the proliferation of service districts at the local level almost guaranteed that the taxpayers would be thoroughly confused about who was taxing them how much, and for what.

Special districts are free-floating units of local government created to deliver a particular service. California has 4,700 such districts, which provide water, sewers, fire protection, parks and recreation, urban renewal, libraries, cemeteries, street lights, garbage collection, soil conservation, flood control, and even mosquito abatement. Few are under direct control of city or county officials. Some are elected; others appointed. Significantly for the tax revolt, many have the autonomous power to levy taxes on property.

Ironically, special districts were created in part to circumvent earlier limits on the power of local government to tax or borrow money. In the Depression, with the erosion of local tax bases and the inability of many local governments to borrow, President Roosevelt encouraged governors to permit the creation of special districts to carry out federally assisted public works.

Getting the voters to approve the creation of a special district turned out to be a lot easier than persuading them to levy a new tax directly, even though the ultimate fiscal effect was the same. But this new form of local government often proved to be substantially less accountable to the voters than an old-fashioned city council or county board of supervisors. With the proliferation of overlapping special districts, a Los Angeles taxpayer might find his property tax bill itemizing upward of twenty different charges, each reflecting a separate rate applied to his assessed property value: a city tax, a county tax, one or two school taxes, and at least a dozen special district taxes.

As long as property values were relatively stable, no unit of government could increase its revenues without increasing the tax *rate*. But with assessments doubling in a single year, it was easy to reap windfalls for pet projects simply by failing to *reduce* the rate.

The property tax on a home, of course, is produced by multiplying the combined tax rate times the assessment.

Of course.

Let's take that again, more leisurely, because it is the key to the whole problem. Rate times assessment equals tax. If a house is worth $80,000, and the assessor has accurately appraised it and assessed it according to the 25 percent formula, then the assessment is $20,000. After each of the little service districts, the county and the city have applied their piece of the tax rate, the total tax rate might add up to 10 percent,* producing a tax of $2,000. The tax is the assessment times the rate.

This seemingly neat bit of elementary arithmetic invites untold mischief and confusion.

Keep the assessment constant over time, as Russ Wolden did, and some taxpayers may be overassessed in comparison with others, but at least local government must deliberately raise the tax *rate* in order to increase revenues. But let inflation create higher and higher assessments, and the rate ceases to be so important. It can drop and tax bills can still rise. Now let there be twenty different taxing districts, each applying its own rate to rising assessments, and the confusion multiplies. Try to figure out which service district is responsible for how much of this year's tax increase.

In California, more than one local government played a cute game of announcing with great fanfare a *cut* in the tax rate, which hid an *increase* in actual taxes, thanks to the higher assessments. The voters might not have appreciated the finer subtleties of the arithmetic, but they understood they were being had.

As a further twist, most local governments in the U.S. typically "back into their tax rate." This means that the city council, for example, determines how much money the city needs for the coming year and what other resources such as state aid it can expect, and then calculates the tax

---

* Expressed as $10 per hundred, or sometimes in mills. A mill is one-tenth of one cent, so $10 per hundred is 100 mills.

rate that will produce the necessary revenue when multiplied by the total assessed valuation. To the average taxpayer, this procedure was clear as mud. He could only read the bottom line, which spelled higher taxes.

Jarvis would convince the voters that these confusing formulas added up to a bonanza for local government. To the individual homeowner, it certainly looked that way, but it wasn't true. Mainly, rising taxes on homeowners were buying tax relief for business.

This happened in two waves. A mild tax shift was created by AB 80, when business assessment ratios were brought into line with assessment formulas on homes. But the legislature largely nullified the impact with the increasingly generous homestead exemptions in 1968 and again in 1972. In the tax year 1972–73, California homes paid 32.1 percent of the state's property taxes—much the same percentage they had paid during the sixties.

In the mid-seventies, however, the tax shift accelerated. The price of housing began to appreciate much faster than the value of commercial properties. As residential housing came to account for an ever higher proportion of the assessed valuation of California property, homeowners bore an ever greater share of the tax load: 34 percent in 1974–75; 40 percent in 1976–77; nearly 45 percent by the time of the vote on Proposition 13. The homeowner share of property taxes increased by a third in just four years. Without Proposition 13, homeowners would have paid more than half the total property tax load by the end of the decade.

THE HOUSING BOOM

California, the home of real estate booms, had never seen one like the housing market of the mid-seventies. Greater Los Angeles was finally paying the price for two generations of sprawl; L.A. was running out of land. People didn't move to Southern California to settle in a high-rise condominium. The preferred style of housing included a ranch house, with yard, fruit trees, and perhaps a swimming pool. If Manhattan had the same density as greater L.A., it would extend halfway to Albany.

With many Angelinos already commuting an hour each way to work, the pressure on the remaining close-in development land grew acute. The first gasoline scare, in 1973, made buyers think twice about living in the fringe areas of Orange or Ventura county. As a consequence, prime development land was fetching $100,000 an acre and up; sometimes the cost of the land exceeded the cost of the house. At the same time, the new environmental laws were making it harder to develop available land. Builders faced new zoning restrictions, sewer moratoriums, and the 1972 coastal zone initiative regulating development along the coast.

The economy, however, continued to boom. When California roared out of the 1973–74 recession, and tight mortgage money suddenly became plentiful again, there was unleashed a pent-up demand for housing which builders were unable to meet. The result was unprecedented inflation in the price of housing.

In the mid-sixties, housing prices in California, as in the rest of the country, rose at 2 to 3 percent a year. By early 1976 they were rising at 2 to 3 percent a *month*. With the stock market flat, the smart money poured into real estate, creating a classic inflationary market that fed upon expectations of further inflation. In parts of Orange County, half of the new single-family houses were being snapped up by speculators, to rent or to hold for future appreciation. On the Irvine Ranch, the developer finally resorted to a lottery to determine who would be permitted to bid on new tracts of townhouses even before they were opened for inspection. Many houses were sold and resold before construction was completed.

With inflation ravaging consumer savings, housing became all the more attractive as an investment. The traditional banker's rule of thumb, allowing 25 percent of income to be allocated for housing, was discarded as young couples spent a third and even a half of their income to get into a house—any house—before the market got away from them altogether. Existing homeowners could sell $25,000 homes for upward of $100,000. They then applied their windfall to the purchase of more-expensive homes, pushing the dizzy climb in housing prices up through the brackets.

In the four years between April 1974 and April 1978, the average price of a Los Angeles single-family house went from $37,800 to $83,200, a rise of more than 120 percent compared with only 48 percent nationally. In December 1975, 31 percent of Orange County single-family homes were valued at more than $70,000. Only eighteen months later, 87 percent were worth more than $70,000. Listings for under $100,000 were very hard to find.

The Federal Home Loan Bank Board, which regulates savings and loan associations, finally issued an order in May 1977 warning its lenders to avoid lending to speculators who didn't intend to reside in a property. But even this failed to deter the rising prices significantly.

Thanks to the reforms of AB 80, these dramatic price rises translated directly into tax increases. The doubling and tripling of property values, however, was largely restricted to single-family housing. While California assessments on single-family houses increased by 110.9 percent between 1975 and 1978, apartments went up only 34.2 percent. Commercial, industrial, farmland, and public utility assessments rose only 26.4 percent.

The resultant tax shift was so massive that it produced an almost unbelievable statistic: While total property tax revenues collected in California during the seventies actually fell—from 7.2 percent of personal income in 1972 to 6.5 percent in 1977—property taxes on *individual* homeowners doubled and tripled.

To homeowners who had gone deeply into debt to clamber aboard the fast-disappearing housing market, the huge tax hikes added insult to injury. Spending an outlandish portion of one's income on homeownership, in an inflationary market, can be justified as a kind of forced savings. Today's cash goes to purchase a hedge against tomorrow's inflation. But it remains a burdensome out-of-pocket expense. The house that sold for $50,000 yesterday may be today's $150,000 house, but it remains the same four walls. The shelter is not suddenly three times better, nor is the psychological satisfaction. The rising nominal value increases your net worth, but the capital gain exists mainly on paper. Unless you plan to live in a tent, you can't buy anything with it. You can always cash in the windfall, but the next house is likely to cost $200,000.

Consequently, the rising property taxes on inflated homes operated as a steadily increasing tax on an *unrealized* gain. Unlike the gain in the value of a stock or a bond, which is taxed only at sale, homeowners were being socked for a purely paper windfall. This windfall increased net worth but not in a form that left the homeowners with ready cash to pay taxes.

The shift in assessed valuation and the rising homeowner taxes produced a world that looked very different to a homeowner than to a local city council or county board. The city got its revenue from many sources —the sales tax, fees, state and federal aid, as well as the property tax. With homes making up on average only about a third of the property tax base, and only a third of properties reassessed each year, the taxes on those homes could double without adding more than a few percent to the city's total revenues.

This arcane arithmetic made little sense to the homeowner. His taxes were doubling! Value received from government was certainly not doubling. Government, obviously, must be squandering the money. To compensate the unlucky homeowner whose assessment had just doubled, government would have to cut the tax rate in half. But with uniform rates on all types of property you couldn't do that. Two-thirds of the homes had not been reassessed. Business property values, accounting for more than 60 percent of the tax base, were not doubling. For local government, there was nothing to be done but to drop the rate slightly, as many cities and counties actually did, and to petition Sacramento for relief. When tax rates were reduced uniformly, the tax shift onto homeowners was only reinforced.

But in the Alice in Wonderland world of inflating property value, where homeowner taxes could double and revenues almost stand still, there was one other diabolical wrinkle worthy of the Red Queen: state aid formulas were inversely related to a community's property values. As assessed valuation went up, state aid for schools, welfare, medical care, etc., went down. From local government's point of view, collecting higher taxes through rising property assessments was like walking up a down escalator. You had to run faster to stay in the same place. Tax burdens not only shifted from businesses to individuals. They shifted from state revenue sources to local ones.

The *state* treasury, however, flourished. California's economy was booming, and the need for state expenditures diminishing. State taxation was entirely different from local. The state did not back into its tax rate. The rates were fixed, and the state backed into a budget surplus. Here again, the process that worked so well during normal times seemed almost foredoomed to produce a tax rebellion once it was mixed with a combustible dose of inflation.

THE GREAT SURPLUS

The state government raises its money mostly from sales and income taxes. AB 80 was entirely in character, since California has one of America's most progressive state tax structures—in both senses of the word: tax administration and enforcement are highly professionalized, and income tax rates are steeply graduated, from one percent in the lowest bracket to 11 percent in the highest. Under the income tax schedule adopted in 1972, the 11 percent bracket begins at the relatively modest taxable income of $15,500.

As money incomes rose with inflation, Californians found themselves pushed into ever higher tax brackets, and the state treasury fattened. The legislature, just as it deadlocked on property tax relief, also failed to pass the indicated remedy of a formula to index the state income tax rates to inflation.

As the inflationary economy stimulated consumer spending, even the state's sales tax receipts, though levied at a flat rate, increased substantially faster than real incomes. In 1977, when personal income rose 11.5 percent, sales tax receipts rose 18.7 percent.

During the Reagan years, the combination of a conservative governor and a liberal legislature led to an odd compromise. Government stopped churning out new social programs, but the state taxing structure became even more steeply progressive. The bipartisan tax reform bill of 1972 not only increased the homeowner exemption; it also broadened sales and corporate income taxes. The highly diversified and resilient California economy began pulling out of the 1973–74 recession just when higher local property assessments were diminishing the need for state aid. Consequently, state officials found themselves with more money than they knew what to do with.

When Ronald Reagan left office in January 1975, he bestowed on his successor a growing state surplus and highly elastic revenue machine that Sacramento veterans said was sufficient to prevent the need for any tax rate increases through the rest of the century.

Every year, about thirty economists and statisticians from California's elite banks, brokerage houses, and academic economics departments hold a closed meeting with officials of the State Department of Finance in the governor's paneled conference room, to project revenues for the coming year on the basis of their projections for the state's economy.

From 1974 on, all the major projections erred dramatically on the low side. In 1974 the Finance Department projected growth in personal income of 7 percent. By year's end, personal income had risen nearly 12 percent. In 1975, '76, and '77, the state's economy grew each year about 20 percent faster than officials had projected. For a while, this embarrassment of riches suited the new governor nicely. The increasing state budget surplus was consistent with Jerry Brown's image as a fiscal conservative. He could continue to balance the state's books at a time when Jimmy Carter's budget was in serious deficit, and still have billions left over to fund pet environmental projects and to redeem his campaign pledge to business to eliminate the tax on business inventories.

But the state taxing formulas proved more elastic than anyone dreamed, and the surplus soon became too much of a good thing. Like Pinocchio's nose betraying its owner, the accumulated surplus grew and grew, from about three-quarters of a billion dollars when Jerry Brown became governor to $4 billion when Proposition 13 passed. And as it grew, it made a liar out of government. The state of California was earning a quarter of a billion dollars a year just from the interest on the surplus.

The surplus was coming from somewhere, of course. It was coming out of taxpayers' pockets. Between 1973 and 1977, personal income in California increased from $103.8 billion to $156.4 billion—better than 50 percent. Personal income *taxes* increased more than 150 percent, sales taxes increased by 188 percent.

Oddly, the rising taxes were not the result of pressure by government to finance new programs. Jerry Brown, much to the consternation of his liberal allies, was holding down spending almost as tightly as former Governor Reagan. Rather, the taxation system had taken on a life of its own. Neither the legislature nor the governor acted to interfere with the soaring trajectory of the revenue curves, which accelerated with each new dose of inflation.

Elsewhere, New York City teetered on bankruptcy while the federal deficit set new records. A surplus was a very comforting thing for a state government in the mid-seventies. In his first post–Proposition 13 speech, Jerry Brown could say, unblushingly, that he had kept his promise to the voters not to raise state taxes. Technically, this was correct. Rates had not been raised, but thanks to inflation, income tax collections soared.

Oddly, too, there was little protest about the unlegislated increases in state income taxes. The state income tax was small compared with the federal tax. Thanks to the payroll deduction system, the tax was invisible for most wage earners. Having your raise all but wiped out when you landed in a higher bracket was cause for chronic grumbling, but not the stuff of rioting in the streets. Though state taxes increased, real spendable incomes were also rising until the late 1970s. In a sense, the rising property tax paid for the sins of the income tax. For most taxpayers, who get a refund on their income tax as often as a bill, the property tax is the sole occasion to sit down and actually write a check to the government.* When that check suddenly doubles regardless of what has happened to earnings, it hurts. In California, the tax is collected twice yearly, in the spring, when thoughts turn to federal income taxes, and in mid-December at the height of Christmas shopping.

Remarkably, the legislature and the Governor failed to deal with the spiraling property taxes despite three years' grace; thanks to the three-

---

* In some states, taxes are "escrowed" and paid monthly along with the mortgage payments.

The bill filed by Petris was a tax reformer's wish list. Petris' "Tax Justice Act of 1977" would restore the traditional balance between taxes on homes and businesses by providing a generous "circuit-breaker" to refund a portion of local property taxes, under a formula tied to income: The lower the income, the higher the percentage to be refunded. Renters also would receive rebates. The Petris bill was to be financed partly out of the state surplus, and partly by adding new upper brackets under the state income tax and removing the income tax preference on capital gains.

The Petris bill, which would cost nearly a billion dollars a year, was backed by a broad liberal coalition—labor, consumer groups, local governments, the grassroots Citizens' Action League, and the California Tax Reform Association. It was strenuously opposed by business interests, because it raised capital gains taxes and concentrated the tax relief in lower brackets.

The approach was also opposed by the Governor, who eventually threw his support to a rival proposal which was introduced by Senator Jerry Smith, a conservative Democrat from Saratoga, and supported by the Republicans. Smith's formula also tied property tax relief to income, but it concentrated more of the relief in the upper-income brackets. It also imposed a revenue limit on local government. Both bills initially passed the senate.

BROWN

In early 1977, Jerry Brown remained as much of an enigma to the legislature as to most everybody else. After a single term as secretary of state, he had led a lackluster field of Democrats in the 1974 primary and went on narrowly to defeat the Republican candidate, state controller Houston Flournoy.

As Governor, Brown baffled and infuriated the traditional liberal-labor coalition, which had worked so closely with his father, Pat Brown. The younger Brown took the cards of Roosevelt's New Deal and gave them a fresh shuffle. Nominally, labor and the urban poor would be part of his constituency—they had nowhere else to go—but more attention was given to the newer additions to the liberal coalition: environmentalists, feminists, Chicanos, gays. These were handed numerous symbolic victories and a spate of radically unorthodox appointments to state regulatory and judicial offices.

Brown's argot reflected the buzz words and fashions of the California counterculture. He shunned the grotesque new Governor's Mansion designed by Ronald and Nancy Reagan and retreated to a bachelor apartment with a mattress on the floor. He was well read for a politician, and his tastes ran to pop social criticism, ecology, and writings on Buddhism. He dated Linda Ronstadt; he had a guru. This was great copy, but it masked Brown's disdain for the bread-and-butter social issues so dear to the old liberal coalition: jobs, housing, health, education. Many of his early liberal supporters left during his first term, some of them quite bitter.

His personal freakiness, his sincere antinuclear stance, and his close ties to a few individual radical notables such as Cesar Chavez and Tom Hayden brought Brown some elbow room that concealed a fairly ordinary, moderate conservatism. Though a genuine ascetic personally, Brown's "era of limits" turned out to apply mostly to social programs, not individual or corporate excess. His approach to education, health, mental health, and social services was barely distinguishable from Reagan's. As time passed, some of his critics on the left saw in his embrace of counterculture symbols more than passing cynicism. His preachings about living modestly also combined oddly with an almost Calvinist summons to greatness. The self-denial was part of a formula for grandeur, not simplicity.

In a remarkable interview shortly after his conversion to Proposition 13, Brown insisted that he was not categorically antigovernment: "There are some areas of spending that should be increased," he said, "like space," and he went on to speak rapturously of space exploration as the last frontier. "We have to decide whether we're a great nation, or just a bigger version of Uruguay," he declared.

And what of those directly hurt by the Proposition 13 cuts, whose welfare checks were not keeping pace with inflation, whose children could not go to summer school, what would they say to this set of priorities?

"What would they have said to Queen Isabella?" Brown replied, deadpan.

Unlike other renowned media politicians, Brown did not complement his public manipulation of symbols with backstage legislative wizardry. He had little aptitude or taste for legislative politics. On most major issues, his custom was to announce a program at a press conference and let the legislature write its own bill. Thanks to the item-veto in the California constitution, Brown still enjoyed some control over the final product.

Rather than cutting deals, the Governor was given to Zen utterances; bargaining with Brown was like pushing on a string. He asked for few favors and he delivered fewer. "What kind of leverage do you have with a governor who doesn't want anything?" said one legislator despairingly, and others used almost identical words.

Though tax reform was given major billing in Brown's 1977 State of the State address, neither Brown nor anyone in his inner circle considered property tax relief a high personal priority in a preelection year. Once the Administration's own 1977 tax relief package, costing $480 million, was unveiled January 10, Brown had characteristically little influence on the development of the bill in the legislature, other than to warn lawmakers to keep down the cost to the state. This changed only when the bill got to conference committee in June.

Two other tax matters, dear to business, were uppermost in Brown's mind. By 1977, businesses enjoyed a tax exemption on 50 percent of their inventories. Over the years, the exemption had been gradually increased to get business support for various tax packages, beginning with AB 80 in 1966. In his 1974 campaign, Brown promised business to get rid of the other 50 percent. Even Reagan, as a conservative, had traded business inventory tax relief for other taxes. Brown, the Democrat, was prepared to give away $450 million in business tax relief and get nothing in return, at a time when homeowners were crying for property tax relief.

The Governor was also waging war with his own tax enforcement officials over their treatment of multinational corporations doing business in California. Unlike most states that put courting business ahead of tax enforcement, California had a long tradition of tough auditing of corporate income tax returns. Most states permitted corporations to book profits according to the corporation's own internal accounting artifices, which minimized the corporation's tax exposure in any one state.

California law, however, required that corporations doing business in the state pay income taxes based on the fraction of total worldwide business done in California, regardless of where the profits were nominally booked.

In 1977, however, the corporate tax lobby nearly succeeded in using a little-known treaty as a device to have the federal government override California's tax enforcement. A provision was slipped into an obscure tax enforcement treaty being negotiated with Great Britain, prohibiting any state from requiring business to account their worldwide profits on a unitary basis.

While Brown was warning legislators to keep down the cost of property tax relief, he was quietly lobbying the U.S. Senate to approve a treaty that eventually would have cost California hundreds of millions of corporate tax dollars. Ironically, the main opponent of the treaty was the multistate tax commission, a cooperative tax enforcement project sponsored by nineteen western states, pioneered by California. (Despite Brown's support, liberals in the U.S. Senate stripped the provision from the treaty.)

A year afterward, Brown and his allies would take their revenge against the state's top tax enforcement official, a career civil servant named Martin Huff, who ran the successful campaign against the tax treaty. Huff is a revered figure to professional tax administrators and the *bête noir* of corporate tax evaders. Countless industrial magnates have maneuvered tax-forgiveness deals with California politicians only to run smack into Martin Huff.

Under California law, Huff, as chief taxation civil servant, had extraordinary protection from political interference. He could not be fired, except by a two-thirds vote of the state senate. This insulation enabled him to run a tough, corruption-free tax administration.

In September 1979, Huff's nominal boss, state comptroller Ken Cory, had his allies in the legislature slip a rider onto a routine bill, giving the three-man Franchise Tax Board headed by Cory the power to fire Huff. Despite widespread indignation that this constituted an underhanded attack on a dedicated public servant, the legislation was signed by Cory's boss, Governor Jerry Brown.

A few days later, Huff received a telegram from former governor Pat Brown. "Deeply regret my son's failure to veto this very unfair bill," Brown Senior wrote. "You are one of the most courageous, independent and fair men that I have ever met. I am proud that you were part of my administration."

On October 2, Huff resigned. It would not be the last time that Pat Brown apologized for his son's tax policies.

THE LEGISLATURE

As the 1977 legislative session wore on, the posturing on the tax relief issue came to resemble the familiar *Perils of Pauline* scenario from years past: the two houses of the legislature would disagree; a conference committee would be appointed; after furious lobbying and bargaining, there would be a compromise tax bill, signed by the Governor at the eleventh hour.

By June the inevitable conference committee was meeting. While the committee in Sacramento struggled to find a formula that would command the necessary two-thirds majority in both houses, a Los Angeles haberdasher named James Earle Christo was also doing some basic arithmetic. Christo went back a long way with Howard Jarvis. He had been fighting tax increases in the city of Bellflower since the late fifties. As vice chairman and cofounder of Jarvis' United Organization of Taxpayers, Christo also got along well with Paul Gann, who headed a conservative group called the People's Advocate, based in Sacramento.

Gann's recent attempt to put his own tax limitation measure on the ballot had collected about 300,000 signatures, nearly all in northern California. Jarvis' effort fell short with more than 400,000, mostly garnered in greater L.A.; 500,000 were necessary to qualify. "Three plus four equals seven," said Christo, and he began working to get Jarvis and Gann together.

The two men had little use for each other. Howard Jarvis disliked the patrician Gann, who considered Jarvis an unseemly buffoon. Negotiations for a coalition had broken down once before, in 1976, when Gann teamed up with Watson and Jarvis had felt double-crossed.

After several weeks of quiet discussions with Gann, Christo was able to enlist the support of others on the United Organization of Taxpayers board. Gann flew in for a Sunday morning meeting at Jarvis' office, and the two men shook hands. On May 31, Jarvis and Gann jointly announced their latest drive. Jarvis would later point to his million signatures in Southern California and insist that he had never needed Gann.

In July the 1977 reassessments came out, fueling taxpayer anger anew.

The deliberations of the conference committee in Sacramento dragged on all summer. Liberals had begun with a good deal of momentum behind their drive for a broadly redistributive tax bill, but the political currents had worked against the Petris bill. With the next general election more than a year away, neither the legislature nor the Governor felt the pressure that had produced the earlier tax relief bills in the election years 1968 and 1972.

The Republican members of the legislature had nothing to lose if the tax bill failed. Of eighty assembly seats, only twenty-three were held by Republicans; several of these were planning to retire, and the remainder were in largely safe districts. Seventeen Democrats, but only three Republican senators, were up for reelection, and all three were expected to retire. "If the voters got angry because they didn't get tax relief and decided to throw the bums out, the bums who would get thrown out were all Democrats," observed Dean Tipps, who as lobbyist for the California Tax Reform Association orchestrated the lobbying for the Petris bill. As the price for supporting a tax reform bill, Republicans could—and did—call the shots.

Finally, on September 2, after marathon negotiation, the conference voted out a bill that allocated $550 million to homeowner relief and $285 million for renters and sought to buy in business and the Governor by spending $450 million to repeal the tax on business inventories.

Nobody really liked the bill. To liberals the formula failed to provide enough money for homeowner relief and gave too much to business. The tax reform coalition withdrew its support for the bill. Some Republicans also objected that the tax relief phased out in the highest-income brackets. And business objected to new fees authorized for local government.

Support in the senate dissolved fast. On the floor, the assembly approved the conference bill by the necessary two-thirds, but in the senate, Petris' own Democrats began defecting from the bill. "Senators from the cow counties complained that too many of the dollars were going to reduce the higher property taxes in the cities," Nick Petris said. "That's four votes. The farmers didn't like the fact that farms were taxed as businesses. That's another five votes. A good friend of mine from a suburban district didn't like the renter relief. And the tax reformers didn't think the bill was redistributing enough."

The center failed to hold, and Petris failed to deliver even a simple majority.

"The average guy doesn't care about my problems," he fumed. "All he knows is that his taxes are going through the roof and we couldn't get a bill out. We looked terrible."

The legislature planned to come back for a last hectic week after taking a recess for Labor Day, to give tax relief one last try.

Brown might have been on the phone to legislators, rounding up the necessary votes, but that wasn't his style. On Labor Day, the Governor spoke at the traditional picnic in Pleasanton. His speech was a tough rhetorical denunciation of multinational corporations, but his mind was on tax relief for business. Chatting with a few legislators, Brown inquired, "What can we do about the business inventory tax?"

Under pressure of adjournment, a second conference committee tried once more. The bill was liberalized, changing the formula for renters and adding another hundred million to homeowner relief. Other business taxes were raised to offset the repeal of the inventory tax. But the support for this last attempt was thin.

Brown was still warning the legislature to keep the total price down; despite the growing surplus, the Governor's main concerns were to keep the surplus free for other pet projects and to avoid raising other taxes to pay for property tax relief.

The *coup de grace* came with the loss of Republican support. The senate Republican leadership blasted the bill as providing too little for middle-income tax relief and too much for renters. The Republican caucus leader, Senator George Deukmejian, pressed his thirteen colleagues to oppose the bill unanimously.

Brown was almost useless in the effort to round up votes. His own support was lukewarm, and buttonholing legislators was not his forte. His tardy attempt to win the support of the senate's most liberal Republican, Milton Marks of San Francisco, failed.

The measure was called up for floor debate on September 15, the final day of the session. Speaker Leo McCarthy had the necessary two-thirds votes for passage in the assembly, but decided to wait for the senate vote. Sponsors needed to hold every Democrat plus at least one Republican.

Late into the evening came a fatal defection when Democrat Walter Steirn of Bakersfield announced he could not support the bill. "I have to go out to Antelope Valley next week to make a speech about this and I really shudder," Steirn began. "I'm going to talk to those people about circuit breakers, split level tax concepts, XYZ funds, marginal threshhold rates." Steirn looked around the chamber and shook his head. "*Marginal threshhold rates?*"

In the end, the sponsors came up two votes short. Steirn voted no, along with all fourteen Republicans. The 1977 session adjourned, with no tax bill.

An editorial cartoon in the Sacramento *Bee* expressed a popular view in the state capital that Republican senators had killed the bill for partisan advantage. The cartoon showed the Republican caucus chairman, Senator Dennis Carpenter, whispering over the corpse of Tax Reform as he handed the smoking gun in a handkerchief to the minority leader, Senator Deukmejian: "Wipe off our fingerprints, Deuk, and we'll blame it on the Democrats."

If Democrats in the legislature saw things that way, the Governor did not. His comment was classic Brown: "The senate," he intoned, "needs a period of reflection . . ."

But in the view of many Democrats, what the senate needed was a swift kick. They felt set up by the Republicans, and wanted Brown to go on the attack. "If Brown had called the legislature back into special session and made it clear that tax relief was being held up by two Republican votes, he could have forced the bill out," said one.

This, however, was neither Brown's form of leadership nor his political interest. An election year was coming up. As a centerist looking for support from suburban homeowners and businessmen who vote Republican as often as not, Brown was not prepared to scapegoat Republicans. In many respects, he found the Republican minority in the legislature more congenial than the carping Democrats to his left. Republican views on tax issues were far closer to his own. The Governor would wait till next year.

Even as the legislature failed to deliver the promised tax relief and the autumn tax bills went out to homeowners, many in Sacramento did not realize just how late was the hour. After all, the election was still a whole year away. There would be plenty of time to vote out a tax bill well before November 1978.

During that fall, after the editorial blasts at the legislature's failure, an eerie calm descended. Tax protest was not dominating the papers. Legislators did not hear much from constituents about tax relief. Some took this as a sign that the fever was quieting down. But there was another explanation: the voters had given up on Sacramento and had taken their tax grievances elsewhere. Jarvis was collecting signatures in record numbers. On December 20, he and Gann qualified their initiative with 1.2 million signatures.

THE PROPOSITION

In the absence of anything better, Proposition 13 offered homeowners a deceptively simple appeal:

All property would be taxed at a flat one percent of actual value.

No new taxes could be raised, either by the state or local government, except by a two-thirds majority vote.

For present homeowners, property assessments would be rolled back and frozen at 1975–76 levels, except for a token 2 percent annual hike for inflation. New homes, and newly bought homes, could be assessed at current market values.

Translated into dollars, this meant that an average Los Angeles homeowner, paying a 1977 tax of about $2,200 on a $70,000 home, would have his taxes frozen at $700 a year, plus a cost-of-living increase far less than the actual inflation rate.

If the taxpayer grievances were amply justified, even the most cursory analysis of Proposition 13's likely effects revealed gross inequities. Local government would either be hobbled financially or newly dependent on Sacramento. On average, local governments stood to lose about 23 percent of their total revenues. With the state surplus then estimated at less than half of the Proposition 13 cuts, there was no apparent means of making up the lost revenues short of massive cuts in services, or new taxes. Since local government's dependence on the property tax varied widely—from 100 percent in the case of some service districts, to about 40 percent for schools and less than 20 percent for some cities and more than 50 percent for others—the axe would fall with random injustice.

And this was just the beginning. While the cause of tax protest was raising *homeowner* assessments, about $3.5 billion of the $5.5 billion savings would go to landlords and business property (ultimately mostly to out-of-state corporate shareholders). Ironically, state and federal government would recapture over $1.5 billion, thanks to diminished property tax deductions against the income tax. In short, Proposition 13 created a remarkably perverse "multiplier," which removed $5.5 billion worth of revenues but saved homeowners only about $2 billion in taxes.

The principle of taxing everybody uniformly would be grossly violated. Because Jarvis' grandfather clause locked in 1975–76 assessments only for homeowners who stayed put, next-door neighbors with identical homes would pay wildly different taxes. This disparity would be compounded over time as market values continued to rise. The result would be a shift of tax burdens from the old to the young: Mom and Pop, who bought their house in the fifties, already enjoyed a housing bargain. Their mortgage payments, perhaps $200 a month, reflected the low housing prices and easy interest rates of those years, while the kids paid $700 and $800 a month to amortize mortgages upward of $60,000, at interest rates topping 10 percent. Now, to add insult to injury, Proposition 13 would grandfather the longtime homeowner's *taxes* as well, while the new buyer would be taxed at ever-increasing market values.

The grandfather clause would also accelerate the tax shift from businesses onto homeowners. Factories and refineries are almost never sold; even small businesses change hands far less often than homes, which sell on average every five or six years. After a decade under Proposition 13, most homes—having sold once—would be assessed at current values, while the clock would be frozen at the 1975–76 levels for most business assessments. Further, sales of business properties are often missed by the assessor because the transfer is of stock rather than the physical property. In short, the tax shift that created Proposition 13 would be exaggerated by Proposition 13.

Two years after Proposition 13, thanks to continued inflation in housing prices, assessments were still rising just as fast as they were on the eve of Proposition 13. Now, however, because existing homeowners were grandfathered at their old assessments (plus 2 percent per year), only newly purchased homes got stuck with the full assessment hikes. The increasing residential share of the tax load was being absorbed almost exclusively by young homeowners, who could afford the hike least.

The Jarvis amendment also raised a thicket of troubling questions of governance and public administration: What kind of strings would the legislature attach to its new local aid? Would Proposition 13, as a reaction against red tape, create new layers of bureaucracy? With no new taxes permitted to pay off new local bonds,* how would localities finance public improvements?

Since many federal aid programs require local matching funds; how much federal aid would be lost? With change in ownership triggering reassessment, would widows be penalized when they inherited property? Would property that decreased in value be frozen at the 1975–76 level? How could localities honor contractually mandated pay increases? In tight rental markets like Los Angeles, would landlords pass along their windfall tax relief to tenants?

As the long list of probable effects began to sink in, virtually every special interest group in the state found good reason to oppose Proposition 13. Big business, the recipient of the biggest windfall, saw long-term risks. Business craves predictability even more than low taxes. The potential damage to government would shake the investment climate. Delayed voter anger at reduced public services and business's large share of the tax relief would create pressure for higher corporate taxes. Builders, already reeling from environmental controls, saw local governments imposing a rash of new fees and losing the ability to finance public improvements with bonds. More seriously, the grandfather clause would produce a housing market in which nobody with a locked-in assessment would ever want to buy a new house. The powerful California Taxpayers Association, representing corporate taxpayers, took a strong position against Jarvis.

Consequently, the coalition of interest groups that cranked up to oppose Proposition 13 was the most far-flung—and unwieldy—in anyone's memory.

---

* General obligation bonds were wiped out as a financing source; some communities could still rely on self-liquidating revenue bonds, which are not guaranteed by future tax receipts.

4

THE CAMPAIGN

SELDOM, IF EVER, was there such a grand coalition of diverse and antagonistic interest groups arrayed against a ballot proposition, and seldom was there a more disastrous campaign.

To nearly every respectable politician in California, Howard Jarvis, even with his million and a quarter signatures, remained, quite simply, a nut. The removal of an estimated $7 billion dollars of local revenue*— nearly 60 percent of the total property tax—was plainly unthinkable. As late as January 1978, Governor Jerry Brown had other plans for some of the state surplus: a new $300 million housing program; an alternative energy scheme; even a state-operated space satellite.

Prodded by Jarvis' unexpected success, the legislature finally overcame its differences in February and brought forth a bipartisan tax relief bill, sponsored by Senator Peter Behr, a courtly, British-born Republican from the old money San Francisco suburb of Tiburon.

At a cost of $1.4 billion, the Behr bill provided a 30 percent across-the-board cut in homeowner taxes, doubled tax credits for renters and the elderly, and authorized different rates for homes and businesses to compensate for the inflation in housing prices tied to a local revenue limit. The bill required a constitutional modification permitting the split rate, which was presented for ratification by the voters as Proposition 8.

Now there were two tax relief items on the June ballot: one drafted by

* The actual cut turned out to be $6.15 billion.

the legislature and backed by much of the state establishment, the other drafted by Jarvis and Gann and put on the ballot by a million and a quarter angry taxpayers.

A comparison proved instructive. Because Proposition 8 targeted most of the relief to homeowners, the $1.4 billion brought virtually the same residential tax reductions as the far more expensive Proposition 13. Seemingly, the legislature's bill also had the political advantage of appealing to the 45 percent of the electorate who rented, who would get nothing from Proposition 13. Liberal tax reformers and their legislative allies suddenly found themselves with a stunning gift horse. Not only had Jarvis finally inspired the legislature to act; the entire state business establishment was horrified by Jarvis, and willing to help finance the No-on-13 campaign.

Kirk West, the influential director of the business-oriented California Taxpayers Association, considered Proposition 13 fiscally irresponsible and potentially catastrophic for the state's economy. West urged the state's business leaders to unite in opposition to Jarvis. Howard Allen, the politically influential vice president of Southern California Edison (which stood to save $53.8 million in taxes under Proposition 13), moved quickly to organize a business-dominated No coalition. In early February, while the legislature was still putting the finishing touches on the Behr bill, Allen called a Los Angeles meeting to plan strategy with other business notables including A. W. Clausen of Bank of America, together with labor, education, and civic leaders and Assembly Speaker Leo McCarthy.

"What business, or others, might win in short run gain they would lose in the long run through offsetting taxes," Allen said at a press conference. "Although business stands to receive at least $4 billion of the anticipated $6 billion in property tax relief, we felt it was time for the private sector, among others, to stand up for principle and fight this measure as unsound."

While many liberals grew instinctively wary of a public utility that shunned tax breaks in the name of principle, Allen was able to broker his grand coalition. A statewide organizing meeting held in a Burlingame hotel February 28 brought together in one room eighty groups representing the entire spectrum of California's power elite: the state association of manufacturers and the AFL-CIO; the liberal California Tax Reform Association and the conservative California Taxpayers Association; every good government group from the venerable League of Women Voters to the upstart Common Cause, as well as consumer, environmental, police, fire, schoolteacher, feminist, minority, and senior citizens organizations.

This gift horse proved to be not quite Trojan, but an ill-tempered, wheezing nag, hauling far too many riders. With business helping to underwrite the No coalition, the liberals were denied their strongest argument: you could hardly tag Proposition 13 as a bonanza for corporations when the Chamber of Commerce was bankrolling your campaign.

From the outset, the No campaign was hobbled by crippling differences of principle and tactic, compounded by personal rivalries. Liberals, for example, insisted that the campaign emphasize Proposition 8. Tax grievances were real, and you couldn't beat something with nothing. The Behr bill should be promoted as the more effective remedy. But many of the more conservative elements in the No coalition didn't like the precedent of taxing business at a higher rate. Proposition 8, as a major theme, was vetoed early. So was a big appeal to renters. The dominant memory of the No campaign, for many of the harried campaign workers, was an endless series of phone calls, with the Governor's office on one line, while the AFL-CIO, Speaker McCarthy, the Chamber of Commerce, the state teachers association, two rival tax groups, and Bank of America champed on hold. It did not make for a zestful, inventive campaign.

Howard Jarvis found himself in a delicious brier patch. The entire state establishment, fat, unruly, and divided against itself, was ganging up on him. When Speaker McCarthy tried to tag Proposition 13 the "Landlords' Enrichment Act," not an unreasonable description, Jarvis had only to point out the honor roll of big contributors to the No campaign: Federated Department Stores ($12,500), Pacific Mutual Insurance Company ($25,000), Southern California Edison ($25,000), Carter Hawley Hale ($12,500) . . . as well as five- and even six-figure contributions from the big and self-interested public employee unions. Jarvis' own list proved to be a long roster of unknowns, mailing in ten- and twenty-dollar checks. The other side had everybody but the people.

THE MEDIA

The campaign also turned into a battle of two rival public relations firms: Butcher-Forde for Jarvis, and Winner-Wagner for the No coalition.

Winner and Wagner were mainstays of liberal democratic California politics. Chuck Winner had worked on Pat Brown's campaigns and had managed Jerry Brown's first try for public office—a campaign for the Community College Board. Bill Butcher and Arnie Forde were younger, with no discernible political convictions. Both had worked for Winner at one time. They set up their own shop in Newport Beach, where they gravitated toward the Right and developed a reputation as direct mail wizards, working largely in local legislative and municipal campaigns.

In early 1978, Butcher and Forde were working for State Senator John Briggs, author of Proposition 6, the antigay initiative. Briggs, one of California's few elected officials supporting Proposition 13, introduced Butcher to Jarvis, who was in desperate need of funds. Jarvis' million signatures had cost only about $58,000 to collect, far less than the sums of a million and up often spent on initiatives, but there was little left for the campaign itself.

"We made two quick decisions," Butcher recalled later. "We decided to put most of our effort into direct mail, and we decided to build the whole thing around Jarvis. Most people thought Howard Jarvis was a goofy old gadfly who would hurt his own cause. We felt he was somebody ordinary taxpayers could identify with. So we said let's not diffuse this; let's make this one guy and his struggles the entire focus. The other side thought that was great. Well, we were right and they were wrong.

"We had a relatively straightforward thing to sell," Butcher reminisced further. "You could reduce your own taxes and jab the politicians in the ass at the same time."

Jarvis had an unerring sense that political figures in California had lost their legitimacy to many taxpayers. Like the useless, ritual deliberations of Petrograd or Versailles, the self-important activity in Sacramento ceased to have meaning for the ordinary property owner. Jarvis calculated correctly that the voters would regard the legislature's rival Proposition 8 as too little, too late, and inherently suspect for its parentage. He had great sport with the Behr bill, which he persisted in calling the "Bare Bill," and made much of the fact that it was written by the politicians. Jarvis also hit two other facts—that Proposition 8 merely authorized a split rate but left the precise tax relief formula to the politicians in the legislature, while Proposition 13 locked the one percent tax rate into the state constitution.

"Proposition 13 cuts taxes two-thirds; Proposition 8 does not," began one of Butcher-Forde's TV spots. "Proposition 13 requires a two-thirds vote for new taxes; Proposition 8 does not. Proposition 13 rolls back assessments; Proposition 8 does not. The People put Proposition 13 on the ballot. The politicians put Proposition 8 on the ballot. Now we know why."

If Butcher and Forde had a clientele of one and some nimble, intuitive appeals, Winner and Wagner reported to a committee. To divine a common theme, Winner began by conducting an extensive public opinion poll. The results did not bode well. It mattered little to most voters that business got most of the tax relief as long as the homeowner got some, too. The loss-of-local-control argument was empty theory, against the hard reality of Jarvis' tax savings. The polls confirmed a deep distrust of politicians. Voters liked Proposition 8—until they found out where it was drafted. And a large portion of the public was convinced that government spending could be trimmed by up to 15 percent without affecting vital services.

Suspecting as much, Butcher and Forde featured Jarvis in a masterful TV spot contrasting the $7 billion Proposition 13 tax cut with the total government revenues exceeding $70 billion. "Proposition 13 will reduce government's money by 9 percent," Jarvis intoned soothingly. "That's all. Just 9 percent." Then came the announcer with the Proposition 13 tag line: "Give the politicians a budget instead of a blank check. Vote Yes."

With such voter attitudes, Chuck Winner's polls suggested only one theme that seemed at all persuasive to undecided voters: Proposition 13 looked a bit excessive and might cut into vital government services. This was also the one concern shared by all the elements in the unwieldy No coalition, from the public employee unions who seemed self-serving to the suspiciously altruistic corporations. From the outset, Winner urged the No coalition to duck the tax issue altogether and stress the loss of services.

Here was the slogan: "It may look good, but it costs too much." Service cuts became the central pitch of the No campaign.

As with the scientifically designed perfect dog food which the dogs wouldn't eat, there was only one problem: the voters didn't entirely believe that vital services were jeopardized. As the state surplus continued to grow, the scare campaign looked increasingly silly.

Many of the liberal groups in the coalition thought the slogan not only risky, but patronizing. "Tax grievances are real," complained Dean Tipps, the lobbyist for the California Tax Reform Association. "When the issue is taxes, we'd better talk about taxes." But Winner's polls told him that tax issues were too complicated to risk commercials contrasting Proposition 13 with Proposition 8. Tipps thought this was absurd, since tax issues were the whole point. "Chuck Winner was a prisoner of his polls," Tipps would say afterward.

Eventually, Winner and Wagner set up a separate Yes-on-8 committee, as well as a statewide renters' committee. But the coordination of so many disparate committees and egos sapped the funds and the energy of the No effort. Every ad had to be cleared with key leaders of the No coalition, and the ads came out bland and unconvincing.

Firemen were posed in front of fire stations, warning about precious minutes lost in alarm response times. Police spokesmen warned about increased crime. This proved persuasive to some voters, but others wondered why the politicians couldn't cut the ubiquitous "fat," instead of police and fire services.

With all its woes, however, the No campaign began to make some lumbering headway. Jarvis, after all, *was* a little nutty. People *did* worry about losing services. In past years, support by the hard-core faithful gave extremist initiatives an early lead, until the wider electorate appreciated the fine print, gradually eroding the lead, and a "crossover" was reached a few weeks before the election.

It began to look as though Proposition 13 just might follow the pattern. By late April, the No campaign was within a few points of Jarvis, and gaining. In May, everything came apart.

Jarvis was making a preposterous claim, pounding away at it day after day. Property taxes, he insisted, would soon double again. This was, of course, unthinkable, since they were already at a level so exorbitant as to have provoked the revolt in the first place.

The 1978 assessments were scheduled to be released in July. Why, Jarvis wondered aloud, can't we see them before the June election?

One of Jarvis' most effective television commercials showed a musical jack-in-the-box; as the music box played "Pop Goes the Weasel," a voice-over said coyly, "The politicians have a surprise for you. But they didn't want you to know about it until after the election." The box popped open, to reveal the message that taxes for many Californians would go up 100 percent.

Butcher and Forde also used computerized public records of property tax payments to devise an ingenious and barely legal mailing to taxpayers in several counties. The bold print on the envelope read simply: IMPORTANT ASSESSMENT INFORMATION INSIDE, suggesting an official notice from the assessor. The recipient tore open the envelope to find a letter from Howard Jarvis, beginning: "I was shocked to learn that your 1977 property tax was . . ." (here the computer inserted the individual's exact tax), and advising that the tax was likely to double within three years. The mailing closed with an appeal for Proposition 13 and a fund-raising coupon.

In his appearances around the state, Jarvis continued to pull assessment projections out of thin air, hoping that one of the county assessors would be pressured into releasing the 1978 figures before the election. "We kept making it more and more outrageous," said one of Jarvis' aides, "hoping that some assessor would crack. We would have settled for Lake County." The No campaign was still gaining. A poll conducted in mid-May had 42 percent of the voters supporting Proposition 13, with 39 percent opposed, and 19 percent still undecided.

Bill Butcher was on the road with Jarvis when the phone rang in his hotel room.

"One of the assessors just broke," Arnie Forde sang out.

"Oh, that's great," Butcher replied. "I hope it's a county with enough growth to make it look reasonable."

"Oh yes, it's one of those," Forde assured him.

"Which one?"

"L.A."

THE DEBACLE

It had been only ten weeks earlier when the Board of Supervisors in Los Angeles had appointed Alex Pope assessor, to replace the controversial Watson and clean up the assessor's office. As a reformer, Pope was up for election in his own right in November. It did not seem right—or politic—to bottle up the new assessments until just after the Proposition 13 vote in June.

On a far less philosophical level, some 1,400 people worked in the assessor's office, and they all had tax-paying uncles, cousins, and neighbors. Inevitably, as rumors flew, some of the new assessment figures leaked out.

With Jarvis' luck running true to form, it was the sizzling real estate in West Los Angeles that came up for reassessment in 1978, some 500,000 parcels in all. Pope's preliminary figures showed that the average assessment would increase 125 percent. Some assessments would triple. Jarvis, the great inventor of statistics, had understated what was coming.

True, the rising assessments would not translate precisely into doubled and tripled taxes, because the rate could be dropped. But you couldn't drop the rate enough to cancel the assessment increases, because two-thirds of the properties would keep their old assessments. Anyway, that distinction was sure to get lost in the furor. It always did.

As Jarvis poured on the pressure to release the assessments early, Pope increasingly worried about his own political future. If Proposition 13 lost and taxes doubled a few weeks later, the anger surely would focus on him. At the same time, Pope and his patrons on the Board of Supervisors strongly opposed Proposition 13.

With election less than a month away, County Supervisor Ed Edelman, one of the key liberals, and Chuck Winner from the No campaign were on the phone to Pope daily, imploring him to keep the assessments bottled up.

Finally, Pope insisted that he had to run an "open office"; despite his own strong feelings about Jarvis, he would not be a party to a cover-up. "It just seemed to me that any homeowner had a right to see his assessment," he said later, chagrined at his role as Jarvis' unwitting accomplice.

In mid-May, Pope announced that any taxpayer was free to look up his assessment at any of his eighteen offices around Los Angeles County.

"We knew that would be devastating," Chuck Winner said later. Winner and Edelman devised a fallback: Pope should mail out notices to *all* homeowners. At least the two-thirds who were not being reassessed might cancel out the anger of the one-third who were stung. But another key vote on the County Board, Kenneth Hahn, was out of the country, and Edelman himself fell ill with pneumonia. The issue of who, if anyone, should get new assessments by mail was unresolved on May 15, when Pope opened his rolls.

The ensuing uproar exceeded Winner's worst fears. With Election Day only three weeks away, thousands of panicky taxpayers lined up daily to get the dread news. Night after night the Los Angeles television news, reaching nearly 60 percent of the state's voters, showed tearful, despairing homeowners outside the assessor's office, reacting to their new assessments, and the papers repeated the angry comments in front-page accounts.

"I don't know if I can walk to the car," said a housewife named Marjorie Jordan, when she discovered that her assessment almost tripled. At current rates her taxes would jump from about $2,000 to more than $5,500. A woman with a small baby told reporters she would have to go back to work to pay the property taxes. Retired people spoke of selling out. Virtually everybody interviewed said they would vote for Proposition 13. One quite typical Los Angeles homeowner paid a tax of $535 on his 1966 assessment of $22,800. By 1970 the assessment was up to $34,900 and the tax had doubled to $1,080. By 1975 the house was assessed at $54,700 and the tax was over $1,800. That was high, but still comparable to national norms. In 1978, however, reassessment valued the house at

$90,800, and the tax nearly doubled again to $3,130. The house belonged to Alex Pope.

With the two strong anti-13 votes on the L.A. County Board absent, the three remaining supervisors borrowed Chuck Winner's idea for a mailing, modified to compound the damage. The board directed Pope to mail assessment notices by June 1, but only to homeowners who were being reassessed. This, Pope refused. "It was totally political and a waste of money," he said, "because if Proposition 13 passed, the assessments would all be canceled anyway."

Supervisor Hahn returned from Athens to find Los Angeles in turmoil. As a desperation ploy, Hahn and Governor Brown contrived to have the Los Angeles County Board instruct Pope to freeze all assessments at the 1977 level. Brown publicly applauded the idea, though it was illegal under the AB 80 assessment reform, which required periodic reassessments at current market values. Freezing assessments in the face of rising values was precisely what generations of assessors did in the old days, but the old days were long gone.

Like so much else in the campaign, the maneuver to freeze assessments backfired. Officials of the *City* of Los Angeles, who had already set their own tax *rate* based on the new assessment projections, now announced that the lower assessments would require a higher rate. The tax break for the one-third of homeowners with canceled 1978 reassessments would translate into a tax increase for the other two-thirds. Now there was something to anger everybody.

In Sacramento, the State Board of Equalization ruled the freeze illegal. Brown briefly tried to get the legislature to change the law, but there was no time. All this frantic maneuvering dominated the Southern California media. In the space of two dizzy weeks, the homeowners of Los Angeles county were told the following by their elected officials:

New assessments are secret until after the election.

New assessments are available now, and some will double.

Assessments will be frozen, but *rates* may double.

Assessments will double after all.

Once again, the politicians were playing clumsy, transparent games with people's homes, in a manner not even Howard Jarvis would have dared to predict.

On May 25, if Jarvis needed anything more, State Finance Director Roy Bell handed him a final gift: The prodigious state surplus was not $3 billion after all, Bell announced; it was closer to $5 billion. Bell was later made the scapegoat for the State's chronic failure to estimate accurately, and demoted to a lesser job. Once again, Jarvis looked like a seer.

During the last two weeks in May, Proposition 13 surged 20 points in the polls.

It was over. The No campaign's emphasis on services had led Jarvis' adversaries into a trap. Jarvis had been transformed from a chronic clown into a prophetic folk hero. As his personal popularity soared, even the anti-13 coalition grew wary of attacking him personally. Butcher was amazed that the No coalition even refrained from hitting Jarvis' greatest vulnerability, his association with the landlords' lobby.

Jarvis possessed the demagogue's ability to articulate *everyone's* frustrations, however incompatible. It didn't matter that he worked for the landlords. Even the tenants loved him. He had assumed the populist mantle, while the state's liberal establishment came to personify the hated status quo. Jarvis crystalized all the voters' economic and political grievances, which he blamed on "the politicians."

His escapades and his misstatements of fact, which would have sunk an ordinary politician, only added to his roguish charm. In a political culture sated with slick media creations, Jarvis' rough-cut authenticity shone, never mind that it was kited by his own media managers.

He remained a homey, unpretentious figure, combining the kindly folk wisdom of a Grandpa Walton and the universal orneriness of a W. C. Fields. Despite his growing celebrity status and the demands on his schedule, he retained the habits of an Outsider. Jarvis astonished his handlers by periodically disappearing in his Toyota to address this or that property-owner's group in obscure Valley towns a hundred miles from L.A. With the national media looking for him, Jarvis would turn up in places like Brawley or Tumecula, because an old friend wanted him to meet with six or eight neighbors to discuss taxes. He stayed up long into the night, answering his own phone, and mysterious events would appear penciled into his busy schedule.

Butcher remembers the standard routine of "Where's Howard?" "Some major event would break, and the networks would be pounding on our door: Where's Jarvis? They thought it was really weird that we'd have him in Carpenteria addressing ten or twelve people when he could have been on CBS talking to twelve million. The Redding *Gazette* got a lot of scoops on the L.A. *Times*."

KABC in Los Angeles found that ratings soared whenever they had Jarvis on debating an opponent, so they gave him his own slot. He became a member of the news team, taking on a different opponent every night, like Bobby Fischer checkmating simultaneous opponents.

He could do nothing wrong. Pat Brown made the mistake of declaring that if he were a Communist he would vote for Proposition 13 because it would weaken America. The Communist party took great offense, pointing out its early opposition to the Jarvis amendment. Since it was a liberal who had begun the red-baiting, Jarvis delighted in noting that the Communists were part of his opposition.

In a televised debate with Darlene Daniel of the League of Women Voters, Jarvis pulled from his pocket a copy of the Communist *People's World*, pointing to an article lambasting Proposition 13. "The Communist party," Jarvis growled, "has an ally in the League of Women Voters."

In the control room, Arnie Forde groaned, "That will cost us a hundred thousand votes." It didn't. Nothing seemed to slow him down. Jarvis was telling reporters he would win 2 to 1. Privately, the No's were hoping they could hold it to that.

The old man was charging around the state growing more outrageous daily, and the voters loved it. One afternoon, the L.A. Board of Supervisors held a press conference to warn that Proposition 13 would cause 80 percent of the libraries in the county to close. Jarvis was asked for a comment. "That doesn't matter," he said. "Why do we need books? The schools aren't teaching the kids to read anyway."

He appeared with the gentle Peter Behr, author of the rival tax relief bill under Proposition 8. Mocking Behr's trace of an English accent, Jarvis bellowed, "I thought we settled this tax thing with the British a long time ago."

In Thousand Oaks, he was arrested for drunk driving. The patrolman asked him to recite the alphabet. Jarvis couldn't. The officer testified that Jarvis pulled out his driver's license, sputtering indignantly, "That's right, I'm Howard Jarvis. You realize what you've done to yourself?"

Long after the election, he would be acquitted by a jury of his peers.

With his full shock of hair, the bull head squashed down on a five-foot five-inch frame, he had all the charm of an angry Muppet. He insulted everybody, without regard to creed or party. Businessmen were "horses' asses; their inventory is cowardice." Republicans, he said, "think like molasses."

"It's going to make my trip to Forest Lawn a goddamned joy ride," he proclaimed. "I'll die knowing I really put the hot rod up the butts of those damned stupid politicians."

He could also be touching, shedding tears at the story of a retired couple in danger of losing their home, and sweetly avuncular when he wasn't raging like a wounded boar. "I'll soon be seventy-five," he told an audience in Long Beach, "and I've found that all the sugar's in the bottom of the cup."

Belatedly, respectable political figures came to bask in his warmth. The Republican state convention in March couldn't decide whether to endorse Proposition 13. Now, Senator S. I. Hayakawa, gubernatorial nominee Evelle Younger, and former Governor Reagan all recognized a sure winner.

In Sacramento, Jerry Brown began waffling, telling reporters that if the voters approved Proposition 13, he would do everything in his power to make it work. The Governor's staff began drafting contingency plans for a post-13 budget. All over California, undecided voters adopted a what-the-hell attitude. Certified liberals even voted for Proposition 13; it was a rare chance to humiliate the entire miserable California establishment from Jerry Brown on down, and save a few thousand bucks besides. The mood turned apocalyptic, even carnival. If it was going to pass anyway, why not really send the bastards a message. To most frightened home-owners, the message was very simple: you can't tax us out of our homes. Against this prospect, confirmed so dramatically in Los Angeles almost on election eve, the firefighters' warning about precious minutes added to alarm responses and the sweet reasonableness of the League of Women Voters preaching local control stood no chance.

5

THE MORNING AFTER

> *Don't go away from here thinking there's a*
> *sugar daddy in Sacramento who will bail you*
> *out if Proposition 13 passes.*
> —Jerry Brown, to a meeting of county super-
> visors, April 26, 1978

WITH THE VICTORY of Proposition 13, by a margin of 65 to 35, the era of limits arrived.

Or did it?

The most immediate effect in California was a severe fiscal crunch for local government, which was suddenly out $6.15 billion. But the cuts were not distributed uniformly. A few rural counties lost little, while some service districts lost their entire budgets. School districts, heavily dependent on the property tax, lost nearly one-third of their revenue. As an emergency move, summer school sessions throughout the state were simply canceled.

City governments, which relied on other taxes and fees, were down about 9 percent but counties on average lost about one-fourth of their funds.

In Los Angeles, Harry Hufford, the county's chief administrator, faced a billion dollar cut in his $3.5 billion budget. Hufford's doomsday figures were no longer a ploy to scare the voters. Without an infusion of state funds, 37,000 county workers would be laid off; more than half of the fire stations would close; and on and on and on.

From all over the state, similar reports poured into Sacramento of impending catastrophes, large and small.

San Francisco, which planned to scrap most of its branch libraries, reported runs on books.

Tax assessors from the state's fifty-eight counties gathered for a funeral session in Sacramento. With assessments frozen at 1975–76 levels by Proposition 13, they would not only collect less money; they would have less to do. As the final indignity, many stood to lose their own jobs.

Statewide, civil service layoffs were projected at anywhere from 100,000 to 450,000.

One study hastily calculated that the Proposition 13 cuts would cause the state to lose an additional $4.4 billion in federal grants that required a local match.

Bond ratings were suspended on most local issues, making them unmarketable.

The voters had gotten the attention of the politicians with the proverbial two-by-four. Talk of raising other taxes to replace lost revenues ceased almost immediately. A bill to recoup $3 billion by raising business taxes failed to pass either house.

THE BAIL-OUT

With most legislators and the Governor up for reelection in November, no politician was willing to let the voters simply suffer the consequences of this protest vote, however irrational.

Despite the bluffing about no state bail-out, the state surplus was now fair game.

Governor Brown ordered an immediate freeze on state hiring and prepared to address an emergency joint session of the legislature. The deadline for the legislature to act was July 1, the beginning of the new fiscal year when the Jarvis Amendment took effect.

It was an odd moment for Governor Jerry Brown.

He had been elected as a new-wave, small-is-beautiful liberal, genuinely believing in self-reliance as a better route to the just society than big government programs. As his first Administration went into its final year, the schism between Brown and the mainstays of the orthodox liberal coalition deepened. Among minorities, labor, the urban poor, public employees, the Governor was increasingly viewed as opportunistic and probably a little flaky besides.

When it became clear that Proposition 13 was a very serious prospect, the anger and sense of betrayal intensified. Despite his nominal opposition, many liberals charged, Brown had helped create the climate for an irrational taxpayer rebellion by his own attacks against government. And, finally, it was Brown who had made the tax revolt almost inevitable by banking an outlandish state revenue surplus, to bolster his personal reputation as a fiscal conservative.

Thus it was rankling to liberals, though not entirely unexpected, when Brown turned around after the election and embraced not just Proposition 13, but with his own reelection campaign faltering and November five months away, embraced the old man, too. A smiling Howard Jarvis paused long enough before he went national to appear with Brown and congratulate the Governor for understanding the verdict of the voters and for endeavoring to "make Proposition 13 work." Eventually, Jarvis would make a tape endorsing Brown, and then when criticized by outraged Republicans, make a second tape endorsing the lackluster GOP candidate, Evelle Younger, too.

In a brief and somber address to the joint session of the legislature June 8, Brown proposed to part with $4 billion of the surplus to reimburse local government for much of the loss. State salaries and welfare payments would be frozen at present levels. Brown advised landlords, who realized a billion dollar windfall, to rebate the money to renters. He urged businesses to reinvest their tax savings in the California economy.

The state's own budget, though not directly touched by Proposition 13, would be cut by as much as a billion dollars to free money to distribute to the hard-pressed locals. The Governor would give up some of his own prized projects, such as the proposed state communications satellite, state-sponsored research on energy, and a reforestation program.

"The voters have told us they want a tax cut," Brown concluded soberly. "They don't want a shell game."

In the audience, just off the chamber floor, Paul Gann listened with satisfaction.

The Governor was reborn in editorial cartoons as "Jerry Jarvis," and though Brown's embrace of Proposition 13 after the fact was one of the most implausible political turnabouts since incumbent New York Mayor Robert Wagner's 1961 reform campaign against his own previous Administration, Brown's conversion helped carry the Governor to a triumphant reelection in November.

Working fifteen- and eighteen-hour days, a special bipartisan joint committee of the legislature hammered out an emergency bail-out bill that eventually totaled $4.3 billion. A year's worth of lobbying and special pleading was telescoped into two dizzy weeks. The Association of County

Supervisors alone booked 200 rooms in the Senator Hotel across the street from the state capitol, to lobby for their share of the bail-out.

"It was one of the most selfish times I've ever seen," recalled one of the key legislators. "The few people who came by and said, Just treat us equally—I wanted to kiss them."

Two weeks proved too short a time to revise the state's spending priorities. Instead, the legislature essentially acted to spread the burden of Proposition 13 around as equally as possible, so that most localities would end up with about 90 percent of their previous year's budget. Each local government would figure out how to close its own gap.

The Governor characteristically had little influence in the ultimate bail-out formula.

Schools got the lion's share, $2.5 billion. Another billion went to have the state "buy out" the local government share of welfare and medicaid.

A billion went into a special revolving loan fund to help local government with cash shortages, and the rest was divided between counties, cities, and special districts.

Some of the local deficit would be made up by new fees. Local governments outdid each other dreaming up new fees or raising old ones; fees on parking, on garbage collection, parks, municipal pools, public tennis courts, health inspections, water and sewer service; higher admission charges to libraries, theaters, museums, zoos, and botanical gardens; higher fees for dog licenses, business licenses, and hotel licenses. The little town of Bell near the Nevada border, faced with a $350,000 deficit, voted to charge $75,000 to license its popular draw-poker parlors. Many cities raised bus fares, ambulance charges, tuition for adult education, grave-digging fees, parking ticket rates, and even library card fines. In San Clemente, ambulance rides were upped to $160 each. Monrovia began charging for street sweeping and the senior citizen dial-a-ride. Modesto increased airport landing fees. The heaviest fees were concentrated on new development, which ironically raised the cost of housing. Even so, though roundly resented by the public, the new fees raised less than a tenth of the revenues taken away by the tax cut.

The winners were the Californians who saved on property taxes. A modest homeowner would save a few hundred dollars. The owner of a Beverly Hills estate would save upward of $5,000. Renters got nothing. And the biggest windfall of all went to the corporate property owners.

Pacific Telephone and Telegraph saved $130 million in property taxes; Pacific Gas and Electric, $91 million; Southern Pacific Railroad, $12 million. In Contra Costa County alone, Standard Oil saved $13.1 million, and several other *Fortune* 500 companies with California operations, including Lockheed, Bank of America, United Airlines, and IBM, tens of millions of dollars each.

The losers were mainly the consumers of public services. Subsidized services can be supported only be general tax levies on the haves. The doctor who saved $3,000 in property taxes would not feel the increased library and museum charges. The elderly and the working poor would. Though seen as nuisance charges by some, the dollar museum charges in Los Angeles were enough to reduce attendance by 60 percent, and the hike in adult education tuition from $3 to $30 kept away thousands of retirees.

Life went on. Budgets would be extremely tight, but the Governor's security blanket, now estimated at $5.3 billion and still growing, had bought California a year or two. Brown appointed a prestigious commission headed by the former chief of the legislature's respected nonpartisan Office of the Legislative Analyst, A. Alan Post, to recommend a permanent, new fiscal structure for the state. The Post commission's recommendations, and the next bail-out bill, due in mid-1979, would not merely be a pro-rata infusion of cash, but would set new priorities.

Brown was enjoying life after Proposition 13. It had accomplished what he now believed he had been advocating all along. Like a reformed sinner, he attacked government with new zest. By late June, the Governor, looking forward to his own reelection, was confident enough to proclaim that Proposition 13 gave "an opportunity to make government in California a model for people across the country." A confused visitor to California might have assumed Governor Brown had thought up the idea.

In fact, Proposition 13 made California *more* like the rest of the country, especially the fiscally strapped older cities of the Northeast and Midwest. Local government went on almost as usual, though there were real, wrenching inequities, of which more later. Though the Golden State's budget crisis was self-inflicted rather than imposed by a shrinking tax base, California's cities have entered a period of austerity and retrenchment whose politics would be very recognizable to anyone who had spent the middle seventies in Newark or Detroit.

WINNERS AND LOSERS

Thanks to the state bail-out, the first wave of program cuts was far milder than feared. All told, local government came through the first year of the Proposition 13 era with slight budgetary increases, although in a period of 15 percent inflation these translated to effective cuts. Total funding for public schools for the 1978–79 year remained at almost exactly the level of the previous year, though now the state was picking up nearly 80 percent of the cost. Cities ended up with an increase in total revenue over 1977-79 of about 3.8 percent, and counties managed to increase their total spending by 9.5 percent.

For most citizens, just the fact that local government continued to function seemed to vindicate Howard Jarvis. Most programs could operate at their previous levels, though this meant a cut in real purchasing power. Yet "fat," however defined, is not evenly distributed throughout government. Programs that had run lean and creative operations were punished. Those with real fat to spare suffered little.

Moreover, the averages belie specific cases of genuine hardship. Because of its declining population and quirks in the bail-out formula, San Francisco, which is both a city and a county, was particularly hard hit. By early 1980, San Francisco had closed 26 schools and laid off almost a thousand teachers. A pre-13 local surplus had been used up, and San Francisco faced a deficit of $126 million. All told, some 5,000 jobs in local government were eliminated, with the service cuts concentrated in libraries, schools, parks, street cleaning, and public works. Mass transit fares were doubled, to 50 cents.

To meet its huge deficit, San Francisco officials proposed local increases in taxes and fees, to be ratified by the voters, as required by Proposition 13. But in a classic illustration of the tax revolt's Catch-22, voters already felt they were paying too much for services that were obviously declining. Key parts of a local tax package were voted down in the June 1980 election, leaving San Francisco facing a true fiscal crisis—and the immediate prospect of far steeper cuts in services.

Elsewhere, the cuts in 1979 and 1980 were somewhat milder but still substantial enough to pinch. Los Angeles eliminated about 2,500 jobs in local government, including about 280 actual layoffs. Four libraries were closed, as were two health centers, three neighborhood service centers, two local district attorneys' offices, and even two local assessors' offices. In general, there was a freeze on new hiring and the purchasing of new equipment. This strategy, of course, works well enough for a year or two, but eventually equipment does break down and must be replaced. And equipment breaks down faster when budgets are reduced for maintenance.

Certainly, Proposition 13 forced local government to economize. While some localities genuinely cut gratuitous expenditures—new fire engines, top-heavy administrative jobs, private use of official cars, unnecessary public construction—the axe fell most heavily on human services, particularly those for politically weak constituencies, and on maintenance of plant and equipment.

Statewide, libraries in particular were clobbered. Most sharply cut hours and laid off staff. Extra services like bookmobiles and interlibrary exchanges were curtailed. Several library systems, including that of Los Angeles, simply stopped buying new books. The Alameda County library system shut down altogether for a month in 1978. One small city, Downey, forced its library to cut elsewhere so that purchases of new books could continue. "Otherwise," the city manager told a reporter, "it quits being a library and becomes a museum."

In many communities, free recreation became a thing of the past, as fees were newly imposed to cover costs. Maintenance of parks, baseball fields, tennis courts, and public beaches also suffered. One annoyed letter-writer to the Long Beach *Independent/Press-Telegram* calculated that the new fees combined with the reduced deductions against his state and federal income tax more than wiped out his Proposition 13 savings.

Beyond the fact that California's cities have less money to maintain their physical plant, the financing of capital improvements is now far more difficult. Because Proposition 13 prohibits property tax increases to pay off new bonds, general obligation bonds are no longer possible. Until Proposition 13, general obligation bonds backed by local governments accounted for some 40 percent of the $12.6 billion in local bonds outstanding in the state, according to *The Wall Street Journal*. No more. California's local governments are either turning to "creative financing," such as creating nonprofit corporations to float their own bonds (usually at costlier interest rates), or they are simply doing without. Schools in particular find it difficult to finance capital improvements and face a growing backlog of deferred maintenance. Pay-as-you-go, which formerly made up about one-third of the capital needs of schools and special districts, is also more difficult because of the other competing demands on current revenues.

Welfare benefits under the first Proposition 13 budget were frozen. A year later, Governor Brown offered a 6 percent cost-of-living increase to cover a two-year period when the the true cost of living increased by nearly 20 percent. (The legislature eventually insisted on 14.5 percent, overriding Brown's veto.)

California's mental health system had been under assault since the Reagan Administration, which shut down most of the state hospitals without replacing them with decent community care facilities. Under Brown, increasing numbers of patients were dumped into rooming houses and inadequate nursing homes.

In late 1977, when the staff of Metropolitan State Hospital near Los Angeles staged protests over chronically inadequate funding and several mysterious patient deaths, Brown made a dramatic visit to the hospital, pledging that 1978 would be the year of mental health, promising $82.6 million to improve community facilities as replacements for locked wards. That sum was among the first cut from Brown's austerity budget.

Dr. Jerome Lackner, Brown's former health director, articulated a widespread view: "When Jerry Brown talks about lowering expectations, he's really talking about lowering expectations for the poor, the mentally ill and the disabled."

One almost invisible constituency whose suffering has been increased by Proposition 13 is California's "developmentally disabled"—the mentally retarded, the autistic, those with learning disabilities. In California a model program of 21 Regional Centers for Developmental Disabilities provides services to thousands of clients, most of whose families cannot afford private treatment. These centers train the retarded and disabled to function minimally in society—to engage in social behavior, to take care of themselves, to hold jobs. These centers are the alternative to far more costly (and brutal) institutionalization.

After Proposition 13, most centers sharply curtailed "nonlifesaving" services. These are, of course, precisely those that make a difference in the lives of clients and their families: physical and occupational therapy, speech therapy, infant stimulation, living skills, recreation, and "respite" (short periods when trained sitters stay with retarded or autistic children so that parents can attend to other needs and get some emotional relief). Subsidies to programs for the retarded in public schools have also been cut. Harbor Regional Center, serving southern Los Angeles County, eliminated all therapy and recreation programs, as well as respite and out-of-home placement in the first half of 1979. In this one center, 500 children were denied desperately needed services.

As a protest vote against bureaucracy, Proposition 13 ironically punished many nonbureaucratic approaches to providing services. Most governments cut grants to nonprofit community agencies before they cut their own employees. For example, when federal revenue sharing came, in the early seventies, the Alameda County Board decided to spend a major portion of the new federal money on community services, including home care for shut-ins, halfway houses for the mentally ill, comprehensive day care, a model center instructing the blind and physically disabled in self-sufficiency, and a string of thirteen nonprofit health clinics providing primary medical care to poor communities. Most of these were community-based, private facilities, nonbureaucratic and innovative in style, receiving reimbursement from the county.

When Proposition 13 hit, revenue sharing was diverted from these community services to plug other holes. Most of these service centers took cuts of 10 percent. A few closed. The county prudently banked a surplus in anticipation of further cuts when the bail-out ends. "We'd rather go through this only once," said the county's budget chief. One clinic shut down; others began turning away patients.

"The services are still in place," observed one health aide. "People are paying by waiting in line longer, or just not coming. The suffering is largely hidden. It's a subtle kind of triage."

Alameda cut its own county work force by more than 1,000 jobs. Typically, most of the layoffs were at the lower end of the ladder. Of 1,060 positions eliminated, only 6 paid more than $25,000. The county work force is 23 percent black, but fully one-third of those dismissed were blacks. In the city of Oakland, the 70 employees laid off as a direct result of Proposition 13 were 84 percent minority.

Minorities suffered disproportionately from Proposition 13, both as consumers and as providers. During the sixties and seventies, government became the principal entree for blacks and Hispanics into professional and white-collar jobs, just as it once served generations of Irish immigrants. This, by itself, may be insufficient justification for continuous expansion of government jobs, but the new era of a no-growth public-sector has blocked a major avenue of minority opportunity. With over 100,000 government jobs eliminated by attrition, including over 16,000 layoffs, and very little new hiring, affirmative action goals in most California public agencies have been rendered meaningless.

In Santa Barbara the county closed the only public hospital. Officials tried to get the area's private hospitals to sign a contractual agreement to take charity patients on a reimbursable basis, but the hospitals would give only verbal assurances. As it turned out, medicare and medicaid patients were accommodated, but others were required to post cash deposits. An autumn hearing revealed that numerous patients were turned away. One man suffering a heart attack was sent home from an emergency room.

The biggest loser was probably public education. The canceled summer school sessions kept a million and a half children out of summer classes and cost 15,000 teachers two months' pay. Wholesale layoffs of teachers began to materialize only in the winter of 1978. San Mateo prepared to let 300 teachers go. Anaheim, in Orange County, sent notices to 426, every teacher hired since 1970.

The first-year freeze in public school funding under Proposition 13 dropped California from one of the leading states in per pupil public education expenditure to twenty-fourth.

Thousands of teacher aides, heavily minority, lost their jobs, and most of those remaining were put on ten-month salaries. With fewer aides to help teachers, class sizes increased as well, giving California one of the worst teacher-pupil ratios in the nation. In Anaheim, 40 eighth-graders in a class were common.

Anything that could be labeled a frill was cut sharply: sports, art, shop, music, library, counseling, and busing. Nonracial busing, that is. The other kind was mandated by the courts. In Foster City, a suburb of San Francisco, parents had to get their children to school catch-as-catch-can, over distances as far as twelve miles. Many districts canceled all buses for athletics and field trips. Others levied charges.

In San Francisco itself, besides the 26 school closings, 16 publicly supported child care centers were shut. Beyond cuts in nonacademic frills, psychologists and social workers were laid off, and a district-wide staff of 50 remedial reading teachers was reduced to 3.

As the school year began in September 1978, the city of Modesto, in the central valley, presented a typical picture of normal frustrations of teaching and learning compounded: textbooks could not be replaced, though some were ten years old. Supplies of everything from crayons and paper to shop rags were not to be had. The school newspaper was gone. No new films could be ordered. The custodian now came only once a week to clean, waste baskets overflowed, and last year's graffiti still graced walls. In one classroom, a buzzing fluorescent light that the harried custodian was too busy to replace was jangling already frayed nerves.

The town of Little Lake canceled all after-school sports, increased class size, reduced supplies, cut school library hours, and stopped purchasing new books and magazines.

"But the most serious consequence of all," said Cal Rossi, of the California Teachers Association, "is the effect on teacher morale. Teachers should be dedicated, looking forward to a bright career. Instead, the prospect is further cuts next year. They're waiting for the other shoe to drop. A lot of them are looking for other jobs. Math teachers are being snapped up by industry."

Cultural programs were also reduced sharply. The State Council on the

Arts, which makes grants to local artists and to community performances, saw its own budget reduced from $3.5 million to $1.5 million, shifting California from one of the nation's leaders to forty-fourth place in funding for the arts. Statewide, according to Joseph Young of the California Confederation of the Arts, public spending on cultural activities dropped by at least $80 million.

Seemingly, Proposition 13 was a vote against statism and for voluntarism. But charitable organizations have been damaged trebly. Many private, not-for-profit organizations, like those providing social services in Alameda, depended in part on local government funding. Though a great many nonprofits are probably more efficient than government agencies, local government looked to its own survival first and cut funding to outside agencies sharply.

But with the cut in government's own services, the demands placed on voluntary agencies were greater than ever. When summer school was canceled, tens of thousands of unexpected kids poured into local YMCA's and "Y" camps.

Finally, though Proposition 13 returned billions to taxpayers, it raised the cost of after-tax charitable giving. With property taxes so much lower, fewer California taxpayers chose to itemize deductions. And those who don't itemize can't deduct charitable contributions.

Politics in California lurched hard to the right. The Governor's own deft conversion, the state rescue, and the limited damage to local government made sitting ducks out of liberal Democratic "spenders" who had opposed Jarvis.

In effect, a Left opposition to the Brown-Jarvis axis ceased to function. Liberals fought over which programs to salvage, but few legislators were proposing new programs or effectively attacking Brown from the Left.

Assembly Speaker Leo McCarthy, a potential candidate for governor, became the closest thing to a rallying figure for dispirited liberals. McCarthy momentarily toyed with a proposal to revise the Proposition 13 formula to take some of the windfall away from business, aid renters, and go Jarvis one better by abolishing homeowner property taxes altogether.

Despite the seeming appeal of this idea, the climate was utterly wrong. Nobody was going to tinker with Proposition 13. Speaker MCarthy quietly dropped the idea. A year later, McCarthy endorsed Paul Gann's initiative to limit the growth in government spending.

In late 1978, McCarthy's main concern was limiting the losses to his Democratic majority, who were up for election, and terribly vulnerable. Jarvis used his new celebrity to punish old adversaries. He targeted ten liberal Democratic legislators for defeat, helping their opponents with fund-raising appeals and making endorsements. He also helped Republicans pick up vacant seats. His familiar scowl graced billboards throughout the state, urging voters to support good old fill-in-the-blank. In all, more than 1.5 million personal letters signed by Jarvis were sent to voters by the Butcher-Forde computer.

In November, seven of Jarvis's ten targets were voted out. Governor Brown, on the other hand, won by a landslide.

On January 9, 1979, a confident Jerry Brown delivered his annual State of the State message, the first of the Proposition 13 era. Brown had good reason to be confident. His election margin of more than a million votes exceeded his most extravagant hopes. By "Making Proposition 13 Work," without catastrophic effect on public services in California, Brown became the most prominent national spokesman for the new austerity, outflanking Carter to the Right as a tightwad—and to the Left as an ecofreak.

"Nineteen seventy-nine is the International Year of the Child," Brown solemnly reminded his audience. "Those born this year will graduate in the class of 2000. What they inherit will depend on the courage and vision we pass on to them." Brown neatly combined an environmentalist appeal for less profligate use of the plant's resources with a conservative call for limits on government. "The depressing spirit of the age ungratefully feeds off the boldness of the past," he added, warning that it was time to consume less and invest more. He pointed proudly to the cuts in state spending, and proposed deeper ones, announcing his support for a federal constitutional convention to require a balanced-budget amendment.

But in effect, California government survived Proposition 13 by feeding off the boldness of its own past.

Meeting with reporters afterward, Brown noted that thanks to Proposition 13, California would drop from third in per capita spending among the fifty states to about twenty-first. But, he insisted, "California will stay in the forefront in its concern for the needy, the blind, and the disabled." Welfare benefits, he declared, placed California third in the country.

How, he was asked, could California continue to be third in welfare benefits, when state spending dropped to twenty-first?

The Governor stared for a moment.

"That's a very good question," he said.

6

SYMBOL AND REALITY

NATIONALLY, the resounding success of Proposition 13 was instantly taken as a profound sea-change in the currents of American sentiment about government.

A Proposition 13 mythology grew up overnight. National political commentators, who had scarcely heard of Howard Jarvis until the Los Angeles assessment protests two weeks before, decided in chorus that June 6, 1978, marked the day American voters put a limit on the rising size and cost of government. The issues of 1978 seemed all of a piece, signaling a sharp swing to the Right.

"Just as the New Deal of the 1930's launched Big Government, the Great Tax Revolt of 1978 may herald a conservative reaction," proclaimed *Newsweek*. According to columnists Evans and Novak, the voters were increasingly coming to see government as an "oppressive burden," and Proposition 13 indicated "no less an anti-government revolt than an anti-tax revolt." Pat Caddell, President Carter's voluble poll-taker, agreed. "This isn't just a tax revolt," he told an interviewer. "It's a revolution against government."

This view was especially congenial to Governor Jerry Brown, whose own conversion to Proposition 13 helped to ratify the national media's interpretation of the event.

The mythology created its own reality as national politicians scrambled to give the voters what they thought was being demanded. Congress resounded with Proposition 13 speeches; members wrapped themselves around Jarvis. A symbolic amendment to cut 2 percent from HEW appropriations, long offered in vain by Republican members of the House, passed for the first time. The Office of Management and Budget grew bolder in its battles with federal agencies over spending requests. Shifting congressional sentiment on taxes turned the 1978 tax reform bill into a giveaway for upper-bracket taxpayers, as concern about the tax deductible three-martini lunch gave way to a stampede to reduce taxes.

When Jarvis triumphantly visited Washington, liberal and conservative politicians tripped over one another to have their pictures taken with the old rogue. Liberal California Senator Alan Cranston, who campaigned against Proposition 13, elbowed out colleagues to escort Jarvis around the Capitol. "You certainly had a big victory," Cranston said, smiling. "You certainly got your ass kicked off," Jarvis replied. As Jarvis entered the Senate dining room, a covey of liberals (Percy, Church, Glenn, and Hatfield) leapt to their feet to shake his hand. Anne Wexler, a White House political aide, reminded reporters, "Jimmy Carter was telling us long before Proposition 13 that the country was in a fiscally conservative mood."

But what, really, was this revolt all about?

As a reconstruction of the California events strongly suggests, the seeds of Proposition 13 lay first in the gross defects in the state's system of taxation, and secondly in the remarkable political default of the Governor and the legislature. (When Jerry Brown deftly changed course to embrace Jarvis, State Treasurer Jesse Unruh observed that Brown was indeed the father of Proposition 13, far more than he knew.) A contributing cause was the general economic malaise and the stagnation in household purchasing power. In California the squeeze on real income was compounded by outlandish housing costs. When inflation blended with tax schedules to push up tax rates, hard-pressed consumers were in no mood to tolerate rising taxes, as they might have a decade earlier when times were good.

The right wing divined in the California vote a vindication of the view that holds government spending and regulation responsible for economic distress. Yet, though Howard Jarvis was the chosen vessel of economic frustrations in 1978, ideology explained a small part of the vote. California voters' supposed conservative allegiance proved utterly empty when the next political expression of economic distress turned out to be—of all things—a successful rent control drive, organized by former SDS president Tom Hayden.

Even the very rhetoric of Proposition 13 was an attack on taxes first, faithless politicians second, and "government" only a distant third. To euphoric conservatives savoring their victory, some aspects of the vote indeed seemed curious. Though Proposition 13 was advertised as a vote against government, the polls did not confirm widespread erosion of public support for government. With the exception of the perennial whipping boy, welfare, California voters did not want to see public services reduced. The polls also suggested growing distrust of all remote institutions —big business, big labor, as well as "big government"—and a far more uniform sense of foreboding about personal economic well-being.

Summarizing the poll results in neoconservative journal *Commentary*, Seymour Martin Lipset and Earl Raab puzzled over the anomaly that voters agreed with generalities about government "waste," but only welfare reductions commanded majority support when interviewers pressed for the details about what should be cut.

The anomaly exists, of course, only if one tries to paint Proposition 13 as an ideologically motivated spasm against government. Is it reasonable to differentiate *antitax* sentiment from *antigovernment* sentiment? (After all, taxes are simply what pays for government.) But in the peculiar California tax system, rising homeowner taxes did *not* purchase appreciably more government. They did enable other taxpayers (businesses) to pay a lower share of taxes, and they bought Governor Brown a handsome surplus. Dean Tipps, the former California Tax Reform Association lobbyist, observes sagely, "People say that if you give a politician a dollar, he'll just go and spend it. In California, you give a politician a dollar and he keeps it."

THE FISCAL CONTEXT

Government expenditures in California grew steadily throughout the entire postwar period—but the growth slowed down markedly during the years preceding the great taxpayer revolt.

Throughout this period, California ranked in the top five states in per capita tax levels. For generations, California pioneered progressive statewide free higher education, mental health programs, and relatively generous welfare and medical care benefits. Traditionally, a majority of Californians supported a level and quality of public services that required public spending somewhat higher than the average. But it was not a reversal of these long-held views of public services that prompted the tax revolt.

The relative size of California's public sector was not significantly different in 1978 from what it was in 1976, the year Jarvis and Watson failed to qualify for the ballot, or in 1973, when a political conservative, using all the prestige of his governorship, failed to persuade California voters to approve a much more moderate tax limitation initiative. The new factor operating in 1978 was gross tax inequity, compounded by economic malaise and political stalemate.

It may be convenient, as Jarvis' disciples do, to lump the whole condition under the heading of unresponsive, bloated government, but this confuses the true nature of the grievances afflicting Californians in the spring of 1978.

According to data assembled by economist Frank Levy of the Urban Institute, local government expenditures in California grew by 9.4 percent per year betwen 1974 and 1977—slightly more than the inflation rate, but less than the growth in personal income and substantially less than the average growth in assessed valuation, which exceeded 15 percent. This, of course, confirms the impact of the tax shift: Local property taxes were rising far faster than local government's total revenues.

Nor were bureaucrats getting rich from the rising taxes. Civil service salaries in California during this period did not even keep up with inflation. In fact, between 1975 and 1977, state and local payroll, measured against personal income, declined 5.5 percent. Most surprisingly, state expenditures measured as a percentage of personal income dropped steadily in California between 1974 and 1978. Their sharpest increase, ironically, came during Ronald Reagan's last year as governor, 1973–74.*

In short, the charge of excess government spending does not stand up, though the charge of political unresponsiveness clearly does.

Given the accelerating inflation, taxes were the one piece of the consumer's budget subject to referendum, and the growing state surplus made it appear a free vote. Hard-pressed consumers did not get to vote on the cost of tomatoes or no-lead gasoline, but here was a rare chance to vote yourself a few thousand dollars.

Against the majority view of Proposition 13 as a generalized protest against government, some liberal political voices offered a minority interpretation: the vote was nothing more than a lightly masked attack on the

---

* State spending as a percentage of personal income increased sharply from 5.08 during Pat Brown's first full year as governor, 1959–60, to 7.87 during Reagan's last full year, 1973–74. It then dipped to 7.60 during fiscal year 1977–78, when Proposition 13 passed.

poor by materialistic and heartless Californians who placed their hot tubs and their BMWs above even their own children's education.

According to Arthur Blaustein, chairman of the National Advisory Council on Economic Opportunity and a Berkeley resident, "No group of middle class revolutionaries ever had it so good, and are so confused about social and economic values. The message . . . is screw you, buddy, I've got mine, you get yours."

Senator George McGovern, in his keynote speech to the national convention of Americans for Democratic Action, saw racist overtones in Proposition 13 and suggested that the haves remember their own debt to government: "Perhaps property taxpayers ought to remember, if only for a moment, how many of them would never have owned a home without a government loan and a mortgage tax write-off."

Indeed, Proposition 13 seemed to confirm the rest of the country's caricature of California as the land of fringe politics and decadent self-indulgence. Columnist Joseph Kraft wrote a diatribe denouncing "populist hedonism" and "middle class greed." Behind the legitimate cause of tax relief, Kraft wrote, "there lurks a cloven hoof—self-indulgence by the relatively comfortable majority at the expense of the poorer minorities." A letter to the L.A. *Herald-Examiner* called Proposition 13 "The Watts riot of the white middle class."

Jonathan Lewis, the director of the California Tax Reform Association, which was on the losing side of the Jarvis steamroller, began a long conversation with the observation: "Howard Jarvis is to the tax field what Joe McCarthy was to civil liberties."

"The tax cut is regressive, of course," he continued, "But the new fees are just as regressive. Most of the services that raised fees hit the poor hardest—museums, libraries, bus service, free recreation, ambulances. And the people paying the higher charges in a lot of cases didn't get any tax relief. Jarvis was just a veiled attack on the poor."

But this devil theory misses the point, too. A revolt of the haves? Certainly. Property owners by definition are haves. The Proposition 13 tax-cut formula disproportionately favored business and the well-to-do. The services that were cut disproportionately hurt the have-nots.

But a revolt against the poor?

That may have been one effect, but it was hardly the driving cause. Proposition 13 was the result of shifting taxes, unresponsive politicians, and unusually opportune timing. So effectively did Jarvis mobilize general economic discontent into an income transfer for the rich, that even the poor voted, by a slight majority, for Proposition 13.

Indeed, the mandate expressed in the Proposition 13 vote was all the more impressive for its uniformity.

Though the tax cuts heavily favored upper-income groups, people with incomes over $25,000 actually voted for Proposition 13 by slightly less than the state average: upper-income voters approved, 61 to 39. The middle class, hard hit by inflation and rising state income taxes, voted yes almost exactly 2 to 1: 67 to 33 for the $15,000–$25,000 group, and 66 to 34 for the $8,000–$15,000 range. The poor, with incomes below $8,000, most of whom rent, supported Proposition 13 by 55 to 45.

Homeowners overwhelmingly approved, by better than 4 to 1. Self-described conservatives approved the initiative 82 to 18, and moderates, 63 to 37. Even ideological liberals split almost evenly. The satisfaction of a protest vote against generalized economic frustrations was enough to enlist the support of many renters, though Proposition 13 provided no direct relief for them. Remarkably, 47 percent of renters, 42 percent of blacks, and even 44 percent of families of public employees voted for Proposition 13.

A sixty-year-old janitor for the Los Angeles school system spoke for many Californians: "I'm for it," said Bill Heckathorn, "Even if they lay me off, because they were taxing me out of my home. I've been paying on it 27 or 28 years. Where am I going to get another home? I'd rather go out and find a new job."

Indeed, spiraling taxes on one's home seemed to crowd out most other concerns. In San Diego, Mrs. Homer Peabody, wife of a prominent and liberal cardiologist, interviewed shortly after the election, voiced dismay for the future of the Anthropology Museum, on whose board she served. The city, hard hit, was cutting off funding to the private museum. Did she vote for Proposition 13? Of course. "We had to show them this couldn't go on."

Even schoolteachers had voted in large numbers to back the Jarvis-Gann Initiative. "We had a four month propaganda campaign to stop it," reflected Hank Springer of the 19,000-member Los Angeles teachers' union. "People are funny, aren't they?"

According to the poll taken by CBS and the Los Angeles *Times*, the very lowest category of support for Proposition 13 was among public employees who did not own their own homes. Even 28 percent of them voted yes. Harvard Professor William Schneider, who helped design the CBS–*Times* poll, observed: "Clearly, self-interest cut across ideology and brought many blacks and liberals over to the yes-on-13 side."

But happily for Howard Jarvis, self-interest was a one-way street; it didn't deliver votes for the opposition. Among many voters whose apparent self-interest was not served by Proposition 13—blacks, poor people, renters, and public employee families—the I'm-Mad-as-Hell infection was also widespread.

A remarkable mandate—but a mandate for what?

STATE TAKEOVER

Neither the causes nor the consequences of Proposition 13 produce a very uniform picture. The electorate voted for tax relief, and tax relief it surely got. But the fine print inadvertently seeded long-term changes in the way Californians are governed: an erosion of home rule; powerful disincentives to California-style sprawl; a new system of sharing tax revenues that levels expenditures for health, education, and welfare, dwarfing even the effect of the landmark *Serrano* decision.

To be sure, the reduction in services and the new fees disproportionately hurt the poor, just as the tax-cut formula favored the rich. But the far-reaching changes in California's fiscal and political structure were hardly congenial to a conservative philosophy of governance. Local government, the level dearest to conservatives, survived only with a whole new dependence on Sacramento. "The voters," quipped civil rights activist James Farmer, "demonstrated against Washington and Sacramento by blowing up City Hall."

Whatever the faults of the property tax—and they are multiple—it has provided historically a local base for fiscal autonomy. That is why the property tax in every state has endured generations of nearly unanimous criticism. But Proposition 13 wiped out about half of the locally generated revenue controlled by California's local government.

With the state contributing upward of $4 billion in new revenue to local government yearly, there must come a whole new order of probing and priority setting. The fruits of the bail-out bill were distributed with satisfying impartiality, but numerous conditions were attached. "Maintenance of effort" was required in police, fire, basic education, and certain health services, causing mayors to concentrate cuts elsewhere. Local budget surpluses were penalized; salary increases were prohibited. New reports were required.

Key legislators began thinking that as long as Sacramento was providing the money, the state might just as well provide the services. The public school lobby had to fight strenuously to kill an idea for statewide collective bargaining for teacher salaries.

As the chief aide to Assembly Speaker Leo McCarthy, Bob Toigo, expressed the thought in fluent Proposition 13 argot: "We're less inclined to bail out and more inclined to buy out." Translated, this meant that the state would pay for more and more services directly, rather than continuing to subsidize local governments.

One mild November day prior to the November 1978 election, Toigo was lunching with Bill Keyser, the affable lobbyist for the California League of Cities, at a popular Sacramento restaurant called appropriately The Lobby.

Several Democratic legislators were losing their races, and the state budget was down a billion dollars, but Toigo's mood that day was up. This is a rare opportunity, Toigo was saying over his salad, for the legislature to set some standards. Keyser nearly choked on his shrimp cocktail. The last thing most California mayors wanted from Sacramento was standards.

Toigo was marveling at how the state had picked up the local share of Medicaid, food stamps, and welfare, thanks to Howard Jarvis. Education would be next. The conservative initiative was opening up liberal possibilities. The whole state taxing system was up for grabs. "We can do things you just can't do in normal times. But these are not normal times," Toigo concluded.

"You just want to attach strings to everything," Keyser grumbled, reaching for the check.

Toigo put his hand on Keyser's. "I always pay for my own lunch," he said, grinning.

As Sacramento attached strings, however, inventive mayors found ways of shaking them loose. For example, several mayors whose contracts with government workers called for cost-of-living raises found themselves in a quandary. If they refused the raise, they could be sued. If the city paid it, they would lose state bail-out money. More than one city neatly got around the prohibition by picking up the employees' share of retirement or health insurance premiums instead, since technically these are not raises. Eventually, the state Supreme Court ruled that local governments could grant raises after all. Since the bail-out formula penalized mayors with large cash surpluses, Proposition 13 prompted a brief but intense spending spree. One school district splurged on forty tons of sand to get the money out of the bank. It will presumably keep school sandboxes full well into the next century.

Not normal times. They are not at all. Local government does not do well under the Jarvis-Gann amendment.

ODD CONSEQUENCES

An even more fundamental shift derived from the seemingly innocent language in Proposition 13 providing that the one percent tax on property would be "collected by the counties and apportioned by law to districts within the counties."

Jarvis offered no guidance on *how* tax moneys should be divided. In the past, of course, each district with the power to tax set its own rate and reaped its own tax revenues. In the frantic two weeks of drafting a bail-out, the legislature had no time to reorder priorities for the thousands of claimants on the public purse. The first state bail-out bill signed by Governor Brown simply allocated property tax revenues within each county based on the historic proportions, and replaced almost 90 percent of the loss with new state aid.

Ironically, this remedy produced tax sharing, another seemingly unreachable goal of progressives. Critics of the property tax have long argued that the tax is unfair because it enables wealthy areas with high property values to generate substantial revenue at a relatively low tax rate. In contrast, poor communities with low tax bases must tax themselves at exorbitant rates to produce fewer dollars. The whole system encourages what has been called "fiscal zoning," as localities try to attract tax-producing developments and keep out low-income housing and other projects that produce more costs than gains for the local public treasury.

Although good government groups advocated regional tax sharing for decades, healthy suburban jurisdictions will seldom surrender tax base to help older, less-affluent areas.

Of all U.S. cities, only in Minneapolis–St. Paul, with its relatively homogeneous population and its progressive tradition of government, has an entire metropolitan area agreed to a voluntary tax-base-sharing plan, under which all communities share in a proportion of regional tax base growth, regardless of where it occurs.

Now, however, as an untended by-product of Proposition 13, countywide tax-base sharing came to California. This will free poor communities from dependence upon their own meager tax base. Increasingly, revenues will be raised according to abilities, and services delivered according to needs, which of course sound more like Marx than Jarvis. Heavy users of services will no longer pay a penalty in the form of higher taxes for the sin of being poor.*

In the past, communities were willing to welcome most new development because the costs to the local government would be offset by the new tax revenues. Under the first bail-out bill, tax receipts produced by a new factory or subdivision were shared with the entire county, although the costs still fell to the school district or city where the development was located.

As a result, local governments grew markedly less sympathetic to new development within their boundaries.

Further, Proposition 13 prohibits new property tax levies to pay off new bond issues. This makes cities still more leery of new developments that require publicly financed streets, sewers, or schools, because there is no means of financing them.

Moreover, most of the new fees imposed to replace lost tax revenues were fees related to construction. The California Building Industries Association (CBIA) estimates that these fees add $2,500 to the cost of a typical new house.

Add this to the grandfather clause that guarantees a cut-rate assessment for those who stay put, and you have the most surprising and unintended impact of Proposition 13: it will probably discourage sprawl in the state that invented sprawl, more effectively than all the environmental policies put together.

In order to get permits to build at all, developers have been forced to pay for all kinds of public improvements once provided by the community. The Hahn Company, a shopping-center developer, negotiated for eighteen months with the city of Fairfield, and finally offered to pay the city $350,000 a year for ten years for off-site improvements, plus a share of the profits. A Santa Monica developer agreed to help the city pay off a bond issue that would have been retired by higher taxes. In Ventura County, north of Los Angeles, a proposed housing-tract development was canceled when the developer refused to meet the city's terms.

The city of Sacramento had projected a net gain in property tax receipts of $1.7 million from a major new housing development. With the impact of Proposition 13 requiring county-wide tax-base sharing, the city esti-

---

* In the 1979–80 bail-out legislation, this was revised to give local California taxing jurisdictions the benefit of increased assessment growth.

mates an annual loss of $4.3 million in extra service costs. Throughout the state, local officials have begun to bargain much harder with developers, who were already reeling from the environmental controls.

Bill Press, former director of California's Planning and Research office, observes that requiring developers to internalize the full cost of development instead of sticking the community with the bill will lead to a radically different pattern of growth in California, including higher-density new construction, and a greater economic incentive to reuse old structures and build new ones within existing communities where infrastructure already exists. Press calls Jarvis "savior of the cities."

Another curious and perverse effect of Proposition 13 was on California's education system. When Proposition 13 was enacted, the public education system in California was in the throes of adjusting to the 1971 decision *Serrano v. Priest*, in which the state supreme court held that students have a constitutional right to substantially equal school expenditure regardless of how rich or poor their local tax base.

Before *Serrano*, inequities had been extreme. Even afterward, wealthy communities continued to generate more tax dollars at lower rates than poor ones. In Beverly Hills in the fiscal year 1976–77, a school tax of $1.00 generated about $770 per pupil; in nearby Baldwin Park the same tax rate generated only $70 per pupil.

The California Court held that under the existing school-financing system, ". . . affluent districts can have their cake and eat it too: they can provide a high quality education for their children while paying lower taxes. Poor districts, by contrast, have no cake at all." In December 1976, after the U.S. Supreme Court ruled that the Federal Constitution does not require equal school financing, the California Court reaffirmed the *Serrano* doctrine under the state constitution.

In the flush years of the mid-seventies, it was considered politically inconceivable that the wealthy districts like Beverly Hills should reduce their per-pupil spending to the level of the poor ones.

It was widely assumed, therefore, that state aid would be increased substantially to bring the level of Baldwin Park up to that of Beverly Hills. In the educational finance jargon, this was termed "leveling up." Within a year, the public school lobby, working with the State Superintendent of Public Instruction, Wilson Riles, obtained a $4.6 billion state aid bill in the same fateful 1977 session (which failed to pass tax relief) to gradually bring up poor districts to the level of rich ones.

Although the 1977 school aid bill was criticized by the *Serrano* plaintiffs as reaching the goal of equal school expenditure too slowly, it was generally hailed as a step in the right direction.

Proposition 13 created a new fiscal climate, without funds to "level up" all the poor districts in California to the standard of Beverly Hills. In the long run, this left the politically unthinkable alternative of "leveling down," in which affluent, suburban school districts where well-educated parents insist on high standards for their children would gradually have revenues withdrawn.

The first year bail-out bill ducked this issue by simply apportioning $2.5 billion in additional school aid funds to replace nearly all the revenue the schools lost under Proposition 13. In the 1978–79 year, public schools in California received a total of about $7 billion—some $2 billion from local sources and $5 billion from the state.

With the state, rather than local property taxes, providing most of the money for public schools, the wide gap in per-pupil spending between rich districts and poor districts became all the more indefensible. Yet the first bail-out bill gave substantially more state aid to rich districts than poor ones. Because Beverly Hills took more of a cut under Proposition 13 than Baldwin Park, Beverly Hills got $1,578 per pupil in state aid, compared with $1,275 for Baldwin Park, leaving the two districts more than $1,000 apart in their total per-pupil spending, a greater disparity than in 1971, when *Serrano* was argued.

This, obviously, could not continue. The second bail-out bill, in 1979, put the public schools on a path that will bring 89 percent of school districts into apparent compliance with *Serrano* by 1983–84, using inflation to gradually reduce the state aid given to rich districts.

This will in time produce the elusive goal of equal spending on public school children, regardless of their parents' wealth. But it may well turn out to be a Pyrrhic victory. In places like Beverly Hills, where local wealth can no longer translate into superior public schools, the constituency for public education is fast eroding, compounded by Los Angeles court-ordered busing.

The most significant long-run effect of Proposition 13 may well be the extension of a *Serrano* standard to all major public services: the State has already picked up the cost of most local welfare and medical care. If the state is paying the bill, how can huge disparities be justified in welfare, health, sanitation, or recreation any more than in education? The equalization of social spending is certainly an outcome that liberals will applaud —unless the result is to further erode the support for public expenditure altogether.

In the topsy-turvy Proposition 13 world, where liberals have achieved several long-sought goals, Howard Jarvis, a spokesman for the Los Angeles apartment owners, can also be credited with—rent control.

Much of the strength of the Los Angeles rent control drive came out of the same middle-class neighborhoods in the San Fernando Valley and West Los Angeles which voted so heavily for Proposition 13. In both cases, the cause was much the same: housing demand exceeding housing supply. For homeowners in the mid-seventies, rising prices translated into heavier taxes. For tenants, the result was steeply higher rents.

Although Jarvis himself asked landlords to pass along their Proposition 13 windfall, demand for apartments was so strong that most landlords continued to charge whatever the market would bear. Before Proposition 13, about 24 percent of the cost of operating a rental building went for local property taxes. With their taxes cut in half landlords should have been able to cut rents by 10 to 15 percent. Few did. As rent control rumors began to fly, some even raised rents, helping to trigger the rent control they feared.

In short order the tax revolt turned into a rent revolt. During June 1978 more than 13,000 calls jammed a governor's "renter hotline," complaining about rent increases. Speaker Leo McCarthy, architect of the bail-out bill, was deluged with mail complaining that tenants were getting nothing from Proposition 13.

"We referred them all to Howard Jarvis," deadpanned McCarthy.

The Los Angeles County Board first enacted a six-month rent freeze, which was converted into a permanent rent control system on May 1, 1979. Even County Supervisor Bernardi, a Jarvis supporter, now voted for rent control. Several other cities rejected rent control referenda in November 1978, but by late 1979, rent control was extended to eight California cities.

Both movements—Proposition 13 and rent control—had scant ideological grounding. Voters who could follow first Howard Jarvis and then turn to rent control were motivated in both cases by economic distress. The right wing had made off with the first round; the left with the second. Rent control also involves monumental red tape, but the supposedly antigovernment voters were willing to turn to government to redress gouging by landlords, just as they had turned on government to reduce oppressive taxes.

Proposition 13 produced for California a very mixed bag of consequences, few of them deliberately intended by the protesting property owners. The voters who supported Howard Jarvis were voting for one thing—property tax relief. They got a good deal more: a highly centralized system of state government, a remarkable leveling of public services county-wide and even statewide; sharp limitation on future sprawl, state financing of education, welfare, and Medicaid, and rent control. Liberals also could take some comfort in the fact that they didn't care much for the property tax anyway, since it operates as a highly regressive tax. After Jarvis, a larger percentage of public services in California were financed by the far more equitable state income tax.

Proposition 13, in short, did not create the advertised conservative millennium.

But it did create a political context in which the age of less was defined under largely conservative auspices. The era of limits dawned first for government agencies and their needy clients.

With Proposition 13 creating few hardships for most California voters, the momentum continued. In 1979, Paul Gann qualified a more careful initiative, Proposition 4, modeled on tax and spending limits adopted by several other states. The Gann initiative restricts future growth of state and local expenditures to approximately the growth in California's personal income.

In California's new fiscal climate, this idea proved so appealing that even Speaker McCarthy joined Gann as a cosponsor. It was too tame for Jarvis, who collected signatures for a rival amendment to cut the state income tax in half. With little opposition, Gann won handily.

Obviously, Proposition 13 did have one consequence that was entirely intended. It cut taxes.

But it is arguable whether or not Proposition 13 made government more efficient.

The new game in Sacramento of allocating a fixed amount of dollars did not please most politicians. Before Proposition 13, it was always possible to find a few more dollars for a pet project. Now, with a limited pie, adding to one program meant reducing another.

But the state legislature did not respond to this new, discomfiting political reality by radically altering spending priorities or applying new scrutiny to programs. From the first bail-out on, it acted to spread the cuts around and preserve a slightly thinner status quo. It was not deemed politically possible to clean house and toss out entire programs.

In early 1979, the blue-ribbon commission on the fiscal future of California appointed by Governor Brown presented a divided report that failed utterly to agree on what should be scrapped, and how government spending might be redirected.

Two years after Proposition 13, most agencies of government simply continued to operate, on lower budgets. Cutting payroll by attrition undoubtedly *reduced* government's productivity since agencies disproportionately lost their senior people, many of whom took early retirement. Other talented employees left public sector jobs, frustrated by the new salary freeze and the limits on career mobility in government.

On the other hand, the fiscal discipline enforced on local budget officials dictated a plethora of little economies. But typically, political muscle, not excess fat, determined what would be cut. Predictably, services with little political clout, such as libraries, free recreation, specialized social services, and maintenance of physical plants, suffered the steepest cuts.

For those who looked to government for services, the services were still there, but the lines were longer and there was little money to innovate. For the believers, who expected Proposition 13 to impose more stringent priorities on government, the new reality looked disappointingly like the old.

PART II

A Short Course on the Property Tax

7

THE CROOKED ASSESSOR
REVISITED

Practically, the general property tax as actually administered is beyond all doubt one of the worst taxes known in the civilized world. Because of its attempt to tax intangible as well as tangible things, it sins against the cardinal rules of uniformity, of equality and of universality of taxation. It puts a premium on dishonesty and debauches the public conscience; it reduces deception to a system and makes a science of knavery; it presses hardest on those least able to pay; it imposes double taxation on one man and grants entire immunity to the next. In short, the general property tax is so flagrantly inequitable that its retention can be explained only through ignorance or inertia. It is the cause of such crying injustice that its alteration or abolition must become the battle-cry of every statesman and reformer
—*Professor Edwin R. A. Seligman, 1895*

THUS SAITH PROFESSOR SELIGMAN, dean of Victorian tax scholars, and with only slight hyperbole.

For at least a hundred years, the property tax has been monumentally and justifiably unpopular. And it has proven remarkably resistant to episodic swells of protest and reform.

Howard Jarvis' novelty lay in his ability to convert the authentic and long-standing grievances against the property tax into a more generalized protest against taxes and government. In this, he had a good deal of assistance from his governor, the inflationary times, and the prevailing cynicism about political institutions. But much of the culpability lay in the property tax itself. As a peculiarly American institution, impenetrable and hopelessly convoluted, the property tax deserves more than passing notice.

The usual charges against the property tax include these:

It is regressive—that is, it taxes the poor at a higher rate than the rich. It tends to be regressive in several ways: the poor spend a higher portion of their income on housing to begin with; expensive housing is usually assessed at a lower fraction of its true value than cheap housing; localities with lots of poor people have to tax themselves at higher rates to provide the same dollars as more affluent jurisdictions; and income tax deductions against the property tax are worth more to those with higher property tax bills; moreover, a landlord's savings on his income tax bill are not necessarily passed along to the tenant, who gets no income tax benefit from the portion of his rent which helps pay the landlord's property tax.

Also, it is administratively messy; the property tax gives enormous discretion to local assessors, which is sometimes abused. Corruption in assessing weakens confidence in the entire tax system. Even where there is no corruption, the complexity of assessment ratios and overlapping tax districts creates enormous confusion, and defies accountability.

All these charges are quite hoary, and quite valid today. As Seligman's great colleague the tax historian Jens Peter Jensen wrote in his opus on American taxation in 1931, "If any tax could have been eliminated by adverse criticism, the general property tax would have been eliminated long ago."

Yet the property tax has survived, mainly because it simply generates too much revenue to give up: $66 billion in 1978. In 1902 the property tax accounted for 84 percent of locally raised tax dollars. Seventy-five years later, it still provided more than 80 percent. Because real estate stays put, a tax on real property is the one source of revenue that local units of government can count on. Most local mayors, city councils, and county boards have suspected, not without reason, that as state or federal authorities have begun providing more of the funds, they would increasingly call the tune. Thus, the property tax is still with us, and with most of its flaws.

In fairness to the property tax, many tax scholars point out that it is, after all, our only significant tax on wealth, as opposed to income. And as such, the property tax might be considered a quite progressive tax, if it could ever be administered fairly. But that is a very big "if." Defenders of the property tax also point out, with some justice, that the property tax is especially vulnerable to public anger because it is so visible. Citizens can go down to the county courthouse and look up which of their neighbors is paying what sort of tax. You can't do that with your neighbors' federal income tax returns. And if people had the same access to the information about income tax inequities, they might well be just as angry.

But all of this is conjecture. The property tax, as it exists in the real world, has been a lightning rod for public protest, and with good reason.

The first tax revolt was, of course, the American Revolution. The new intolerable taxes, including the hated tax on tea, were tariffs and excise taxes. But the familiar tax, the mainstay of public finance in many of the colonies, was the property tax. In the eighteenth and nineteenth centuries, long before income and sales taxes, a tax on property was crudely progressive. In some colonies it was known as a "faculty tax," meaning that the tax collector took into consideration a citizen's total ability to pay; a lawyer's practice, as well as a cigarmaker's inventory, was fair game for the assessor.

The colonial property tax was also much more comprehensive than the modern property tax, since most of colonial America's wealth was held in the form of real estate and livestock, and therefore most of the total wealth was taxed. Some colonies exempted a basic farmstead from taxation, so that the burden of the property tax fell more heavily on the well-to-do. An early colonial tax, levied on farms in Long Island in 1674, exempted the first 1,000 guilders of value ($400), making it a tax exclusively on the well-off.

By the time of the Revolution, the property tax was the main source of local finance in New England, and to a lesser extent in the Middle Atlantic colonies, which also used excise taxes and tariffs. The more aristocratic South, whose landholding classes resisted taxes on real estate, relied more heavily on the poll tax.

As the young country began to industrialize, more and more of the national wealth shifted to plant, equipment, personal property, and what tax experts like to call "intangibles"—stocks, bonds, patents, savings accounts, and other forms of paper. During the republican Jacksonian era, a number of states attempted to capture this shifting tax base, by extending the property tax to all forms of wealth; hence the designation "general" property tax.

In the early days of the Republic, it was common practice to tax different kinds of property at different rates, with surprisingly fine distinctions. An early history of taxation in New Hampshire records that sheep were taxed at 5 shillings, while swine were taxed at 10. Two-year-old steers commanded 25 shillings, and three-year-olds 40.

The early property tax was a crazy quilt of different rates for different kinds of property, and selective exemptions inherited from colonial times, The Massachusetts Bay Colony, foreshadowing modern attempts to lure industry, offered bounties for producers of hemp, flax, and glass and reduced taxes on commercial brewers whose production exceeded 100 barrels annually.

More informally, assessors were wont to adjust for circumstances. A widow or a farmer who lost his crop could have an assessment lowered. So might a politically influential merchant, while an absentee-owned property could expect to pay more. The motivation might be charitable, or corrupt, but the result was a tax roll that only remotely reflected reality.

REFORM

By the mid-nineteenth century, reformers were clamoring for a more rational and equitable system, based on a *general* property tax, with uniform assessments and equal tax rates on all forms of wealth. The idea had wide appeal. Taxing all forms of property would lower the tax burden on the common man, and at the same time the merchant class could be assured that populist legislatures would not tax commercial and industrial wealth at higher rates. Several state constitutions were amended to include these twin requirements of universality and uniformity, which became widely accepted principles of property tax lore.

The reform was admirable in theory. But it strained the enforcement machinery to the breaking point.

The enforcement machinery was of course the local assessor. It was hard enough for the underpaid and undertrained cadre of part-time assessors to accurately value farms, homes, livestock, watches, pianos, and family jewels. Now they were called upon to include as well stocks, bonds, mortgages, and bank accounts.

Despite the mandate for uniform assessment, most assessors continued to value property at a fraction of its true worth. The practice dates to the earliest days of the English colonies, when the colonial legislature set the rate but the local assessor valued the property. Obviously, the assessor found it in his interest to undervalue his neighbors' holdings and let yeomen from outlying districts carry the heavier burden.

As county and township assessors came to compete with each other to undervalue property, colonial and, later, state authorities were established to supervise local assessors and "equalize" assessments. This was done by independently surveying actual market values, which produced a ratio indicating how much each township or county had undervalued its property relative to others. In theory, this multiplier applied to the local assessor's figures would "equalize" values throughout the state.

As early at 1668 the Massachusetts general court appointed a special committee to equalize assessments from the Bay Colony's several settlements.

By the mid-nineteenth century, most states had established boards of equalization to spot-check local assessments and devise formulas presumably to reconcile disparities. Until well into the twentieth century the property tax produced a large portion of state as well as local revenue, giving the state a good reason to determine whether localities were pulling their weight. As states began giving localities financial aid for schools and other local needs, the equalization formulas became even more important, because local property wealth (or its absence) often dictated the amount of state aid.

But the equalization formulas could serve to rectify only average disparities, and a particular taxpayer with a relatively high valuation who happened to live in a district whose average valuation was low, was doubly punished: overassessed in the first place in comparison with his neighbors, he was clobbered a second time when the equalization formula was applied.

While most states have continued this strange and little-understood process of equalization, most tax scholars have long agreed with the findings of a turn-of-the-century commission, that "equalization so called, does not equalize, and in the nature of things cannot equalize."

The last decades of the nineteenth century were a kind of golden age of tax policy, in which several states created tax policy commissions to modernize tax administration, and scholarly conferences debated tax issues to a fare-thee-well. Although government a century ago spent a much smaller fraction of national income, tax theory was surprisingly sophisticated. Most of the property tax issues that perplexed nineteenth-century reformers were the same ones under discussion today: What kinds of property to tax? What should be exempt? Whether to tax at differential rates? How to limit the local right to tax? What level of government should assess, collect, and distribute revenues? Whether to appoint or to elect tax officials? And what to do about the perennial problem of inequitable or corrupt assessments?

During the years when most states attempted to tax all forms of property, assessment presented an especially thorny problem because it was inconceivable to hire enough officials to assess everything. Virtually all assessors were part-time, usually locally elected and untrained circuit riders—as they still are in many parts of the country. A century ago, many states paid their assessors on commission as an incentive, and several devised systems of self-assessment that foreshadowed modern internal revenue enforcement. A number of states required the householder to swear an oath attesting to the accuracy of his list of property; Vermont permitted assessors to increase incomplete lists "fourfold" and to keep half of the increase as a fee. The hard-pressed legislators of the territory of Illinois in the year 1812 enacted a law providing that any taxable property deliberately omitted from a citizen's sworn list would simply be forfeited to the state.

Throughout the Midwest, tax officials were assisted by a system of "tax ferrets" or "tax inquisitors," who did just what the labels imply. These privateers operated on commission, tipping assessors to the existence of unreported property, like modern contract companies who tow away illegally parked motorists; and they were about as popular. In Ohio, inquisitors' commissions ran as high as 25 percent of the tax owed.

Had the nineteenth-century property tax been consistently enforced, it surely would have provoked open rebellion, just as California's attempt to apply consistent assessment standards overloaded the system a century later. By the turn of the century, nominal tax rates were as high as 2 percent of value. This meant that a $100 bond earning a yield of $4 would have to pay $2 in property taxes, for a real tax of 50 percent on the income.

For the system to work at all, however, it was necessary that property seldom be taxed at its full value, regardless of the principles of the state constitutions. Yet this wide discretion subjected citizens to the whims of assessors and contributed to the perception that the property tax was arbitrary and grossly unfair.

A dismayed assessor from Indiana named Fred Sims balefully described his plight to a 1916 tax convention:

If the assessor were to investigate the true owners of mortgage security, he would drive millions of dollars from the state and send up the interest rate. If he were to assess corporate property at true value, he would create many fat receiverships. If he were to list the true value of stocks of goods, he would decrease competition by the number of merchants put out of business. If he were to put on the roll the "true cash value" of lands and improvements as well as other property, he would destroy the income value of millions of these investments and send values towards Davy Jones' locker. If he were to institute an inquiry into the base amount of intangible property, he would start an exodus of citizens of Indiana to homesteading in other states.

Although this discretion in the hands of an honest assessor produced a crude check on the system's worst inequities (in a manner that California's ultramodern computer formulas failed to), it nonetheless put citizens at the mercy of assessors and brought the entire system into disrepute.

To the scientific, reformist mind of the progressive era, the general property tax, untidy and irrational, constituted a gross affront. An 1886 Illinois commission termed the system "debauching to the conscience and subversive of the public morals."

For the system was quite plainly a charade. In an age before adding machines, let alone computers, the small and amateur cadre of local assessors was called upon to perform feats of enforcement that were plainly beyond their powers. For a period of about seventy-five years, beginning in the mid-nineteenth century, every conceivable variety of property was supposed to be evaluated and taxed at uniform rates: not just real estate, but "personalty"—meaning household goods, business plant and equipment, rolling stock, mineral wealth, timber, and business inventories, as well as "intangibles," such as stocks, bonds, patents, and mortgages. (Even in today's climate of high taxation and taxpayer backlash, the authorities do not attempt to apply the property tax to so broad a base.)

Obviously, this was unenforceable. At the turn of the century, the tax fraternity regularly gathered to lament the sorry state of tax administration. Pocketwatches, supposedly taxed as personal property, intrigued the contemporary critics as a symbol of how low the system had fallen. A tax collector named E. T. Miller dejectedly reported to a 1917 convention of tax experts that in the city of Austin, Texas, "of a population of over 34,000, only 605 persons were honest enough to declare their watches for taxation."

The tax historian Jens Jensen, with meticulous scorn, noted that the watches and clocks taxed in Cook County, Illinois, declined from 7,571 in the year 1867, to 6,281 in 1927, an implausible ratio of "one watch or clock per 400 or 500 persons."

"The forms of the assessor," Jensen concluded, "usually specify in considerable detail the items to be listed, such as horses, watches and clocks, pianos, radios, sewing machines, automobiles, and so on. . . . The records show that in some localities there is a fair listing, while in others there is scarcely any at all. It is reported in some assessment districts that no attempt is made to assess a great variety of items. The assessor's good sense tells him that it is futile to try."

In Massachusetts, where household property was taxed well into the present century, it was common practice for families in the western part of the state to transport the family silver across the line into New York at assessment time. In Illinois, where savings accounts were taxed, savings were customarily transferred to banks in Indiana once a year. A version of this maneuver still goes on in California, where business inventories are taxed. Warehouses just over the line in Nevada do an especially brisk business at tax season.

This system, in which the reality was far removed from the nominal principles of universality and uniformity, gave the assessor an unusual degree of power that far exceeded his nominal responsibility to value and list taxable property. His highly subjective assessments, all of them far below the nominal full market value, could favor one property owner over another, one industry over another, long-time residents over strangers. And more significantly, the total size of his assessment roll determined local government's ability to tax.

The locally elected assessor, seeking to ingratiate himself with the voters, often came to see himself as a force for fiscal restraint. Far be it from him to track down the poor devils in the county so the politicians could levy taxes on their pocket watches! Far be it from him to bring assessed values up to the latest market trends, so that a corrupt gang in City Hall could rake in more tax receipts without having to raise the rate. Throughout the South, conservative assessors opposed to increased funds for public schools often kept new schools from being built simply by restricting the tax base through low assessments. Year by year, assessed values dropped further and further behind actual values, making a shambles out of the system.

The disparities in the quality of assessment, and the incidence of the tax, varied enormously. As a generalization, homeowners as a class probably received favorable treatment in most states, but some homeowners were overassessed compared with others. Industrial real estate in most states was assessed at relatively higher fractions, but given the enormous assessor discretion, favoritism was endemic.

The assessor regularly found himself pressed to consider external economic events that had nothing to do with tax administration—depressions, financial panics, crop losses. Somehow, the property tax seemed to operate perversely in such circumstances.

For example, the financial panic of 1907, like so many others, brought commerce to a temporary standstill. In Seattle, the salmon catch, usually a brisk export item to other states thanks to the innovation of factory canning, was piling up in local warehouses. Under the general property tax, the salmon became taxable as inventory, and just when the canning industry was hard pressed to meet payroll and pay bills. The city fathers came up with the ingenious theory that the salmon tins gathering dust in the city's warehouses were really goods in transit. But the assessor, who happened to be a reform type, would have none of it. He became a hero to his colleagues.

Reform assessors were always getting elected, because the system was endemically and hopelessly in need of reform; and they invariably failed to make much of a dent. True equalization was unthinkable. Some of the disparities chronicled by the tax study commissions of the nineteenth century were quite extraordinary. New York, for example, nominally required all property to be valued and taxed equally; in practice, personal property—meaning mainly business machinery—paid as little as one percent of the tax, though it was estimated to be half the state's property wealth.

Despite the handwringing of the reformers, there were too many good reasons to let assessments lag. Every sort of economic season provided its own special rationale. In inflationary times, it was folly to increase the assessments, because this would only produce windfall revenues for City Hall. By the same token, during depressions, when property values (and wages) actually fell, leaving citizens hard pressed to pay their taxes, there was even less reason to honor the mandated full-value assessments.

At the same time, certain types of property were favorite targets for local assessors. Railroad property, for instance. It couldn't very well pick up and move, and it seldom was locally owned. During a period when the railroad magnates fairly bled America dry, hundreds of unsung county and township assessors struck a blow in return for the little man by socking rolling stock and trackage for every last penny of its market value. And the railroads spent untold millions to have their high-priced lawyers haul local assessors into court.

Fearing to dismantle this convoluted system and shift tax burdens onto homeowners, the courts performed remarkable contortions of logic to harmonize the long-standing custom of fractional assessment with the quite straightforward language of the nineteenth-century uniformity clauses, which required full and equal assessments.

When a homeowner complained that he was overassessed compared with his neighbors, most courts simply ducked. Occasionally, a bold state judge might order the plaintiff's assessment reduced to the level common in his jurisdiction, but not until the 1960s did the courts begin to tamper with the entire system.

Most judges followed the logic of the Massachusetts Supreme Court, which offered a disingenuously literal reading of the state's uniformity clause in an 1890 case. "The question," declared the court, "is whether the property has been valued at more than its fair cash value, and not whether it has been valued more or less than similar property of other persons." Obviously, since *all* property was underassessed, this reasoning nicely sanctioned the grossest sort of discrimination.

In a similar decision, memorable for its candor if not its logic, the Oregon Supreme Court conceded that the assessor had plainly valued the plaintiff's property at far more than comparable properties, but observed that since the assessment did not actually *exceed* the true value, no relief would be granted. "Invalidation of a single assessment," sniffed the court, sounding remarkably like a Gilbert and Sullivan court, "may operate like the loosing of a stitch that causes the entire fabric to unravel."

In a marvelous controversy that worked its way to the U.S. Supreme Court, the Nashville, Chattanooga, and St. Louis railroad complained that the state of Tennessee stuck the railroad's property with an assessment at about 75 percent of its true value, while other property got off with far less. Despite the Tennessee constitution's long-standing (and long-ignored) uniformity clause requiring taxes to be "equal and uniform," the Court breezily declared that "the Company makes no claim that its property is singled out from other public service corporations for discrimination. Its asserted grievance is common to the whole class." This, of course, was the essence of the complaint. (One can imagine the Court advising the plaintiffs in *Brown v. Board of Education* that since *all* Negroes were discriminated against, there was no merit to the individual complaint.) Acknowledging quite frankly that long-standing custom violated the Tennessee constitution, the Court concluded: "Deeply embedded traditional ways of carrying out state policy, such as those of which petitioner complains, are often tougher and truer law than the dead words of the written text. . . ." *The dead words of the written text.* So much for the Tennessee constitution.

Thus, taxpayers wronged by their local assessor, whether homeowners or businessmen, seldom found relief through the courts.

The nineteenth-century debates about uniformity and tax equity have a quite contemporary ring. The issues involved far more than abstract theory, since they determined how the tax load would be divided up. Uniformity was an attractive ideal; if all forms of wealth were assessed and taxed equally, as they were supposed to be in theory, the burden would be spread more widely and the effective tax on ordinary people would drop.

But this reform was not to be, at least not in nineteenth-century America. (Interestingly, the call for a universal property tax on wealth has been revived in recent years. M.I.T. economist Lester Thurow argues that since disparities in wealth are far more extreme than disparities in income, a truly redistributive tax system requires a tax on wealth. While a general wealth tax was far beyond the enforcement technology of nineteenth-century America, the Swedes in recent years have enforced a wealth tax quite efficiently. Professor Donald Hagman of UCLA estimates that the present U.S. property tax captures only about one-fifth of the total wealth, and half of what's taxed is housing.)

Instead, most progressive era reformers concluded with Seligman that the general property tax was hopeless and farcical; it could not be enforced without an unacceptable degree of administrative centralization and new armies of assessors, and the pathetically inconsistent tax enforcement undermined respect for the law.

So the reformers turned their energies to inventing substitute taxes—in particular, two new taxes, radically different from each other: the single tax and the income tax. The search for a more feasible form of wealth tax led first to the single tax, the invention of an authentic native radical, Henry George. The single taxers proposed to tax away all the "unearned" appreciation in the value of land. One strand of this idea derived from the French Physiocrats, who had argued that land is the source of all wealth, and that the surplus rent from land is the only true addition to society's net wealth.

George combined this theoretical premise with his observation of what was quite evident in late nineteenth-century America—a stampede toward development that raised land values chaotically, producing windfalls for promoters and speculators, and frequent hardship for the productive users of the land.

George argued that to tax away the portion of the gain that was not the result of the landowner's own labors would have multiple benefits. It would not tax production or construction. It would eliminate purely speculative acquisition of land; it would force development to proceed more rationally and intensively, since idle property surrounded by productive property would be prohibitively expensive to hold. And it would neatly solve the enforcement problems of the general property tax, because unlike the family silver or can of salmon, "land cannot be carried off." Economists, then and now, widely agreed that the incidence of a tax on land cannot be shifted; it must be paid by the landowner, because the supply of land is fixed. Thus, the tax truly would fall on its nominal recipient. According to George, other taxes might even be abolished, thanks to the high yields of this new, single tax.

George and his teachings enjoyed a wide following. He was nearly elected mayor of New York. But the single tax never quite became a mainstream idea. There is still widespread interest in a less heroic version of the idea, site-value taxation, which taxes land rather than improvements; a version of site-taxation is used in Pittsburgh, with apparently beneficial effects on development patterns.

Instead of espousing a perfected property tax, however, most reformers turned increasingly to the income tax. Yet despite the eventual success of this movement, culminating in the Sixteenth Amendment, and the subsequent addition of sales taxes beginning in the Depression, the property tax endured.

Property taxes did cease to be a main source of revenue for *state* governments, replaced largely by income and sales taxes after the thirties. And gradually, the sillier levies on property were repealed, de jure as well as de facto. Tax scholars no longer count pocket watches. Most states abandoned taxes on household goods and intangible wealth; business pressure has also caused several states to repeal the far more defensible personal property tax on plant, equipment, and inventory.

But the property tax, as a tax on real estate, survived as the mainstay of local public finance. And it survived with most of the irrationalities and inequities described so scathingly by Professor Seligman and colleagues still quite intact.

Since Seligman's day, state tax commissions, boards of equalization, and, more recently, the courts have continued to wage heroic battles to rationalize this remarkable relic, the property tax. The nineteenth-century remedy, comprehensive and uniform taxation, failed utterly. To compensate for the failure, modern tax officials devised one offsetting gimmick after another, until the property tax system became an almost incomprehensible Rube Goldberg contraption.

MODERNIZED INEQUITY

By the eve of the tax revolt, the property tax in a typical state worked like this:

In all but one state (Hawaii), property continued to be assessed at the local level, by a county or township assessor. Assessment continued to be fractional—that is, at less than true value. Most states tolerated *differential* fractions for different kinds of property. Sometimes, the assessor published a target figure, say 50 percent for business property and 25 percent for homes; sometimes the ratios were merely informal and customary.

To compensate for these inequities, equalization authorities at both the state and county level conducted their own surveys of property values, publishing tables showing each locality's average assessment ratio. This was converted into an "equalization factor" supposedly reflecting the degree to which property in each jurisdiction was underassessed. Before the tax rate could be applied and the tax actually levied, the assessment would be "equalized." In some states, this was done by type of property; in others, it was done simply by jurisdiction.

But despite the unflagging efforts to equalize, assessment ratios and tax burdens tended with time to become more and more out of whack. The degree of disparity between assessment ratios among towns or counties in a given state or within the same town can be measured statistically. This so-called "coefficient of dispersion" indicates the degree of unequal treatment. According to the Census Bureau, which surveys assessments every five years, disparities were slightly worse in 1976 than in 1971, and worse in 1971 than in 1966.

Obviously, the greater the inequity, the greater the need for reform. But the *greater the inequity, the more taxpayers will be affected by any significant attempt to redistribute tax burdens, and hence the greater the political resistance to fundamental reform.*

Thus, assessment inequities have persisted precisely because there is such little political appeal in improving tax administration, and even less in conducting a mass reassessment. There is a very simple iron law of tax assessment: officials who preside over reassessments don't get reelected. "You make more enemies than friends," says Ned Pattison, who served as county treasurer of Rensselaer County in Upstate New York before moving on to Congress. "The people who end up paying higher taxes scream bloody murder, and those who benefit keep very, very quiet because they think they're getting away with something."

"Fractional assessment" also helps insulate the system from accountability. Assume, for example, that your house is worth $70,000. You are dimly aware that your town customarily assesses at 20 percent of actual value, which would produce an assessment of $14,000. Your assessment comes in at $12,000, presumably a bargain. But backyard gossip has it that the assessor is actually lagging further below the customary 20 percent and your neighbors got off with only $9,000.

What to do? Most people would hesitate to appeal, because it seems as though they are getting away with something. If the assessor came around, he might discover the new kitchen and push the assessment to $16,500 if only out of spite. Conceivably, he could hike the assessment all the way to $70,000, since fractional assessment in most places is only a matter of custom, not law. Usually the taxpayer grouses and does nothing, becoming another potential convert to the tax revolt. Few individuals have the sophistication to protest a $16,000 assessment on a $70,000 house. Some states even require the petitioner to hire an appraiser at his own expense to survey surrounding property before they will entertain an appeal.

In practice, assessment appeals are something for sophisticated property owners, like railroads, manufacturers, and landlords. As Diane Paul observed in her shrewd study of assessment procedures in Boston and San Francisco, "The structure of property assessing in most big cities favors homeowners over businessmen. This favoritism is mitigated to some degree, by the assessment appeals process. And because those businessmen with the resources and incentives to upset the system are most likely to apply for tax reductions, the appeals process functions to maintain the status quo. It provides the slack without which many of the extra-legal and informal assessing structures which have developed in most big cities would probably collapse."

Helping local businesses challenge assessments has become a legal subspecialty. As a general rule, the more antiquated the city's assessment apparatus, the easier it is to negotiate a settlement. In New York City, where the semblance of systematic, periodic reassessment remains a fantasy, almost any plausible application can win a reduction. A part-time appeals board with a token staff sifts through tens of thousands of applications annually. For two decades, Boston put off its day of reckoning by settling assessment appeals case by case. Invariably, these tend to be appeals of business property assessments.

ASSESSMENT POLITICS

The impenetrability of property taxation is compounded by the variety of approaches to assessment.

In theory, the fair market value of a property is the price that a willing buyer pays a willing seller in an arm's-length transaction. This is fine when you have a transaction. When property does not change hands, the assessor turns to his formulas. He considers "comparables"—that is, similar properties that have recently sold. In the case of rental real estate, he can consider the capitalized value of its rent roll, or its replacement cost. For commercial and industrial property, which seldom changes hands, the exercise becomes even more arcane. One can attempt to calculate the property's historic cost, allowing for depreciation, and obsolescence, or its present market value, or the capitalized value of its power to generate income. But how to compare a jewelry shop with a supermarket, which require very different floor space to generate the same income? And how to value a steel mill? Much of this, of course, is highly technical, and the subject of an extensive, dense literature.

When faced with requirements for periodic mass reappraisal, local assessors sometimes turn to private appraisal companies. The most prominent of these firms, Cole-Layer-Trumble, holds contracts with numerous counties to reassess the entire property roll periodically.

Such firms are often denounced by the assessor himself when the result of the reappraisal proves politically unpalatable. The assessor of Nashville, Tennessee, Clifford Allen, who later became a U.S. congressman, went after Cole-Layer-Trumble for apparently undervaluing commercial properties, and also pointed to an apparent conflict of interest: at the time, CLT was part of a holding company that also worked for industries that were seeking to keep assessments as low as possible.

Private mass-appraisal firms are often attacked for hiring poorly trained temporary employees, who might be local college students. CLT has taken considerable heat for its assessments in cities as diverse as Cleveland, Cincinnati, Quincy, Massachusetts, Wilmington, and Atlanta, where a local judge in 1971 threw out an entire mass reappraisal. In Boise,

Idaho, a 1976 mass reappraisal by an outside consulting firm raised home-owner taxes an average of 50 percent, while leaving commercial assessments almost untouched. In Troy, New York, the appraisal consultant was bitterly denounced for hiring "a bunch of kids from Rensselaer [Polytechnic Institute] who never even went inside the houses." Subsequently, city officials revised commercial assessments upward.

In late 1979, a reassessment by an affiliate of CLT in Waterbury, Connecticut, led to a brief taxpayer revolt. The firm, Trumble McGuirk Associates, conducted a revaluation that produced sharp tax hikes of several hundred dollars each for homes in blue-collar neighborhoods but tax *cuts* for the city's major businesses. A major Waterbury firm, Century Brass, stood to reap a tax cut of some $250,000. Taxpayer indignation forced the newly reelected mayor to delay putting the assessments into effect. Taxpayers demonstrated at Trumble's offices, carrying signs reading: "Make Trumble Tremble!" Eventually, a new assessor was appointed, and many homeowner assessments were cut.

The latest wrinkle in the assessment business is something called "computer-assessed mass appraisal" (CAMA), in which a computer is programmed to consider as many as 100 different characteristics of a property, including its age, size, location, condition, as well as sales of comparable properties, and from these spit out an estimated selling price, or E.S.P. Critics, however, have suggested that assessment usually is more related to the other kind of ESP. At a recent convention, one property appraiser was seen wearing a button with the letters S.W.A.G., standing for Society of Wild-Assed Guessers.

The computerization of assessing in California, of course, was one factor in the tax revolt, because it removed the element of human discretion, however arbitrary, which has traditionally kept this ramshackle system from collapsing of its own weight. The fact that a tax rebellion occurred in California, with its model system of tax administration and its ultramodern computers, has prompted much hand wringing in the tax fraternity.

Yet the old system of rough and ready guessing is also a kind of time bomb, because it fosters the entirely accurate perception of unequal treatment. For the small homeowner, the local assessor's valuation is usually the last word on the subject. For big landowners and corporations, who have the sophistication and financial means to challenge the assessor, their appraisal is typically a negotiated process. In small cities, assessors often treat prominent local companies quite gingerly.

In Gary, Indiana, the Democratic city administration of Mayor Richard

Hatcher fought a running battle with the crusty Republican township assessor over the valuation of the city's largest taxpayer, the huge U.S. Steel works. The city's finance advisor compared the figures in the company's annual report with value claimed for property tax purposes and calculated that the steel works was undervalued by between $92 and $152 million, costing the city up to $25 million a year in property tax revenues.

Neither the company nor the assessor, Tom Faddell, would give Gary access to company records on which the assessment was based. Under questioning from a Senate subcommittee investigating assessment practices, Faddell insisted that the city's campaign against him was politically motivated, but readily conceded that his assessment took into account U.S. Steel's own financial needs as well as its property value for tax purposes.

"It is my responsibility," Faddell explained, "to see that the taxpayer is not placed at a competitive position with his neighbors and in this particular instance you are faced with not only foreign steel competition but you are also faced with Bethlehem Steel in a $4.81 tax rate area and Inland in Youngstown in a low tax rate area."

This, of course, may be so, but it has nothing to do with the assessor's supposed job. The Senate subcommittee investigation also found that ghetto areas of Gary, where property values had been dropping typically, were assessed at a higher fraction of their true worth than more expensive homes.

Although the city of Gary lacked standing to challenge the assessment when it seemed too low, U.S. Steel has recourse to both the state tax board and the courts if it feels its assessment is too high. And this prospect, as well as simple favoritism by the local assessor, helps explain the outcome. Often, the contest is an unequal match. For example, according to the subcommittee investigation, U.S. Steel went to court both in 1968 and in 1969 to reduce its assessment, and in both cases, rather than go to trial, the state tax board settled for a figure lower than the one calculated by its own staff auditors.

As recently as 1977, the government of the District of Columbia was embarrassed when an independent-minded deputy city auditor, Carl Bergman, went public with the disclosure that the city's prime commercial real estate was enjoying remarkably static assessments during the unparalleled boom years of the middle seventies when property values in the District soared and homeowners got hit with ever-spiraling taxes. Between 1974 and 1978, the assessment on Connecticut Avenue's Universal Building was raised a paltry 7 percent. The assessment on the city's single most valuable property, appropriately enough the Watergate, was raised only 12 percent. The Capitol Hilton's assessment was unchanged. And the assessment on the Washington *Post,* at a prime downtown location, was actually reduced. During the same four-year period, the average assessments on homes jumped 68 percent.

Although Washington, D.C., recently reformed its property tax in many respects, including periodic reassessment at full value along with exemptions to shield homeowners against inflationary tax hikes, the reforms did not make the local assessor an equal match for big downtown property owners, their accountants and attorneys.

Matthew Watson, D.C.'s chief auditor, blames the continuing mismatch on understaffing and primitive assessment techniques, which lead to seat-of-the-pants valuations that won't stand judicial scrutiny. "Assessors are still very timid," Watson believes, "because in commercial property even a slight increase is a lot of money and it's worthwhile challenging. Bureaucratically, assessors cave in, not because of corruption, but because they're afraid of suits that can't be defended. A very low assessment is easier to defend in court, and it heads off litigation in the first place."

In other cities, however, the explanation *is* corruption.

In Albany, New York, assessments have been used in a transparently corrupt manner to bolster the sagging local Democratic machine. Surveys by a consumer group found that the assessor systematically jacks up the valuation of newly purchased homes. Shortly afterward, the homeowner is visited by the local party committeeman, who innocently inquires whether the resident has encountered any problems. When the homeowner tells of the high assessment, the committeeman hands him an appeals form and offers to take care of the problem. In short order, the assessment is lowered to its old level. Investigators for the Public Interest Research Group, a Nader affiliate, found that many of the grievance forms contained no more information than a name and address, but won reductions anyway.

Possibly one of the most inventive assessors of recent years was P. J. (Parky) Cullerton, boss of the 50th Ward and longtime assessor of Cook County, Illinois. Cullerton was notorious for allegedly arranging favorable assessments on property owned by investors close to the Daley machine and for Democratic party campaign contributors. Despite press exposés of his dealings, Cullerton easily won reelection in 1970. In 1974 he became a sufficient embarrassment for Mayor Daley to force him to withdraw from the ticket. Cullerton himself escaped prosecution, but six subordinates faced grand jury indictments. In 1979 and 1980, under the regime of a new "reform" assessor, press investigations uncovered the same sort of political favoritism.

Beyond the activities of a Cullerton or a Russ Wolden is a more pervasive, systematic sort of discrimination in assessment.

For more than a century, assessment studies have documented that although housing as a class is often assessed at a lower fraction than commercial property, the poor man's house is typically assessed at a higher fraction of its actual worth than the rich man's. A paper presented at a 1919 tax conference revealed that real estate in Indiana valued at less than $2,500 was assessed at over 40 percent of actual value, while property worth $50,000 or more was assessed at only about 27 percent.

In Minnesota, during the same period, less-productive land fetching between $50 and $75 per acre was assessed at 124 percent of its actual sale price, while prime land selling at $200 an acre and up was assessed at only 67 percent of true value. This pattern has persisted in most states to this day.

In Boston, an extensive study by Professor Oliver Oldman in the mid-sixties revealed gross inequities in property assessments. In the white, middle-class neighborhoods of West Roxbury and Roslindale, where large concentrations of city employees lived, property was assessed at below 30 percent of value, while in the poor black wards of Roxbury, property was assessed at upward of 100 percent ot its market value.

A recent Chicago study found that small homes were assessed at a much higher fraction than larger ones, a striking exception being the politically potent 11th Ward on the South Side, which enjoyed a maximum assessment of 17 percent of market value. In general, according to the Chicago study, homes in the very lowest price range were assessed at the highest fraction of value.

A national survey by George Peterson of the Urban Institute confirmed that in most major American cities, poorer neighborhoods tend to be taxed at a far higher rate than more affluent ones. According to Peterson, housing in "blighted neighborhoods" in Baltimore were taxed at 14.9 percent of their actual value, while the rest of the city paid only 1.5 percent.

While political favoritism and racism explain some of the overassessment of poor neighborhoods, in part this is a natural result of the system. Prosperous communities typically enjoy stable or rising property values. Inner city and minority neighborhoods may have falling values. But the failure of many property tax systems to constantly adjust assessments to current market values typically leaves inner-city communities overassessed, even without influence-peddling or bigotry.

It is bad enough that citizens living in similar houses pay different taxes because of the vagaries of assessment. An even more fundamental inequity of the property tax is the direct relationship between the poverty of an entire taxing jurisdiction and the local tax burden. Poor people who live in poor cities pay a double penalty, which is compounded by the fact that the poor tend to spend a higher percentage of their income on housing to begin with and poor cities tend to require more services.

Residents of Baltimore had to pay a tax rate twice that of surrounding suburbs—not just because services were more costly in the center city, nor because the Baltimore government grew profligate. The disparity existed because the suburbs now enjoyed more than twice as much assessed valuation per capita.

Older cities generally, especially those with stagnant populations, are paying higher tax rates to raise fewer dollars. Boston, Chicago, Cincinnati, Cleveland, Detroit, Milwaukee, New Orleans, Philadelphia, and St. Louis—all these have substantially lower tax base per capita than their suburbs. Many older metropolitan areas as a whole have a relatively static tax base.

This translates into a higher effective tax burden, for reasons that have nothing to do with local government's profligacy. But the individual taxpayer, who sees higher taxes buying fewer services, might be forgiven for concluding (erroneously) that local government is at fault. In reality, the blame belongs to the larger system of taxation.

Thus between 1975 and 1977 the city of Detroit had to hike its property tax rate by 23 percent to produce only a 6 percent increase in revenues.

At the other extreme are manufacturing enclaves like Emeryville, California, and Green Island, New York which can coast along on their revenues from industrial property, while surrounding communities with little industry must tax themselves at substantially higher rates.

In theory, the entire process of assessment and equalization is independent of the process of setting the tax rate and collecting the tax. Taxing, as opposed to assessing, is the responsibility of local government—the town, the county, the school district, and any other districts with the power to tax. In some states, New York, for example, the same property will be assessed by different jurisdictions, and actually carry more than one assessment.

The property tax rate is set, usually annually, only after the local government has determined its budget needs, calculated its other resources such as fees, sales tax revenue, and state and federal aid. But since the amount of aid is governed in part by the relative impoverishment of the local tax base, the process feeds back upon itself.

During the seventies, as the property tax base eroded in many older cities, the cry often went up at city council and school board meetings that the "numbers don't work," meaning that the property tax simply could not produce enough revenue at politically tolerable or legally allowed rates.

In such circumstances, inflation was a godsend. It pushed up assessed values and permitted local governments to balance their budgets. It also pushed the assessor back into the position of fiscal watchdog, a role he falls into quite naturally. Though many assessors agreed with Phil Watson's contention that assessment should be an entirely separate function from budgeting and rate setting, Watson himself believed he had a duty to keep assessments down in order to keep tax bills within reason. And while some assessors like San Francisco's Russ Wolden or Parky Cullerton of Chicago, have used their great discretionary powers to feather their own nests, others have been content to translate it into fiscal (and hence political) influence.

In those states where counties equalize assessments, assessors who serve at the pleasure of local government often find themselves under pressure to bring in the assessed valuation so that the local town council can raise enough revenue to balance the budget without increasing tax rates. The equalization process compounds this pressure. If a town next door has a growth in assessed valuation which exceeds your town's, the county equalization authorities are likely to compensate by lowering your equalization factor. In some states, this reduces your town's share of state aid. In others, including New York, a low equalization ratio also causes an increase in the local tax rate. The town council, which will get the blame for the higher taxes, typically leans on the assessor to make sure that the local growth in assessed valuation does not lag behind neighboring communities. In many places, this translates into what assessors facetiously call a Welcome, Stranger policy, where newcomers to a community are socked especially hard.

As Edgar Swartz, assessor for the town of Schodack in upstate New York, describes the process, "The assessor will go out and grab all the assessed valuation he can, because that will keep the equalization rate down. That protects the rest of the town from a tax increase, but the poor slob who you hit really takes a beating."

Bill Schroeder, assessor of Ada County, Idaho, was elected to the job because his predecessor had the misfortune to preside over a reassessment. Schroeder has no intention of repeating that mistake. "A lot of people don't understand the process," he mused. "The assessor's only function is to appraise the property, put a market value on it. The ratio is set by state law. I certify the value to the county commissioners. Then all these little agencies—the schools, the county, the highway district, the sewer district, the drainage district, fire, and so on, they sit down in their own little meetings and decide how much money they need. They get a levy based on the assessed valuation to bring in the money.

"It puts the assessor in the position of having to be the budget officer for all these little agencies. Because they all have their needs, and if I go out and raise values, they're going to reap the windfall and I get the blame. So I'm going to keep those values down and come next election I'll still be a good guy."

Thus the property tax system has yet another defect, which persists to this day. It tends to jumble tax administration, supposedly a neutral, professional function, with political decisions about how much public money to spend. Obviously, the IRS does not trim its enforcement activities to monetary or fiscal policy; if it did, the income tax would be a joke. But property tax assessors do. Operating against the theoretical pressures to rationalize tax administration is the practical concern that assessing everything at full value will only ignite higher spending, scare away industry, or drive out the middle class; assessors, often elected from a wider district than a city council or a school board member, tend to sympathize with taxpayers.

As the discerning reader may have gathered by now, the steady deterioration of the fairness of the property tax, both real and perceived, provided a standing ingredient for a tax revolt. The actual revolt awaited the addition of a more combustible ingredient. Good candidates were unprecedented inflation in housing prices—or a new, activist generation of judges and legislatures willing to tamper with the tax system—or a fiscal erosion of urban demographic and tax bases, requiring higher property tax levels to produce the same level of services. During the past decade, all these events occurred. Another contributing cause might have been a sudden increase in local government's appetite to spend money. Though widely cited as an explanation for the tax revolt, that did not occur.

8

LIMITING TAXES

IN THE ARCANE REALM of the property tax, there is nothing new under the sun. Long before Jarvis, Gann, and Watson, earlier generations sought to compensate for defects in the property tax by adding constitutional limits on tax rates, tax levies, expenditures, and debts. Like Jarvis' Proposition 13, these arbitrary limits tended to compound the inequities.

Nobody branded these early measures a "tax revolt"; they were part of the continuing and largely futile effort to impose some fairness and coherence on the property tax. In fact, state and local legislatures continued quietly to adopt tax and spending limits, right through the 1970s, when the media pronounced Howard Jarvis a brand new phenomenon.

Actually, Proposition 13 was a surprisingly close replica of Ohio's Smith Law, a one percent ceiling on property tax rates, enacted in quite similar circumstances in the year 1910. Like the seventies, the first decade of the twentieth century was a period of inflation. After several decades of slowly declining prices, the gold discoveries and the quickened pace of commerce began to push prices upward. As property values rose, assessments grew wildly inaccurate, and reformers were pressing for mass reassessment. In Ohio, there was widespread concern that once assessments were increased, local governments could not be trusted to drop tax rates proportionally, which could drive up actual taxes. (This, of course, was what happened in California during the seventies as the tax burden shifted from businesses onto homeowners.)

To allay these fears, the Ohio legislature passed the Smith Law, prohibiting localities to tax at a rate greater than one percent without a direct vote of the local electorate. Now surely, the taxpayers would finally accept the full and equal assessment the reformers were clamoring for.

As it happened, the Smith Law eased the way for the reassessments of that era, but almost immediately there was wide outcry that it encouraged localities that were below one percent to *raise* their rate, while creating severe hardship in places with smaller tax bases. Three-quarters of a century later, Ohio assessments are still well below full value, and industry still sues to force local assessors to lower their ratios. Today, Ohio's limitation of property taxes to one percent, except where the voters override the limit, serves mainly to help defeat local school levies.

Limitations in state constitutions on the local power to tax and incur public debt date back to the 1830s. While the ideal of local self-government is a dearly cherished American totem, reformers of the nineteenth century increasingly looked to state government to rein in local fiscal excess. Appalling corruption and the reformist impulse surged in tandem during this era of municipal overconfidence, in which every local hamlet saw itself as a future metropolis. To finance the grand schemes of the mid-century, local governments often sold bonds. Sometimes the intent was honorable. Just as often, bribes found their way from the entrepreneur to the local officials. Railroads played off one township against another, promising a financial boom along the track right-of-way. Towns went deep into debt to finance concessions, to induce the railroads to favor their route. And when financial panic struck, when the railroad went elsewhere, when the canal never was completed or the market collapsed for the municipal grain elevator, the citizenry was left with a staggering debt and no new enterprise to help pay it off.

In time, every state amended its constitution to limit debts that could be incurred by cities, counties, and towns. Sometimes, their limits were expressed as a percentage of assessed valuation, typically 5 to 10 percent since the total value of a township's property was seen as a rough proxy for its fiscal capacity. As bust turned back into boom, however, some towns began to finance capital improvements out of current expenditures, driving up taxes. From debt limitation it was a short step to tax limitation. The first state limitation on local taxing powers was enacted in Rhode Island in 1870, a depression year that left individuals as well as municipalities hard pressed to pay their bills. Several other states shortly followed suit.

The debt and spending limitations turned out to be rather like locking the barn door after the horse got out: not only was the damage done;

worse, the horse was likely to tromp into the shed, or chew up the garden, and the locked barn quickly became its own major nuisance. As soon as prosperity returned and the need for revenues increased, towns and legislatures devised ways around the constitutional limits. Indeed, the main memorial to the tax and debt limitation schemes is a welter of subterfuges that made local government only more convoluted, such as those special taxing districts that so confused California voters.

Municipal fiscal necessity mothered countless inventions besides special districts: special assessments, which were pledged to pay off an extraordinary bond issue for some pressing need; "revenue bonds," in which the full faith and credit of the state were not invoked; tax-increment financing, where the increase in taxable value generated by a project was pledged to that project; free-standing port authorities, which had immense powers and few public obligations; "service contracts" to convert a long-term debt, which might violate the limit, into annual payments, which do not; long-term leases, eliminating the need to finance a capital expenditure (although the lease can be far more costly than direct purchase and just as conducive to corruption); and more recently, as New York residents will recognize, moral obligation bonds, revenue anticipation notes, tax anticipation notes—and near bankruptcy.

It is no accident that local public finance is littered with gimmicks and fully comprehensible only to bond counsel. As the most prominent legal textbook on public finance delicately depicts the opportunities for inventive evasion, "The challenge of coping with [increasing demands for public services] has called forth the specialized knowledge and experience of bond attorneys to develop new, or to adapt old, legal concepts and techniques of public financing." Yes, indeed.

John Petersen, the executive director of the municipal finance officers trade association, points to the amnesia of state legislatures in setting ground rules for local public finance. "There seems to be a thirty or forty year cycle in this country. First, overexuberance: you get overextended in railroads, canals, public works. Then there's a debacle, and the state legislature puts a stop to it. And then, times get better and the cycle starts all over again. A new generation of legislators comes in and, well, we really do need those sewers. So you go down to the state capital and dial yourself up a little special authority."

In prosperous times, tax and spending limits are widely regarded as silly barriers to progress. Though the courts occasionally intervene to throw out the worst of the subterfuges, judicial interference usually leads only to more inventive, more Byzantine sham.

In a turgid legacy of municipal finance case law, the courts, wherever possible, have helpfully tried to turn a blind eye to the subterfuge, over-ruling only the most transparent evasions.

After wrestling with a complex case where the Washington State housing finance agency essentially concocted an installment purchase of apartment buildings disguised as a lease, the state supreme court, virtually apologized for holding that this financing arrangement violated the state's debt limitation:

> We recognize the housing problem with which the state is confronted. Nevertheless, we cannot permit the exigency of the situation to override the constitutional safeguard against improvidence and the integrity of the state's economy. We cannot resort to dexterity of judicial thinking in order to assist the state in its problem. We cannot close our eyes to what is actually being attempted . . .

LIMITING THE LIMITS

In general, tax limitation hasn't been much more successful than debt limitation. As new fiscal needs arise, government finds ways around the old limitations, which survive mainly to make municipal life more complicated. For example, Arizona pioneered a strict tax limitation law in 1921, limiting the growth of the local property tax, prohibiting any county or city from increasing expenditures more than 10 percent above the previous year's level. But over the years, as demands for government services overtook the passion for fiscal control, the limit proved impossibly rigid. Population grew in some counties faster than others, requiring bigger budgets; the legislature gradually granted exemptions, to the point where more than half of the local budget outlays are no longer covered by the cap. Jurisdictions declaring fiscal emergencies can obtain waivers from the state tax commission. In small towns, the annual "cap" can prove especially ridiculous, since hiring a policeman can double the town budget. The limit has also led to creative accounting gimmickry, such as padding accounts not subject to the limit in order to save money in accounts that are covered. Many towns frankly keep two sets of books, one that nominally complies with the letter of the law, and another that reflects true budget allocations. The League of Arizona Towns and Cities even publishes a manual on how to evade the limit legally.

These gyrations, of course, do not result from municipal profligacy.

The problem is simply that the limit is too blunt an instrument to fit all cases. But once in place, the limit becomes a sacred cow, which politicians are reluctant to challenge. Like other limits, it also has the perverse effect of turning the ceiling into a floor: prudent local officials make sure they raise budgets the permitted 10 percent whether they need to or not, because next year they might really need 12 percent and not be able to get it.

But tax and spending limitation continues to appeal to the voters. In 1978, the year of the great tax revolt, the Arizona legislature passed yet another constitutional amendment limiting state expenditures to 7 percent of state personal income. The voters ratified the amendment by better than 2 to 1. Now, creative accounting will come to Arizona's state government as well as to its local governments.

In 1974 the state of Florida garnered widespread publicity and self-congratulation when officials devised a contemporary-sounding tax limitation law with the catchy Naderesque title "Truth in Taxation." Under this law, all local tax rates are automatically reduced by the amount of inflation in property values, to make this year's total tax levy identical to last year's. No California-style free ride on inflating property values. Any action by a municipal government to raise the rate must be deliberate, undertaken at an open meeting after due publicity. This is almost precisely what the Kansas legislature devised in 1908, after a general assessment quintupled the values shown on the assessor's rolls; in response, the legislature required rates to be reduced, so that total tax revenues in 1908 would exceed the 1907 levy by no more than 2 percent. Kansas reinvented a tax cap in 1970; Kentucky also devised something quite similar in the sixties, terming it a "Rollback Law."

Sometimes, these early laws had perverse consequences. An early Idaho provision, which required the rate to drop in proportion to the increase in assessed valuation, had the unintended effect of reducing revenues. As a result, the State Board of Equalization, supposedly in charge of pushing assessments up to accurate levels, worked hard to keep assessments unrealistically low, so that the rate could remain adequate.

With the Great Depression came another round of tax limitation laws, stimulated by a wave of foreclosures and the fear that high real estate taxes would only further collapse real estate markets. As during the late nineteenth century, assessments lagged behind market values; but now values were *falling*, leaving homeowners to pay an ever higher rate of tax on their property's actual worth. Local governments were themselves hard pressed, and reluctant to lower assessments or rates. In several states the legislatures imposed limits on property tax rates and moved to replace some of the lost revenues with new sales and income taxes.

These limitations on *rates* served their purpose until property values began inflating again, when rising assessments did the dirty work of raising additional taxes.

In recent years, the increasing financial aid by states to municipalities has created an additional rationale for property tax limitation. State aid was designed to relieve local fiscal hardship, or to equalize expenditures among rich and poor communities for basic necessities such as public education. Many towns, however, were tempted to view the new state aid as a windfall and to keep local taxes at whatever rate the traffic would bear. This, of course, frustrated not only the attempt by the state to relieve local property tax burdens, but also the effort to equalize spending for services. As a condition of the aid, therefore, legislatures often attached new limits on local property taxes.

Where states failed to do this, the new aid often failed to lessen local property tax burdens. In 1977, Massachusetts Governor Michael Dukakis leaned hard on the state legislature to sharply increase aid to the cities and towns, to answer voter demands for property tax relief. But the generous state aid package failed to require the cities and towns to use the new state aid for property tax relief. In 1978, an election year, Dukakis looked in vain for voter gratitude. The state aid program was pure carrot and no stick; in most places, taxpayers were still paying their old, high taxes, while the mayor suddenly had a lot of new money for pet projects and a mysterious grin on his face. Dukakis was not reelected; his opponent, arch-conservative Ed King, campaigned successfully almost as a Johnny One Note on the issue of—property tax relief. Dukakis thought this a quite unfair turn of events. Once in office, King moved almost immediately to propose a freeze on local outlays. This the legislature liberalized to a 4 percent annual growth limit, which would have seemed draconian had it been suggested by Dukakis. Now, however, even the liberals in the legislature have learned a lesson: the mayors would not get away with the same game twice of making off with the aid, leaving the state holding the bag for tax relief demands.

The inflationary seventies saw a whole new spate of tax limitation initiatives. Eighteen states, beginning with Kansas in 1970, imposed a wide variety of new controls on the local power to tax and spend. As George Peterson, the Urban Institute's prolific tax scholar, observed pointedly, Proposition 13 was not the beginning of a tax revolt, but the culmination of a decade's quiet efforts to limit tax burdens, and more broadly, to hold the total amount of government spending at roughly its present share of personal income. Unlike Proposition 13, most of the earlier tax limit laws were fairly moderate and fairly technical measures, aimed at rationalizing a hopelessly irrational system.

The federal government's interest in property tax reform also surged briefly in the early seventies. In the 1972 campaign, President Nixon took note of the issue, pledging federal aid for local property tax relief. This was introduced in 1973 but never enacted. "Tax Revolt" was already a popular phrase by the early seventies. The regional press wrote countless stories of property tax outrages, featuring low-income or retired families being "taxed out of their homes." The polls showed that 70 percent of Americans thought property taxes were too high. Public consciousness was growing about *Serrano*-type inequities in school finance.

The new program of federal revenue-sharing failed to reduce property tax burdens, much as state aid to local governments often failed. All of this stimulated Washington's interest in the issue. In early 1973, Senator Edmund Muskie, then chair of the Senate Subcommittee on Intergovernmental Relations, offered a bill giving states financial inducements to "modernize" property tax administration. This reflected the concerns of the federal Advisory Commission on Intergovernmental Relations (ACIR), a permanent agency set up in 1961 as a watchdog, research center, and lobby to strengthen state and local government within the federal system.

The ACIR is dominated by governors, mayors, and state legislators and can generally be counted on to argue for "fiscal balance" to bolster the states and locals against the behemoth in Washington, and the locals against the states. Its staff performs yeoman research labors, regularly issuing reports much in the spirit of the earlier property tax critics, documenting the sorry state of property tax administration.

The Muskie bill proposed new federally funded property tax relief, to be conditioned on reforms that would bring state property tax systems up to a minimal level of competence and equity. It set forth a long list of criteria, including exemptions and credits for the poor, and a variety of reforms. The bill also offered federal technical assistance grants to help states improve their property tax systems.

Muskie, in effect, was arguing for reform, rather than simply relief. This opportunity, however, was missed; the Muskie bill produced a voluminous and useful hearing record, documenting that taxpayer grievances were already perking along merrily in 1972 and 1973, but even the ACIR was hesitant about supporting federal ground rules for state and local property taxes. Muskie, the one prominent senator positioned to have great influence on local tax policy, lost interest (as well as the 1972 Democratic nomination), and after 1973, Muskie's fiscal attention turned from property tax reform to sunshine and sunset laws, and to the landmark Federal Budget Control Act, requiring Congress to agree on the size of the budgetary pie first, and the pieces afterward, which was also part of the quiet movement of the early seventies to rein in the growth of government spending. It undoubtedly tempered what might have been a more serious tax revolt at the federal level.

But in the growing clamor throughout the states to restrain the excesses of the property tax, the initiative shifted to those who were demanding relief pure and simple, not reform.

ACIR continued to issue its reports trying to differentiate the *inequities* in the property tax from the *size* of the property tax. ACIR viewed arbitrary tax and spending limits as a dangerous assault against local home rule.

As opposed to the conservative approach to property tax limitation— which limits permissible taxes in order to limit government spending, liberals have generally backed measures to limit the impact of property tax burdens on hard-pressed taxpayers, typically low-income homeowners, the elderly, or all homeowners as a class. These measures take a variety of forms. Under a so-called "circuit-breaker" approach, the local property tax is limited to a percentage of the homeowner's income, and the state makes up the difference. A second approach, the homestead exemption, exempts a portion of the value of a house from the property tax, which has the effect of taxing homes at a lower effective rate. And some states tax housing at preferential rates directly, by classifying property into different types, and setting separate rates. ACIR has advocated that states provide some form of tax relief for homeowners.

A 1962 ACIR report recommended the lifting of all constitutional and statutory limits on the local power to tax and spend. A follow-up report in 1977 viewed the growing trend toward tax limits with some alarm, but conceded that limits were defensible when they were intended to make sure that new state aid accomplished its objective of relieving the property tax.

Further, the commission advocated more professionalized tax administration, disclosure of tax increases on the Florida truth-in-taxation model, and "fiscal notes" attached to all new state programs, disclosing their effects on local budgets. "What is required," said the commission, "is Marquis of Queensbury type rules to govern state-local fiscal relations, thereby assuring that neither side hits the other below the fiscal belt."

The Marquis of Queensbury, of course, was not quite what Howard Jarvis had in mind. As the seventies wore on, few states reformed their property taxes along the lines advocated by the ACIR. In general, tax administration remained a mess, and tax incidence grossly unfair. By 1978, the year of Proposition 13, the campaign for tax and spending limitation had grown less technical and more plainly ideological.

The few states that had reformed their property tax earlier found themselves battened down quite effectively when the winds of tax revolt struck in the late seventies. Florida's truth-in-taxation law succeeded in holding down the growth of property taxes in that state to politically acceptable proportions. A Dade County (Miami) version of the Jarvis initiative fizzled badly in September 1979, partly because it was sloppily drafted, but mainly because the grievances just weren't there. (Proposition 13 was no master of draftsmanship either.)

Wisconsin, for instance, adopted a circuit-breaker approach in 1964, followed by a moderate levy limit in 1975. The latter was the response of a liberal Democratic governor, Pat Lucey, to local demands for property tax relief. Under Wisconsin law, the total property tax revenues levied by a locality may not exceed last year's levy by more than the statewide average increase in assessed valuation. This approach is not perfect; fast-growing areas are restrained from collecting revenues they need to spend on services, and stagnant areas are tempted to increase their levy by the maximum amount in case next year's limit drops. But on the whole, the Wisconsin law kept property tax increases in that state modest enough to take the wind out of extremist tax protest.

California, on the other hand, had tried something similar in 1972, only to realize too late that this was an inoculation against the wrong disease. California's 1972 law, which ironically was hailed by the ACIR as a model, strictly froze the tax *rate;* tax collections could increase only with growth in assessed valuation. This turned out to be useless when assessed valuations in the Golden State followed housing prices through the roof. Interestingly, the very first of the frankly ideological tax and spending-limit attempts was California Governor Reagan's proposal of 1973. It failed, but became the model for the tax limitation drives of the late seventies prompted by the National Tax Limitation Committee, the conservative group headed by Lewis Uhler, who designed the Reagan proposal.

NEW JERSEY

The most stringent of the pre-Jarvis tax limitation laws was fashioned in New Jersey. The genesis of New Jersey's tax cap, tightly limiting the growth of both state and local outlays, was entirely different from the circumstances in California.

As with California in the *Serrano* decision, and Texas with the *Rodriguez* case (later reversed by the U.S. Supreme Court), New Jersey in the mid-seventies was wrestling with court-ordered school finance reform. In the 1973 case *Robinson v. Cahill,* the state supreme court held that property-tax financing of New Jersey's public schools led to disparities that grossly violated the provisions of the New Jersey constitution guaranteeing a "thorough and efficient" system of free public education for school children throughout the state. The decision resulted from a 1970 suit by Kenneth Robinson and his parents contending that the distribution of the state's taxable wealth denied a thorough education to children who happened to live in poor school districts. For example, the town of Secaucus taxed itself at a rate of $1.10 per hundred dollars of valuation to produce $1,184 per pupil in school funds, while nearby Jersey City was paying the much higher rate of $2.82 per hundred to raise only $897.

The following year, 1975, the legislature and the new Democratic governor, Brendan Byrne, responded by increasing state aid to public schools by some $400 million, tied to a complex formula that "capped" public school budgets to assure that some of the new state aid would translate into property tax relief, while allowing for more-liberal growth of low-expenditure school districts to gradually bring their per-pupil outlays up to the level of more affluent districts. (Studies four years later showed that the school aid program had had only minimal success in equalizing public school expenditures in New Jersey.)

The immediate concern, however, was how to pay for the new state aid. The local fiscal crunch by 1976 was also growing severe because of the erosion of the tax base in the state's older cities. At the time, New Jersey was one of the few industrial states without an income tax, and an income tax was the obvious remedy. But to get an income tax through the conservative state legislature, Governor Byrne and his liberal allies from urban North Jersey had to include assurances that the new income tax would produce real property tax relief and not just higher spending.

As the legislature grappled with the proposed income tax in the summer of 1976, the new school district spending cap from the previous session was available as a rough model. Interestingly, the extension of the cap to local government as a trade-off for an income tax was sponsored by Assemblyman Willie Brown of Newark, the most overtaxed city in the state. Newark was desperate for the new state aid. More to the point, Newark was already at the extreme limits of what could be raised from the property tax. To Brown, offering to forgo future increases in property taxes was something like giving up spinach for Lent. The trade-off, therefore, was acceptable to many urban liberals.

But the downstate Republicans kept demanding more concessions, and the final bill, approved on the morning of July 7 after a hectic all-night session, turned out to be somewhat more stringent than intended. Local government budgets were strictly capped at 5 percent of the annual growth rate. The cap applied not just to the property tax, but to all local outlays except for federal aid, debt service, new fees, services newly mandated by state or federal government, and revenues produced by taxing new construction. To make state government appear to sacrifice along with the towns and counties, the legislature also imposed a cap on the state. But the state cap came out far more generous, giving increases in state budgets in proportion to the annual growth of New Jersey per capita income. Thus, in its 1978–79 budget, the state could spend 10.4 percent more money than in the previous year, while the locals were stuck with 5 percent. Unlike the earlier limits, which restricted property tax revenues, New Jersey's restricted all local spending. The cap came on top of New Jersey's stringent local budget law, which prohibited New York–style accounting gimmickry. By 1979, Newark, the most fiscally pressed city in the nation, was laying off teachers and police, despite a $20 million surplus which it wasn't permitted to spend.

During the first two years under the cap, Newark's budget kept up with inflation, thanks largely to new federal antirecession aid. But in 1978, when Congress refused to extend the aid, Newark's budget fell from $125 million to about $122 million; with inflation, this represented a loss of purchasing power of more than $12 million.

Mayor Kenneth Gibson cut the city's 4,800 employees by 600, laying off about 400, and paring the rest by attrition. Two hundred policemen lost their jobs; health and social services also lost heavily. In a badly dilapidated city, maintenance of streets, bridges, and physical plants was deferred.

Newark's budget chief, Tom Banker, finds the cap idea fine in theory. "Conceptually you can't argue with it, but the idea that there will always be fat to cut is wrong. Once you reach bone, the constraint is still there. You have to decide how severe you want to get."

Supposedly, the cap law was designed to place a 5 percent annual growth limit only on those items within a municipality's local discretion. But in practice, the cap also applies to outlays in several areas where increases in excess of 5 percent are beyond the city's powers to control. The city has to pay utility rate increases ordered by the state's public utility commission, but this portion of the city's budget is covered by the cap. Newark spends upward of $2 million a year just on street lights. If rates go up more than 5 percent a year (and they do, thanks to rising energy costs), Newark must adjust by making deeper cuts someplace else. Likewise, pension increases are calculated actuarially, but they are also "in the cap." And the city is stuck with health insurance premiums for its workers. Rate increases rise with soaring medical costs, but the premiums must come out of that portion of the local budget subject to the cap.

Shortly after the legislature approved the cap law, it passed a bill giving binding arbitration to local police and firemen. If the local patrolmen opt for an arbitrator in a wage dispute, Newark must pay whatever increase he orders. If this exceeds 5 percent something else has to suffer. That, of course, is not quite playing by the Marquis of Queensbury.

"If you want cost containment, you don't go with binding arbitration," Banker groans at the legislature. "If you want to give the police and firemen pro-labor legislation, that's nice, but then put it outside the cap. Hey, guys, choose your poison."

Unlike some of the other cap laws, New Jersey's had precious few loopholes. In its first year, 1977, county and property taxes rose only 5.7 percent, far less than inflation. By 1978 the increase had dropped to 4.6 percent, the lowest rise in twenty-three years. The shoe was pinching local government enough for a Governor's Blue Ribbon Commission on Government Costs and Tax Policy to recommend that the cap on local government be liberalized to put the locals on the same formula as the state. But in that year few New Jersey politicians wanted to stand accused of "messing with the cap."

(One of the urban liberals who voted for the 1976 tax package was a young state assemblyman named Peter Shapiro. Three years later, as a newly elected reform county executive of Essex County, Shapiro found that the perpetual budget crisis imposed by the cap offered him both frustration and opportunity. It meant that services had to be cut back in several areas, where increases were sorely needed; but, Shapiro discovered to his delight, it also meant he could fire people. "We could finally take on sacred cows, like the Sheriff's Office," Shapiro said later. "They never did very much, but the office was loaded with political appointees and nobody dared to go after it. Last year," Shapiro added with a touch of pride, "we came in a million dollars *under* the cap.")

But the New Jersey experience places Proposition 13 in a context largely ignored by the national commentary on the meaning of Jarvis. New Jersey's limits on state, local, and school-district spending grew out of efforts to make the state's system of public finance more equitable. It was certainly not the result of a tax revolt. The intent was to equalize school expenditures, relieve excess dependence on the property tax, and provide for a more balanced and progressive tax structure. The sharp controls on the growth of total spending emerged as a by-product.

Not surprisingly, New Jersey had no tax revolt in 1978.

TENNESSEE AND COLORADO

Interestingly, the first deliberately ideological state caps turned out to be far more moderate in its impact. The Tennessee tax limitation amendment tying the growth of state spending to the growth of personal income, was added to the state constitution by a constitutional convention ratified in March 1978. Its sponsor, State Senator Dave Copeland, has become a great hero to the tax-revolt groups; after his victory, Copeland joined the National Tax Limitation Committee as director of organization, and he finds himself on the lecture circuit several days a month promoting tax limitation in other states; in the conservative tax pantheon, he ranks second only to Jarvis. As Copeland tells the story, he essentially shanghaied the state constitutional convention, which had been called by the general assembly to deal with several other pressing issues. Probably the most pressing was Tennessee's outmoded 10 percent usury ceiling, which was causing bank capital to flow out of the state to higher-yield areas. As a condition of voting for the convention call, Senator Copeland insisted that tax and spending be added to the list of permissible subjects. He then set about quietly lining up delegates to support a tax limitation provision, while the state's media focused on more pressing controversies like the usury issue.

By the time the convention met, Copeland had commitments from more than half the delegates to support a spending limit. But unlike New Jersey, where the legislature wrote a draconian provision almost inadvertently, Tennessee's cap amendment—approved with great fanfare—is something of a mouse.

Under the Tennessee cap, which applies only to state spending, total state outlays financed by tax revenues are limited to the same percentage of state personal income as in the base year, 1977–78, unless the state legislature votes an override. Many legislators feel the override provision renders the Tennessee cap a meaningless piece of symbolism. But at the same time, there is substantial political pressure not to vote an override barring a real fiscal emergency. The cap is designed so that the legislature cannot evade the intent by voting an override for a single deserving purpose, say widows, orphans, or fire protection. The entire budget must be within the cap limits or be overridden as a whole. Thus far, it has stayed within the limit.

According to the director of the legislature's Fiscal Review Committee, state outlays in Tennessee are growing at about 2 percent less than they would have without the cap, something like 10 percent per year. This is enough to force a more careful consideration of budget priorities, but not to inflict real hardship.

The Colorado legislature enacted a similar measure in 1977, and for essentially similar reasons.

In Colorado, as in California, the quirks of the assessment machinery had riled up the voters. Typically, assessments were lagging far beyond actual value, especially in the booming suburban counties outside Denver. Colorado's relatively generous state school-aid formula is based on the relative poverty of a district's property tax base. The poorer you are, the more you get. In effect, the less-affluent citizens of Denver, whose assessments more accurately reflected their real tax base, were sending tax dollars to subsidize richer suburban districts, whose true tax base was understated.

Like countless equalization authorities before it, the State Board of Equalization ordered several counties to reassess, triggering widespread concern that the higher assessments would produce higher taxes.

In suburban Jefferson County, the assessor, Dave Braden, subscribed to the Welcome, Stranger approach. Braden was keeping his assessment ratios on homes at about 10 percent. At the time, the state average was close to 30 percent. Braden responded to pressure from the State Board of Equalization to raise his ratios by giving new homes higher values. When the Equalization Board, whose members included the governor, finally compelled Braden to reassess the whole county, homeowners found a note from Braden attached to their reassessment notice inviting them to direct any inquiries to Governor Dick Lamm.

The mini tax revolt that followed was one more casualty of the assessment maze; it had little to do with public sentiments about government spending.

Tax relief, however, soon became the main issue of the 1977 legislative session. The Republican majority proposed a package of tax bills freezing assessments at 1975 levels and providing a 10 percent tax rebate on local property taxes, to be paid by the state general fund.

One key Democratic member of the legislature's joint budget committee, Jim Kadlacek, urged the Republican members to include authorization for a classified property tax, lowering the rate on homes. When he failed to make headway, Kadlacek decided to go the Republicans one better. Very late in the session, at about 3 A.M., he proposed that state spending be limited to annual increases of 7 percent, plus 4 percent for a reserve, and all excess state revenue be put into a property tax relief fund.

Both the legislature's Republican leadership and the liberal Democratic governor, Richard Lamm, were caught totally off guard. But the cap idea soon became popular, and despite the absence of organized support, became an inviolable part of the bill.

As the inflation rate rose well beyond 7 percent there were calls to increase the limit, but serious hardship has not yet resulted. Kadlacek intended the cap law to produce more state funds to relieve local property taxes, but Colorado also has a new law indexing the income tax for inflation.

The indexing prevents state income tax receipts from growing faster than the rate of inflation. Colorado also recently repealed its sales tax on food, as part of a general tax reform bill. The result is that state revenues have not increased fast enough to significantly boost local fiscal aid for property tax relief. This is ironic, because it was the demand for property tax relief that generated Kadlacek's spending-limiting bill.

In this climate, the more ideological of the tax rebels saw Colorado as an ideal climate for a Jarvis-type referendum. To the right-wing tax limitation movement, there was only one flaw in the Colorado cap: it was statutory, not constitutional. The general view of Jarvis, Gann, the National Tax Limitation Committee, and other right-wing groups is that legislatures cannot be trusted to abide by statutory limits for very long.

In mid-1978 a constitutional cap initiative was circulated by Palmer Burch, a well-known Colorado conservative, who had served as state treasurer for several terms before being ousted by antiwar activist Sam Brown in the post Watergate 1974 election. Burch is a crusty, outspoken figure, of personal frugality, who refused to hire a secretary for the state treasurer's office because he insisted on typing his own letters.

In some respects, Burch's initiative was more moderate than the cap law, because it permitted state spending to rise with the cost of living. But it covered fees as well as tax revenues, and also extended the cap to local government, which aroused the ire of public school groups throughout the state. Though the Burch initiative qualified for the ballot, most of the state political establishment concluded that yet another limit was too much of a good thing. Kadlacek became chairman of the group opposing Burch. In November 1978 the constitutional limitation initiative went down to defeat. The inoculation had done its job.

9

SHIFTING TAXES

IN MANY RESPECTS, the homeowner tax revolt of the late seventies followed (and partly resulted from) a much quieter tax rebellion—by business taxpayers. The business tax revolt was fought out in state legislatures and state courts, and it made few headlines.

Steady business pressure for tax concessions has eroded the business share of property taxes, especially in older industrial states. Industry has become enormously skilled at playing off one state legislature against another in a tax-concession war. Very few states have been able to resist this pressure, lest they be accused of a "bad business climate." Ironically, before Proposition 13, one of the very few was California, with its tough tax-enforcement bureaucracy, no competing industrial state on its borders, and a huge natural market.

Less visibly still, the shift in property tax burdens was the result of inflation in housing prices nationwide, coupled with changes in assessment ground-rules dictated by legislatures and courts. At a time when the outcome happened to benefit business, lawmakers at last dusted off the reformer wish list and got serious about enforcing requirements for periodic reassessment under nominally uniform standards.

The growing business pressure for tax relief, and the intervention of the courts in the assessment machinery, steadily reduced the business share of the property tax load from 45.1 percent in 1957 to 39.5 percent in 1967 to 34.0 percent in 1977.

The taxes shed by industry, of course, were paid by homeowners. And the tax revolt was nothing if not a homeowners' revolt. The tax shift is a largely unrecognized factor in the tax protest, and not surprisingly, it was most pronounced in the states where the voters finally rebelled, even though they rebelled at the wrong target.

The sole state to ratify a virtual imitation of Proposition 13 in 1978 was the one state with an even sharper tax shift than California's, the state of Idaho.

IDAHO

Anybody who looks to gross increases in public expenditure to explain the tax revolt will be utterly baffled by Idaho. It is a sparsely populated and fiercely independent state, where the grizzlies probably outnumber the bureaucrats. (While I was visiting Boise, my taxi driver had to radio his dispatcher to find City Hall.) Idaho ranks fiftieth in per-pupil expenditures for public schools, according to the state education association. Total public outlays have grown less than the rate of inflation, and in 1977 the property tax took a far lower fraction of gross personal income than it did a decade earlier. Welfare spending per capita is about one-third the level of California's. But Idaho's tax revolt was a corker. Without any sizable state surplus to cushion the impact, Idaho voters ratified an amendment limiting property taxes to one percent of value, which reduced property taxes by 60 percent.

The simple explanation for the voter anger is that Idaho's tax load had massively shifted onto homeowners. In 1969, residential property in Idaho had contributed about 24 percent of the tax load. By 1978, the year of the great revolt, residences were paying 44 percent.

The story begins in 1965, when the Idaho legislature tried to legalize the informal system of classification then commonly used throughout the state. The Idaho constitution requires uniform assessment of property, but at that time, homes were typically *appraised* at a small fraction of their true value, and then *assessed* at about 10 percent of that. Some parcels of land had never been reassessed. The Idaho legislature wanted to reform this mess, but, like other legislatures before it, feared the consequences of a mass reappraisal. To prevent a tax shift, the legislators specified target assessment ratios for several classes of property. This infuriated the state's utilities, which were to be assessed at the highest rate. The Idaho Telephone Company immediately filed suit challenging the new assessment ratios under the state's uniformity clause, and in

1967, the state supreme court ruled that the utilities were indeed overassessed compared with everybody else and that the 1965 law was unconstitutional. In response, the legislature passed a bill putting local assessors on a schedule to equalize assessments gradually by 1982, at 20 percent of the market value, thus spreading out the impact of the inevitable shift. The big winners were the public utilities, whose share of the property tax declined from 28 percent to about 14 percent by 1979. The state's assessors did not like this at all. Rising assessments equal unhappy homeowners. In Ada County, the state's largest, the tax commission kept doing surveys and finding that the residential assessments were not even near the mandated schedule. Finally, the utilities sued again; the state tax commission lost patience and ordered a comprehensive reassessment; and rather than trust the offending assessor, the commission brought in out-of-state appraisal consultant, Max Arnold Associates of Denver. Arnold performed his task with the magnificent detachment of a good technician. All assessments were equalized in a single year.

This meant that homes, whose prices had accelerated sharply since the late sixties, were hit with steep increases. Predictably, there was hell to pay. Businesses, assessed according to an income-capitalization formula, stayed at about the same level.

"My taxes exactly doubled," complained a Boise homeowner named Dick Eardley. "We had been in the process of a gradual tax shift for years, but the reassessment compounded it. Commercial and industrial didn't go up, but residential went sky-high."

Eardley should know. He is the mayor of Boise. Boise is reeling from the consequences of voter indignation.

Besides this shift from commercial and industrial property onto residential housing, farmers had been getting a break not available to homeowners. Like other businesses, farm properties are assessed according to the income they generate. The assessor begins with his idea of a reasonable rate of return, say 5 percent. The supposed value of the property tax is then calculated by simple arithmetic: with a "capitalization rate" of 5 percent, a farm that posts a net earning of $5,000 is presumed to be worth $100,000. But in inflationary times, the assessor adjusts his rate upward, say to 10 percent. Now a farm with a net income of $5,000 is "worth" only $50,000.

There are innumerable variations to the income capitalization method of assessment, but they all tend to shelter business property from the impact of inflation. According to the assessor of Ada County (Boise), farmland that would cost between $2,000 and $3,000 to purchase, is typically appraised at only $500 or $600. Thus, Idaho farmers enjoyed spectacular protection against inflating property values.

The Arnold firm, however, began tinkering with the farm assessments too. Small parcels of farmland deemed suitable for development were reclassified residential and suddenly assessed at their full market value. Some small farmers enjoying assessments in the hundreds of dollars, now found their land assessed in the thousands.

Enter a retired insurance salesman named Don Chance. When the reassessment struck, Chance was living with his wife on a small farmstead four miles outside Boise, dreaming of planting his four acres in raspberries and enjoying a quiet retirement. Instead, Chance organized his neighbors and revolutionized public finance in Idaho.

Chance's favorite example of how the reassessment misfired is the Boise Front, a range of scrubby ridges just to the city's west. "The land is covered with sagebrush and junipers," Chance says. "It's steeper than a cow's face, good mainly for grazing jackrabbits and field mice. They assessed that at $10,000 an acre."

At fifty-nine, Chance is an image out of the Old West. He displays the sort of weathered, mournful countenance that suggests harmonicas wailing quietly, off mike. He could be the Marlboro Man's uncle. Chance was the perfect Idaho counterpart of Howard Jarvis.

The present Ada County assessor, Bill Schroeder, whose luckless predecessor suffered the wrath of Boise's voters, recalls the pandemonium when the 1976 assessment notices went out. "Usually, we get a dozen or so appeals," says Schroeder. "That year, we got seven thousand."

The Arnold firm had less than one year to revalue every parcel of property in Ada County. "Oh, there were problems," says Schroeder, "but given the time limit, he did a pretty good job."

"They hired the track team," scoffs Don Chance. "Their only qualification was that they could run the hundred in ten seconds. Can you imagine doing 66,000 parcels in one year? It was all done on the run: windshield appraisals."

By late 1976, Chance was spending much of his time helping Boiseans appeal their assessments. The appeals process, such as it was, only fueled taxpayer anger. "We had to run them through one every five minutes," Schroeder admits.

"A young farmer comes before the Board of Appeals," Chance says, pulling on his cigarette. "He raises hay to feed his cattle, but they've assessed him residential because the land can be subdivided. The assessor says, 'Look, you can subdivide this, make a bunch of money off it.' The man says, 'But I just want to farm it.' ''

As farmland, the land is assessed according to the income it produces, at perhaps $500 an acre. But as a potential subdivision, it can be assessed at $10,000 an acre.

Chance's indignation rises as he recalls the scene. ''Finally, one of the commissioners says, 'Well, would you take five thousand for it?' The farmer figures he's got his assessment cut in half and he says, 'Yes, I suppose I would.' 'Fine,' says the commissioner, 'I move we assess this man's land at $5,000 an acre. Next case.' ''

It was not a bad climate for a tax revolt. To compound the damage, a few jurisdictions took advantage of the skyrocketing assessments and failed to lower rates proportionally. The county highway district, for example, doubled its revenue.

Nineteen seventy-seven produced another 4,000 appeals in Ada County. In the meantime, Chance discovered that other counties were going through the same ordeal, and he went statewide just about the time Proposition 13 qualified for the California ballot. Interestingly, he had never heard of Howard Jarvis.

Nor was it necessary that he should have. The Idaho statistics tell their own story. Thanks to the 1976 reassessment, Ada County homeowners as a group were hit with a 50 percent tax increase in one year, on top of a long-term tax shift.

Even as Howard Jarvis was gearing up for Proposition 13, Don Chance was still casting about for a remedy. As in California, the Idaho governor and the legislature failed to agree on a tax relief package, and voter anger was rising. At first, Chance and his Idaho Property Owners' Association proposed the simplest of solutions: abolish the property tax.

''They didn't take me seriously, of course,'' says Chance. ''After some discussion, I felt we should propose something less drastic.''

Finally, in early 1978, ''a real estate lady told me about Proposition 13.'' Chance got his lawyer to draft a nearly exact copy, complete with the misspellings and references to provisions that didn't exist in the Idaho constitution. The Idaho one percent initiative, ''Proposition 1,'' qualified for the November ballot with the signatures of one Idaho voter in three. At one point, Chance invited Jarvis into the state to campaign, then changed his mind.

''I decided we didn't really need either of them,'' says Chance.

Obviously, Chance didn't. With a thoroughly home-grown grievance, the initiative coasted to victory in November by a 60 to 40 margin.

Few states experienced a tax shift quite as extreme as Idaho's. But in most other states, a similar shift took place, and with essentially the same ingredients: legislative and judicial reform of tax assessment, sharp inflation of housing prices, and effective business pressure for tax relief.

Moreover, as the Idaho episode illustrates, the new, supposedly uniform system of assessment has actually traded an older double standard that favored homeowners for a new one that favors business. In their uniformity rulings, the courts required uniform assessment *ratios*, not uniform *methods*. Consequently, only homes are truly assessed according to their current market worth. Like Idaho, most states and localities continue to value business property indirectly—by capitalizing its current income stream, or by estimating its depreciated construction cost or its replacement cost.

For prime commercial property whose value is steadily appreciating, the income-capitalization method rarely states the true price the property could fetch at a sale. And this disparity does not show up in the surveys of state equalization authorities, because the local assessor can claim he is assessing commercial property at "full value"—according to his capitalization formula. Thus, a building that sells for $5 million may have a "full value" for tax purposes of only a million or two.

According to Professor Oliver Oldman of the Harvard Law School, who conducted the landmark surveys of assessment inequities in Boston in the mid-sixties, "By using a low capitalization rate to set a supposed value for commercial property, assessors make it look like they are really socking commercial property, but really office and apartment buildings are getting off very easy. Assessors capitalize the rental income using the *current* rents, but anybody who invests in rental property is counting on future rent increases, and the assessors don't consider that. So they seriously understate the value of the property."

The *Idaho Telephone Company* case was one of the first in an obscure series of successful lawsuits during the sixties and seventies, in which state supreme courts gradually insisted that nineteenth-century uniformity clauses must be enforced. With the exception of New York's landmark *Hellerstein* decision, which resulted from a suit by a tax scholar and his wife to challenge the assessment on their summer cottage on Fire Island, most of these lawsuits were brought by business taxpayers.

Until this recent series of rulings, courts were willing to grant some assessment reductions on a case-by-case basis, but refrained from pronouncing on the fairness or the constitutionality of the system itself. As early as 1923, the U.S. Supreme Court was willing to overturn a state court ruling, in order to grant relief to a bridge-building company that had been assessed at full value while neighboring businesses were assessed fractionally.

But for nearly forty years the *Sioux City Bridge* case marked the limit of judicial intervention. Plaintiffs who could afford to conduct assessment surveys could and did win reductions. But the courts, like the Oregon court of several decades earlier, remained reluctant to pull too hard on the string that might unravel the entire fabric.

In the late fifties, however, the New Jersey Supreme Court took a close look at the sorry condition of property assessment in that state and ordered some comprehensive reassessments. Similar rulings in Connecticut, Idaho, and Kentucky followed.

The courts moved slowly at first in deference to the fact that this is an obvious political minefield, but step by step they have grown more assertive. In Ohio, where the state supreme court first struck down preferential homeowner assessment in the 1964 *Park Investment* case, the plaintiff has gone back to court on three subsequent occasions, because local assessors balked.

The Massachusetts Supreme Judicial Court first struck down extralegal fractional assessment in a 1961 case, in which the court ordered the city of Springfield to assess all property at full market value. But not until 1974, in response to a suit brought by the town of Sudbury, did the court take the next logical step and direct the state revenue department to require all assessments throughout the state to be brought up to full market value. Sudbury had sued because its practice of assessing at full value made the town seem more prosperous than it was, which had cost it state aid.

New York got a similar ruling in 1975. Like the courts in Massachusetts, the New York courts previously had been content merely to provide relief to individual plaintiffs. The 1975 case was unusual. The plaintiff was not a business taxpayer, but the owner of a summer cottage on Fire Island, Long Island, who happened to be a prominent tax scholar. The Hellersteins carefully drafted the complaint in the frank hope of having the entire ramshackle assessment structure torn down. And they succeeded. The *Hellerstein* suit asked the court to invalidate the entire assessment roll of the town of Islip, not because their summer cottage was overassessed in comparison with others, but because the entire system patently violated the uniformity requirement of New York state law.

Finally girding itself to face the issue squarely, the New York Court wrote:

> . . . for nearly 200 years our statutes have required assessments to be made at full value, and for nearly 200 years assessments have been made on a percentage basis throughout the state. The practice has time on its side and nothing else. It has been tolerated by the Legislature, criticized by the commentators and found by our own court to involve a flagrant violation of the statute. Nevertheless the practice has become so widespread and been so consistently followed that it has acquired an aura of assumed legality.

The court gave Islip, and by inference every other jurisdiction in the state, until December 31, 1976, to assess all properties at full value. Almost immediately the New York State Legislature, fearing a massive tax shift and political uproar, acted to postpone the deadline five years. New York, like Massachusetts, is only now gearing up for full-value assessment.

While some states have postponed the day of reckoning, the era of the friendly, and sometimes corrupt, local assessor is clearly ending. In the long run (when we are all dead) this will improve tax administration. But the immediate result in several states was to strip assessors of their admittedly extralegal but politically crucial function of keeping homeowner taxes within politically tolerable limits, precisely when housing prices were inflating astronomically.

The shift in the tax burden might have escaped the attention of the national commentators trying to divine meaning from the Jarvis revolt, but in the tax politics of several states it has not gone unnoticed.

PROTECTING HOMEOWNERS

Alongside Jarvis-style generalized rage, homeowner protest in several states has taken the form of demands for homeowner tax relief, rather than wholesale cuts in government outlays. For example, property can be taxed at varied rates. Thirteen states and the District of Columbia now have classified property tax systems; the oldest and most complex is Minnesota's, which sets up thirty-one different classes and tries to fine-tune the rate structure to keep the distribution equitable. Business critics contend that this opens the property tax to political interference—as if abatements for industry were something different.

Minnesota has been fairly successful in stabilizing its tax load, although the residential share crept up by about 10 percent between 1974 and 1977. Nonetheless, Minnesota has avoided an extremist tax revolt even though it has one of the most highly graduated tax structures and taxes business at a relatively high rate.

Even a classified property tax, however, is no guarantee against a tax shift.

South Carolina, in 1976, adopted a classification amendment to quell political protests by homeowners. South Carolina now mandates industrial property to be assessed at 10 percent of value, and homes at 4 percent. But state tax officials believe that the historic extralegal gap between assessments on homes and businesses might have been a lot wider, and the cure may turn out to be worse than the disease.

The most popular form of tax relief, the homeowner exemption, dates to the Great Depression, when states were compelled to legislate reductions in local property tax burdens. Today, most states exempt some portion of the value of owner-occupied property from taxation, the most generous being Louisiana, which exempts $50,000. Louisiana, with its huge revenues from severance taxes on gas and oil, can afford to be generous with the property tax. In most states, however, the relief provided by homeowner exemptions is only token relief.

Homeowner exemptions are also tricky because they must be constantly adjusted upward to maintain their value in the face of inflation. California's exemption remained fixed at $1,750 through the middle and late seventies, while the legislature failed to agree on a remedy for soaring property taxes. As assessments rose higher and higher, and rates dropped, the exemption became worth less and less. The other problem with homestead exemptions is that they provide the same dollar amount of tax relief to all taxpayers. In order to target increased relief to those who need it most, it is necessary to spend huge sums on everybody else.

The third form of homeowner aid gets around this problem. The so-called "circuit breaker," pioneered by Wisconsin in 1964, refunds a portion of the property tax when the tax becomes excessive in relation to income. This approach is more economical than a homeowner exemption, because it targets the relief to the most overtaxed homeowners. It also introduces an income criterion, which makes the property tax more progressive. And, since the state usually provides the refunds to relieve local tax overloads, it also helps balance the fiscal inequities among local taxing jurisdictions. While some states provide circuit breakers only for the elderly, or for veterans, only four—Michigan, Oregon, Minnesota, and Wisconsin—use this approach for general tax relief.

Michigan, which has the most generous circuit-breaker program in the country, has used it to keep tax shares relatively stable over the last decade. Michigan was one of two states to reject imitation Jarvis amendments, in favor of a more moderate form of spending cap tied to the growth of personal income.

But even circuit breakers fail to compensate for the psychological sense of property tax overlaod, because in most states, the refund comes as a credit against the state income tax. The taxpayer, therefore, suffers the pain of paying the full amount of the property tax and gets a credit only later. Other states require the taxpayer to file a form to get a cash rebate, and many elderly and low-income property owners forget to file. And with the fiscal crunch growing, few states can finance circuit breakers.

Even in fairly progressive states willing to risk business ire by shielding residential property from a shift, the erosion of business property taxation has continued, and in several ways. In Wisconsin, which pioneered the modern circuit-breaker idea in 1964, the decline in industrial property tax revenues has far outstripped the residential relief provided by the circuit breaker. According to the state Department of Revenue, residential property taxes increased 126 percent between 1968 and 1978, while industrial taxes dropped 2 percent (during a period when consumer prices about doubled). During the same period, the share contributed by industrial property declined from 18 percent of total property taxes to less than 9 percent while the residential share rose from 50.6 percent to 57.3 percent.

Part of this decrease was deliberate; in 1974 the legislature voted to exempt part of manufacturers' machinery and equipment from property taxes, which reduced taxes from this source by some $16 million.

In the same year, the state took over from the local assessors the function of assessing industrial property. Although this was not expected to significantly reduce taxes on industrial property, it turned out that local assessors had been valuing businesses at a higher fraction of their actual worth than homes. When the state took over, it applied equalization formulas to the industrial property, and the result was a reduction of industrial assessments. In several parts of the state, this caused substantial consternation, because the decreasing industrial tax base led to pressures for increased taxes. In an ironic turn, local assessors were admitted as parties with standing to appeal industrial assessments in their locality when they felt the state's figure was too low.

Thus, despite the popularity of tax classification, homeowner exemptions, and circuit breakers, the tax shift has continued. For example, Oregon, with a $50 million circuit-breaker program, nonetheless experienced a tax shift; in 1978, homeowners paid an estimated 53 percent of the tax load, up from 45 percent in 1974. During those four years, the industrial and commercial share dropped sharply, thanks to a phase-out of the personal property tax and the relatively greater inflation in housing prices relative to commercial property. Oregon narrowly rejected a version of Proposition 13 in November 1978.

Because of continuing corporate pressure to "improve the business climate," only a small number of states have moved decisively to offset a tax shift. Even where there is general agreement on the need for homeowner relief, there is often dissension over what form the relief should take (witness California).

States can be divided roughly into four groups, according to how they have tried to meet voter demands for relief in the face of shifting tax burdens. Some, like California and Idaho, did nothing about the shifting tax load, and suffered the consequences. A second group, including Colorado, Tennessee, and New Jersey, voted across-the-board limits on taxes or spending generally. A third group, made up of mainly midwestern and western states, adopted a mix of circuit breakers, homestead exemptions, and classification schemes, to focus tax relief on homeowners. But the states that will undoubtedly have the stormiest tax politics in the coming years are those where politicians have tried to preserve the status quo by keeping antiquated assessment systems in bare working order.

NEW YORK

New York, as always, is a special case. Especially in New York City, where 120 field assessors are responsible for valuing some 840,000 properties, the system is a museum piece, much the way it was in the days when Professor Seligman and his colleagues excoriated the general property tax. New York City has *never* done a mass reassessment. The city's assessors work with ledgers rather than computers, and they simply can't keep up. The system invites all kinds of favoritism, but it has one plain virtue. It fails to reassess small homeowners. Throughout the seventies, when California taxpayers were rampaging, the real tax rate on New York homeowners lagged nicely behind inflation.

Depending on your perspective, this is either a blessing for Bensonhurst or a fleecing of midtown Manhattan. Nominally, New York levies a stiff $8.75 for every hundred dollars of property value, but in the Archie Bunker neighborhoods of modest single-family houses throughout Brooklyn and Queens, the homes are so underassessed that the effective rate is about 2 percent.

New York's last bargain, however, will shortly go the way of the nickel ride on the Staten Island ferry, thanks to an odd coalition of landlords, judges, and tax professionals. Two landmark court rulings of the mid-seventies signaled an end to this archaic system, though the blow has been stayed temporarily. In the *Guth* case (1974), the state appeals court ruled that a business taxpayer could use the state equalization surveys to calculate how much his assessment ratio exceeded the average ratio in his community, and have his assessment reduced accordingly.

A year later, in *Hellerstein*, the court declared illegal the entire system of fractional assessment.

Politicians in the Empire State, however, were either more prescient or more primitive than their cousins in California. The reaction of most New York lawmakers to the prospect of a modernized assessment system was neither quite liberal nor exactly conservative, but Luddite. Computerized reassessment might make for a more just system in the long run, but in the meantime it would rejigger everybody's taxes. When the dust settled, the big property owners would get tax relief, and the voters would get mad. No thank you.

The New York legislature postponed the effect of the *Hellerstein* ruling five years, created a commission, and went home.

In the early eighties, however, the clock, will run out. New York's liability for tax refunds to overassessed commercial property under the *Guth* doctrine is approaching $2 billion. No fewer than five task forces and committees at various levels of government are now wrestling with the question of how New York can somehow modernize its relic of a property tax without setting off an insurrection in the process.

The status quo favors two kinds of property owners—small homeowners who are never reassessed, and big downtown commercial landlords with the sophistication and the connections to appeal their assessments. The New York City Tax Commission considers about 40,000 appeals yearly and reduces assessments by a total of $300 million, most of which goes to downtown landlords. Because assessment is so primitive, the assessors have difficulty defending their figures, and fear being reversed in court. As a consequence, most big landlords appeal their assessments routinely, and often win reductions.

As in Idaho, the income capitalization method of valuation tends to understate the real value of prime rental property. A landlord can show a very low rate of return on his building, but make a fortune on the leveraged capital gains, while he enjoys the generous depreciation allowances against his federal income tax liability.

In places like midtown Manhattan, where property values soared far faster than rents during the late seventies, the capitalization method produced low property taxes in relation to actual values. According to the former president of the New York City Tax Commission, Marshall Kaplan, "The property tax is supposed to be an *ad valorem* tax—a tax on value. For the small homeowner, it doesn't matter whether he has three kids in college and he just lost his job and his wife had a stroke; he pays the tax or else. But if the same guy owns a rental property, and the vacancy rate is high or his oil bill goes up, he can get a reduction from the tax commission."

Through the capitalization method, the tax base, in effect, is used as a reservoir to guarantee the landlord's rate of return. If it drops, for whatever reason, his tax can be adjusted downward. There is a term for this sort of tax, of course; it is called an income tax. But this isn't how the *property* tax is supposed to operate.

"Assessing commercial property according to its income rewards bad management," says Mary Mann, who succeeded Kaplan at the New York City Tax Commission. "Why should a bad manager pay a lower tax?"

New York's large property owners, of course, disagree. From their perspective, it's the small homeowner who has gotten the tax breaks, because the failure to reassess has kept his tax burden low in relation to real value, too. Says Louis Fischoff, president of the bar association of real estate tax lawyers, "Why should my client bust his pants for a 6 percent return when he can get 12 percent from the bank?"

But in the real estate business, a net return of 6 percent can be feast or famine depending on where the building is. In hot midtown Manhattan, where values are soaring far faster than rent rolls, an investor can show a nominal 6 percent return and make a fortune on highly leveraged appreciation. Uptown, where values are stagnant, it is easy to go bankrupt on a 10 percent return. That's why a property assessment calculated according to income is so arbitrary.

As New York shifts to "full value assessment"—whatever that turns out to mean—it is hard to imagine a system that will treat homeowners, small landlords, and big-time property owners equitably.

A circuit breaker is not a likely remedy, because using a circuit breaker to limit local tax burdens on New York homeowners after a revaluation would cost the state treasury billions of dollars, which New York State doesn't have.

And a classified tax system flies in the face of efforts by both city Mayor Ed Koch and Governor Hugh Carey to improve the state's business climate—or at least its image.

Most professional tax administrators today have an almost theological reverence for the idea that all property should be assessed and taxed at uniform rates. The officials of the New York State Division of Equalization and Assessment repeatedly point to the 31 small, upstate communities that went to full value assessment in the late seventies without experiencing major tax shifts or tax revolts. But these were largely small towns with little industry, or communities that had kept their assessments much more up to date than had New York City.

According to calculations by a task force on real estate taxations created by the state assembly, a move to full-value assessment in New York City would increase homeowner taxes by 113 percent, while reducing commercial and industrial taxes an average of 28 percent. This, of course, is just what the big real estate owners want; they argue that for years the big downtown properties have been paying taxes properly owed by the small homeowner.

The temporary commission on real estate taxation created by the New York state legislature after the *Hellerstein* decision was dominated by spokesmen for the large property owners, and essentially subscribes to this view. All four of the New York City members of the original temporary commission represented landlords—three tax appeal lawyers, plus the Albany lobbyist for Harry Helmsley, one of the city's biggest landlords. In its first report, the commission expressed sympathy for homeowners, but warned that a classified property tax couldn't work.

New York City Mayor Koch responded by appointing his own team of assessment experts to recommend how the City could modernize its property tax, without shifting the burden onto homeowners. In the meantime, City officials have implored the legislature to delay the deadline. Koch wants to preserve the status-quo distribution of the tax load between commercial and residential property, while eliminating the inequities within classes.

Like California's tax experts of a decade ago, the professionals working on New York's system are placing great faith in the new computerized assessment techniques that can factor in sales of comparable properties, net income, replacement costs, and whatever other variables seem to determine a property's actual value. And undeniably, there is no way 120 assessors working by hand can calculate the changing values on New York's 840,000 properties. Technological modernization is the obvious precondition to any rational property tax in New York.

But the ultimate questions are political. Shall the historic allocation of New York's tax burden be redistributed? To whom? On what basis? Even if the authorities figure out a way to retain the historic distribution among residential, commercial, and industrial classes of homeowners, the disparities within these groups are even worse than the disparities between groups. Regardless of the "fair" distribution between classes, some landlords are clearly overassessed compared with others; the same is true of homeowners. Any conceivable revaluation must increase taxes on some and lower taxes on others. Worse still, New York's property tax is being jerked directly from the nineteenth century into the twenty-first, during a very austere fiscal period with little slack in the system. In retrospect, California's failure to adjust its system while the state funds were overflowing looks all the more egregious next to New York's present situation.

Ultimately, New York will get a much fairer property tax, but in the meantime the Empire State is a very likely candidate for the next outburst of tax revolt.

A hearing in late 1979 provided the opening skirmish. Faced with pressure from the courts, New York State Assembly Speaker Stanley Fink and New York City Mayor Koch reluctantly proposed a quite admirable plan to gradually reassess all of New York's properties at full value, and then shield homeowners from excessive increases by taxing them at preferential rates.

But *any* reassessment is poison to the millions of small homeowners now protected by the antiquated system. The small homeowners came out in force to lambaste the tax technicians. The initial hearing was held in the ornate Wall Street hall of the New York Chamber of Commerce, an unfortunate bit of symbolism not lost on the tax protestors.

Former State Assemblyman Vito Battista, who would like to be New York's Howard Jarvis, rose to the occasion. "Outrageous," he rasped into a portable bullhorn. "A hearing for small homeowners. During working hours. On Wall Street!" About forty Battista supporters from such organizations as the Bay Ridge Pothole Committee carried signs reading: TAXES ARE REVOLTING, WHY AREN'T YOU? and chanted, "Support the Esposito Bill."

The Esposito bill is the quick fix, sponsored by Republican Assemblyman John Esposito of Queens. It would simply freeze the status quo by repealing the state law requiring uniform assessments. Homeowners would continue to be underassessed, some far more than others. By throwing out state standards and legalizing inequities, Esposito's bill would almost surely be thrown out by the courts. It was also widely considered a Republican ploy to take votes away from marginal Democratic legislators up for reelection in 1980, who were loyally supporting Speaker Fink.

But after the hearing, the pressure from homeowners mounted, to the point where Fink and Koch soon abandoned their more legalistic approach for a Democratic version of the Esposito bill. New York's politicians may not be as up-to-date as California's technicians, but they know when to duck.

 ## MASSACHUSETTS

New York seems to be closely following a script written in Massachusetts, with a lag of about two years. The prospect of a massive tax shift surfaced as a hot political issue in Massachusetts almost immediately after the *Sudbury* decision requiring all jurisdictions to assess every property at its full value. Studies calculated that compliance with this standard would shift about $265 million in annual business property taxes onto homeowners.

Massachusetts property taxes were already the nation's highest. Nominally, Boston residents paid an astronomical tax rate of $252.90 per thousand dollars of assessed valuation, but homes in Boston were usually assessed at a fraction of their actual value. Since assessment ratios varied widely, a new, uniform assessment would be a roll of the dice certain to hurt homeowners as a group and some homeowners more than others. The city's mayor, Kevin White, used every trick at his disposal to avoid moving toward 100 percent valuation. Mainly, the city refused to hire enough assessors to conduct a full-scale reassessment. Applications by business taxpayers protesting high assessment were simply settled out of court.

By 1977, however, the courts were putting increasing pressure on Boston. At one point, a local judge enjoined the city from collecting its property taxes unless it provided evidence of a good-faith effort to move toward a comprehensive reassessment. Mayor White responded to this potential disaster by supporting a constitutional amendment authorizing a classified property tax, with homes assessed at 40 percent of value, commercial property at 50 percent, and industrial at 55 percent. In addition, the amendment provided a $5,000 exemption for residences. The intent of the amendment was to roughly maintain the extralegal status quo. Despite a campaign by business groups to defeat classification, Massachusetts mayors joined with consumer and labor groups, in one of the few instances in which a progressive coalition was able to seize the initiative and articulate voter frustration about taxes. In November 1978 the classification initiative was ratified by a margin of almost 2 to 1.

There is a footnote to this story, however. As of this writing, most Massachusetts cities still have not reassessed. As always, a mass reassessment is a severe political risk to incumbent officials. Boston Mayor White has hinted that he will not be a candidate for reelection after his present term expires, and most political observers expect that now he will finally bite the bullet and order the reassessment. Although the classification amendment ensures that the share of property taxes paid by homeowners as a group will not increase very much, there are still bound to be a lot of angry taxpayers, because the disparities within the homeowner class are so great. Privately, city officials concede that neighborhoods favored by assessors in years gone by will face what seem to be staggering tax hikes once they are reassessed.

Interestingly, it was not the *Sudbury* decision that finally pushed the city of Boston into gearing up for a reassessment, but rather the slow fiscal drain caused by business applications for reduced assessments. For decades, commercial and industrial property owners applied, one at a time, for reductions in their assessments, on the ground that they were improperly assessed compared with homeowners. And for decades, the assessor conceded the point and reduced the assessments for whoever bothered to apply.

In 1979 the drain suddenly turned into a hemorrhage. The owner of a downtown office building requested that his assessment be reduced—not merely to 50 percent of its actual value, the average for all Boston property but to 25 percent, the average for *residential* property. In March 1979 the State Supreme Judicial Court ruled for the property owner, Norman Tregor, and ordered his tax bill abated by 75 percent. This new standard, which took city officials by surprise, will cost the city treasury something like $50 million a year. Unlike the *Sudbury* case, the *Tregor* hits Boston directly in the pocketbook. And if every business taxpayer applies for the abatement permitted by the court, Boston residential taxes will have to increase by 55 percent just to maintain the same level of revenue.

Until the *Tregor* case, Boston had been able to maintain the status-quo distribution of the property tax by settling abatement applications here and there, while keeping homeowner assessments far below the average for all types of property. Now, suddenly, a *reassessment,* coupled with the classified ratios authorized by the 1978 initiative, became the lesser evil.

At least, that's what the always-canny Mayor White says. The actual reassessment is still to come.

THE MYTH OF BIG GOVERNMENT

The shift in the tax load contributes to the illusion that taxpayers are squeezed because government is growing fat. At best, this is a half truth. Certainly, some government agencies are overdue for a trimming, but the statistics of government outlays in recent years simply do not bear out the charge of accelerating growth.

Indeed, the tax revolt of the late seventies was oddly out of phase with the real growth of public expenditures in the United States. The relative size of the public sector at all levels of government was essentially stable during the seventies. Government spending, of course, exploded during the New Deal and the World War II years, but federal expenditures dropped back to about 17 percent of gross national product in 1956 in the middle of the Eisenhower Presidency. Federal outlays crept up to almost 21 percent of GNP by 1968, and they have been essentially stable ever since, peaking at 23.3 percent in the recession year, 1975, and dropping back to 21.9 percent in 1979. According to President Carter's budget officials, the Carter Administration aimed to reduce the federal total to below 20 percent.

State and local spending also grew rapidly during the postwar period until the late sixties, when it stabilized at between 10 and 11 percent of GNP. Both federal and state and local outlays have dropped as a share of GNP since 1975. This, of course, reflects the new budget controls at the federal level and the pre-Jarvis limitations at the state and local. Therefore, unless one believes in rather long lags between causes and effects, it is hard to hold the excessive growth of government directly responsible for the tax revolt of the late seventies.

Property taxes, as a percentage of gross personal income, actually dropped in all but eight states between 1972 and 1977. The incidence of the property tax burden, however, shifted dramatically from business onto homeowners, and while *total* revenues grew at a slower rate than total income, taxes on homes typically increased.

The shift in who pays the property tax comes on the heels of a similar shift in the distribution of income taxes. Twenty years ago, corporations were paying about one-third of total income taxes, at both the state and federal level. Today, the corporate share is down to one-fourth. The individual share of the income tax has risen from 68 percent to 75 percent for federal income taxes, and from 61 percent to 73 percent for state and local.

Politically, the shift of the tax burden onto consumers was a double carom shot for business. Not only did it buy business some tax relief, but when consumer frustration at the rising homeowner taxes boiled over into tax revolt, business lobbyists deftly took advantage of the new fiscally conservative mood—to demand still more tax breaks for themselves.

FISCAL FACTORS

If the tax revolt should not be seen as merely a backlash against the *level* of government spending, other fiscal trends, however, are worth noting. In many jurisdictions, taxpayers have been getting less for their tax dollars. This has occurred, not because government has grown more wasteful, but because of shifts in the tax base and other long-term economic trends.

Most of America's older big cities suffered economic reverses, which accelerated in the late 1960s. These included loss of population and especially loss of economically productive population; loss of private sector jobs; slower growth of property values; shrinking per capita income as compared with their own suburbs and other regions of the country. At the same time, these older cities found themselves saddled with two costs that few incumbent mayors find politically rewarding to emphasize in their budgets—pension liabilities and maintenance of physical plant.

There is, of course, a great debate over whether New York City's financial woes were the result of fiscal erosion or financial mismanagement. I tend to agree with those who cite both. There was ample mismanagement, but even without political irresponsibility, the erosion of New York's manufacturing base, the increase in New York's dependent population, and the relatively large share of New York's welfare costs that are borne by the city rather than the state or federal government, all provided ample cause for a fiscal squeeze.

Most other large old cities found themselves squeezed by the same forces, and in order to maintain services at existing levels, they had to tax themselves at higher effective rates. By 1970, according to Thomas Muller of the Urban Institute, cities with populations of more than one million had effective local tax rates of 7.6 percent of income; smaller cities with populations between 50,000 and 100,000 had average local tax rates of only 2.8 percent.

Many cities, like New York, made up for the loss of private sector jobs by creating additional jobs in the public sector. New York, for example, lost about 400,000 manufacturing jobs between 1958 and 1975. The growth of the public sector could make up for this loss only for so long.

While some free-marketeers credit the growth of the South and the West to the friendlier attitude toward business in those parts of the country, the fact is that older cities are simply more costly to maintain than newer ones. Land is more expensive, densities are higher, infrastructure is older, all of which add to the cost of basic public services. Moreover, the older cities have political traditions of providing jobs through local political machines, and more liberal attitudes toward the poor. In the absence of national standards for social programs, it is somewhat self-defeating for older regions to provide more generous benefits than newer regions, but this has been the reality. As Senator Pat Moynihan has observed, a middle management executive in New York would increase his salary by a third by taking the same job in Houston, while a welfare family would decrease their benefits by a third by making the same move.

In addition, the growth of the sunbelt region has been promoted by public policy—through grants in aid, government contracts, and tax benefits that promote relocation rather than reinvestment in existing facilities. No other advanced industrial country has such a casual, laissez-faire attitude toward the decline of its built-up regions.

To a degree, many older cities were able to delay the day of fiscal reckoning by turning to increased federal aid. After the big increase in social programs under Lyndon Johnson, federal expenditures under Nixon added another round of new money through general and special revenue sharing. This enabled cities to postpone dealing with fiscal reality for another decade. In 1967, for example, federal aid to 15 big cities averaged only about 5 percent of the money generated locally. By 1978 the federal aid percentages had risen to: Cleveland, 60 percent; Buffalo, 76 percent; Detroit, 77 percent; Philadelphia, 53 percent. According to John Petersen of the Municipal Finance Officers' Association, locally generated revenue in the 45 largest cities increased at an annual rate of

6.3 percent—less than the rate of inflation—between 1967 and 1977. But these cities were able to maintain services mainly because intergovernmental payments increased at nearly 22 percent annually. By the mid-seventies, many older cities were depending on federal aid, not just for social programs, but to pay for basic public services like police, fire, sanitation, and parks. Cleveland's parks department was made up of a few civil servants and hundreds of CETA workers.

But during the late 1970s, about the same time the general economic slowdown contributed to the tax revolt psychology at the state and local level, stagnation and political backlash increasingly cut into Washington's ability to make up the gaps in local budgets. According to the Tax Foundation, total federal grants to the states grew by only 4 percent in 1979—far less than the rate of inflation—after rising by about 15 percent in 1978. By 1980 Congress had cut CETA, revenue sharing, and countercyclical fiscal aid. And as the temporary budget surpluses of 1978 and 1979 were rapidly depleted in state after state, most states found themselves unable to maintain services at existing levels without raising taxes. Whatever "fat" existed that could easily be pared away was excised in most states by 1980. In that year no fewer than 23 states were considering increases in their sales taxes.

As the voters finally faced the fact that they had to choose between losing public services or adjusting their tax systems, the issue of the distribution of the tax load began to surface again. The Connecticut legislature, facing a huge budgetary deficit, levied a 2 percent gross receipts tax on oil profits. A similar proposal was narrowly rejected in a 1980 California referendum. As the conservative Tax Foundation reported in its March 1980 bulletin, "In contrast to the tax-cutting mood of the past two years, state legislators in 1980 are seeking ways to raise taxes."

10

THE ABATEMENT GAME

INTRODUCING THE NEW AND IMPROVED
NEW YORK
Let's face it. The old New York was a prod-
uct with problems. And its attitude towards
business was nothing to shout about.

But today, New York State is new and im-
proved. It comes complete with a better atti-
tude. More tax incentives and better tax
credits than ever before. And for the first time
in a long time, newspapers, magazines and
people everywhere are talking about our new,
improved state. The fact that companies are
starting to move back into New York instead
of just leaving it. That more jobs are opening
up than closing down. And that, in the last
few years, the state legislature has revamped
the tax laws to create a package in favor of
businesses, both large and small.

WE'VE CUT MORE STATE TAXES THAN ANY
STATE IN AMERICA!

THE ABOVE TEXT is from one of a New York State series of ads aimed at
inducing businesses to locate in New York. The most stilted Marxist
rhetorician could hardly fabricate more revealing prose to cast the state
as the executive committee of the ruling class. The supposed antibusiness
attitude of the bad old New York refers to a fifteen-year period when
the governor was Nelson Rockefeller, a man not noted for a hostility to
industry.

But the abatement game is being played with increasing ferocity, especially among older states competing both with one another and with the sunbelt region for a relatively fixed supply of manufacturing jobs. Democratic governors like New York's Hugh Carey are especially attracted to tax concessions, to balance their liberalism on social issues with a demonstrated friendliness toward business.

The competition to award tax concessions also plays off city against suburb within the same state.

Virtually all the studies show that business decisions to locate here rather than there are motivated mainly by factors other than property tax concessions: convenience of location, availability of trained labor force, cost of land, and interestingly, quality of public services. Ironically, the erosion of the tax base to attract industries often depletes the money to pay for good schools, parks, police protection, and other things that make cities attractive to corporate executives contemplating where to locate. Schools, which are heavily dependent on the property tax, pay a disproportionate price for abatements granted to business.

But this has not stopped the tax concession war.

It is almost impossible to calculate how much of the tax burden has been shifted onto other taxpayers because of business tax concessions, since very few states keep "tax expenditure" budgets that add up all the tax concessions granted.

But it is clear that abatements, credits, and exemptions are a key part of the erosion of the business tax load.

Business tax concessions come in a variety of forms. Several states, led by New York, periodically revise their tax laws to provide across-the-board tax relief to all business. Sometimes, the tax breaks are provided to all new business investments. In addition, many states authorize local governments to negotiate property tax abatements with businesses, one at a time. According to David Gaskell, the director of the New York State Division of Equalization and Assessment, the state doesn't even keep a comprehensive list of the dozens of tax concessions available to industry. His office is working on one.

New York's major tax incentives include a 4 percent new capital investment tax credit against the state business franchise tax, plus an additional credit when new jobs are created or "saved"; extensive pollution control credits; and property tax exemptions that usually exempt any increase in real property up to ten years. New York City provides additional credits for firms relocating from out of state.

The state law authorizing cities to set up local property tax abatement programs, the Steingut-Padavan Act, was passed in 1976, in the aftermath of the most serious recession of the postwar period and New York City's own fiscal crunch. At that time, thanks to a previous cycle of overbuilding, Manhattan was awash in unrented downtown office space, and construction had come to a halt. "Not a twig was being put in the ground," insists Peter Solomon, the City's Deputy Mayor for Economic Development.

In the late seventies, under this new tax act, New York City, through its Industrial and Commercial Incentive Board, rubber-stamped virtually every plausible application for tax abatement. In the eighteen months from February 1977 to August 1978, the board approved 131 out of 145 applications, even though the city's real estate market was clearly rebounding on its own. Ninety percent of the dollar value of exemptions went to Manhattan, and although the rationale of the program was the creation of permanent jobs, only 2 percent of the tax savings went to industrial projects.

The beneficiaries included the City Racquet Club, the New York Health and Racquet Club, as well as a McDonald's hamburger outlet and a bowling alley. But the biggest winners were large midtown office towers, despite the fact that by 1978 New York was enjoying an unprecedented boom in midtown construction. IBM, which had been assembling land for a new sales and service headquarters since 1936, talked the city into a $7.2 million tax exemption. A second office tower, at the prime location of 52nd Street and Madison Avenue on Manhattan's East Side, received a $5.5 million exemption.

At the time, the city board scrutinizing the abatement applications lacked the staff to review the developers' claims. For example, the Palace Hotel got a $6 million exemption on the assumption that its breakeven point was 61 percent occupancy, at a time when city hotel occupancy rates were then running at 79 percent and soon reached 90 percent. The vacancy rate for prime downtown office space, declined from nearly 7 percent in 1976 to under 3 percent by mid-1979, and rents nearly doubled during the same period. But the city kept handing out abatements.

The classic defense, of course, is that these incentives stimulate commerce and bring in other revenues. However, a full abatement on a big downtown office building, even if passed along to the tenants, reduces rents by only about a dollar a square foot. And prime rental space in midtown Manhattan rents for upward of twenty dollars. The subsidy is too slender to significantly influence demand. In most cases, it simply operates as a windfall to the property owner.

An audit by the city comptroller, Harrison Goldin, subsequently concluded that of $84 million in tax exemptions granted during the eighteen-month period, $56 million needlessly went to subsidize projects that probably would have gone forward without the tax subsidy. All told, New York City has $15 billion worth of property on its rolls which is not taxed, thanks to one exemption program or another. Between 1973 and 1979, the exempt portion of the city's tax base increased from 35 percent to 41 percent. And the taxes forgone equaled more than a hundred million dollars yearly.

In 1979, Deputy Mayor Solomon, a former investment banker, came under bitter attack from some of his former colleagues when he cautiously attempted to limit the abatements. So accustomed were developers to abatements as a matter of right, that when Solomon's board refused to rubber-stamp a tax break for a $90 million office restoration on Park Avenue, *The New York Times* put the story on page one, headlined: CITY DELAYS $90 MILLION PROJECT, as if the entire deal hinged on the abatement. There were no headlines a few months later when the project went forward with a much smaller abatement.

"I have a bias against abatement," Solomon confesses. "I don't know of anything that wasn't built because the developer couldn't get an abatement. But you won't know what the market really is until we turn down an application and something doesn't get built."

Solomon, who is sometimes outvoted by his own board, believes that public officials often get taken to the cleaners by private entrepreneurs. "The city tends to get paranoid in transactions," he says. "Most people in government haven't worked in the private sector; they don't have a sense of the dynamic of negotiation, so they're frightened of a deal falling through."

But even under Solomon's new, hard line, most abatement applications are approved, although a developer sometimes gets a lower abatement than he asked for.

New York City also has the nation's most generous tax deals for new and restored housing. Under a 1978 law, any house subsequently built in the city gets a full tax exemption for the first two years, regardless of the need, the site, or the cost, with a gradually declining exemption for six additional years. And New York recently liberalized what was already the nation's most generous tax subsidy for renovated housing.

That program, under the so-called J-51 law, is a classic case of how a good idea is taken over by the smart money. J-51 was originally enacted in the fifties to subsidize the modernization of New York's "old-law" tenements, most of which date to the nineteenth century. Under J-51, the owner of a building not only is exempt from being taxed for most improvements, but he can deduct from his *present* taxes 90 percent of his costs. This tax subsidy is automatic, anywhere in New York City, regardless of the need for the subsidy. It has cost the city tax revenues of $200 million since its inception, $41 million in 1979 alone.

In 1978 the law was liberalized to allow abatements on conversion of commercial space into apartments, although loft conversions were already booming without any tax incentive. Indeed, illegal conversions have continued to boom, even though these cannot qualify for the tax subsidy, which seems to prove that the subsidy is not necessary.

In the past several years, most of the J-51 tax subsidy dollars have gone to landlords in prime residential neighborhoods, who are evicting tenants so they can restore older buildings for occupancy by young professional singles and couples at much higher rents. Since this process also gets the landlord out from under rent control, the tax abatement is pure windfall. And because the J-51 incentive is a tax subsidy rather than a housing program, the city takes minimal responsibility for the workmanship, and tenants in numerous buildings have complained in vain when roofs leak, elevators don't work, and doors fail to fit in newly renovated, tax-subsidized $500-a-month studio apartments.

In 1979, in response to protesting tenant groups, Mayor Koch agreed to limit J-51 to "partial" renovations, meaning that no more than 40 percent of the tenants could be evicted. But at the same time, he extended the abatement period from twenty to thirty-two years.

The problem for officials like Deputy Mayor Solomon who want to slow down the abatement game, is that the city treasury leaks from more than one pocket. When Solomon refused to grant abatement on a commercial building that the blue chip auctioneer Sotheby Parke-Bernet planned to convert into its central warehouse, the developer threatened to convert the building instead to residential lofts, where J-51 abatements would be available as a matter of right.

And if Father won't come across with some tax subsidy, there is always Mother. Solomon can bargain tough at City Hall, but if the developer's rate of return turns out to be low, he need only go across the street to the Tax Commission, where the capitalization formulas will dictate a cut in the property tax bill.

"It's not a closed system," Solomon muses. "Sometimes I say to myself, why am I making myself the heavy; they'll just get it somewhere else."

Tax concessions not only favor business, they favor *big* business. A small merchant can't persuasively threaten a city council to pack up and leave unless he gets a tax abatement. But General Motors can, and does. As North Dakota's populist tax commissioner, Byron Dorgan, has observed, "You'll never see a welder or a barber or a punchpress operator who's thinking of moving to Buffalo or Cleveland saying, 'Well, let's see. What kind of tax deal are you going to give me first?' " In addition, special tax concessions are increasingly part of large-scale, high-visibility, tax-exempt, bond-financing package deals, which typically include other subsidies such as site improvement and job training, not the sort of ventures suited to small business. A survey by Ralph Nader's Public Interest Research Group found that more than two-thirds of tax exempt industrial revenue bonds and pollution-control financing went to corporations employing more than 5,000 people. Yet study after study has shown that most new job opportunities are produced by small, new firms, not by the *Fortune* 500.

Obviously, when tax concessions are granted to corporate taxpayers, somebody else must pick up their share of the tax burden or go without some public services. It is often argued that the income and sales tax revenues produced by the new enterprise will more than compensate for the tax concession, but these statistics assume that the tax concession produced the new investment. Obviously, if the enterprise was going to be developed anyway, then the tax concession simply amounts to a giveaway, at the expense of other taxpayers. Usually, those other taxpayers are individual small businesses, because the gimmickry is aimed mainly at big companies and downtown developers who are sophisticated enough to take advantage of them.

OHIO

Among the states most generous with their business tax concessions, New York probably shares first place with Ohio, which *The Wall St. Journal* has called "a candy-store of tax incentive programs." Ohio's Impacted Cities Act, enacted in 1973, permits cities to abate taxes on new development for a period of up to twenty years. The idea is to give older, poorer cities a competitive advantage in the struggle to attract new development. During the first four years of the Impacted Cities Act, Ohio cities granted tax concessions that will save business taxpayers about $123 million over a twenty-year period.

In 1977 the state legislature decided that suburbs and rural areas should not be denied the right to bargain away their tax base, too. So, under the Community Reinvestment Area legislation, any community may set up a special, tax-abated district. The rationale of the original law, to give older cities a competitive advantage, was overlooked, and industry is now free to play city off against suburb.

Although these tax abatement laws were billed as job incentive measures, both have stimulated mainly downtown office buildings and suburban shopping malls, not industrial development. In several cases, tax abatement was sought to move a plant from one Ohio location to another. And the Impacted Cities Act has gone to subsidize primarily commercial developers, not industry. In its first five years, the Impacted Cities Act was used for just one industrial plant, a Copperweld Corporation mill in the town of Shelby, Ohio, population 9,300.

The tax abatement legislation requires a city to declare an area "blighted" before tax concessions may be granted, but as Norman Krumholz, Cleveland's acerbic city planning director, observes, "Blight can strike anywhere." In Cleveland, blight first struck the city's most prime piece of real estate, at the corner of Ninth and Euclid, a parcel National City Bank had been assembling for years to build a new headquarters tower. There was no risk that the bank would take its business elsewhere, since it is chartered to operate in Cleveland. But in June 1977, the bank successfully persuaded the administration of Mayor Ralph Perk that a tax concession was necessary to build the office tower at a price that would produce competitive rents. The city council dutifully granted the bank a tax concession that will cost the city treasury $14 million over a twenty-year period. (It was National City Bank that ungraciously pulled the plug on Cleveland's finances less than two years later by refusing to roll over some $4 million of notes.) The biggest loser in the deal was the public school system, which gets most of its money directly from property tax revenues. The abatement cost the Cleveland schools $8.8 million in potential taxes.

According to Planning Director Krumholz, National City Bank's abatement equaled a rent subsidy of 57 cents a square foot—not enough to significantly affect the rental market for the space. In Cleveland, prime downtown office space has been renting at a premium in recent years.

It took only three weeks for the city council of this fiscally strapped city to approve the abatement for National City Bank, which then ranked as the most profitable of the country's fifty largest commercial banks.

Two weeks afterward, a consortium of developers applied for an abatement to renovate the old Cleveland Sheraton as a luxury hotel. A week after that, Standard Oil of Ohio came in for abatement to build *its* new headquarters. By August the city council had given away more than $38 million in future property tax revenues "faster than the average Cleveland resident can get a sewer cleaned," as one disgruntled consumer activist complained.

In Cleveland, at least, the abatement craze backfired. Mayor Perk seemed determined to give away the city's downtown tax base. A coalition of neighborhood, consumer, and trade union groups began a protest campaign, and City Councilman Dennis Kucinich, one of the votes against the abatements, made them the central issue of his mayoralty campaign. After Kucinich's election as mayor in November 1977, no new abatements were granted in Cleveland—and the downtown office-building boom has continued—unabated.

In most of Ohio, however, tax abatement has become a way of life. In the town of Parma, General Motors has a Chevrolet plant, with almost a billion dollars invested. GM needed a new warehouse. Although the idea that GM might pull out its entire plant was inconceivable, the company used its influence with city officials to get a tax abatement. The town agreed to abate the warehouse under Ohio's Community Reinvestment Act, the law that extended tax abatements to suburbs and small towns, although it was clear that the abatement was not creating any investment that could not have otherwise occurred. "The trend of industry to migrate outside cities is there anyway," says Jack Nicholl, Cleveland's director of economic development. "This law just makes it more attractive to put an industrial park in a cow pasture twenty miles outside town. All they're doing under the guise of stimulating new investment is to lower the share of taxes paid by corporations and office buildings."

Nicholl contends that the main obstacle to industrial location in big cities is assembly of land. His office, which refuses tax abatement requests, has sought to attract industry by helping to assemble sites, and by subsidizing their cost. "Land costs have a much greater impact than tax abatements," says Nicholl. "You subsidize it directly on the front end, and you don't prejudice your future revenues."

Cincinnati officials take an entirely different view.

For example, U.S. Shoe Corporation, a seventy-five-year-old company employing about 1,000 workers, worked closely with Cincinnati economic development officials to get a $7.8 million federal grant to build a modern factory in a new industrial park, intended to anchor the revitalization of an old Cincinnati neighborhood, Madisonville. At the last minute, in January 1979, U.S. Shoe approached officials of two suburbs, Blue Ash and

Sharonville, and dangled the prospect of giving them the new factory if they would abate the property taxes. Armed with a commitment from Blue Ash, the company then went back to demand tax abatement from Cincinnati, as a condition of going forward with the Cincinnati site. At the time, U.S. Shoe was reporting that its profits were up 40 percent over the previous year, to $27 million.

Despite protests of blackmail from labor and consumer groups, the city council took less than two weeks to give U.S. Shoe a $5.6 million abatement. The council added a provision, which is probably unenforceable, giving residents of Cincinnati first claim on jobs at the plant.

In Columbus, the state capital, tax abatement has become closely identified with urban redevelopment. The first major tax-abated redevelopment project under Ohio's Impacted Cities Law was a new worldwide headquarters for Nationwide Insurance Company (which was previously located in Columbus). Under the abatement agreement, the company "refunds" to the city a sum equal to the abated property taxes, which the city must use to upgrade Nationwide's site. Through this agreement, the city neatly converts $20 million in tax revenues, $14 million of which would have gone to Columbus public schools. Now, these funds go to the city—and effectively to Nationwide, for public amenities in connection with the building. Ultimately, Cincinnati may benefit from the infusion of new commerce, but the Cincinnati schools are short the tax revenues. Thanks to burdensome school tax rates and the shrinking tax base, Columbus voters have turned down four school levies since 1970.

It isn't just taxpayers who make up the difference when taxes are abated on big commercial developments. The combination of tax abatement and urban renewal can be lethal for small businesses, which often thrive on the moderate rent districts on the fringes of downtown—the sorts of areas that attract big-time developers and their allies in urban renewal agencies.

Columbus is relying on tax abatement deals to promote the redevelopment of one such area, adjacent to the state capitol, called Capitol South. Far from looking like a center of blight, the Capitol South district was a thriving district of gift shops, delis, clothing and book stores, convenient for a daytime trade of white-collar shoppers who work in the nearby commercial center. Under the redevelopment plan, the city uses its power of eminent domain to condemn property in the three-square-block area and convey it to the Capitol South Development Corporation, a private nonprofit corporation that is assembling the land for an eventual redevelopment site for hotels, shopping malls, and the like. Like a great many such projects, Capitol South is wired into the city establishment. One member of the city council is a partner in the law firm that represents the Capitol South Development Corporation. This is classic fifties-style urban renewal—supercharged by eighties-style tax abatement. As the city takes title to the land for the development corporation, the land ceases paying property taxes. And abatements will be extended to the new shopping malls and hotels—if they are ever built.

Columbus already has one colossal failed urban renewal project on its hands—the Market/Mohawk area, which was once an old-fashioned market center. Hundreds of homes and small businesses were condemned there for a redevelopment scheme that never materialized. The process of taking properties for urban renewal is painfully slow, and as more and more properties in the Capitol South area are vacated, it is gradually turning into the blighted slum the city claims it always was. Eventually, if the grand design for Capitol South materializes, Columbus will forgo about $70 million in property taxes over a twenty-five-year period.

John Meysenburg, who runs a florist shop a few blocks from Capitol South, considers the whole project bad for his business and unfair to small businesses generally. "I've already been through one very costly forced relocation, when they extended Interstate 90," Meysenburg explains, between customers. "Even after Capitol South is redeveloped, the only businesses who can afford to come in are the big chain operators. Small, owner-operated businesses are being systematically excluded from the area. It's a land grab, almost like a feudalization. The city is promoting a corporate takeover of prime real estate. They're taking away the foundation of the American economic system, the small independent entrepreneur."

This, of course, is the classic plaint against urban renewal grand schemes. But the injury is especially insulting to the tax-paying entrepreneur who is displaced to make way for a tax-abated project. Meysenburg has organized a Downtown Fair Deal Association, representing about fifty small merchants in and near Capitol South. Despite this opposition, the Capitol South district is slowly turning into a wasteland, to make way for the bulldozer.

Overblown claims are often advanced that new development will produce new jobs and expanded sales and income tax receipts, which will cancel out the property tax reductions. But these claims seldom pan out. New businesses often simply replace older businesses.

In Columbus, the city council counted on income and sales taxes produced by new jobs to compensate for a property tax abatement granted to a West German firm, L. Schuler GMBH company, a manufacturer of pumps, motors, valves, and presses. But one immediate result of the Schuler abatement was the acceleration of the shutdown of a domestic competitor, the Abex Corporation's Denison Division, which employed some 230 workers in its Cincinnati plant, producing an almost identical product line. In announcing the shutdown of Abex-Denison's Columbus plant, the company's industrial relations director said the unfair competition created by the tax abatements to Schuler played a major role in Denison's decision to close. The new jobs produced by Schuler will just about replace the jobs lost by Abex–Denison—and the city will be out hundreds of thousands of dollars in property tax revenues.

The most dubious of Ohio's recent tax deals is the Ford Motor Company exemption. Since 1950, Ford has operated an automatic-transmission plant in Fairfax, Ohio, near Cincinnati. The plant was built to turn out the big clunky automatic transmissions that auto makers introduced in the years after World War II. The machinery is mostly thirty years old. Workers on the line figured Ford would have to spend millions of dollars to retool Fairfax for the front-wheel-drive cars and the new transaxles of the eighties.

Instead, word spread in mid-1977 that Ford was planning to build a new computerized transmission factory from the ground up. It was natural to keep transmission assembly in southwest Ohio, with its machine tool industry, its trained engineering and assembly-line work force, and its distribution system already in place. Ford eventually settled on a site in nearby Clermont County, insisting that the older plant in Fairfax would continue. But the men on the line knew better. Ford didn't need two transmission plants, and the failure to retool Fairfax was a sure sign that it would be shut down.

Negotiations for the Clermont site were far along when Ford officials began raising the subject of tax abatement. Company executives hinted they were considering rival sites across the state line in Kentucky. Perhaps they were. In any event, Ohio Governor James Rhodes obliged by ramming through the legislature a bill reducing the property taxes on *all* new business machinery and equipment by more than 50 percent. At the last minute, after protests by local school officials, the law was modified to take the revenues out of state rather than local funds.

Few Ohioans were surprised when Ford announced plans to go ahead with the new plant, but Governor Rhodes rushed into print full-page newspaper ads proclaiming FORD PICKS OHIO! and claiming that the new state law was "a deciding factor" in Ford's decision, and lavishly praising the state's solicitude for business.

The new tax abatements, which might or might not have influenced Ford's decision, will reduce Ford's property taxes by about $2 million a year. But other manufacturers, who presumably were not debating a move to Kentucky, will save some $60 million annually. In other words, Ohio sacrificed $60 million in property tax revenues in order to channel a $2 million subsidy to one company.

The rationale for this gift was the prospect of new jobs; but inevitably, less than a year after it had "picked Ohio" for its new plant, Ford announced that it would phase out the old transmission plant after all. The new plant, which was supposed to create 3,500 new jobs, would employ 2,900, Ford said, and most of these would be workers transferred from the obsolescent factory in Fairfax. Total subsidies for the new Clermont facility include about $3 million in personal property taxes lost yearly, $1.1 million lost in local property tax abatement, $5.3 million spent from state funds to acquire and improve the site, as well as highway, water, and sewer improvements. These funds will come from other Ohio taxpayers.

In effect, Ford has replaced an existing taxpaying plant with a new tax-abated one. And the long-term effect of the Ford exemption will reduce taxes on virtually all plant machinery and equipment in Ohio as well. Although the state law reducing the assessment ratio from 48 percent to 20 percent nominally applies only to new machinery, industrial machinery rarely lasts more than a few decades and is often fully depreciated much sooner. In Ohio, approximately 12 percent of industrial machinery turns over each year. Within ten years, most, by far, of the taxpaying industrial machinery and equipment in Ohio will be "new" for tax purposes, further eroding the business property tax base and increasing the tax burden on everybody else.

These tax deals are being offered in a state that already has one of the lowest state and local tax levels in the country, and far lower than in surrounding industrial states—which are also drawn into the abatement competition by Ohio's generosity. According to Professor Frederick Stocker, a tax scholar at Ohio State University, "These tax concessions convey the idea that if you hang tough and hold off, you can always get a better deal. It creates a negotiating climate where a businessman won't make an investment until he gets a tax concession. Taxes in Ohio are really very low. But our citizens have been led to believe by a generation of politicians that our taxes are the highest in the nation."

The psychology of tax abatement is nicely self-propelling. Every time business shifts part of its tax load to other taxpayers, it reinforces the illusion that Ohio is a heavily taxed state—which lends credence to business's next demand for still more tax abatement.

Ohio periodically generates headlines when citizens of this or that city vote down a school tax levy, shortening the academic year or even closing down schools. To put those gifts in perspective, consider that Ohio is one of a very small number of states where tax levies are subject to referendum, thanks to the 1910 Smith Law, the granddaddy of Proposition 13. Moreover, only the local property tax is subject to a popular vote. There are no plebiscites on other taxes. Given the increasing share of the tax burden paid by residential housing, small wonder that voters express their frustration through the one available outlet.

But the school levy votes also paint a misleading picture of Ohio as a high-tax state. The reality is a state with a badly apportioned tax distribution.

In 1978 the treasurer of Cuyahoga County (a Democrat) and the county auditor (a Republican) jointly released figures showing that the residential share of property taxes in that county increased from 50 percent in 1964 to an estimated 78 percent in 1979.

Some Ohio localities, however, are beginning to follow Cleveland's lead. Tax abatement votes are not quite as certain as they once were. The issue has become controversial, thanks to the opposition by the trade unions and the Ohio Public Interest Campaign. In Clermont County, where the new tax-abated Ford transmission plant is being built, county commissioners tried to ram through a fifteen-year tax abatement for the Eastgate Mall, an eighty-five-store shopping center. This was pure windfall, since the mall was already half completed. The vote came Christmas week 1978, with no prior notice. Threatened with a vocal outcry including a lawsuit by one local township that stood to lose tax revenues, the commissioners voted to rescind the abatement a week later.

William Osterander owns a Cleveland precision-machine-tool shop, called Universal Grinding. It is the kind of small enterprise, employing about 100, that has been the backbone of Cleveland's now-faltering industrial economy. In late 1978, Osterander was thinking of building a new, larger factory.

Twenty miles outside Cleveland, in Brunswick in Medina County, city officials were trying to promote development of their new industrial park. Under Ohio's new Community Reinvestment Area legislation, the city council proposed to designate the park a tax-abated area and offered Universal a million-dollar tax-exempt revenue bond, to finance the factory, to be coupled with a fifteen-year tax abatement. According to Osterander, the tax abatement was key to the deal. Supposedly, of course, Ohio's tax abatement law was intended to promote new development, but this was clearly a raid by one community on another city's industry. Much of the land for the site was owned by Nationwide Insurance, which had enjoyed the huge abatement for its Cincinnati headquarters.

In this case, Cleveland counterattacked, and on several fronts. The city economic development director, Jack Nicholl, offered to help Universal assemble a new site in Cleveland, and the Ohio Public Interest Campaign, the auto workers, and the steelworkers, all close allies of Kucinich, helped mobilize opposition to the abatement. In Brunswick the abatement became a major local issue, opposed by many Brunswick small businessmen, school officials, and other local luminaries. The county auditor warned the city council that abatement was a dangerous precedent for the city's fiscal health. The former Brunswick city law director testified emotionally, "Who has the deeper pocket? Nationwide with its millions or Brunswick, which has to beg voters to pass levies?" The council delayed action.

In the end, Osterander accepted Nicholl's offer to help Universal assemble another site in Cleveland, and the whole Brunswick tax abatement scheme fell through.

For Jack Nicholl, who wants to promote development of Cleveland's economy, suburban tax abatement just makes his job harder. "It only encourages a trend that is happening anyway. Under the guise of stimulating new investment, Ohio makes it even more attractive for industry to move to the suburbs," he says.

Citizens groups in Toledo filed signatures for a local initiative to force that city council to overturn a twenty-year tax abatement proposed for Toledo's largest bank, Toledo Trust Company. The city council had also approved an abatement for a new office building for Owens Illinois. Faced with the prospect of a referendum reversing both votes, the city administration entered into negotiations and ultimately repealed the tax abatement for the bank, which will restore $2.2 million to Toledo tax rolls over a twenty-year period. Toledo Trust, which had insisted the tax abatement was necessary for the building to go forward, plans to build the new headquarters anyway.

Tax abatement in Ohio was originally an import. The Ohio Impacted Cities Act was modeled on a Missouri statute that combines twenty-five-year tax abatement with urban renewal (Missouri, at least, limits tax abatement to its big cities).

MISSOURI

The Missouri Urban Redevelopment Corporation law, Section 353 of the Missouri Revised Statutes, is the earliest and most permissive law of its kind. Section 353 was enacted during World War II, to stimulate "slum clearance" and construction of desperately needed apartments in St. Louis and Kansas City. When the federal government began financing urban renewal projects in the fifties, the Missouri law served as a handy companion. But unlike federal urban renewal, the Missouri law gave extensive powers to private, for-profit developers, with virtually no controls.

Under the law, a private redevelopment corporation requests the city council of St. Louis or Kansas City to declare an area "blighted"; the private developer then may take all land within the area through eminent domain and enjoys full tax-abatement for ten years and partial abatement for fifteen years more on whatever he builds there.

The abuses of urban renewal have been amply documented elsewhere, but St. Louis has carried it to unparalleled extremes, thanks to the extra ingredients of tax abatement and private eminent domain. In 1971 the city declared its entire downtown "blighted" and invited tax-abated redevelopment of the whole central business district. "What a wonderful gesture," exclaimed the president of Downtown St. Louis Inc., "to hand me a completely blighted downtown St. Louis."

One of the city's biggest developers today is the former mayor, A. J. Cervantes, the official who decided to blight downtown. Under Chapter 353, the prospect of acquiring land cheap via eminent domain and then enjoying tax-abated development fueled an orgy of bulldozing unparalleled in any other city. Entire sections of the city were razed, with little guarantee that anything would be built in their place. Today, no American city has a higher percentage of idle land, or a steeper decline in population. Around a few islands of tax-abated high rise redevelopment in the city's new Downtown near the Eero Saarinen Gateway Arch, are vast tracts of rubble, awaiting development that may never come.

At the time of its passage, Section 353 was intended to promote housing. Metropolitan Life and the other big insurance companies, which had pioneered development of such middle-income housing projects as Stuyvesant Town and Parkchester in New York, dictated the terms of Missouri's redevelopment law as a condition of financing similar developments in St. Louis. The first application of the law, in 1962, did produce a $24 million middle-income housing project, called Plaza Square. But with the exception of that first project, tax-abated redevelopment in St. Louis has produced little housing.

Instead, tax abatements have gone to hotels, sports arenas, commercial office buildings, convention centers, and malls. Thanks to the decision by Mayor Cervantes, in 1971, to "pre-blight" all of downtown, the real estate business in downtown St. Louis has enjoyed a bonanza that contrasts sharply with the poverty and genuine blight of the rest of the city.

One project alone, Mercantile Center, was built on a prime downtown site that was never "blighted" in any sense of the word; yet the $30 million Mercantile Trust building, Missouri's largest, will add not a penny to St. Louis's tax base until the next century.

The sole other housing project built under Section 353 is something called Mansion House, which stands as a textbook housing scandal. Mansion House was originally built as a luxury high-rise apartment complex, with a mortgage insured by FHA. The deal was put together as a massive tax shelter for such prominent absentee partners as Henry Ford II. Federal investigators found that the developer diverted project funds for a variety of inflated expenses, including payments to subsidiary corporations he also controlled. The project fell behind on its mortgage almost immediately, leaving the federal government holding the bag for $36 million. Eventually, despite the $400,000 annual tax abatement from the other taxpayers of St. Louis, part of Mansion House was converted into a hotel, and the rest of it is the subject of extensive litigation between FHA and the developer.

Tax abated redevelopment in St. Louis has scarcely touched genuine slum areas, or stimulated creation of new industrial jobs, save for one major plant expansion in which the company, Amax Aluminum, engaged in a well-worn maneuver, threatening to move to another state unless St. Louis could produce subsidies. The city readily agreed to tax abate the $10 million plant addition (built on land already owned by Amax) for twenty-five years.

In sharp contrast to St. Louis, where the city council has been all too eager to give downtown developers a blank check, Kansas City carefully negotiates each tax-abated project and rarely grants the legally maximum twenty-five-year abatement, which St. Louis provides routinely. One exception, however, was made in the case of the giant Crown Center development, which was sponsored by the Hallmark Corporation, one of

Kansas City's most influential local employers. The Crown Center abatement will cost Kansas City and surrounding Jackson County $400,000 a year in revenue, of which nearly half would have gone to local schools. But, unlike St. Louis, most of the new office building construction in Kansas City has gone forward without tax abatement. In St. Louis the total cost of tax abatements of projects built will exceed $200 million over a twenty-five-year period; assuming constant tax rates (the total property taxes *paid* in St. Louis are slightly less than $100 million a year).

It is also very difficult to calculate the effect that subsidized redevelopment of newer office buildings has had on the ability of older, unsubsidized buildings to compete for commercial tenants. But the St. Louis rental market has remained softer than that of comparable cities, which has led some observers to conclude that taxed buildings are in effect subsidizing tax-abated buildings by supplying them with tenants, at a cost to their own rent roll.

As of 1978 the total value of exempt and abated property in St. Louis, $2.8 billion, almost equals the value of taxable property, $3.2 billion, and the taxable roll has been decreasing in value every year, while the tax rate has been increasing. Slightly more than half of St. Louis's property taxes go to finance the public schools. For the homeowners and small businessmen of St. Louis, tax-abated downtown development offers the stark choice of higher taxes or reduced services. In recent years, St. Louis has gotten both.

Unlike in Cleveland, where a whole city administration turned against tax abatement, tax abated redevelopment remains highly popular in St. Louis as a key component of the revolving door of the political and real estate professions. Only one alderman consistently opposes tax abatement, Bruce Sommer, and he is as popular at city hall as the proverbial skunk at the lawn party.

In April 1978, President Carter's National Commission on Neighborhoods held a series of field hearings in St. Louis and inadvertently stumbled into the local controversy over tax abatements. St. Louis was on the verge of receiving an $18.5 million urban development action grant from the federal government, to build a massive suburban-style shopping mall in the middle of downtown. Or more precisely, the mall is being built in the last old-fashioned downtown area that is not yet urban-renewed.

When the Neighborhoods Commission obliquely criticized St. Louis's tax abatement policy, the city fathers bitterly denounced the commission as a tool of Alderman Sommer, whom Mayor James Conway called a "dog in the manger." Fearing that the federal grant might be held up,

Conway turned to the Missouri congressional delegation and succeeded in getting Senator Thomas Eagleton to blast the commission, and the local congressman, Joseph Gephardt, to threaten its appropriation.

The Gateway Mall, to be developed by the May Company at a total cost of $150 million, includes an enclosed shopping center, a new 1,000-room hotel, and an "entertainment mall," all to be linked by a system of "skyways," and of course all tax-abated. Without tax abatement, the tax on a project of this value would be about $3 million a year.

The mall is being built on a site that was the last thriving section of St. Louis's old downtown business section. Several retailers unsuccessfully filed suit to block condemnation of their stores, including Woolworth's, whose St. Louis outlet was its fifth most profitable store in the country.

Woolworth is not in the habit of taking on local business establishments, but Woolworth executive J. T. Marziotti testified angrily before the Neighborhoods Commission, "The mall will destroy the only remaining successful, diversified shopping area in downtown St. Louis." Marziotti added that the redevelopment would evict the retailers from the area for a period of at least three years while the mall was being built, and "even then, they might not be able to obtain or afford the costly space in the mall. Most of the present businesses will be forced to relocate out of the city or cease operating altogether."

Marziotti also pointed to the example of other grand designs that were left half-completed once the developer had built his own portion, leaving acres of land vacant that once housed taxpaying business.

"The city has accelerated the decline of downtown," Marziotti said, "by giving developers all the benefits of Section 353 without requiring any firm commitment that the projects be completed."

For example, the Mercantile Trust Company, using tax-abated eminent domain, built phase one of the promised $150,000,000 project, a huge headquarter tower for itself, and then ignored phases two and three, a hotel and three other buildings. All that was risked was a $500 performance bond—which the city did not bother to collect. Mercantile is now sitting on prime redevelopment land with the option to build—or sell—if and when the market seems right. In the meantime, this piece of once-thriving downtown sits truly blighted.

St. Louis style tax-abated urban renewal is Henry George's worst nightmare come true. Instead of using tax provisions to discourage land speculation and reward productive use of land, St. Louis gives speculators inducements to keep massive amounts of land idle. For this act, they receive full tax abatement, while productive existing businesses and homes are punished, by being charged their own full taxes plus whatever the developer has failed to pay.

Does any of this actually attract industry? Mainly, the tax abatement game serves to erode the business tax base and increase business net profits at the expense of consumers and workers. Studies of business decision-making overwhelmingly conclude that regional differences in tax levels are not a significant consideration in corporate decisions where to locate. In the first place, most employers stay put most of the time. Those that do move are concerned about labor costs, energy availability, and access to markets. Tax considerations may be the frosting on the cake when a decision is all but made. An official of Church and Dwight, recipient of a $60,000-a-year abatement for a new $20 million sodium bicarbonate plant in Seneca County, Ohio, confessed to a *Wall Street Journal* reporter, "The tax abatement was a nice kicker at the end, but we chose Ohio mainly for its strategic location for distribution and market growth."

All told, state and local taxes usually are less than 5 percent of a company's sales, while labor costs may be 50 percent.

Moreover, the studies of where new jobs come from suggest that most new jobs are generated by small new companies, the sort that do not choose their locations on the basis of tax considerations. A widely recognized study by economist David Birch of MIT prepared for the U.S. Department of Commerce found that small firms, with fewer than twenty employees, produced 66 percent of all new jobs generated in the U.S., and that medium-sized and large firms accounted for few new jobs. Birch attributes this to the life cycle of firms: small, new firms, though many fail, are more aggressive and inventive. As firms mature, they stabilize and produce few new jobs. Birch concludes, "In short, the firms that can and do generate the most jobs are the ones that are the most difficult to reach through conventional policy initiatives. . . . it is no wonder that efforts to stem the tide of job decline have been so frustrating—and largely unsuccessful. The firms that such efforts must reach are the most difficult to identify and the most difficult to work with. They are small. They tend to be independent. They are volatile. The very spirit that gives them their vitality and job generating powers is the same spirit that makes them unpromising partners for the development administrator."

While the total cost of tax incentives is impossible to calculate for the whole country, just the expense of administering tax concession programs stretches well into the millions. States spend an estimated $7 million just on magazine advertisements trumpeting their inducements. In 1975 the Massachusetts taxation commissioner calculated that six of the tax incentives enacted in a package program called "Mass Incentives" cost the commonwealth $80 million a year. While these incentives add up to a big drain on state and local treasuries, they rarely mean enough to influence decisions made by particular companies.

For example, Massachusetts has a major tax incentive program that permits a manufacturing or research and development firm to deduct 3 percent of the cost of new investment from its annual excise tax due. But MIT economist Bennett Harrison takes the hypothetical example of a medium-sized firm with annual costs of $6.7 million and a new investment of $800,000. The value of the credit is $24,000 (3 percent of $800,000) or less than one-fifth of one percent of the firm's total costs. The incentive in this case, a trivial one, is unlikely to change corporate behavior; yet in the aggregate the Massachusetts incentive costs the commonwealth millions.

The firms in the business of advising other companies where to locate are themselves highly skeptical about the value of tax incentives. "The vast majority of firms are much more concerned about markets, labor availability, labor-management climate, transportation, and increasingly energy and environment," explains Charles Pollak, senior consultant at the Fantus Company, which helps companies identify sites for expansion and relocation. "Taxes may be a very fine divider at the end of the process, but the broad divider is—what do I need to operate, what kind of market am I serving, what are my energy needs. A guy with an aluminum rolling mill is much more interested in environmental factors and energy costs than taxes, and this is a guy who's going to own 1,500 or 2,000 acres of property."

According to Pollak, "Take South Dakota. Their advertising pushes the fact that they have no income tax and no personal property tax, but they're far away from the big markets and they haven't had much success in attracting industry. Texas has done very well attracting new industry. They have no personal income tax, no corporate income tax and very low property taxes, and of course lots of other advantages. But North Carolina has done very well too, and they have a 6 percent corporate income tax, a business inventory tax, and no program of across-the-board tax breaks. But they've attracted lots of new industry with a superb labor market and a great location that can reach the Northeast as well as Midwest. When you come right down to it, taxes are not a prime consideration at all."

North Carolina's economic development chief is one of the very few to risk this viewpoint: "Existing industries in most cases pay for incentives, and we don't burden our industries with that. We treat everybody equally." Another of the few other states to shun tax abatement gimmicks is Idaho (which is shifting its property tax burden away from business at such a rapid rate that it may not need the more overt form of incentive).

An extensive literature surveying business motivations to locate or relocate overwhelmingly confirms that tax incentives are of very limited importance. In virtually all the surveys, business executives place tax incentives near the bottom of the list. An extensive 1958 study of firms moving out of New York City found that only fourteen even mentioned taxes. A series of interviews with executives of fifteen Massachusetts companies that had applied for state "job creation tax credits" revealed that in every case, the company had made decisions based on its internal needs, and subsequently learned of the tax credits. An independent set of interviews in Connecticut yielded the same results. The tax loss to both states was pure windfall for the companies.

A 1979 study by Roger Vaughan of Citibank concluded that "the level of business taxes has had very little impact on the local growth rate or on the interstate locational decisions of firms . . . Firms are rewarded for doing what they would have done even in the absence of the incentive."

The number of abatement and exemptions offered by states has grown dramatically in recent years. Between 1966 and 1975, the number of states offering tax exemptions on machinery and equipment rose from fifteen to twenty-seven, while the states where exemptions on land and capital improvements were available increased from eleven to twenty-one. Obviously, as more and more states offer benefits similar to their neighbors', any incentive effect washes out altogether.

Tax-exempt development bonds, a story that has been amply told elsewhere, also provide a subsidy to industry at the expense of other taxpayers. Surveys also demonstrate that this form of tax subsidy has scant influence on corporate decision-making.

SELECTIVE REDUCTIONS

Business taxpayers also benefit disproportionately from abatements, in another sense of the term. If a taxpayer feels that compared with others he is overassessed, he may apply to have his assessment lowered. But in some states, assessors are reluctant to roll back an assessment, because reductions in the total assessed valuation of the city requires a compensating increase in the general tax rate. Instead, the city agrees to *abate* the tax due, on the overassessed property, usually on a year-by-year basis.

This was the system in Massachusetts for over a decade. After a comprehensive revaluation ordered by the state supreme court caused angry voters to throw out the incumbent mayor in Springfield, mayors of other large cities grew determined to do almost anything to avoid a similar fate.

For example, Boston tax officials during the sixties and early seventies simply settled cases rather than risk the lawsuit that might bring down the whole system (the suit finally came in 1979). There developed an "abatement bar" of politically well-connected lawyers, blue chip as well as sleazy, who specialized in winning tax reductions. The lawyers operated on a contingency basis. The usual fee was one-third of the tax reduction. For a big commercial building, which could bring in a fee in the tens of thousands, the costs to the attorney were well worth the risk. But there was little profit in taking the case of a homeowner, where the entire abatement would be less than a thousand dollars. The tax savings won through the curious labors of the Boston abatement bar were virtually all savings for business.

Every large property owner, of course, enjoys an equal right to appeal his assessment—just as the rich and the poor observed by Anatole France had an equal right to be punished for sleeping beneath the bridges of the Seine. In most big cities, particularly those with antiquated assessment systems, tax appeals are something for big, commercial landlords.

In New York, as in Boston, tax appeals are also an unbelievable bonanza for a select fraternity of tax lawyers. New York currently has 121 lawyers specializing in real estate tax appeals, known collectively as the "certiorari bar." As in Boston, cases are taken on a contingency basis, which effectively rules out small homeowners. With more than 40,000 cases filed yearly and only thirty-two hearing days set by the city Tax Commission, each case gets about one minute. The top certiorari lawyers file more than a thousand cases *each,* and the good lawyers file only those appeals they expect to win. The president of the certiorari bar association, Louis Fischoff, boasts a success rate of better than 95 percent.

The 1979 league leader among tax-appeal lawyers, Hubert Brandt, won assessment reductions for his clients totaling more than $58 million, according to Tax Commission records. Before he takes a case, Brandt makes a quick calculation to determine whether the landlord paid more than 5 percent of the building's value in property taxes. If he did, Brandt figures he has a winner.

In New York, the lawyer's share of the savings runs between 10 percent and 50 percent of the total tax reduction, depending on its size, according to former Tax Commission president Marshall Kaplan. The established certiorari lawyers split their fees with an extensive network of referring attorneys. Even with only a 10 percent share of the proceeds, several of the more diligent members of the certiorari bar can easily earn six-figure fees for a few months' work.

Of the $297 million in assessment reductions awarded by the New York City Tax Commission in 1979, the lion's share went to big downtown commercial properties. Most of the *Fortune* 500 headquarters buildings won big reductions, as did the New York Stock Exchange. Topping the list was Mobil Oil's headquarters on Forty-second Street. Mobil, hardly a candidate for public alms in 1979, got its assessment reduced by $7 million.

Many of the landlords and lawyers who do well at this system are politically prominent. Hubert Brandt, who won the biggest reductions, is also a member of the temporary state commission recommending reforms in the property tax. His father, Peter, was a close associate of former Mayor Robert Wagner. Others among the most successful tax-appeal lawyers include the law firm of former Brooklyn Congressman Bert Podell, and the well-known Democratic party fund-raiser Abraham (Bunny) Lindenbaum.

By the same token, the politically connected landlords win a high percentage of their tax appeals. In 1978 a group of city public employees from the social service employees' union, angered at cutbacks in services resulting from the fiscal crisis, descended on the Municipal Building to conduct an ingenious study of who wins assessment appeals. Combing public records, they compared assessment reductions won by politically influential landlords with other reductions obtained by buildings on the same block.

The survey showed that Lewis Rudin, one of New York's biggest landlords and a close ally of Mayor Koch, appealed more of his assessments and won more of his appeals than comparably located properties owned by other landlords. Thirty-two percent of Rudin's buildings obtained reduced assessments, compared with 7 percent of buildings owned by others. And while other nearby landlords won 20 percent of their appeals, Rudin won 33 percent. For Harry Helmsley, another influential landlord, the disparity was of the same order.

But it misses the point to conclude that insiders simply get special treatment from the Tax Commission. Other big landlords with no apparent political ties do almost as well, mainly because they have the sophistication and the resources to appeal. And several small-time lawyers, with no special access other than a thirty-year familiarity with the Tax Commission, make out very nicely, too.

"Years ago, there may have been political influence," says attorney Fischoff. "Today it's much more subtle. The big property owners win reductions because they hire the best lawyers."

Fischoff's view is seconded by Marshall Kaplan, who as Tax Commission president won the enmity of the certiorari bar when he sought to institute some mild procedural reforms: "Nobody comes in and says, 'That's Rudin's building, take care of him,' " Kaplan says. "The problem is the whole system.

"These lawyers are selling an aura of expertise and they're selling access. They do a little grade school math; they jerk around the numbers on the balance sheet. But are they 'experts'? The definition of an expert is the guy who gets the business. I have seen this process from the inside, and it's horse shit. But you tell the average guy, 'This is a certiorari matter,' and he says, 'Holy Jeezus, get me an expert!' "

Kaplan found himself reviewing tax reduction appeals at the rate of about one per minute, without enough information to know what he was doing. When he sought to make applicants file a standardized profit and loss statement that was subject to penalties for fraud, the other lawyers retained a blue chip firm to sue Kaplan. He was widely considered a peculiar bull in a delicate and lucrative china emporium; and when his term expired, Kaplan was not reappointed by Mayor Koch.

Landlords seeking reductions on property taxes still file a rudimentary balance sheet. If the net profit as a percentage of the assessed value seems to produce a low rate of return, the landlord can usually win a reduction. The commission's calculation of rate of return does not consider the landlord's mortgage. The Tax Commission does not audit applications, and does not normally prosecute cases of fraud.

Picture the IRS handing out tax refunds without spot-auditing tax returns, and you have a good picture of how the New York City Tax Commission operates. A property owner who inflates his expenses to win a tax cut runs little risk. "Nobody has ever gotten in real trouble, and nobody ever can," Kaplan says.

Kaplan's widely admired successor, a professional tax administrator named Mary Mann, speaks a far more diplomatic language than Kaplan, but feels the same frustrations. The process affords all the careful deliberation of a tobacco auction.

"I sit in front of the hearing room with a pile of cards stacked in front of me," Mann says. "The assessor has made a few notes on the back. I skim the card, consider where the property is located, its rate of return. If it's making more than 20 percent on its assessed valuation, I won't even consider it. If the rate of return is low, I'll usually make an offer."

Each case takes less time than a traffic ticket. Commissioner Mann usually handles Manhattan cases herself. The other six commissioners, who are part-time patronage appointees, sit in New York's four other boroughs. The landlord has ten days to decide whether to accept the commission's offer. If he doesn't like it, he can go to court, and many do. The courts, though they require a little more preparation on the part of the lawyer, tend to be even more charitable than the commission. One tax appeals judge, recently assigned to other duties, was renowned for never refusing at least a token tax reduction—and seldom explaining why.

As of this writing, assessors in New York City still lack the authority to require property owners to supply figures, and still lack the manpower to conduct audits. Commissioner Mann's wish list includes subpoena power and more hearing days to consider applications. She also proposes to require that profit and loss statements be filed in a format that can be keypunched, so that figures can be verified. And she wants to charge a filing fee to finance the cost of audits.

"This system has never been policed," Mann points out. "It's unnatural not to puff up your figures if you know there's no audit. Everybody who files should be subject to random audits."

According to Mann, the present system makes it impossible both to treat taxpayers equitably and protect the city's beleaguered tax base. But the constituency for tax enforcement is very limited nowadays. Tax reform has been redefined as tax cuts, and to most people tighter assessment and collection procedures smack of higher taxes, which are hardly in vogue. New York City is under immense pressure from the state, the banks, the bondholders, and Senator Proxmire to balance its budget. Nearly all the scrutiny has focused on outlays; hardly any on tax enforcement.

Eventually, after New York modernizes its property tax administration with computerized assessments, the certiorari bar may fall on hard times. But that day seems decades away. Nobody can program a computer with enough sophistication to resolve definitively the market value of a commercial building, because the value is ultimately a subjective product of the assumptions made by the humans who run the computer. And with or without the computer, these are the same assumptions that have been disputed in courts for centuries.

"You would think that a sale would be a pretty good test of market value," says Marshall Kaplan. "But nobody knows what a sale is. I've seen sales where the seller actually paid the buyer to buy the building, sales with leasebacks, sale-exchanges, and 'thin' sales with a dollar down and two million in paper. Then you have all this foreign money pouring into New York, which inflates sales prices beyond all reason. If a guy buys bricks rather than stocks to shelter his money from inflation, is that a sale? They think they're going to replace the assessor with a machine, but mainly it'll make a fortune for the lawyers. My advice to any young lawyer is—get yourself a piece of this business."

The president of the certiorari bar discreetly agrees: "When they go to full-value assessment," says Louis Fischoff with a shrug, "you will have nine million people filing application for reductions."

11

WHO REALLY PAYS
THE PROPERTY TAX?

ECONOMISTS DATING BACK to at least the French Physiocrats have recognized that the person who receives the tax bill is not necessarily the
one who ultimately pays the tax. The tax may be shifted "forward" to
consumers of a company's products or to the renters of a landlord's
apartment house, or it may be shifted "backward" to suppliers, depending on the tightness or slackness of the market. Some degree of tax shifting takes place no matter whether the tax is levied on property, income,
gross receipts, or sales.

Conservative economists argue that it is essentially futile to tax business, since business taxes are reflected in higher prices, and thus all taxes
are eventually paid by consumers. But if taxes are so readily passed
forward to consumers, it is surprising that business fights so vehemently
against paying its share of taxes. As a generalization, most economists
agree that the ability to shift a tax depends on how competitive the market
is, and the "elasticity" of demand for a particular product. If, for example, housing is in very tight supply, increased taxes on landlords will be
largely passed along to tenants. And as in California, a tax reduction like
the one provided by Proposition 13 will benefit landlords, who know that
the market is so tight that they have no need to drop their rents. But if
demand is slack and the market won't tolerate rent hikes, then much of a
tax increase is likely to come out of the landlord's pocket. In theory, the

market tends toward equilibrium: low returns will cause landlords to quit; the housing supply will shrink; and rents will rise. Or increased populations attracted by the low rents will drive up rentals. But the persistent variations in actual prices and rentals in different housing market areas suggest that textbook equilibrium theory is often a poor proxy for reality.

Until about 1970 it was widely agreed that the property tax is a highly regressive tax. In recent years, that theory has been challenged by a number of revisionist economists, and the debates have raged back and forth in the scholarly journals. The so-called "new view" of the property tax as a progressive tax was first put forward by the economist Peter Mieszkowski on entirely theoretical grounds, and refined by Henry Aaron of the Brookings Institution, who added empirical supports.

In simple terms, the new view relies on equilibrium theory to argue that since the property tax is a tax on capital, eventually it must filter through the economy to reduce the rate of return on *all* capital. Since by definition the owners of capital are wealthy, the property tax must be a progressive tax. Henry Aaron makes the further empirical point that the statistics of *annual* family earnings do not accurately reflect true economic condition, and that many people who statistically show up as "poor" one year may really have substantial wealth. Since investment in a house is a long-term decision, Aaron contends, we should compare the property tax against the long-term income, not the annual income. By making this comparison, Aaron concludes that the property tax is not nearly as regressive as previously assumed.

Aaron's view of the property tax as progressive leads him to take a skeptical view of circuit breakers. According to Aaron, circuit breakers pay benefits to those members of a given income class who own the most property. A $10,000-a-year wage earner with a $60,000 house and a higher property tax bill gets more circuit-breaker relief than his fellow worker with a $30,000 house.

In addition, other economists have argued intuitively that any tax on wealth logically must be progressive, because it falls proportionally on the wealthy. "If one wants to escape the property tax," observes Mason Gaffney, a tax scholar of populist leanings, "there is no simpler route than being too poor to buy real estate."

Gaffney also points out that far more of the value of real estate is in the land than tax assessors normally calculate. And all economists agree that a tax on land must be absorbed by the owner of the land, since no more land can be created. Thus, the portion of the tax that falls on the land is entirely progressive.

Changing housing-consumption patterns in recent years also suggest that property tax is not as regressive as once thought. Housing, increasingly, is serving not just as shelter, but as investment. Once, people did not increase their housing expenditures proportionally as their income increased, but today a family with an income of $50,000 spends almost as large a fraction of its income on housing as a family with $10,000.

Politically, the view of the property tax as progressive began seeping into policy journals about the same time the Nixon Administration began proposing to replace the property tax with revenue sharing or a value-added tax. The proposed value-added tax, a national sales tax, has also prompted reconsideration of the property tax as a regressive tax. It may have some regressive features, people like Gaffney argue, but compared to what?

It is quite tempting to embrace the simple view that the property tax is progressive after all, because this nicely confirms that the tax revolt was simply a revolt of the haves, a rebellion by the rich against paying their share. A look at the distribution of the Proposition 13 savings is consistent with this thesis: the wealthy, who were paying taxes in proportion to the value of their homes, saved thousands; the poor saved hundreds. But even this conclusion must be qualified. The property tax is indeed proportional to income for the broad middle class, but it becomes regressive at both extremes. It punishes homeowners of modest means and taxes the wealthy more modestly in relation to their income.

As noted, it is doubtful whether general equilibrium analysis is a useful tool for viewing the property tax. Even conceding that the "average" property tax rate nationwide ultimately operates as a tax on all capital, a particular tax increase in a particular place at a particular time is absorbed by the person who pays the bill. Moreover, Aaron's view of long-term income as a more appropriate measure of ability to pay has theoretical appeal, but in the real world a pensioner who might have enjoyed high average earning once in his life must pay this year's property tax bill out of this year's income. Against the theoretical appeal of the lifetime income hypothesis is the very real appeal that he not be taxed out of his home.

Economists like to point out that homeownership is such a good deal that it ought to bear a heavy share of the property tax; homeowners benefit from their mortgage tax deduction, the imputed rental value of their house (which is not taxed), and an inflation-proof investment, all of which is true. But in recent years, an increasing portion of the net worth of ordinary people is the equity they have in their homes. Consumer savings have declined in comparison with housing values. This is both a cause and an effect of the inflation in housing prices. The result is that most of the wealth held by working people is taxed at increasing rates, while the large proportion of the holdings of the well-to-do—fine art, gold, stocks, bonds, expensive furniture—are not taxed as property.

And as economist Dick Netzer and others have pointed out, the most devastating refutation of the "new view" of the property tax is that it largely ignores the property tax *as it works in practice*. Arguably, if all property were assessed uniformly and all jurisdictions paid the same tax rate, the property tax might be progressive or at least proportional to income. But in practice, poor people's homes are assessed at a higher fraction of worth than the houses of the rich, and poor communities pay at higher tax rates than rich ones. In addition, not all wealth is taxed. Netzer has written: "It is possible to grant virtually all of the points of the revisionist critics and still maintain that the property tax in practice in most metropolitan areas is distinctly regressive."

Federal income tax shelters provide a useful analogy. In theory, the federal income tax is highly graduated. But most economists agree that the income tax in practice is virtually flat, thanks to tax shelters that primarily benefit the well-to-do. At first glance, the property tax seems mercifully free of shelters, which lends credence to the idea that it is a progressive tax. If your house is worth $100,000, you pay tax on $100,000. But the fact that cheaper housing tends to be both assessed and taxed at higher rates shelters the wealthy from paying their full share of the load. Further, abatements on commercial and industrial property taxes have become the property-tax equivalent of income tax shelters. All of this makes the property tax far more regressive than it first appears.

Most likely, the property tax is proportional to income in the middle and upper-middle ranges of income. That's why it hurt those California homeowners. But it is a particularly bad deal for the poor and the near poor, those who have managed to scrape together the money to buy a home and have trouble hanging onto it during lean years. It also falls lightly on the very wealthy. A well-to-do physician may keep trading up to bigger and better houses as he climbs the income ladder. But beyond a certain point, housing soaks up substantially less than the benchmark 25 percent of income. Most millionaires don't build castles. And most states don't tax Renoirs.

As for the supposed ability of commercial and industrial taxpayers to shift their property taxes onto consumers, in the real world this varies widely with industry, company, and location. In theory, public utilities whose rates of return are regulated shift virtually all their property tax to consumers. Yet utilities have been the most litigious of taxpayers in struggling to reduce their property taxes. Regardless of the ultimate incidence of commercial and industrial property taxes, the pertinently political fact is that in recent years residential housing has picked up an increasing share of the tax burden once paid by business taxpayers. It doesn't really matter that some business taxes may ultimately be paid by consumers, because the shift has increased the felt burden of the property tax, on consumers here and now, and that is what counts politically.

The theoretical debates on the incidence of the property tax can reach absurd lengths, which become a kind of modern scholasticism that leaves the real world far behind. At a recent colloquium on the effects of Proposition 13, one economist used equilibrium analysis to demonstrate that Proposition 13 could be regarded as highly progressive, because it increased the effective rate of return on capital investment in California, which made California more competitive compared with other regional economies, which in turn lowered the cost of goods and services in California, which helped the poor, who spend relatively more of their income on goods and services.

Under this approach, it doesn't matter who got how much of the Proposition 13 windfall. And under questioning, this theoretician indeed revealed that he had performed almost every conceivable calculation other than considering the actual distribution of the tax cut, which of course was highly regressive.

It was never the theoretical equity of the property tax that was at issue—but its practical application. Professor Seligman and his brethren also recognized that the property tax could be a marvelous instrument of public finance, if it ever could be administered well and allocated equitably.

And that, of course, was the whole problem, as it remains nearly a century later. In practice, the property tax was—and is—a mess. The economists of Seligman's day did not have the benefit of the elaborate formal modeling that dominates the economics profession today, but they were far shrewder observers and critics of the political economy around them.

PART III

Haves
and
Have-Nots

12

THE SHATTERED KEYNESIAN CONTRACT

The harvest is past
The summer is ended
And we are not saved.

—*Jeremiah*

THE GATHERING ECONOMIC CRISIS of the late seventies produced the most unlikely political ramifications. For the first time since the Great Depression, large numbers of ordinary people suffered a real decline in their living standards. Yet this time, economic discontent did not create political pressure for more equity. Instead, the economic gloom nurtured a reaction against government intervention and a resurrection of pre-Depression trickle-down economics.

Stagflation—the logically impossible combination of rising prices and declining production increased discontent among all economic groups. Inflation hit people of moderate means with added force, because prices rose fastest for the basic goods that make up most of the family budget —food, housing, energy, and medical care. But the well-to-do also had cause to complain. Inflation seemed to raise prices everywhere but on Wall Street. The real value of investment portfolios, far from accumulating at the benchmark 6 percent per year, eroded more than 50 percent in a decade. The shrinking value of the dollar also helped debtors at the expense of creditors, and creditors tend to be haves.

The income of many of the poorest people, those on welfare, failed to keep pace with inflation as fiscally pressed states made their budget cuts in the programs commanding the least public support. In New York the legislature failed to raise the basic monthly allowance of $258 for inflation between 1974 and 1980, a period during which purchasing power dropped 50 percent. In Connecticut, welfare benefits rose 44 percent between 1972 and 1980, while the cost of living rose 76 percent. The pattern was the same in most industrial states. While family income *as a whole* kept slightly ahead of inflation until stagflation worsened in 1979, the income of many population groups did not. Blue-collar wage earners generally had lower purchasing power in 1979 than in 1967. Boston's substitute teachers have had no pay raises since 1975. California's public-hospital nurses have seen their salaries fall further and further behind those in private hospitals. The averages simply fail to tell the story.

But if inflation hurt the poor more than the rich, it produced some relative winners and losers at all income levels.

Moderate-income people who happened to have cost-of-living clauses in their pensions or wage contracts were hurt less than other wage earners. Real social security increases reduced the percentage of elderly poor. Moderate-income people who already owned homes benefited from the inflation in housing prices, while wage earners who rented did not. In general, small savers with interest rates limited by federal regulation found their savings eroded, while more-affluent investors were better able to find money-market investments to stay even with inflation. Those haves who invested in real estate did quite well indeed.

The urban professional class found itself nicely ahead of inflation thanks to the new popularity of feminism and two-income families. Female labor participation rates among the poor increased far less, because wives were already working. And they were working as secretaries and dime store clerks, not lawyers and doctors.

Within these murky currents and countercurrents a few trends stood out unmistakably: most people, contrary to their expectations, ceased to earn more real money every year. Inflation played havoc with people's economic planning, at all income levels. The slight redistribution of income toward the poorest Americans was paid for by slightly higher taxes on the middle class, not the wealthy. And the economic technicians suddenly lost their powers.

For two generations, the mainstream assumptions of American economic policy rested on the Keynesian bargain: prosperity would buy increasingly generous social benefits, and public spending for those benefits would stimulate prosperity. To a society accustomed to the frugal economic precepts of Calvin or at least Benjamin Franklin, Keynesianism cloaked the social pork barrel in a patina of legitimacy and moral purpose. Not only would the public spending purchase a more just society, but it would actually energize the private economy. Deeper, darker distributional conflicts would be mooted by the expanding pie. In John Kennedy's loftier metaphor, the rising tide would lift all the boats.

This convenient Keynesian social contract informed the American political economy—as long as the economy continued to prosper. When the economy faltered, Keynesian intellectual dominance collapsed.

Throughout the steady postwar boom, as long as most people continued to make real economic gains, the relative size of the public sector was not a major issue, except to ideological hard-core conservatives. The manipulations of aggregate demand and the money supply worked—and nothing succeeded like success. Even Nixon pronounced himself a Keynesian.

By the mid-seventies, however, the after-tax income of most people stopped increasing. Not because taxes were so much bigger, but because the economy as a whole slowed down.

The tax burden, however, was a magnificent scapegoat.

The signal success of political conservatives was to convince a growing public that stagflation resulted from excess government size as well as misguided government policy, and that a revived version of trickle-down would get the economy moving again. (In the 1980s Americans have come to view inflation as erosion of income. But of course, it does not have to be. For the wage earner, the issue is not whether his paycheck has inflated in nominal dollar value from $100 to $110, but what the $110 buys. If it buys only $95 worth of goods, he is in trouble. If wages stay ahead of prices, nobody really minds. Some countries such as Brazil and Japan have managed to combine inflation with real economic growth for decades, and indeed galloping inflation in Brazil has been entirely compatible with a real boom for the middle and upper classes, which scarcely touched the living standards of the poor.)

But as real purchasing power stagnated in the United States, the psychology of inflation made government spending a logical scapegoat. As Lester Thurow has observed, if your wages go up $75 and inflation takes $60 of that away, people feel cheated; they feel that something they "earned" was taken unfairly. It does not occur that without inflation, wages would have gone up far less than $75. Whom to blame? Blame the government.

"Everybody thinks they earn their money by merit, and somebody must be taking it away. In a noninflationary world, you would have to blame income drops on yourself or your own bad luck. In an inflationary world, you can say, 'I would have made it if those bastards hadn't screwed up the system.' Inflation converts personal problems into social problems,'' Thurow says.

STAGFLATION AND TAX REVOLT

Blaming inflation on excess public spending is the centerpiece of the new trickle-down dogma, which has capitalized so skillfully on generalized economic frustration. The conservative critics are right about one thing: expectation of steady economic gain is so entrenched in the national psychology that both the government and the private sector resisted making hard distributional choices as the economy slowed down.

Whether you're General Motors or a federal agency, it is much less painful to pass along the costs of inflation to the larger economy than to tighten your own belt. Raising wages or social program budgets to compensate for the last round of inflation admittedly sows more inflation—but the alternative is to make the lower and middle classes pay disproportionately for the real economic slowdown. The last time deflationary policies were applied to a stagnating economy was during the first years of the Great Depression.

''The government'' as the arbiter of national choices can be blamed for continued inflation in this sense: throughout the seventies both of the two Republican Presidents and the one Democratic President resisted curing inflation by turning stagnation into depression. The biggest deficits of the decade—in 1975 and 1976—were incurred under President Ford, whose advisors warned that failure to stimulate the economy would only cause it to sag further. The deficits occurred not because Ford had expanded government programs—but because the recession led to reduced production, and diminished tax receipts.

But the case that excess public spending *caused* stagflation in the first place is much harder to make. The relative size of the federal budget has hovered around 21 percent of gross national product, give or take a point, for over a decade. The peak year was 1969, at the height of the Vietnam War, and even the 1969 budget absorbed only 3 percent more of GNP than the 1961 budget. Of the real increases in public spending since 1961, the biggest share went to social security payments to the elderly, which are widely considered neither wasteful nor inflationary. But with the number of retired people steadily growing, as compared with the number of working people, even modest increases in pension levels are very costly to the rest of the society.

There is a far more plausible (and discomforting) explanation than "government spending" for the maddening condition of stagflation. The thirty years of steady economic growth and widening prosperity, which Americans came to regard as natural, were really an exceptional period, characterized by conditions unlikely to recur so fortuitously ever again: American domination of the world economy, weakened competition from Europe and Japan, and falling commodity prices, especially energy. Given these remarkable conditions, the American economy could enjoy steady growth with moderately rising prices.

Under these circumstances, the electorate could graciously accept a small degree of income redistribution, mainly from the middle class to the poor. This was not terribly painful, because real per capita income was rising substantially. In constant dollars, per capita income rose from $2,696 to $3,515 between 1959 and 1969. And the number of people officially classified as poor dropped from 22 percent to 12 percent of the population. But during the same period, the dollar earnings of poor people fell further behind those of the nonpoor.*

An entire generation of economists came of age believing that economics had become a science, and steady growth was merely a matter of keeping the machine precisely tuned. In the fifties the main worry for American macro-economic technicians was a persistent surplus in the U.S. balance of payments. As late as the mid-sixties, a best seller in Europe could be titled *Le Défi Américain—The American Challenge—* warning that the towering dominance of the American economy was in danger of overwhelming Europe's control of its domestic resources.

Until the late sixties the industrial West, the United States in particular, dominated the world economy. Technological advances, high capital investment, and effective political domination over the economies of weak Third World countries produced a very high rate of return for the investing companies, improving terms of trade between producers of manufactured goods and suppliers of raw materials, with plentiful materials at low prices, for the West. In 1971 the index of world commodity prices stood below where it had been in 1956; it had hardly fluctuated for two decades. Petroleum was selling for $3.50 a barrel. But by 1980 the commodity

---

* In 1959 the official poverty level stood at 49 percent of median income. By 1979 it had dropped to 34 percent. There were fewer poor people, but they were poorer relative to everybody else.

index quadrupled, and the price of oil was up eight fold, taking $60 billion out of the American economy in 1979.

The reversal of the long postwar trend of falling commodity prices was not just the result of growing political power of the Third World. Gradually, the economics of Western Europe and Japan gained strength compared with the U.S. economy. Their expenditures on new capital investment were higher; their machinery was newer. There were now nearly a trillion relatively affluent consumers throughout the industrial world, all demanding a U.S.-style standard of living, bidding up prices of raw materials, undermining the U.S.-dominated *Pax Economica*.

Suddenly, it seemed, several other advanced countries enjoyed consistently higher growth rates than the United States, and by the late seventies, these translated to higher per-capita incomes. This meant that the dollar had to fall in relation to other currencies. It meant that imported products sold in the U.S. became substantially more expensive. Although most other industrialized countries are far more dependent on trade than in the United States, prices on imported goods have risen faster in the U.S. than in most other countries. Using 1967 as a base year, the index of import prices had risen from 100 to 258 in the U.S. in only nine years, more than in France, Germany, and even in trade-dependent Britain.

These long-term global changes cannot be blamed on the burden of taxation in the United States, or on the size of the federal deficit. But they changed the economic game within the United States. They put upward pressure on prices, while the real rate of domestic economic growth slowed down.

Incidental events, which have been fully recounted elsewhere, also set the stage for spiraling inflation. In brief, these included the attempt in the late sixties to have both guns and butter with no tax increase; crop failures overseas, which encouraged the U.S. to remedy its balance of payments deficits with increased grain exports, raising food prices domestically; and of course OPEC. Johnson's delay in imposing a tax surcharge to pay for the war overheated the economy and set off the only true episode of textbook demand-inflation during the past decade. Later, the other external events kept the inflationary momentum going.

By the time OPEC moved to raise its oil prices in 1973, American economic technicians were already living in a new, uncomfortable world where the textbook remedies no longer worked. The supposedly precise trade-off between unemployment and inflation now functioned only at the extremes: a depression would certainly bring down prices; conversely, massive deficit spending might put some jobless people back to work. But in the politically acceptable middle ranges of moderate inflation and tolerable unemployment, the fine-tuning was gone, and the prospect was for more of both.

The monetarists fared almost as badly as the Keynesians. Just as the United States ceased to dominate trade, it no longer controlled monetary movements—other people's or even its own. Beginning in the early sixties, dollars held outside the United States became a significant international financial reserve. These so-called Eurodollars—dollars on account in European banks—could be borrowed by multinational corporations. American regulations did not extend to these holdings. Interest rates on Eurodollar loans fluctuated independently, regardless of what the Federal Reserve Board and the world's other central bankers did to tighten or loosen credit. By 1978, dollars held outside the United States exceeded the domestic money supply, and the total value of Eurocurrencies (currencies held in countries other than the issuing country) ran into the trillions. With so much currency floating freely, the world's central bankers, in effect, had lost half of their monetary rudder.

Raw materials presented another unprecedented problem. Until the seventies, the neo-Keynesian economic models concentrated on the manipulation of *demand*. Government spending could manipulate the total demand in the economy to the point where nearly full employment and full use of productive capacity would be reached; when the machine began overheating, the screws would be tightened just enough to damp down demand, but without setting off a depression. Now, suddenly, the problem was *supply:* long-term scarcity of just about everything that an advanced industrialized economy needed to function. Supply problems did not lend themselves readily to Keynesian manipulation. The price of oil could quadruple, but there was only so much oil in the ground. And there were other industrial countries with bigger bankrolls. If the price rose high enough, eventually people would cut down their consumption, and in the long run, new competing energy technologies might prove economic. But in the meantime, the rest of the economy could sputter into stall speed because of all the resources being diverted to pay for energy and other newly expensive raw materials. Rather than being antithetical, externally imposed price inflation and domestic stagnation could reinforce each other.

Domestically, much of the American economy had become indexed for inflation, almost by inadvertence. Union contracts contained cost-of-living escalator clauses. Social security was automatically adjusted to the cost of living. Rising prices created a spend-now psychology, because goods were a more effective hedge against inflation than dollars. Neither the stock market nor, by the late seventies, interest rates kept pace with inflation. Saving became a foolish strategy, borrowing a shrewd one. All of which fueled inflation further.

Consequently, the Federal Reserve could raise interest rates in the late seventies, but this did not have a depressing effect on economic activity; rather, the public just kept on borrowing. Consumers took out auto loans at 14 percent because the high interest rate signaled that cars would only become more expensive next year. Corporations continued borrowing, because the high interest rates could be passed along in the form of higher prices. Consumer credit had replaced government spending as the engine that kept aggregate demand at full tilt.

In the years before the Great Depression, business cycles were steeper, depressions occurred periodically, and prices fluctuated down as well as up. But after World War II, the expectation of stability and mild price inflation had become so well entrenched that economic behavior changed, and some degree of inflation became a permanent condition of the economy. Because companies and workers both expect recessions to be shallow and temporary, firms continue to invest and workers maintain their wage demands even during periods of economic slump.

Inflation, in short, had become chronic. The last episode of inflation that resulted substantially from overheated demand was the guns-and-butter inflation of the early Vietnam War years. The inflation of the seventies occurred during a period of relatively high unemployment and significant idle productive capacity. Since this inflation is not primarily the result of overheated demand, it is not a phenomenon that responds dramatically to cuts in public-sector spending. According to the congressional budget office, each reduction in federal spending by $10 billion would reduce the rate of inflation by just one-tenth of one percent. Only if the federal budget were cut so deeply as to induce massive unemployment would there be a significant easing of inflation.

TRICKLE-DOWN REBORN

Politically, however, it didn't matter much that the inflation of the late seventies was created by events and trends independent of the size of the federal deficit or the level of taxation. The Keynesian party was the party in power, and the party in power was failing to make the economy work.

The opposition, except for a rather weak left opposition, was the party of trickle-down economics, which blamed inflation and most other economic ills on high taxes, redistribution of income, and government spending. Economists have continued to debate the logically contradictory condition of inflation combined with stagnation, its cause, cure, victims, and beneficiaries. But surely one beneficiary is a reborn laissez-faire economics. If most observers remain baffled by stagflation, political conservatives seem quite certain of a series of interconnected postulates:

Never mind OPEC, inflation is caused by the U.S. government. Federal deficits create excess demand in the economy, and when these deficits are monetarized the government prints too many dollars for the available supply of goods and services. Politically, the deficits and hence the inflation are the result of too much democracy: Congress cannot resist pandering to all the demands of newly enfranchised special-interest groups (who of course tend to be have-nots). Rather than exercising self-restraint, Congress tries to dish out more than 100 percent of the available pie, creating deficits and inflation for all.

The taxes required to pay for this largesse destroy initiative, the true source of all productivity. Regulation hobbles American productivity. In particular, taxation of the well-to-do retards productive investment (capital formation), which is necessary for economic growth. Economic growth, in turn, is the precondition of better living standards for the have-nots. Therefore, those who want equity for the have-nots, had better begin by lowering taxes on the haves.

Government is addicted to inflation, not only because it produces a bigger pie to distribute to special interests, but because inflation is the tax collector's best friend. Under the graduated income tax, inflation pushes wage earners into ever higher brackets, producing more revenue without the need to raise tax rates.

Thanks to the frustrations of stagflation, this new laissez-faire doctrine is taken very seriously. It has gained surprisingly wide currency in editorial columns of major newspapers, as well as the corporate op-ed advertising. It is increasingly accepted in Congress and the budget office, as well as in the more traditionally conservative Treasury and the Federal Reserve. And it fills the pages of the neoconservative policy journals— not just *Commentary, The Public Interest,* and the American Enterprise Institute's new shelfful of publications, but such formerly liberal magazines as *Harper's* and *The Washington Monthly.*

A lobby pressing for lower tax burdens on the well-to-do calls itself the American Council for Capital Formation, since "capital formation" is a far more virtuous objective than just plain wealth. All of this is as old as the Protestant Reformation. The wealthy classes have traditionally justified a highly unequal distribution of wealth and income with the claim that they are doing good by doing well. (On the other hand, the fainthearted liberals in the permanent professional class that populates Washington have grown far less confident of their right to do moderately well by doing good.)

The reason trickle-down economics is being taken seriously again probably has more to do with the stagnation part of the present economic malaise. Inflation was tolerated and even welcomed as long as it seemed to be stimulating economic growth and most people stayed ahead of it. One political scientist used to justify the mild, tonic inflation of the Kennedy-Johnson years by inviting students to choose between a 1947 Sears catalog with 1947 wages and a 1967 catalog at a 1967 wage. Plainly, even though the currency had inflated, the money bought more in 1967, and the products were better. But the same choice between 1967 and 1977 would be a much closer call. And the issue is not so much the higher and more unsettling price inflation of the last decade, as the stagnation in real economic gains. Nineteen seventy-nine wages barely bought what 1969 wages bought. During 1979, when wages rose 8.7 percent, consumer prices jumped 13.3 percent.

The conservative diagnosis rests on the assumption that the tax level in the United States is excessive, that there has been so much income redistribution at the expense of the well-to-do that the most talented among us are not putting forth their best efforts because most of the money would only go to the tax collector, and that inflation has been a means for government to redistribute income and wealth from haves to have-nots. Each of these assumptions is worth considering in careful detail.

TAX BURDEN

In reality, the United States ranks eleventh out of twelve major industrial nations in the share of personal income taken by the tax collector. Only Japan has lower effective tax rates. And while neoconservative economists attribute Japan's phenomenal growth to its low taxes, other nations with a much higher tax bite also have highly dynamic economies. West Germany, with the healthiest economy in Europe, taxes about 44 percent of its GNP, compared with 34 percent in the U.S. Indeed, using 1955 as a base year, the public sector share of the economy has grown at a slower rate in the U.S. than in any other industrial country in the world. Using 1962 as a base, the U.S. has had the least government growth of any country save France. In the U.S., federal spending increased from 29.5 percent to 34.0 percent of gross domestic product between 1962 and 1975. During the same period, public spending in Germany, Britain, Italy, every Scandinavian country, Canada, Australia, Holland, Belgium, Austria, and even Japan, increased at a faster rate—and most of these countries enjoyed higher rates of economic growth as well.

The more-telling figure is that while taxes were rising faster in Europe than the U.S., after-tax income was also rising faster, thanks to Europe's higher rate of growth. Real spendable wages increased at an annual rate of 1.5 percent in the U.S. during the sixties, compared with an average for all industrialized democracies of 3.2 percent; and between 1969 and 1975 the annual rate of increase in the U.S. dropped to only two-tenths of one percent, compared with 2.9 percent for the other countries. Moreover, only in Britain and the U.S. are public employee salaries on average lower than private sector salaries.

A favorite claim in the tax revolt rhetoric is that "you have to work until the end of May just to pay the government"—as if the money expended through the public sector somehow left the economy. In reality, tax dollars pay for services, and they also pay for all or part of many Americans' salaries. Much of the reason that Japan's tax bite is low is that social services, including pensions and medical care, are financed largely by Japanese corporations, but the proportion of national income spent on these services is quite similar to that in the United States.

Far from radically redistributing income, the tax system in the United States alters the income distribution only slightly. Tax reforms enacted in 1969 and 1976 made the federal income tax slightly more graduated, mainly by lowering the rates on the poor and closing some loopholes. But the 1978 tax legislation erased many of the earlier gains. The incidence of federal spending is also mildly redistributive. But a closer look at the statistics suggests that the improved income for the poor provided by government has come largely at the expense of the middle class.

Tax shelters continue to limit the effective tax burden for the well-to-do, while effective rates for the middle class have crept up. A comparison of the tax load on average-income families and high-income families is quite instructive. In 1953 an average-income family with earnings of $5,000 paid a total tax of 11.8 percent. A family with four times the income ($20,000) was taxed at nearly twice the rate (20.2 percent). By 1966 the average family was taxed at 17.8 percent, but the upper-income family's total tax had risen only slightly, to 23.4 percent. By 1977 the respective figures were 22.5 percent and 31.4 percent. Instead of twice the rate of tax, the wealthy family was taxed at only half again as much.

The classic study of the distribution of the total tax burden, Pechman and Okner's *Who Bears the Tax Burden?*, concludes that despite graduated income tax brackets, the true tax burden in the United States is virtually flat at all income levels, rising slightly for the very poor and the very rich. That is, most income groups pay about the same share of their real income to the tax collector. At the upper end, graduated rates are substantially offset by tax preferences; at the lower end, consumption taxes, payroll taxes, and property tax disproportionately increase the tax burden on the poor. This remains true, regardless of what assumptions one uses about the final incidence of taxes.

While the distribution of federal taxes became slightly more graduated during the sixties and seventies, the federal income tax burden, as a share of the average family's income, remained virtually constant. The big increases came in the form of higher sales taxes, property taxes, and social security payroll taxes, all of which fall most heavily on people of moderate means.

SOCIAL SECURITY

Much of the increase in the tax load on low- and middle-income Americans is the result of higher social security taxes, which have skyrocketed in recent years. Payroll taxes have gone up as a result of both higher rates and steep increases in the wage base.

As recently as 1965, employees paid a tax of 3.625 percent on income up to $4,800, for a maximum annual social security tax of only $174. By 1980, the tax rate had risen to 6.13 percent, and the wage base had skyrocketed to $25,900, for a maximum tax of $1,588. This meant that a moderate-income family with two $12,000 wage earners and several children could pay more social security taxes than income taxes.

During the seventies, these social security increases hit middle-income voters with special force. A low-income wage earner was already paying maximum social security taxes on his earnings. And even with a social security wage base as high as $25,900, a $60,000-a-year professional still escaped taxation on more than half his earnings. But as the wage base crept up during the seventies, most moderate-income wage earners who had been accustomed to avoiding social security taxation on at least part of their paycheck now found substantially all of their income subject to rising social security tax rates. In FY 1979–80, social security taxes brought in $139 billion, or 29 percent of the federal budget, up from 10 percent in 1954 and 20 percent in 1964.

Why did social security tax burdens rise so sharply? In part, the population was growing older, leaving fewer wage earners to support the pensions of retirees. Secondly, only in the sixties did the social security system "mature," meaning that all retirees finally had spent enough years paying social security taxes since the system's founding in 1935 to qualify for their maximum benefit. Finally, thanks to the new political influence of the growing legions of senior citizens, Congress regularly extended coverage and raised the minimum benefit.

The increase in real purchasing power of the average social security check was fairly modest, but coupled with the larger ratio of retirees to workers, even modest increases required sharply higher taxes.

And in an era of supposed tax revolt and heightened budgetary consciousness, the obvious remedy of delaying the retirement age failed to win the most perfunctory hearing, let alone win enactment.

Social security is probably the most valid—and the most costly—example of what right-wing critics have attacked as the pork-barrel state, defined as a political climate in which Congress can't resist increasing benefits for this or that special interest group. Over the years, Congress has gradually raised the minimum social security benefit to guarantee a basic pension, regardless of the retiree's actual contributions to the retirement system. Average benefits have increased modestly, and coverage has been broadened to include nearly all elderly persons in the United States. In 1966, Congress approved a flat monthly benefit for all retirees at age seventy-two, a provision championed by Republican Senator Winston Prouty. And in 1972, social security benefits were indexed, to provide automatic increases. Between 1969 and 1972, real benefits, adjusted for inflation, increased 23 percent.

In 1951 the average monthly old-age benefit paid out by social security was $43.86—about 80 percent of the average *weekly* wage earned by privately employed workers. The ratio of social security benefits to wages crept up every time Congress amended the Social Security Act. By 1971 the pensioner's monthly benefit surpassed the worker's weekly wage. This increase was hardly lavish, but combined with the growing ratio of pensioners to workers, it caused the current social security tax to sky-rocket.

While it is popularly claimed by tax rebels that rising taxes are caused by government's insatiable appetite to expand its own activities, this largest component of the increasing tax burden, social security, is nothing but an income transfer from working people to elderly people.

Despite the universal unpopularity of welfare, with its connotation of unwed mothers immorally breeding litters of bastards in order to collect welfare checks, or able-bodied men idly reaping unemployment benefits, the fact is that most income redistribution in the U.S. takes the form of social security pensions to the elderly—and the biggest real tax increases have been social security taxes.

This is likely to worsen in coming years as the population ages—and the pension liabilities for 12 million World War II veterans now reaching retirement age is also likely to increase tax pressures in the working population.

Even at the current, seemingly exorbitant payroll tax rates, American social security taxes remain among the lowest in the Western world. In the U.S., worker and employer split a total payroll tax of 12.6 percent, which finances old-age benefits, disability pensions, benefits for widows and orphans, and medicare. But this remains far below payroll tax rates in Germany, France, Britain, Italy, all the Scandinavian countries, Belgium, Holland, Austria, and only a shade higher than in Japan, where many social benefits are paid directly by the *zaibatsu*. Social security benefits are also substantially higher as a percentage of gross national product in every major industrial country but Japan.

Indeed, the U.S. is more miserly than any Western European state save Ireland in its outlays for all income maintenance purposes, not just social security. In the U.S., total spending on all forms of income main-tenance—unemployment compensation, welfare, veterans' pensions, etc., as well as social security—consumed approximately 7 to 8 percent of gross domestic product in recent years. Western European countries typically spend in the range of 12 to 15 percent.

Other advanced countries not only provide more-generous basic bene-fits; they provide whole categories of cash transfer benefits that do not exist in the United States, such as universal child allowances and pay-ments to compensate for short-term sickness. The countries of the Euro-pean Common Market, for example, spend about one percent of their entire domestic product on child allowances, which is twice what the U.S. spends on its highly controversial Aid to Families with Dependent Children.

Moreover, the rate of increase in income maintenance outlays was also higher during the sixties and early seventies in other industrialized countries. Only if we measure the rate of increase in transfer payments against the increase in national income per capita is the American increase slightly above average. And this, of course, again suggests that our problem is not an increase in welfare spending so much as a slowdown in economic growth, and that the slowdown in growth cannot fairly be blamed on an increase in social programs or tax levels.

Europe, with a much faster rate of economic growth, is also far more generous toward its needy.

POVERTY AND INCOME DISTRIBUTION

Neoconservative critics have had a field day manipulating statistics in their effort to prove that the United States is suffering the effects of an orgy of egalitarian income redistribution. The classic of the genre was entitled "How Much More Equality Can We Afford?," written by Edgar Browning in *The Public Interest* magazine in 1976. Browning took the official "poverty gap"—the total deficit in the income of officially "poor" Americans—and compared this figure with the amount spent by the government on social welfare programs, which came to $1,139 per poor person. Browning then breathlessly reported that when federal cash transfer payments were added to in-kind transfers such as subsidized housing and medical care, the total expenditure more than equaled the poverty gap.

He concluded: "When in-kind transfers are counted as income, the average poor family had an income that was approximately 30% above the poverty line. In terms of the average income of officially poor families, there is practically no poverty—statistically speaking in the United States today; and, indeed, there has not been for several years. It remains only for our accounting procedures to be modified to record this achievement!"

The only problem with this heartwarming statistical elimination of poverty was that many of the social welfare dollars counted by Browning in his figures went to Americans who are not poor. For example, a large share of housing subsidy dollars flow to people not officially counted as poor, and most poor people live in unsubsidized housing.

By 1978, even with increased cash transfer payments, 25 million Americans were still officially classified as poor. And the in-kind transfers, such as food stamps, medicaid, and public housing, went only part of the way toward making up the gap.

But this statistical sorcery remains a favorite device of the trickle-downers. In a full-page *Wall Street Journal* ad paid for by the Smith Kline Corporation, former Treasury Secretary William Simon, who certainly should have known better, proposed to take the total federal "social welfare" *increases* between 1965 and 1975, amounting to $209 billion, and simply give them to the poor. According to Simon, this would have produced $8,000 a year for every poor person in America. Unfortunately, Simon's calculations include virtually the entire federal domestic budget, even social security. In reality, most of the increase in federal spending of the past fifteen years did not go to the poor. In one of the most careful studies of antipoverty programs, economist Henry Aaron calculates that expenditures on poor people increased from $6 billion in 1965 to $34.5 billion in 1976. As a percentage of federal spending, programs directed at the poor increased from 5.2 percent of the federal budget in 1965 to 9.4 percent in 1976, down from a peak of 11.2 percent in 1973. However, something like five-sixths of federal domestic spending goes to people who are not necessarily poor—social security, medicare, public health, education, veterans' programs, transportation, urban renewal, environmental and energy spending, all of which benefit middle- and upper-income people as well as the poor.

On balance, neither the distribution of tax collections, nor the pattern of federal spending, significantly redistributed income or wealth in America.

The actual redistribution of income accomplished by antipoverty programs was slight and temporary. Between 1960 and 1965, according to the Census, the income after redistribution realized by the poorest fifth of the population increased from 4.8 percent to 5.2 percent. It peaked at 5.4 percent in 1970 and dropped back to 5.2 percent by 1977. The income of the richest fifth dipped briefly during the sixties and early seventies. By 1977 it was 41.5 percent higher than its 1960 share.

If these figures fail to take into account some of the in-kind income of the very poor, they also leave out some of the real income of the very rich, such as income from tax-exempt bonds, tax deductible meals and vacations, autos, and other perks that are not reported.

At the very lowest end of the income spectrum, the number of people officially counted as poor declined from 39.4 million in 1969, when the federal government began collecting such statistics, to 24.7 million in 1978. All told, the Federal government now spends about $50 billion on outlays aimed primarily at the poor—about 2 percent of gross national product. As noted, this slight income redistribution has been financed mainly by increasing taxes on the middle class.

But even this accomplishment is deceptive. As many studies have documented, the increase in cash transfers and in-kind subsidies serves mainly to offset the growing disparity in pre-tax of dollar earnings, not to effectively redistribute final income.

All told, the United States has one of the least egalitarian distributions of income in the industrialized world, both before and after the slight redistributive effects of the tax system. According to a study published by the Organization for Economic Cooperation and Development (OECD), the United States ranks second only to France among major industrial countries in its income inequality. Salary and wealth inequalities in America are changed only slightly by the impact of taxation. Before taxes, the poorest fifth of the U.S. population received 3.8 percent of total U.S. income; after taxes their share increases to only 4.5 percent. At the other extreme, the wealthiest tenth of the U.S. population received 28.4 percent of the total income before taxes, and only a bit less, 26.6 percent afterward.

In West Germany, the bottom fifth of the population received 6.5 percent of post-tax income, 40 percent more than the poorest fifth in the U.S. And the pre-tax distribution of income in Germany was also substantially more egalitarian than the American. Even Japan, with a lower total tax load, also had a much more egalitarian income distribution than the U.S., both before and after taxes.

Much of the disparity results because wage and salary differentials between workers and executives, or between low-skill and high-skill jobs, are simply greater to begin with in the United States, and are not significantly changed by the allocation of taxes or services.

Another international study compared the ratio of high-income families (at the 95th percentile) to low-income families (at the 5th percentile) in major industrialized nations and found that the ratio in the U.S. was 13.3 to 1, compared with 5.9 to 1 in Britain and 3.0 to 1 in Sweden. The U.S. had the worst maldistribution of income of any industrialized nation.

According to the Swedish tax scholar Nils Mattsson, when the redistributive effects of both taxation and transfer payments are taken into account, the disparity between the average income of Swedes in the top 10 percent and the bottom 10 percent drops to below 2 to 1. And this occurs in a country with a higher rate of economic growth than our own.

Although a number of economists contend that productive efficiency and social equality are incompatible and must be viewed as a trade-off, cross-country comparisons prove very revealing. The reality is that a high rate of economic growth is quite compatible with either a high degree of income equality or a low one. Productive investment depends on what fraction of total national income society saves and how wisely it is invested. Many countries with far higher rates of savings and productivity growth than the U.S. also have much more egalitarian distributions of wealth and income. Despite the odd vogue of the new "supply-side economics" promoted by Dr. Laffer and others, the fact is that inequality is only one of many possible strategies for economic growth.

TOO MUCH EQUALITY?

Despite the unfortunate condition of the stock market, several developments have combined during the seventies to limit the supposedly relentless march toward greater income equality. Social welfare spending on the poor has declined as a percentage of gross national product, after increasing during late sixties. The 1978 "tax reform" act concentrated most of the tax reduction in upper-income brackets, reversing the trend of earlier tax bills which gave more benefits to low- and middle-income taxpayers. After the civil rights gains of the sixties, black household income ceased increasing in relation to white household income, then began to decline again, dropping to only 57 percent of white income. And several social trends left upper-income consumers better protected against stagflation.

As economists Leslie Nulty and Gar Alperovitz have shown, the cost of basic commodities has increased at a faster rate than inflation generally. According to Nulty, 70 percent of Americans spend 85 percent of their disposable income on food, shelter, medical care, and energy. These "four necessities" have increased far faster than the consumer price index average. Discretionary items have appreciated in cost at a slower rate. Thus, working people as a group have suffered more erosion of their purchasing power than the official statistics show, and the well-off have suffered less.

In addition, feminism and the two-income, professional couple have kept innumerable upper-middle-income families well ahead of inflation. The working wife has traditionally been a far more common fixture of blue-collar families—as a matter of economic necessity, and female labor-force participation has been highest of all among blacks. As real income stagnated and prices continued to soar during the seventies, many lower-income families simply did not have the option of sending additional members out to work, because they were already working. But the newly enlarged class of professional women helped more affluent families stay well ahead of inflation.

Between 1969 and 1973, for example, the labor force participation rate of wives whose husbands earned $6,000 to $9,999 rose 30 percent. But in the $15,000 to $24,999 group, it rose 52 percent. And for husbands earning more than $25,000, wives' entry into the job market went up 79 percent.

By the same token, changing social patterns have increased discretionary income disproportionately for the better-educated and generally more-affluent classes. Any retailer or adman aiming for an upscale market knows where the discretionary income is: single professionals (or professional singles), gays, and highly educated couples deferring childbearing or having small families.

The result has been a strange, last-days-of Rome psychology, for the well-to-do. As economic confidence has worsened, spending has increased, especially among upper-middle- and upper-income Americans, who have been able to maintain their standard of living.

The consumption patterns of the late seventies invite a revealing comparison with those of the fifties. In *The Affluent Society,* John Kenneth Galbraith looked at the new, mass-consumption society of the early postwar period and saw in it an almost sinful gluttony of private excess while public needs starved. But in those years, at least, passenger railroads still ran and cities did not go bankrupt. And in retrospect, the new consumption of the postwar decade served mainly to bring middle-class amenities to masses of working people who had never before enjoyed them—a modest home of one's own, a car (or even two), basic household appliances and a TV, and later such luxuries as a dishwasher, occasional restaurant meals, and holiday travel. This new mass-consumption was diffused fairly broadly.

Compared with the lavish, elite consumption of the late seventies, the junk economy decried by Galbraith looks almost Spartan. As real economic growth has stagnated and real purchasing power has declined for many Americans, the continuing maldistribution of income has forced producers to dream up the most outlandish baubles to keep the haves spending their incomes. While the economy as a whole is faltering, Bloomingdale's continues to thrive.

High consumption today no longer means the diffusion of consumer products to a broader middle class. It means elite versions of basic goods, and expensive substitutes for products *whose original virtue was their economy:* Cuisinarts for mixers, designer jeans for Levi's, running shoes for Keds, the twenty-dollar styling-and-blow-dry for the three-dollar haircut, urban cowboy boots, gourmet cookery, and even imported water.

The cruder suburban shopping malls of the fifties are increasingly giving way to more fashionable downtown bazaars, often blending satisfyingly with architectural landmarks such as Boston's restored Quincy Market, to make the act of consuming seem less crass and more urbane. These in-town malls are obviously aimed at an upscale market, and despite stagflation, they continue to break records.

If the society is suffering from an excess of income redistribution, you couldn't tell it from Quincy Market. Somebody is staying nicely ahead of inflation—and it isn't the poor.

The egalitarianism of the sixties has been supplanted by counterculture consumption. Even former radicals have mellowed into hip consumers, who differentiate themselves from bourgeois society not by their greater compassion but by their more discerning taste. One well-known radical, after a New York dinner party, paraphrased Camus, wondering aloud whether one could love the revolution and still love Brie.

This is a dilemma that need trouble only a rather limited class. While elite consumers are having trouble finding new things to buy, prices continue to rise faster than wages for the poor.

Even as public opinion polls showed declining confidence in the economy, consumer spending continued to increase, especially for the luxury trade. *The New York Times* led its financial section, in early January, 1979, with an optimistic story headlined: RETAILERS' OUTLOOK BRIGHTENS, and recounting how sales were increasing faster than inflation. And according to a *Business Week* article describing buyers' preferences during the Christmas 1978 season, the upscale items were selling fastest: " . . . not only snug sacks (a zippered lounging blanket), but silk tunics, designer jeans, and microwave ovens.'' Orders for Mercedes-Benz autos and the new Cadillac Seville model far exceeded factory output.

Inflation also produced a special boom in the sales of luxury durable goods—the kind that hold their value. Fine art remained in high demand; jewelry sales soared; and furriers' sales broke all records, despite the fact that prices easily doubled between the middle and late seventies.

A *Wall Street Journal* article nervously appraising the outlook for sales of consumer durables during the coming recession concluded with the observation that "the only part of the furniture industry unlikely to be hurt is the most expensive furniture. That's also true of appliances.'' An executive of the high-quality, high-price Amana appliance company provided the tag line to the article. "We're on the higher end," he said. "The Cadillac doesn't follow the trend up and down. Companies that feature price will get hurt more than we will."

HOUSING

Although the rising cost of housing has produced almost as much editorial hand-wringing as the rising cost of oil, housing inflation is more of a blessing than a curse for the haves. Unlike soaring energy prices, which benefited only oil producers, housing inflation had a silver lining. If you owned a house (or could buy one) when prices started to soar, you had it made. The bigger the house, the bigger the appreciation in its value. The more assets you had, the easier you could command mortgage money, so that the capital gain would be financed by borrowing somebody else's money.

By the late seventies, tens of millions of American families had increased their net worth by tens of thousands of dollars each, simply because they happened to own homes in the early seventies.

So lucrative were the capital gains from homeownership that Congress was compelled in 1978 to liberalize the capital gain exemption to $100,000, and lower the minimum age to fifty-five, so that most middle-class emptynesters could sell their house and realize a capital gain of as much as $100,000 without having to pay the tax collector a nickel.

In a funny way, not acknowledged by the capital formation lobby, the soaring housing inflation added to the real capital formation problems. Higher real estate prices, both commercial and residential, soaked up enormous amounts of capital that would otherwise have been available for more productive uses. More directly, middle-class couples with heavy consumer debts and no money in the bank could reassure themselves that they really had substantial net worth—thanks to the entirely unearned equity in their homes. This, in turn, dampened the motivation to save. In 1970 the total value of housing owned by homeowners was $570 billion, compared with $729 billion held in stocks. By 1979 the value of the housing had soared to $1.8 trillion, while the value of stocks had increased only slightly, to $790 billion.

But the other side of the coin provided a very bleak picture indeed. Most people who rent are poor. For renters, the inflating real estate prices did not equal more money in the bank, but more money down the drain. And for those not yet in it, trying to get into the ever-appreciating housing market was like running after a bus. As you ran faster, the bus accelerated twice as fast.

The housing market of the late seventies hardened class lines between haves and have-nots in several ways. A generation ago, almost any blue-collar worker with a few hundred dollars for a down payment could get an FHA or VA loan, and buy a house, often for less than his apartment rental. Indeed, the steady shift during the fifties and sixties into home-ownership reduced demand for apartments, kept the rental market depressed, and caused rents to lag well behind inflation. (Here trickle-down worked, though only temporarily.)

By the late seventies, FHA was financing less than 10 percent of all home mortgages, and a down payment often required cash of upward of $10,000. By 1980, only 15 percent of the families could afford the payments on an average-priced new house. For many young people, home-ownership was possible only if there were enough money in the family to finance the down payment. Instead of an attainment financed by one's own labors, homeownership had become a perquisite for the class that already owned homes in a previous generation, or was otherwise wealthy. The growing condominium conversion movement further divided apartment dwellers into haves and have-nots. With fewer people moving into homeownership and more affluent young professionals favoring in-town living, the value of prime apartments began to increase faster than the general rate of inflation. Suddenly, condominiums, which have been a fixture of the tight European apartment market for generations, became economically attractive in many American cities and suburbs. Once again, for those who owned enough wealth to readily convert other net worth held in stocks, bonds, or savings into condominium equity, this was a great deal. It provided tax breaks, a guarantee against rent increases, and an inflation-proof investment. But millions of others without money for the down payment found themselves displaced into an ever-shrinking pool of available rental housing commanding higher and higher rents, with the prospect of being condo-ed out again as soon as tightened demand made their new apartments sufficiently attractive to the condo converter.

13

INFLATION AND TAXES

IF, AS LORD KEYNES WROTE, inflation "engages all the hidden forces of economic law on the side of destruction," it has distorted the tax code like a fun-house mirror. Inflation mixes poisonously with the graduated income tax to push wage earners into ever higher tax brackets far faster than their real income goes up, turning a raise into an after-tax pay-cut. And that is only the most obvious effect. Big corporations don't have that problem, because they are taxed at a nearly flat rate, but inflation seriously waters down the value of their depreciation write-offs. Machines that must be replaced at next year's higher prices are depreciated at last decade's cheaper costs. Inflation also distorts corporate "inventory profits": if a good is produced at a cost of $100, and sits in a warehouse for a year before being sold at $110 during a period of 10 percent inflation, the taxable profit is $10. But the real profit is zero.

Similarly, inflation disastrously hypos the capital gains tax on sales of stock, bonds, or houses. A stock bought for $100 in 1970 and sold for $150 in 1980 (if you could find one) lost value in real dollars. But the IRS taxes the $50 "gain" just the same. And as California voters noticed, inflation does very strange things indeed to the property tax.

The effects are quite different on different classes of taxpayers. At one income extreme, inflation plays havoc with capital gains. At the other, the effect of inflation on the income tax is particularly harsh on low-income wage earners. At lower-income levels, tax brackets are "narrower" and increase more steeply. But at the very upper end, once a wealthy taxpayer reaches the top bracket, there are no further rate increases, no matter how much further income rises due to inflation.

Thus, for example, in 1974, inflation increased income taxes by 6.6 percent on persons earning between $3,000 and $5,000 a year, but only 5.4 percent for those in the $50,000–$100,000 brackets, and just 2.6 percent for persons with incomes over $100,000.

On average, the effect of inflation on the federal income tax increases tax revenues by about $1.60 for every increased dollar of personal income because a graduated income tax taxes higher incomes at increasing rates. Take the case of a middle-income wage earner, with an income of $12,000 in 1975. In that year, his federal income tax was $1,089. If he received a 6 percent raise and earned $12,720 in 1976 that boosted his tax to $1,201. In other words, a 6 percent raise triggered a 10 percent tax hike; and in terms of real purchasing power, he was slightly worse off. Most of the cancellation of the man's raise, of course, is the result of inflation itself, but the higher tax rate frosts the cake.

Inflation so potently increases the flow of tax dollars by pushing taxpayers into higher brackets that much of the tax-revolt literature quite earnestly accuses the government of deliberately promoting inflation in order to reap unlegislated tax revenues.

This view, if slightly conspiratorial, is not entirely wrong. There is a simple enough remedy to inflationary tax-bracket creep—indexing the tax brackets—which politicians tend to shun for reasons that are partly valid and partly just convenient. Indexing the income tax would automatically adjust rates, brackets, and standard exemptions and deductions, in exact proportion to the annual rate of inflation, so that a taxpayer with the same effective purchasing power would continue to pay the same tax, unless the tax was deliberately changed by Congress.

Indexation was strenuously resisted by California Governor Jerry Brown, because Brown found it useful to watch state surpluses pile up while he kept his election pledge not to increase taxes. In California, the indexation issue cut across ideological lines, with the eventual support of both the liberal California Tax Reform Association, and the business-oriented California Taxpayers Association. It finally passed the California legislature—after voter anger erupted in Proposition 13. In the end, Brown both lost his surplus *and* had to live with indexing. By 1980, five other states—Arizona, Colorado, Iowa, Minnesota, and Wisconsin—had indexing laws.

At the federal level, indexation of the income tax has been embraced mainly by conservatives, although some reformers find it attractive too. It has been strenuously resisted by both the Treasury Department and Democratic congressional leaders, largely on three grounds.

First, obviously, from the Treasury's point of view, indexation would be "expensive"; that is, it would reduce revenues and worsen the federal deficit. It would substitute a rigid formula for an "elastic" system.

Second, many liberals and conservatives argue, indexation would weaken the government's resolve to combat inflation. Once something as basic as the income tax were automatically rendered inflation-proof, inflation would become hopelessly accepted as a given. But, goes the reply, who is kidding whom? Inflation is already hopelessly embedded in the economy. And some groups already *are* protected by automatic indexing —social security pensioners, those employees with cost-of-living escalators in their contracts, so why not the taxpayers, too?

The third objection has been stated most succinctly by that fiscal conservative Senator Russell Long. "Why give away something once," Long likes to lecture his colleagues, "when you can keep giving it away over and over again?" Congress seems to prefer adjusting the tax code every few years to compensate for inflation, rather than substituting a mechanical formula. In the absence of indexation, inflation does the dirty work of raising taxes, leaving Congress to rescue taxpayers with a "tax cut" that is seldom a true tax cut at all. With indexation, the periodic headlines would have to read: CONGRESS RAISES TAXES, rather than: CONGRESS VOTES A TAX CUT. Except for the temporary Vietnam War tax surcharge in 1969, the last time Congress actually legislated an increase in income tax rates was 1952. But Congress has rolled back rates five times since 1964 to compensate for inflation.

And in fairness to Senator Long, the rate reductions have compensated quite effectively for the impact of inflation on the income tax. Thanks to these adjustments, the average income tax rate rose only from 10.7 percent to 11.3 percent between 1960 and 1975. Virtually all the real increase occurred during the four years between 1965 and 1969, even if rising social security taxes are added in. During those four years, personal income and social security taxes taken together rose from an average 12.5 percent to 16.8 percent of income. But after 1969, effective tax rates have fluctuated narrowly, moving back to the same 16.8 percent in 1978.

According to Benjamin Okner, one of the senior tax economists at the Treasury Department, the laws enacted by Congress between 1964 and 1978 actually "overindexed" for inflation. That is, taxpayers on average got bigger rollbacks from Congressional action than they would have received under an automatic indexing formula tied to the rate of inflation.

So why all the fuss about rising taxes? In the first place, Congress might have effectively erased much of the inflation-fueled tax hikes *on average,* but the shape of the tax load had changed. Middle-income wage earners —especially those families with two workers struggling to stay ahead of inflation—got clobbered by the social security tax hikes. And state legislatures, despite their reputation for conservatism, did not act to roll back income tax rates to compensate for inflation. Like the U.S. Congress, the state legislatures resisted indexation, but, unlike the Congress, they did not regularly adjust rates and brackets downward. During the sixties and seventies, state legislatures felt growing pressure from the fiscally strapped cities to increase state aid, which gave legislators good reason to leave the rate structure alone, or even increase it. For the voter, of course, this equaled rising taxes.

Did Congress really overindex for inflation? Only for the elusive "average" taxpayer. For the real taxpayer, the impact varied for different income and population classes. During the sixties and seventies, as Congress adjusted tax rates for inflation, the tendency was to take the opportunity to make the tax system more progressive at the lower end. But because the well-to-do were so successful in resisting a shift of tax burdens to them, this meant a shift of burdens onto the middle class.

As an antipoverty measure, millions of very poor Americans were removed from the tax rolls altogether. Effective tax rates on low-income, blue-collar workers, increased only slightly—from 5.2 percent of total income in 1965 to 7.8 percent in 1979, for a family of four with half the median income. But for a family of four at the median income, rates increased faster than for any other group, rising from 9.4 percent in 1965 to 16.0 percent in 1979. This was a much sharper increase than for low-income families, high-income families, or singles at any income level. Some of the increase was simply a reflection of the fact that real income was rising, and higher real income is taxed at a higher rate. But for the middle-income family of four, even with the rate adjustments, the real tax burden increased faster than real income gains:

FAMILY OF FOUR AT MEDIAN INCOME
(one wage earner)

	ACTUAL INCOME	% TAX	TAX	AFTER TAX INCOME	AFTER TAX INCOME IN CONSTANT 1972 DOLLARS
1965	$ 6,957	9.4	$ 635	$ 6,322	$8,200
1979	$18,870	16.0	$3,019	$15,851	$9,724

If this family had two wage earners, then the tax burden rose even faster, because both paid increasing social security tax. In addition, a 1977 law increasing the standard deduction as a tax-simplification measure lowered effective tax rates for millions of moderate-income taxpayers, but it also eroded the middle class's favorite tax shelter, the deduction for mortgage interest and local property taxes. Thanks to the higher standard deduction, only about 25 percent of taxpayers still bother to itemize deductions, and of course these tend to be the wealthier ones. Consequently, the home mortgage interest is no longer effectively tax-deductible for the majority of moderate-income homeowners, while it continues to be a lucrative tax write-off for the wealthy.

Further, according to computations by Rudolph Penner of the conservative American Enterprise Institute, inflation increased the effective tax rate between 1963 and 1979 on incomes below $76,000. But for the very wealthiest, the effective rate in 1979 was lower than in 1963.

Inflation's distortion of the *personal* income tax is quite mild and easy to cure, compared with what inflation does to business accounting and business taxation. For the individual income tax, the remedy is simply to adjust rates, brackets, and exemption amounts to correct for inflation, either by congressional action or through an automatic formula. But businesses, by definition, produce or purchase something at one time and sell it at a later time. If the value of the dollar changes in the interim, what is the real "profit"? And suppose the value of the dollar fluctuates at different rates over time? Then what?

Congress's resistance to indexing the individual income tax may be simply a matter of political prerogative; the problem of indexing business income, deductions, capital gains, etc., presents far more intractable policy issues and technical problems.

A conference of tax scholars and economists convened by the Brookings Institution in late 1975 to discuss possible approaches to indexation identified a rat's nest of problems. Even a matter as relatively simple as indexing the capital gain on a bond provoked an extensive discussion of different accounting methods and indexation formulas, and no clear consensus on which was fairest.

Because firms in different industries vary widely in their use of capital, and their relative use of equity capital and debt capital, any consistent form of indexation would produce widely different effects on different industries. It would also, as a general rule, redistribute real income to creditors and take income away from debtors. One study concluded that if corporate accounting methods were permitted to adjust for the rate of inflation, General Motors' billion-dollar profits would suddenly be transformed into "losses," while AT&T's $3 billion profit would almost double. The problems are almost infinite, and of a technical nature beyond the scope of this book.

At bottom, the problem is that if one thing is to be indexed, then fairness dictates that everything be indexed. In a summary of the conference's findings Brookings economist Henry Aaron questioned whether America is ready for "a world in which all the effects of inflation were neutralized."

> In such a world all nominal quantities in laws or contracts would be adjusted automatically and frequently for changes in prices that had occurred since the preceding adjustment. When prices rose 10 percent the borrower who previously owed $1,000 would owe $1,100; the Congressional appropriation that had been $1 million would be $1.1 million; the personal exemption under the income tax that has been $750 would become $825; the bank account balance that had been $100 would become $110; each $10 bill would be exchanged for an $11 bill . . .

No country has indexed its economy to quite these lengths, but several countries, including Canada, Denmark, and the Netherlands, have indexed their tax systems. Even these countries, however, have continued to resort to ad hoc adjustments of tax rates, brackets, and exemptions.

Other countries, with more chronic inflation problems, such as Brazil and Israel, index wages and loans to a far greater degree than the U.S. But while this practice is creeping up on the American economy piecemeal, there is a great resistance to adopting it uniformly. The only kind of tax indexation with substantial use in the U.S. has been the sort of property tax rollback laws in effect in several states (see Chapter 8), which automatically reduce rates to compensate for increases in property assessments. As a policy matter, the problem for the U.S. is that the one form of indexation—adjustments in income tax rates—which is easiest to accomplish, is probably the least necessary because Congress makes adjustments already. The other problem—namely, inflation's distortions of business taxation—is much more in need of a remedy, but almost impossible to achieve without resorting to indexation of the entire economy.

Consequently, indexation had not won wide support either in Congress or at the state and local level by the time tax revolt broke out.

Big business's version of the tax revolt, which took Congress by storm in 1978, was primarily stimulated by inflation's frustrating effects on corporate accounting systems, and taxes on profits and capital gains.

Thanks to inflation, business enjoyed great credibility when corporate executives, their lobbyists, and academic retainers flooded Congress with statistics showing how inflation exaggerated inventory profits, reduced the value of depreciation write-offs, scared away investment capital, and depressed the stock market.

Congress was not prepared to index the entire economy, nor unfortunately was there any widely acceptable method for precisely adjusting corporate taxation to compensate for inflation. So Congress resorted to a remedy not exactly suited to the problem, but highly popular with business and wealthy investors just the same.

Congress cut taxes.

14

THE LIGHT TAXES OF THE RICH

The prosperity of the middle and lower classes depends on the good fortune and light taxes of the rich.

—Andrew Mellon, 1923

Tax reform is dead.

—Joseph Pechman, 1979

THERE IS NOTHING NEW about the claim that low taxes on the well-to-do are the key to abundance for all. The idea had great appeal during the 1920s; it formed one basis of Treasury Secretary Mellon's national economic strategy, until it was discredited by events that began in 1929—the stock market crash and the the Great Depression.

Nineteen seventy-eight, the year of the great tax revolt in the heartland, was also the year business conservatives regained the initiative in Washington, intellectually as well as tactically, and won substantial tax concessions in the name of a newly refined trickle-down economics.

In 1978 the legislative calendar began with the Carter Administration's bold program to advance tax equity and end once and for all the tax deductible three-martini lunch. It ended with a radically transformed Revenue Act of 1978, which expanded some old loopholes and opened new ones, almost exclusively for the well-to-do. By 1979, Congress's agenda of still-pending tax issues was totally transformed. The tax reform spirit of the late sixties and early seventies lay quite dead, and Congress was preoccupied with tax reduction. Not Howard Jarvis' brand of tax reduction, either. Sweeping cuts of the Jarvis variety commanded great rhetorical support, but in the end it was nicely targeted capital gains cuts, reductions in corporate taxes, and other tax preferences for the well-off that commanded votes.

If the revolt of California property owners against an oppressive property tax was something of a populist uprising, the quiet ambush of the federal capital gains tax by well-heeled business lobbyists was more like a *coup d'etat*. Until 1978, tax reformers enjoyed a decade of steady progress against tax preferences for the wealthy. Although rising payroll, property, and sales taxes raised tax burdens on working people, the distribution of the federal income tax load during the seventies did grow slightly more equitable.

The two major tax reform measures of the decade, oddly, were signed by Republican Presidents—Nixon in 1969 and Ford in 1976. Both bills were mainly the work of Congress. The 1969 act was the product of labors begun during the previous Democratic administration, combined with growing public indignation at legal tax evasion by the wealthy. Essentially, the evolution of tax gimmicks for the rich has kept pace with the evolution of the supposedly progressive income tax. In practice, the incidence of the tax system taken as a whole remains almost flat. The very wealthy, who supposedly paid taxes up to the admittedly astronomical rate of 91 percent, in fact pay perhaps 30 to 35 percent. A plethora of tax shelters are still available to any high-income person with the wit to hire an accountant: accelerated depreciation gimmickry for real estate investment, tax-free municipal bonds, and a vast array of other tax-sheltered investments could sharply reduce taxable earnings. If all else fails, the tax-writing committees of the Congress occasionally oblige well-to-do tax avoiders by writing custom-made loopholes, the most infamous of which was a specially written provision for Hollywood magnate Louis B. Mayer, which enabled him to avoid paying a tax on his lump-sum retirement benefit.

Wealth is taxed far less than income. To the extent that one's stock of wealth is held in the form of investments and not cashed in, it is never taxed. When stocks are sold, they are taxed at preferential capital gains rates, and losses could be manipulated to cancel taxes on gains. A variety of shelters assure that great wealth could be passed along from one generation to the next with minimal taxation.

Several good books written during the sixties, most notably Philip Stern's 1964 best seller *The Great Treasury Raid*, indignantly laid bare the tax gimmicks used by the affluent to escape paying a fair share of the tax burden.

During the same period, a new concept, "tax expenditures," helped the Congress and the public understand just how tax preferences worked as a form of subsidy to the rich. The term "tax expenditure" was coined by Stanley Surrey, the Harvard law professor who served as assistant treasury secretary for tax policy under Presidents Kennedy and Johnson. At the time, Congress and the Johnson Administration were grappling with how to finance the Vietnam War. By late 1967 it was clear that taxes would have to be increased or spending cut. But neither the Congress nor the White House possessed an adequate tool to identify what had long been termed simply "backdoor spending"—namely, expenditures in the form of tax preferences.

Partly in response to this frustration, Surrey's first "tax expenditure budget" in 1968 meticulously tallied all the loopholes and their public cost; it identified the capital gains exclusion as the biggest preference item, costing the Treasury some $8 billion a year in revenues, followed by deductions for state and local taxes, tax deferral on pension fund contributions, and the homeowner deduction on mortgage interest.

Surrey hoped that Johnson would seize on the tax expenditure issue as an alternative to the politically unpopular 10 percent tax surcharge. If loopholes benefiting mainly the well-to-do could be closed, there might be no need for a tax surcharge raising everyone's taxes. But Johnson was unreceptive to the plan, and the surtax became law in 1968. Nonetheless, a new idea had taken on a life of its own. There was great interest among congressional liberals and among tax scholars.

Finally, on the last day of the outgoing Johnson Administration, Surrey and his boss, Treasury Secretary Joe Barr, having failed to sway Johnson, turned over their best ammunition to Congress. In widely publicized testimony, Secretary Barr disclosed that hundreds of very wealthy Americans paid little or no federal income tax and warned of a "taxpayers revolt" by ordinary Americans resenting legal tax evasion by the well-to-do.

Ironically, when the revolt came, it would be neatly co-opted by the well-to-to and turned back against the tax reformers.

But a decade ago, the timing was excellent. The voters in 1969 were indeed resentful both of the recent tax surcharge and of the inflation that had resulted from Congress's failure to pay for the unpopular war earlier. Supporters of tax reform went on the offensive in Congress, aided by massive mail backing measures to close loopholes for the rich.

The first fruit of this agitation was the Tax Reform Act of 1969, which was carefully drafted to increase taxes only on the well-to-do: the 1969 act lowered the maximum rate on wage and salary income, but raised the effective tax rate on income from investments. Money earned by labor should not be taxed more highly than money earned by money, went the slogan. Congress left alone the 50 percent exclusion of capital gains income, but limited an alternative 25 percent capital gains rate to the first $50,000 of capital gains.

And rather than dismantle tax preferences one by one, Congress added a new "minimum tax," to be paid on most income otherwise sheltered from taxation. (Even this new minimum tax had some loopholes, however, as President Carter later found to his great embarrassment, when an investment tax credit on new peanut-shelling machinery reduced his taxable income to zero. The minimum tax, it turns out, covers only certain deductions, and doesn't affect tax credits.)

After 1969, the tide continued to run with the tax reformers.

The most respected tax policy journal was a newly launched publication called *Tax Notes,* published by the reform-oriented Tax Analysts and Advocates. Consumer activist Ralph Nader created his own formidable public interest lobby called the Tax Reform Research Group, headed by a talented young lawyer named Robert Brandon. The fledgling tax reform lobby threw an unwelcomed spotlight on the dealings of the congressional tax-writing committees, which were long accustomed to quietly writing special tax legislation for influential campaign contributors or well-connected lobbyists. It made very good copy, and the press and the tax-reform lobby fed on each other.

For example, when the upstart billionaire H. Ross Perot tried to custom-order a special loophole during the 1975 session, the ploy ended up on the front page of *The Wall Street Journal,* causing great embarrassment to both Perot and the Senate Finance Committee.

Despite the Republicans' control of the White House, and the basically conservative majorities on the tax-writing committees of both houses, the tax reform momentum continued. After several years of experimentation with control of tax expenditures, the 1974 Budget Control Act formally required a tax expenditure budget to be submitted as part of the annual budgetary process, indicating the cost of each tax preference item in lost revenue.

In 1975, Congress sharply reduced the oil depletion allowance, long a symbol of tax inequality and a prime source of legal tax evasion for the wealthy.

Again in 1976, Congress enacted a broad tax-reform measure. The main impetus for the 1976 act was the mass-marketing of artificial tax shelters, which added fresh fuel to the tax reformers' indignation. Typically, these shelters enabled a high-tax-bracket investor, often a doctor or a lawyer, to become an absentee partner in a venture that raised its own capital literally by selling shares in paper losses. These inflated artificial losses were generated by the manipulation of accelerated depreciation formulas.

Thus, a doctor could invest in a cattle ranch or a citrus grove, and in the first year alone, his share of the "loss" would save him more money on his other taxes than the total cost of the investment. Because the law permitted investors to take these losses even where their investment was borrowed money, much of the new capital raised through tax shelters wasn't really new capital at all, but money loaned by banks to the investor and then forwarded to the tax-shelter venture in exchange for the tax write-off.

Despite cries from the tax-shelter industry that this was an important way for new ventures to attract capital, feeling ran strong in Congress that mass-marketed tax shelters were abused, and after nearly three years of effort, Congress in 1976 sharply limited most tax write-offs on artificial accounting losses. The 1976 act also tightened the minimum tax provisions.

The most controversial section of the 1976 act was a provision forcing heirs to pay capital gains tax on appreciated stock they inherited. Generally, capital gains are taxed only when the gain is "realized," in other words, when the stock is sold. But the tax is avoided altogether when a stock is left to an heir. If grandfather buys a stock for $10, and wills it to grandson when the stock is trading at $100, grandson is deemed to have acquired it for $100. If the stock further appreciates to $105 and is sold, the heir pays tax only on the $5 gain. This treatment has long been attacked by tax reformers as a classic gimmick that enables the very rich to pass along tax-free wealth from one generation to the next.

In the 1976 tax reform mood, however, liberals at last gathered enough votes to change the ground rules. Henceforth, Congress decreed, the heir would inherit the old man's purchase price along with his stock. The original acquisition price, called the "basis," would carry over to the heir —hence the provision's name "carry-over basis."

Though reformers didn't get everything they wanted in the 1976 law, the prospects looked even better for 1977. Now the Democrats were retaking the White House, and under the banner of a new President whose populism might be ambiguous on other fronts but who was clearly a champion of tax reform. Carter had campaigned against the tax deductible three-martini lunch as a symbol of unjustifiable privilege, and even branded the tax code a "disgrace to the human race." His new IRS commissioner, Jerome Kurtz, was a charter member of the tax reform lobby. And the new man in Stanley Surrey's onetime job as assistant secretary of the treasury for tax policy was an inspired appointment, Lawrence Woodworth, the universally respected director of Congress's professional tax policy staff.

In his fourteen years as staff director, Woodworth had earned the respect of all the senior legislators, and he conducted himself with scrupulous professionalism; he was frequently the only man in the room who fully understood the legislative intricacies. Yet Woodworth's advice, when sought, was often discreetly shaded against tax loopholes, and Congress watchers detected in him a closet tax reformer, who might be highly influential once he was cut loose from his staff role. Woodworth brought with him to Treasury several other tax reform types for the subcabinet positions.

THIN ICE

Yet the apparent ascendancy of the tax reform mood was already deceptive. The strength of the 1976 law was more a reflection of legislative luck than strong sentiment among the electorate. Congress, in a sense, backed into the 1976 law, almost by accident.

Under the new budget process begun in 1975, Congress must decide in advance how much revenue to raise and how much to spend, before settling on the pieces of the pie. Tax expenditures are part of this process. In 1976, the new budget procedures were still unfamiliar. As the legislative year wore on, the tax-writing committees discovered that in order to make the numbers come out, they were obligated to reduce "tax expenditures," i.e., loopholes, by some $2 billion. Worse still, for the numbers to balance, some of the loophole closings had to take effect retroactively, which particularly riled up affluent taxpayers, who had already planned their annual tax-avoidance strategy.

The 1976 legislation caught most business lobbies asleep at the switch. Yet one reform against which business mounted a serious attack was easily defeated, suggesting that support for tax reform was quite soft once a serious opposition lobby mobilized: the tightening of the rules against tax shelter gimmicks originally proposed to limit artificial accounting losses in real estate investments, by tightening up depreciation schedules and limiting the paper loss to an investor's own money, as opposed to money borrowed from the bank. A hastily assembled coalition of real estate developers, brokers, and investors wrapped itself around low-income housing, which presumably stood to lose investment if the reform was enacted, and disingenuously carved out an exemption for *all* residential real estate.

Congressmen went home for the Christmas 1976 recess, to find that mass public support for tax reform was thin indeed. The provisions of the new law were extremely complicated. The only voters who knew anything about accelerated depreciation, "limitation of artificial accounting losses," and "carry-over basis," were those who *needed* to know. And they were incensed.

Most congressmen won little praise from the masses of voters who benefited slightly from the greater degree of tax equity, but they caught hell from the wealthy few who would now pay higher taxes.

In Washington, as the Carter Administration took office, the business lobbies took the candidate at his word and began bracing for the next battle. Candidate Carter had spoken of getting rid of the biggest loophole of them all, the exclusion of 50 percent of capital gains from taxation. Of all the tax preference income that Congress sought to capture by subjecting it to a minimum tax, about 75 percent came from the capital gains loophole. Any serious attack on tax inequities would go after the capital gains exclusion.

The bulk of stocks and bonds, of course, are owned by the well-to-do. The "ordinary investor" referred to in the business literature is already a lot better off than the ordinary citizen. Out of the 67 million tax returns in 1978, only 4.7 million even had taxable capital gains.

Reformers managed to tighten the capital gains loophole slightly in 1969 and again in 1976 by including capital gains in the list of items subject to a minimum tax. This meant that, in theory, a very wealthy investor with a very dumb accountant could conceivably pay a tax rate as high at 49 percent on a capital gain, although the business groups failed to find a single live, warm taxpayer who actually paid that amount. In practice, investors could still manipulate other tax preferences to plan a tax strategy, and the average capital gains rate actually paid was only about 16 percent. In 1976, only 7 percent of taxpayers with capital gains paid more than 25 percent.

But business groups generally and Wall Street in particular had reason to fear total elimination of the 50 percent capital gains exclusion. The stock market was in dismal condition, a victim largely of inflation. It had been close to a decade since the great bull market of the sixties. The little guy was out of the market, and the smart money was in real estate; new issues of stock were unmarketable. With inflation, investors paid capital gains tax on gains that were actually losses when expressed in real purchasing power. The solution to this problem, however, was indexing, not a liberalization of capital gains rates.

But indexing seemed politically impossible. Because inflation overstated the true capital gain on a stock, investors tended to hang on to what they had, rather than trade. Many on Wall Street feared that any increase in the capital gains rate would be the *coup de grace* for the flattened market.

Therefore, as President-elect Carter, the newly influential tax reform groups, and prominent legislators including Senator Kennedy laid plans to go back for what they failed to get in the mild 1976 reforms, business groups began organizing in earnest against an expected drive to get rid of the capital gains exclusion.

Capital formation, at the time, was not a sexy issue; Nixon's treasury secretary, William Simon, had sought to sound the alarms about a capital shortage, but had not found a receptive audience. Simon, a former partner in the Wall Street firm of Salomon Brothers specializing in Treasury securities, was worried that government borrowing would drive out private borrowing. He argued that the new, record peacetime deficits produced by the 1974 recession would soak up so much money from the capital markets that little would be left to finance private investment. But Simon turned out to be quite wrong, and even financial leaders took exception to his logic. Walter Wriston, chairman of Citibank, cautioned that the excess of investment needs over available capital produce a kind of permanent optical illusion. "Pick any year," Wriston commented; "compile a national shopping list of capital investment aspirations and the estimate of the financial resources to fulfill them would always fall short."

As it turned out, real interest rates stayed fairly close to the rate of inflation (in other words, the effective cost of borrowed money was close to zero), suggesting no excess demand for capital.

But where Simon's theoretical capital shortage produced mostly yawns from bankers who knew better, the threat of higher capital gains taxes hit the well-to-do where they lived, and galvanized business and financial groups into an effective lobby that would pay back the tax reformers for their successes in 1976, 1969, and then some.

Established business lobbies like the National Association of Manufacturers and the U.S. Chamber of Commerce, were not unduly upset about capital gains taxes. *Fortune* 500 corporations preferred to use their influence to bargain for investment tax credits (which mainly benefited the biggest corporations), and for a reduction in the corporate income tax.

Thus when "capital formation" finally caught on with a vengeance, the issue was orchestrated, not by the venerable business trade associations, but by newer, go-go lobbying groups formed during the early seventies —the Business Roundtable, made up of the chief executives of some 180 very large corporations, and a new group called the American Council for Capital Formation.

WALKER'S COUNCIL

The capital formation council began life with a much less sexy (and more revealing) name, the American Council on Capital Gains and Estate Taxation. In late 1975 the fledgling council enlisted as its chairman Charls Walker, probably the shrewdest business lobbyist in Washington.

Walker and the capital formation crusade were made for each other. A Ph.D. economist from north-central Texas, Walker had worked for Eisenhower's Secretary of the Treasury Robert Anderson, spent eight years as chief lobbyist for the American Bankers Association while the Democrats were in power, and then joined the Nixon Administration as deputy secretary of the treasury. Walker, watching Democratic tax reform legislation make surprising headway under a Republican administration, became convinced that business wasn't fighting hard enough. He resigned in early 1973 to form what soon became Washington's hottest lobbying-consulting firm for big corporations, Charls Walker Associates.

Within a few months, Walker had signed up as clients, GM, Ford, GE, Gulf Oil, Bethlehem Steel, Procter & Gamble, Union Carbide, Time Inc., and several other corporate giants, as well as several trade associations, including the new Business Roundtable, which he had helped to launch while still at the Treasury.

Though unmistakably Republican, Walker courted Democratic contacts with great care. James Rodney Schlesinger, Jr., aged seven, son of Carter's energy secretary, is Walker's godson. Walker boasts an intimate friendship with Democratic Representative Thomas Ashley, the floor leader of the Carter energy bill. Not surprisingly, Walker soon became an indispensable business lobbyist on energy.

Walker's astuteness as a lobbyist rests on his ability to forge coalitions. At any one time, he has dozens of projects simmering away for a diverse array of powerful corporate clients. These can be marshaled to cross-promote one another's interests, making the whole far more powerful than the parts.

The president of the capital formation council (Walker is chairman) is a man named Robert Keith Gray, whose name is even less of a household word than Charls Walker's. The council's letterhead lists Gray as "former Secretary to the Cabinet," a job he held under Eisenhower. More importantly, Gray heads the Washington office of Hill and Knowlton, the leading corporate public relations-cum-lobbying firm in the capital. Whatever corporate connections Walker lacked, Gray was likely to have. In making capital formation into a broad, national-interest issue, Walker also salted his board with prominent liberals: lawyers Edward Bennett Williams and Clark Clifford (both with big corporate clients), as well as the quixotic Eugene McCarthy.

As tax rebel, a Charls Walker is the polar opposite of a Howard Jarvis. Whereas Jarvis turned property tax reduction into a populist crusade with the endearing buffoonery of a total outsider, Walker is an insider's insider. With his formidable corporate contacts and his knowledge of Congress and the business press, Walker was positioned almost uniquely to work the three pressure points of a successful lobbying campaign—the Congress, the press, and the grass roots.

Walker brought to the business-lobbying scene a Texan flamboyance that roused the older trade associations out of their mannered eastern ways. For better than a decade, big money had been losing the tax battles; the new, effective lobbying techniques had been devised by the brash public interest groups: orchestration of grass-roots pressure on a congressman from his district; skilled development of allies in the press; cultivation of junior members of a congressional committee, leaving the once-potent chairman neutralized like a helpless Gulliver.

For a time, the public interest groups had their inning; when business came back to bat, it would come back with all of its latent influence mobilized and the new lobbying techniques perfected, by men like Walker. One astute member of the House Ways and Means Committee on the losing side of the 1978 tax battle, observed, "Here was this young Nader kid, Bob Brandon, fresh out of law school, standing the tax bar on its head. They all just got mad. Well, Charlie Walker didn't get mad. He got even."

Throughout 1977, as the Carter Administration thrashed out the details of its own tax reform bill, the business groups geared up for an epic battle to hold the line against the expected proposal to increase capital gains taxes. Walker and his executive director, Richard Rahn, crisscrossed the country with speeches to local business groups and got favorable play in the regional financial pages. Media kits were assembled; other trade associations were mobilized. Academic studies were commissioned to show how a capital gains tax hike would depress economic growth. Walker's own council retained Chase Manhattan's subsidiary, Chase Econometrics. The Securities Industry Association hired Data Resources, Inc., a Cambridge firm headed by former LBJ economic advisor Otto Eckstein, to calculate the effects of various capital gains tax levels on investment.

These studies used very sophisticated, computerized econometric models to make the case that higher capital gains taxes would depress stock prices, and lower capital gains taxes would boost the stock market, creating a myriad of other benefits. The Securities Industry Association study contended that eliminating all capital gains taxes would increase capital investment by $81 billion and GNP by almost $200 billion, and as a consequence federal tax revenues would actually increase by $38 billion. But these conclusions all flowed from the arbitrary assumption that eliminating the capital gains tax would increase stock prices by 20 percent. Later, Harvard economist Martin Feldstein, president of the prestigious National Bureau of Economic Research, predicted that lower capital gains taxes could enable investors to trade stocks they had held onto for tax purposes, "unlocking" new reservoirs of capital. Though the complicated algebra merely extrapolated assumptions based on investors' historical behavior, these studies did have influence.

About the same time, Dr. Arthur Laffer began publicizing his wondrous curve. The Laffer curve, which enjoys enormous popularity in conservative circles, argues that beyond a certain rate, higher taxation will produce lower revenues, because taxpayers will stop bothering to produce more wealth that the government will only tax away.

Thus, according to Laffer, there are two tax rates—a low one and a high one—that will produce the same amount of revenue for the government. Obviously, with the lower tax rate everybody is better off. The government does at least as well, and the taxpayer gets to keep more of his earnings in take-home pay. This is the elusive free lunch, for which economists have been searching in vain.

Laffer has even argued that reducing taxes will liberate so much productive energy that government will ultimately raise more revenue, not less.

Nobody disputes that there is some conceivable tax rate so burdensome—say 95 percent—as to make taxpayers simply give up. But most economists, including most conservative economists, believe that the current U.S. income tax rate, which is perhaps 35 percent for the very wealthy and far less for most taxpayers, is nowhere near that theoretical point. Tax rates would have to be far higher for cuts to stimulate so-called feedback effects. And even if lowering taxes did lead some taxpayers to work harder, it is inconceivable that the economy would grow so much faster that government revenues would actually increase, as Laffer insists.

The use of tax cuts to stimulate the economy is not a new idea. Keynesian economists have long recognized that in certain circumstances where the economy has slack because demand is low, pumping money into the economy through a tax cut will stimulate production, but most economists don't expect this to increase net revenues, and a budget deficit is normally anticipated as one of the consequences of a tax cut. Obviously, if government spending were also cut to pay for the tax cut, there would be no deficit, but there would be less economic stimulus, too.

Laffer, on the other hand, argues that tax cuts are potent, not because they increase demand, but because they stimulate *supply*. People will simply work harder because they get to keep more of the paycheck after taxes. Laffer, who has been promoting this idea for several years, has not tested it empirically as of this writing. In fact, some economists argue that just the opposite occurs: people work harder when taxes are *raised*, in order to maintain their prior standard of living. Lowering taxes is just as likely to encourage people to substitute leisure for work. The main empirical evidence to refute Laffer is the fact that other industrial countries with far higher tax rates are also far more productive than the United States.

In one embarrassing test of Laffer's "supply-side" models, Laffer, while on the staff of the Council of Economic Advisors, forecast a sharp increase in the gross national product on the basis of the premise that an easing of the money supply would increase productivity. After Laffer's prediction of a boom was cited by President Nixon, the preliminary figures released in early 1972 turned out to be about $20 billion less than Laffer had predicted.

Other economists disputed Laffer for relying on just four indicators in deriving his estimate—money supply, federal spending, stock prices, and interest rates. Econometric models normally factor in dozens of variables.

Despite the fact that Laffer's methodology was widely considered to be primitive and speculative, he suddenly found himself a new prophet of great influence, thanks largely to an editorial writer for *The Wall Street Journal,* Jude Wanniski. As Wanniski recounts his discovery of Laffer in his own book, *The Way the World Works,* the Laffer curve had a striking influence in Wanniski's own thinking. The two became close friends, and Laffer's work soon became a fixture of the *Journal'*s editorial page.

One devastating refutation of Laffer's economics was Proposition 13 itself. Laffer has repeatedly pointed to the 461,000 new private sector jobs created in California's economy in the twelve months after Proposition 13. He does not mention that 634,000 jobs were created in the California private sector in the twelve months *before* Proposition 13.

Interestingly, the best squelch of Laffer came in the pages of the same *Wall Street Journal,* and it came not from an outdated Keynesian but from Nixon's former chief economic advisor, Herbert Stein. "Despite the tone of much of the current argument," Stein wrote, "the propositions of supply-side economics are not matters of ideology or principle. They are matters of arithmetic. So far one must say that the arithmetic of any of the "newer" propositions is quite doubtful. Supply-side economics may yet prove to be the irritant which, like the grain of sand in the oyster shell, produces a pearl of new economic wisdom. But up to this point the pearl has not appeared."

THE BATTLE

By late 1977, as the Carter Administration continued to work on its overdue tax legislation, the business press was issuing dire warnings about the effect of further tax equity on "capital formation," many of them adroitly generated by Charls Walker and his American Council for Capital Formation.

Even before the battle began, Administration strategists sensed that the wind was changing. When the long-awaited tax package was finally unveiled in January 1978, it included many of the reforms Carter had promised, including sharp restrictions on tax deductible entertainment, and tax cuts for moderate-income taxpayers. But it also proposed to reduce the corporate tax rate, make permanent the investment tax credit, giving business some $6 billion in tax cuts. And in place of the anticipated elimination of the 50 percent exclusion on capital gains, there was a far milder proposal to get rid of a 25 percent alternative tax on small capital gains.

This victory in advance of the fray left Walker and his troops all dressed up with no place to go. As one congressional insider remarked, "They were braced for an attack; when the attack never came, they decided to invade!"

Walker soon found a willing ally in Representative William Steiger, a widely respected forty-year-old moderate Republican from Oshkosh, Wisconsin.

A former Steiger aide, Mark Bloomfield, had recently come on as Rahn's assistant. Steiger was concerned about the plight of small entrepreneurs seeking venture capital. Walker, through one of his trade association contacts, had just the right approach to Steiger. On March 7, Bloomfield dropped by Steiger's office with a man named Ed Zschau in tow. Zschau was president of a California electronics company, scheduled to testify that day before the House Ways and Means Committee on behalf of his trade association. His topic was venture capital, and he even had a song about it:

> We've got those old risk capital blues,
> Folks don't invest, consume is what they choose.
> The gains are what attracts 'em
> But not when we high-tax 'em.
> And there's high risk they could lose . . .

Zschau brought with him a survey of electronics firms, showing that new capital investment had dropped sharply after 1969, the year Congress raised the capital gains rates. Steiger was impressed and offered to sponsor legislation rolling back taxes on capital gains.

The Securities Industry Association, representing Wall Street brokerage houses, launched a massive mailing, spearheaded by Merrill Lynch, and E.F. Hutton, to investors who stood to save if capital gains rates were reduced. Mail began pouring into Congress.

Now, the studies that had been commissioned by various trade associations to show the dire consequences of a capital gains hike were equally useful to show the benefits of a cut.

On March 22, Steiger and three cosponsors introduced his bill to roll back capital gains rates to their level before the 1969 tax reform act, about a 20 percent reduction. Walker and his staff began quietly enlisting additional cosponsors. With a war chest contributed by his board of big companies, Walker masterminded a classic grass-roots lobbying campaign, using the members of his board and his contacts with other trade associations to have major industries in key congressional districts win pledges of support from their congressmen.

Getting Steiger to lead the charge counted for a great deal. Steiger, who died later that year of a heart attack, was very well liked. He had joined the liberals on several earlier tax reform initiatives. He was not the sort of Republican who could be bought for campaign contributions. If he was carrying water for capital formation, it was because he genuinely believed it would get the economy out of the doldrums.

Once engaged, Steiger worked fiercely. He told Treasury lobbyists, almost apologetically, that he was putting in the bill just to get a discussion going. But in practice, Charlie Walker was playing for keeps. "The Capital Formation Council became a virtual extension of Steiger's staff," recalls former Walker aide Bloomfield.

Nobody was overlooked. Representative Abner Mikva, of Illinois, then one of the most reform-minded Democratic members of the Ways and Means Committee and now a federal appeals judge, marveled at the subtlety of the approach. "I got phone calls from several people back in my district who had been supporters of mine, and contributors," Mikva recalled. "People who seldom asked for anything. Progressive members of brokerage houses. Public spirited bankers. First, they asked if we could have lunch. There was no arm-twisting. They were polite, thoughtful, erudite. They had their facts. We have to do something for the economy; look at the low rate of savings. The letters I got were not mass mailings. They were intelligent letters from people who knew me well. Now, obviously, somebody back in Washington was masterminding this, but I'm sure that some of it did sway me."

Mikva recalled, "When I first came to Congress in 1969, lobbying was a matter of getting to the administration and getting to the committee chairman. The 1974 reforms took a lot of power away from the chairmen. This new kind of lobbying captures members one at a time, and overwhelms a chairman. Lobbying used to require choosing up sides. Something for me and nothing for you. All of a sudden, the ground rules are very different. On an issue like capital formation, where you only hear from business, it isn't something for me and nothing for you; it's something for me, and this doesn't concern you."

By early April, Steiger had the support of nearly half of the thirty-seven-member House Ways and Means Committee. Walker and his chief of staff, Richard Rahn, were sufficiently confident to request a meeting with Representative Al Ullman to tell the Ways and Means Committee chairman what they had.

Meeting with Rahn and Bloomfield on April 14, Ullman was absolutely stunned. Several Democrats, even liberal members like the southern populist freshman Jim Guy Tucker of Little Rock, had been gotten to by key industries back home in their districts. The bill had not even had a hearing, and it already seemed almost assured of passage.

"The President is already very unhappy with me," Ullman sighed. "This is going to make him a lot more unhappy." Ullman temporarily suspended the committee markup of the Administration tax bill, looking for a compromise that might peel away some of Steiger's cosponsors.

Now, Walker intensified his public relations campaign. The Chase Econometrics study by Michael Evans was released April 17, claiming that a capital gains cut would do everything but cure dandruff. According to Evans' crystal ball, which was later challenged even in the business press, a cut in the capital gains rate to a maximum of 25 percent (the Steiger proposal) would raise stock prices by 40 percent by 1982, and produce 440,000 new jobs by 1985. As a result of this bounty, Evans claimed, the federal deficit would be $16 billion less by 1985. This study used highly sophisticated equations to predict these outcomes, but the equations were based on an essentially intuitive assumption about how investors would respond to the tax cut. Later, during the two weeks after the bill passed, the stock market *dropped* 10 percent.

Nonetheless, the Evans study had impact. The *Congressional Record* of that week was filled with capital formation rhethoric. A stampede of congressmen assured business constituents back home they would support the amendment. The ever helpful Jude Wanniski, Arthur Laffer's promoter, contributed a lead *Wall Street Journal* story entitled "Stupendous Steiger." "The Carter tax package, already reeling from other setbacks, has been stopped in its tracks by the Steiger amendment," Wanniski declared. "The key to Mr. Steiger's sudden success is one argument: a lower tax on capital gains will raise more money, not less, for the government."

That, of course, was Laffer's theory, and it remains unproven. After the fact, there has been very little evidence that investors rushed to cash in capital gains under the inducement of the new tax cut. But Wanniski was right on the money in his conclusion. "Everybody should know that the Steiger amendment is not one tax provision among many, but the cutting edge of an important intellectual and financial breakthrough."

That it was.

The constituency for tax reform, always thin, was in tatters. Business lobbying suddenly enjoyed an intellectual as well as tactical edge, and Walker managed to exploit both in the press. "Within a relatively short period of time," Walker later observed, "capital formation has entered the lexicon of 'good' words—not quite equal to Home and Mother, but still a public policy goal few would disagree with."

The strong suit of the Carter Administration had never been legislative finesse, and relations with Congress on tax issues were a special debacle. Against the advice of many congressional allies, Carter had pressed forward with his $50 tax rebate plan during the 1977 session. Like a good soldier, House Ways and Means Committee Chairman Al Ullman reluctantly steered the bill through the House. When the Administration encountered stiffer opposition in the Senate, and suddenly jettisoned the bill, Ullman got the word listening to a newscast on his car radio.

Again in the autumn of 1977, the Administration badly fumbled its energy legislation, much of which was really tax legislation. The Treasury and the Energy Department openly undercut each other. Again, Ullman tried to be loyal to the White House position, not quite knowing from day to day what it was.

In effect, the energy debacle wrecked the tax reform package in a number of subtle ways. First, the energy bill undermined the Administration's credibility. While railing against tax loopholes out of one side of its mouth, the Administration was strenuously promoting an energy bill made up mainly of new tax preferences. Worse, the tax provisions of the energy bill had to navigate the congressional tax-writing committees. The debilitating legislative battle over energy used up the Administration's few IOUs with key tax legislators, and exhausted the first team at the Treasury even before the tax reform legislation came up.

In early 1978, Ullman and other congressional leaders warned Administration officials that the timing might be disastrously wrong for another push on tax reform. Many congressmen were still getting fallout from the 1976 act. The last thing most moderate Democrats wanted in 1978 was another head-to-head battle with the business groups back home. So when the Administration tax package began to unravel, producing a humiliating insurrection from the back-benchers on Ullman's own committee, he was not about to pull the Administration's chestnuts out of the fire yet again. Instead, Ullman supported the efforts of Representative Jim Jones to tone down Steiger's capital gains bill and see whether the Democrats could get a bit of credit for it. Ullman politely told the Administration to salvage what they could.

Suspending the committee markup sessions, Ullman let Jones assemble a compromise. Daily, the compromise looked more like the original Steiger bill, because Steiger had the votes. In the Senate, Steiger's ally

Clifford Hansen of Wyoming, already had fifty-two cosponsors. Ullman unsuccessfully sought to make the size of the capital gains cut the issue, but this already conceded the point that a cut was necessary. The liberals were fighting on the other side's turf.

As Ullman continued to look for a face saver in the form of a basically Republican bill with a Democratic label, unusual rumblings began reaching Washington from the hinterland. It was May 1978. On June 6, Jarvis' success with Proposition 13 made national headlines, just in time to stampede more votes behind Steiger and Jones, and further isolate the liberals, even though capital gains taxes had nothing whatsoever to do with the grievances in California. But it was all part of what was taken for a national mood. "At that time we needed a psychological boost," recalled Richard Rahn of the capital formation council. "Proposition 13 gave us a lift. It helped give tax reduction a broader credibility."

Eventually, on August 10, the House passed a tax bill with little resemblance to the Carter tax package. It contained Representative Jim Jones's variation on the Steiger bill, known as the "Jones compromise." The bill not only lowered the maximum capital gains tax to 25 percent, as Steiger had proposed, it removed capital gains from the list of tax preference income subject to a minimum tax, and it indexed corporate stock and real estate for inflation. Finally, the bill altogether exempted from taxation the first $100,000 profit from the sale of a house.

Such a bill would have been unthinkable even six months earlier, and it signaled a total reversal of congressional attitudes. While much of the antitax sentiment in the country came from people of modest means feeling the pinch of inflation, the capital gains provisions of the House bill benefited the wealthy almost exclusively.

Close to 90 percent of the tax savings of the capital gains liberalization went to taxpayers with a 1978 income over $50,000. More than half of the benefit went to taxpayers with an income over $200,000.

Yet the capital formation lobby was singularly successful in translating the general demand for tax relief into an effective demand for tax relief for the rich.

Politically, the Administration took the position that the indexing of stock purchase prices was even worse than the capital gains cut; Administration economists believed that to index one key financial sector such as the stock market would lead inexorably to indexation of the entire economy; and this they believed would make the society more tolerant of inflation.

At this point, Senator Russell Long shrewdly suggested an idea once advocated by John Kennedy, to increase the exempt portion of capital gains from 50 percent to 70 percent.* This would cut capital gains taxes about as much as the Steiger amendment, but would give slightly more of the cut to upper-middle-income investors, as opposed to the very wealthy. In exchange for the cut in capital gains rates, Long proposed to continue to subject the capital gains preference income to the minimum tax, "to assure that no millionaire would escape taxation."

This time, Merrill Lynch Economics, a subsidiary of the brokerage house, supplied the now predictable econometric projection, arguing that the cut would so stimulate investment that production would soar and the Treasury would end up with more, rather than less, revenue.

According to Merrill Lynch's crystal ball, Senator Long's proposal would increase stock prices, reduce unemployment, reduce the deficit, and increase revenues even more successfully than the House bill, providing 312,000 additional jobs by 1980.

Long agreed to kill the House's indexing proposal, but as his price he exacted a total capital gains cut that was even larger than the House bill.

"We were totally unprepared for Charlie Walker and his troops," recalled Ben Okner, one of the Treasury's top tax officials. "Once it started going, they had plenty of money to keep it going."

On October 10, when the Senate took a roll call on whether to reduce capital gains taxes, only ten senators voted nay.

The barrage of seemingly sophisticated academic studies by prestigious researchers also helped Walker win the day. Harvard's Martin Feldstein offered a paper predicting that the capital gains cut would unlock massive amounts of securities whose owners had hitherto been reluctant to sell because of the taxation rate on gains.

Many of these studies later were shown to be based on unverifiable assumptions about how the market was *likely* to respond to a cut in the capital gains rates; yet they were presented as scientific fact, and by the time the liberal economists reassembled their forces and challenged the methodology in the various tax journals, the political battle was over and Charlie Walker's capital formation council had moved on to other issues.

The final compromise, worked out in a hectic all-night session, increased the exempt portion of capital gains from 50 percent to 60 percent and cut the top capital gains rate to 28 percent. The minimum tax was substantially watered down. In addition, Congress postponed the effec-

---

* What Long did not say was that the Kennedy proposal was part of a package that increased the taxes on appreciated stock left to heirs.

tive date of the carry-over basis reform, and eventually killed it in the 1979 session.

Interestingly, while Congress enacted a tax reduction targeted to the very rich, the final bill rejected the more purely ideological proposals for budget balancing or across-the-board tax cuts, the Kemp-Roth amendment and even the more moderate Nunn amendment.

Evidently, the more amorphous demands for a balanced budget, though closer in spirit to Jarvis fever, packed far less punch in Congress than the aggressively lobbied campaigns for a cut in capital gains rates.

The distribution of the capital gains tax cuts suggests just how remarkable a coup it was for the corporate lobby. Although Charls Walker could testify that "a lot of hard working, typical Americans are being hit hard by the capital gains tax burden," the reality is that one percent of the population owns about 50 percent of the stock, and only about 7 percent of the nation's taxpayers are even affluent enough to have taxable gains at all.

The result of the bill is to enable a millionaire with hundreds of thousands of dollars in capital gains to pay a lower tax rate than a salaried worker earning $20,000 a year. More startling still, Congress was willing to lighten the tax load on the very, very wealthy in a year when social security taxes were raised, increasing the tax load on working people still higher.

So highly skewed is stock ownership in the U.S. that the wealthiest 2 percent of taxpayers got about 75 percent of the $2 billion of the capital gains cut provided in the 1978 tax bill. The wealthiest one-tenth of one percent of the population received estimated benefits of $850,000,000, or almost half of the total tax cut.

Putting together all the provisions of the Revenue Act of 1978, the 75 percent of taxpayers with earnings of less than $20,000 got less than 37 percent of the benefits of the bill. The top 8.6 percent, with incomes over $30,000 a year, got more than a third of the benefits. Stated another way, the lower half of taxpayers got 21 percent of the tax savings. The upper half got 79 percent.

15

THE CAPITAL FORMATION THEOLOGY

DESPITE THE FANCY ALGEBRA, the essential premises of the capital formation dogma of business are straightforward enough: Greater prosperity requires greater productivity; productivity, in turn, depends on increased investment; the source of investment is savings. Our economy is lagging largely because we save and invest too little and consume too much. Thus, we need policies to stimulate investment.

So far, the argument is all but irrefutable, although some economists will point out that the rate of capital investment is only one of several determinants of economic growth. Next, however, the argument turns to the tax code as a remedy, and here we should keep our hands on our wallets.

According to the capital formation theorists, the most effective way to stimulate investment is to increase the after-tax return on investment. In other words, make investment more profitable by lightening the tax load on wealthy investors. Several recent changes in the tax code effectively lobbied by business interests do just that: the capital gains cut, the liberalized investment tax credit, the repeal of carry-over basis, as well as a general flattening of tax rates and the proposed huge depreciation write-off provision, 10-5-3.

These provisions undoubtedly make the rich richer by lowering their tax burden, but do they really stimulate capital formation? There are, of course, two obvious side effects to this strategy. With capital contributing fewer tax dollars, government gets less revenue, and the tax system as a whole is rendered less progressive. But a third, less obvious side effect is that incentives are created for particular uses of capital, which may or may not be efficient uses. Consequently, tax subsidies favored by business may or may not further the supposed goal of increased productivity and growth. They may just make the rich richer.

Along with the highly selective use of empirical evidence, the capital formation argument depends on a series of unproven, heroic assumptions. In the capital formation lobby's extensive polemical literature put forth as scholarly research, one looks in vain even for a consistent definition of the term "capital formation." The phrase seems to mean net investment in manufacturing plant and equipment, but in the political debate it is used almost interchangeably to mean simply higher after-tax profits for corporations and higher after-tax yields for wealthy investors.

Here, the unstated assumption is that higher profits will automatically translate into greater investments, or into more productive investments. But for every textbook capitalist of the deferred-gratification variety whose increased earnings only beget redoubled Calvinist effort, there must be a dozen coupon-clippers. And for every company that reinvests its higher earnings into new technology, there are several that simply use the additional cash to buy up other companies. Moreover, the real estate boom has soaked up vast amounts of investment capital, which has not improved productivity at all.

Even if tax preferences can be targeted to reward corporate investment in new machinery and equipment, the presumption is that this form of capital accumulation is inherently preferable to other forms such as investment in infrastructure, basic research, education, transport, or public services.

While Charlie Walker and his troops have effectively persuaded Congress that corporate capital is the only kind worth forming, widely accepted economic studies indicate that only about one-fifth or one-sixth of economic growth is contributed by capital at all.

Undeniably, light taxation of capital income at the expense of society's other needs is a proven recipe for one style of rapid economic development—the sort experienced by Korea and the Philippines. Its hallmarks are a high-growth, high-profit manufacturing sector, low wages, a myriad of social problems, and a grossly unjust distribution of wealth. But as the social democratic countries of Western Europe demonstrate, there are other paths to economic growth that include a higher level of social benefits and fairer distribution of society's economic rewards.

CAPITAL SHORTAGE

Despite the rhetoric, the fraction of gross national product spent on private investment in the U.S. has been remarkably constant over the last several decades. Since the early fifties, investment as a percentage of GNP has averaged about 9.6 percent with very little fluctuation. And despite the claim that the U.S. has failed to modernize its plant and equipment, the average age of America's capital stock has fallen—from 14.2 years in 1950 to 11.6 years in 1960 to 9.8 years in 1973. On average, the share of the economy spent on investment has been slightly higher since 1964 except during the 1974–75 recession. In fact, investment in domestic plant and equipment took 10.5 percent of GNP in 1978, the highest rate since 1946, with the sole exception of 1969, when the rate was a shade higher.

How is it possible to reconcile the fairly stable level of investment with the clear slowdown in productivity and economic growth? First, of course, the terms of trade have worsened against the U.S. More of our real income is consumed by the purchase of raw materials; and our own industrial trading partners have caught up with American technological superiority. Secondly, changes in the labor force also account for the fact that the same share of investment packs less of a punch today. With more of the population in the labor force, there is less capital per worker and hence less statistical growth in worker productivity.

Further, there is evidence that technological breakthroughs are cyclical; the explosive progress of the fifties and sixties was fueled in part by civilian applications of military and aerospace research (funded mostly through tax dollars, by the way). Today, this has subsided, and we may be in a period of less dramatic technological gain, where the same dollars will not buy the same sort of dramatic progress. This is not a uniform phenomenon, of course. Despite scant technological gain in many basic industries, newer fields such as computer science continue to grow very rapidly, with little evidence of a capital shortage. Indeed, the main bottleneck in the high-tech industries today is a shortage of physicists and engineers, not capital.

Finally, the demands of pollution control have soaked up some capital, about 4 percent of private, nonresidential investment in recent years. This may be a declining claimant in the future, as new generations of machinery and equipment come with pollution control technologies "designed-in."

On balance, a case can be made for a modest increase in the share of national income allocated to investment. This was the conclusion of a panel of economists representing various orientations, quoted in a recent report by the Joint Economic Committee of Congress. But the report concluded:

"Today's problem, however, is not one of business investment demands outstripping the supply of savings. On the contrary, today's situation is one in which business is not committing itself to new investment projects it recently regarded as urgent, even though it has adequate funds at its disposal."

This raises an intriguing chicken-and-egg question: Does investment "cause" economic growth, or does economic growth cause investment? The capital formation lobby contends that lower taxes on profits will leave more money available to be invested. But can we trust business to invest those dollars? And will they invest them in those projects society needs most?

If recent history is any guide, the answer must be—not necessarily. During the booming fifties and sixties, when America's trackbeds and rolling stock were slowly deteriorating, the railroads made sizable profits. But these were not reinvested substantially in modernizing plant and equipment; they were invested least of all in passenger service. Much of the Penn Central's profit went into "diversification," meaning mainly real estate, where there is no capital shortage. During the capital formation debates of five years ago, the steel companies were leading proponents, pointing to tens of billions needed to increase capacity and modernize plants. In practice, the steel giants were insulated from foreign competition by monopolistic pricing policies, which shielded them from the need to modernize plant, even during the flush years. Instead, they used their profits to invest heavily in the chemical industry. Today, with slower growth of demand for steel, lighter autos, and strong foreign competition, the plans for expansion have been shelved, and steel mills are shutting down. And there is no shortage of capital.

Detroit behaved similarly. During the booming postwar years, when there was no capital shortage, automakers invested massive amounts of capital into styling changes and almost none into improving engine efficiency until ordered to do so by Congress. The energy industry has successfully lobbied Congress to allocate massive amounts of publicly subsidized or guaranteed capital to development of expensive, capital-intensive (and profitable) synthetic fuels, even though the same net energy gains could be achieved by softer, renewable technologies. During the postwar period, when capital was plentiful, there was no interest in expanding energy technology.

Totally apart from the motives of individual businessmen, the experience of the past thirty years suggests that no matter how high the level of after-tax earnings or how plentiful the reserves of capital, business will invest, quite understandably, in areas where it thinks demand exists or can be created. If the goods can't be sold, the investment won't be made. All the investment capital in the world would not have made Detroit produce a VW Rabbit, or Houston a solar-heated house, in the year 1960.

PRODUCTIVITY

There is no doubt that productivity, defined as output per worker, has grown at a slower rate in the U.S. than in most other industrialized countries. Between 1963 and 1973, productivity growth averaged only 1.9 percent annually and has been virtually stagnant since. This compared with comparable rates of over 4 percent in most of Western Europe during the sixties and early seventies, and nearly 9 percent in Japan.

But the analysis of productivity statistics is a very slippery business, especially when one tries to compare one country with another. During a period of falling energy prices, such as the fifties and sixties, the investment in more efficient machines to replace workers makes the remaining work force more "productive" in a statistical sense: thanks to the machinery, each worker generates more output. But when prices of energy and raw materials rise relative to other costs, as during the seventies, the capital equipment becomes relatively more expensive to build and to operate, and suddenly the worker ceases to generate new output so rapidly. This shows up as a decline in productivity.

The causes of economic growth and of productivity are not easy to sort out. One of the most sophisticated bodies of work on productivity is the extensive research assembled over two decades by Edward Denison of the Brookings Institution. Denison found that not more than 20 percent of the economic growth enjoyed by the United States between 1948 and 1969 was the result of "capital formation" at all. Most of the increase was due to more efficient resource allocation, onetime technological breakthroughs, rising levels of worker education, and the changing composition of the work force. For example, when a farmhand migrates to the city to take a factory job, he suddenly becomes more "productive" in a statistical sense, because factories generate more output-per-worker than farms. But even heroic amounts of capital will not enable him to repeat this onetime jump.

The faster growth of European productivity during the postwar period is primarily the result of the fact that Europe had a lot of catching-up to do. Europe possessed all the ingredients of a highly industrialized society —trained manpower, educated population, basic distribution systems. But after World War II, Europe and Japan had to replace most of their plant and equipment to revive as industrial economies, which produced impressive growth rates. In addition, Europe was also better positioned to gain from demographic shifts; by 1950 the American labor force had almost completed its historic shift from the farm to the factory, and these statistical gains were behind us. In 1950, only about 12 percent of American workers were still farmers. But Europe still had 28.5 percent of its workers employed in agriculture. By 1975 this had shrunk to 3.9 percent in the U.S. and 10.2 percent in Europe, giving Europe faster productivity growth from this source.

During the 1960s the integration of Europe's national economies through the Common Market also resulted in marketing and distributional efficiencies that were already in place in the United States. And European industry was in a position to gain rapidly by applying technologies already known in the U.S.

It is widely believed that the era of rapid growth of Western Europe is already slowing down, because these onetime gains that made for Europe's transformation into a U.S.–style mass-consumption economy are now largely completed.

The known technology has been applied and new breakthroughs will be more costly; the migration from farm to factory is almost complete, as is the relaxation of trade barriers. And Europe is facing the same higher raw material costs as the U.S. Totally apart from savings rates or capital investment rates, the statistics are already showing a marked slowdown in Europe's rates of growth.

According to data compiled by the Organization for Economic Cooperation and Development, productivity growth dropped sharply after 1973, not just in the U.S., but in every major industrial nation. West Germany, with its high social welfare budget, suffered less of a slowdown than any other country.

PRODUCTIVITY GROWTH

	1963-73	1973-77
U.S.	1.9	0
Japan	8.7	2.8
Germany	4.6	3.2
France	4.6	2.7
U.K.	3.0	0.5
Canada	2.5	0.5
Italy	5.4	1.8

It is also noteworthy that while the capital formation lobby has focused on the need for greater profits to promote investment in manufacturing, the U.S. productivity growth in that sector is very close to historic levels, and the steep declines have come elsewhere. Productivity growth in manufacturing stayed at an annual average of 2.3 percent between 1969 and 1978, down only slightly from the 3.0 percent of 1959-69, and virtually the same as the 2.4 percent of 1949-59. Most of the drop during the seventies can be attributed to the 1974-75 recession, which was the most serious of the postwar period.

SAVINGS

U.S. households save far less of their income than their counterparts in other advanced countries, and this has been true for decades. The very low household savings are offset somewhat by savings through pension plans. But the overall rate is still far below that of most Western countries and Japan. U.S. household savings have averaged about 6 percent since World War II, and dipped below 5 percent during 1978.

Europeans, in contrast, are prodigious savers, with an average rate of better than 10 percent, which rises to 14 percent in Germany and 16 percent in France. The Japanese are a remarkable 21 percent.

There are numerous theories to explain why, and none is entirely satisfactory. The U.S. does not provide any tax break to promote household savings, other than the so-called IRA and Keogh plans, which enable savings accounts earmarked for one's retirement to defer taxation on their annual contributions. IRA and Keogh users tend to be relatively well off. France and Japan do provide tax exemptions for personal savings (though other countries with high savings rates do not).

More significantly, federal regulations artificially depress the interest rate on small savings—in order to save banks and bank borrowers higher costs on borrowed money. This limit on interest rates, which is called Regulation Q, dates to the Great Depression, when it was imposed on the theory that banks should be protected from "ruinous competition." The result is that even during a period of 12 percent inflation, small savers are limited to 5¼ percent interest on passbook accounts, which can hardly be seen as an inducement to save.

In fairness, however, most studies have shown that small savers are chronically insensitive to interest rates. For example, the biggest savings institution in Washington, D.C., Perpetual Federal Savings and Loan, until recently did not as a matter of policy offer certificate accounts paying higher rates. Yet over a billion dollars in small savings were kept on deposit at Perpetual, much of it from savers who surely could keep some of their money on deposit for 90 or 180 days to qualify for higher rates. But they just didn't bother.

Interest rates on household savings in Japan, the world's champion saver, are notoriously low, as they are in Germany, where they have barely kept pace with the low German rate of inflation.

Also, and here is one of those "cultural contradictions of capitalism," the U.S. spends more of its household savings to finance consumer debt than most other countries. Consumer debt has grown at a faster rate than government debt or private investment. For example, between 1975 and 1980, when inflation increased by less than 50 percent, the increase in credit-card debt totaled 137 percent. In striking contrast, government debt, the great bugaboo of conservatives, has dropped steadily in relation to gross national product throughout the postwar period. Federal debt gradually dropped from 103.5 percent of GNP in 1946 to only 27.1 percent in 1979. During the same period, total consumer debt rose steadily from 16 percent of GNP to 54 percent. Business debt, presumably reflecting productive investment, rose far more slowly. This means that an ever greater share of private savings go to finance *consumption* rather than productive investment, and this is one reason why America's net savings rate is so low.

You don't hear much about excess consumer debt from the capital-formation lobby—because the banks enjoy making 18 percent on consumer loans, and corporations need to move the merchandise.

American capital depends on self-denial for its productive investment —and self-indulgence to peddle its wares. Indeed, the same corporations who have retained Charls Walker to bemoan the low savings rate spend billions on copywriters to induce the American consumer to go deeper in debt. And the corporate managers who wonder at the high absenteeism and the falling productivity bombard the same workers, off hours, with slogans like "You deserve a break today."

Another favorite capital-formation doctrine is the idea that the social security system is one of the main causes of the low American savings rate. The prime author of this theory is Harvard's Martin Feldstein, who rates notice as one of the brightest stars of the capital formation galaxy. Feldstein is an entirely different sort of economist from Arthur Laffer. While Laffer is widely dismissed as a polemicist in the economics profession, Feldstein, president of the National Bureau of Economic Research and a leading member of Harvard's economics department, is one of the most subtle and sophisticated of the econometric modelers. Feldstein publishes prodigiously in the scholarly journals, and until recently was considered a political moderate.

Yet many of his colleagues wonder at the role he has played in the capital formation debate, in which Feldstein has used his research products to justify the crudest of policy remedies, and has become a central academic cheerleader for the capital formation crusade.

Feldstein rightly points out that social security "savings" are not savings at all, though for most households they constitute the largest share of assets anticipated for future consumption. But, unlike the reserves of a private pension fund, in which the income from invested capital pays for current benefits, the "wealth" of anticipated social security checks is not wealth at all, because the American social security system is *unfunded*.

Current social security taxes do not create a pool of capital to be used for investment. Rather, they go to pay benefits to current pensioners. And unlike a private nest-egg, social security wealth does not exist as tangible assets which can be reinvested in the economy, but only as a claim against future taxpayers. Thus, instead of adding to the stock of national savings, social security is a purely paper nest-egg, which paradoxically increases a worker's ability to consume more now and set aside less. He can do this because his pension will be paid by future generations of workers.

Here, Feldstein and the capital formation ideologues are on solid ground. But what is the remedy? Feldstein himself concedes that many individuals would save nothing even if there were no social security. And despite the public's new receptivity to trickle-down, the capital formation lobby has wisely refrained from calling for abolition of social security in the name of self-discipline.

If, as Feldstein insists, social security "induces individuals to reduce their own personal savings," this effect oddly vanishes on the other side of the Atlantic, where pensions and other social benefits are higher but individuals nonetheless save more.

At the same time, it does seem that the *form* of our social security system indeed allows society as a whole to save less. But here, the most obvious remedy is to fully fund the system and convert social security into a true means of national savings. This would require increasing contributions or other taxes to gradually build up a permanent social security fund, whose current income would be paid out as current benefits, much in the way a private pension fund or annuity operates.

One country that operates its social security system in just this manner is Sweden. Under Sweden's National Pension Insurance Fund, which was created in 1959, annual payments to the fund during its early years far exceeded annual payouts. Today, the fund is Sweden's single largest source of capital formation, with 131.5 billion kronor in accumulated assets at the end of 1978 (about $31 billion), which is equal to about one-third of Sweden's gross national product.

The fund's assets are, naturally, invested—in government and private bonds, in housing mortgages, and since 1978, in stocks of private companies. This system enables the Swedes to maintain a high level of capital formation—which ought to appeal to the American critics of our low national savings rate. But, of course, Sweden's funded social security shifts investment decisions to a publicly accountable body, something that is utterly anathema to American conservatives.

Interestingly, the Swedish social security funds (there are four separate funds) are managed quite conservatively, and while some investments are channeled in accordance with national policy to housing and municipal government finance, very little of the investments go to high-risk ventures. The yield on the Swedish social security funds compares favorably with the earnings of most American private pension funds, even though much of it was invested in low-risk instruments such as municipal bonds and mortgages. At the end of 1978 the funds' investments earned an average rate of 8.14 percent—slightly above the rate of inflation, and the funds' assets totaled about eleven times their annual outlays. In other words, income from the invested capital is almost sufficient to finance current pensions (This will require tax increases in coming years, as the percentage of retirees grows.)

The broader point here is that there are many forms of capital formation and many approaches to stimulating investment. In Western Europe, where public ownership has ceased to be a bogeyman, railroads, telecommunications, public utilities, and even some basic industries such as steel and coal are publicly owned to a far greater extent than in the U.S. Consequently, more capital formation takes place in the public sector. Because there is far less ideological opposition to state planning, capital allocation is much more subject to public policy in Europe than in the U.S. As a consequence, investment decisions are far less captive of the autonomous decisions of individual wealthy investors, bankers, and corporate boardrooms.

The lack of private capital investment in U.S. railroads, steel mills, and energy innovation during the booming sixties suggests that relying on the wisdom and efficiency of the private market to make investment decisions for society is not necessarily the best approach.

Ultimately, a society's total rate of savings and investment depends on multiple factors. There is no simple correlation between the tax level and the fraction of total output that society sets aside to invest. Total investment is determined by how much is saved and how those savings are put to work.

Nonetheless, the capital formation lobby has had great political success arguing that the rate of productive investment is mainly a function of how lightly society taxes its well-to-do. It is a tribute to the gullibility of the U.S. Congress that a favorite prop in the capital formation repertoire is the higher productivity growth of Western Europe—which after all has a larger public sector, more government allocation of capital, more generous social benefits, more publicly owned industry, a higher total tax level, and a more egalitarian distribution of income!

FOREIGN TAXATION

Because modern tax systems are so intricate, cross-country comparisons are very difficult to sort out. Other countries may tax consumption at a higher rate, yet offset this by using the proceeds to finance high welfare benefits. The capital formation theorists have selectively pointed to specific features of taxation abroad, which seem to show that most other industrial countries tax capital and capital income more lightly than the U.S. Yet this is offset by the fact that other countries have fewer loopholes, and the net result is a more egalitarian tax system just the same. Taking the tax system as a whole, wealthy Americans pay a lower portion of their incomes to the tax collector than their counterparts in most other advanced industrial nations. Moreover, European tax subsidies to capital are targeted far more narrowly than such American devices as the investment tax credit.

Consider West Germany, a favorite example of a more productive economy. Nominally, the West German tax schedule is slightly less graduated than ours; the top rate is 56 percent compared to our 70 percent. Yet very few Americans actually pay 70 percent, thanks to our loopholes. According to *The Wall Street Journal,* lowering the top U.S. rate to 50 percent would reduce total revenues by only about $1.6 billion.

Income from capital is taxed at slightly lower effective rates in West Germany than in the U.S., though nowhere near enough to account for Germany's superior economic growth. German corporations pay a tax rate of 56 percent, compared with 46 percent in the U.S., but the rate is only 15 percent on dividends paid out to investors. Long-term capital gains on the sale of stock by private investors are not taxed as income— but real estate capital gains and capital gains realized by corporations are taxed at far higher rates than in the U.S. Moreover, the investment tax credit, a favorite capital formation gimmick that saves U.S. corporations about $13 billion yearly, does not exist in Germany. And German depreciation formulas, another source of tax shelter in the U.S., are far stricter than ours.

According to one study, if tax rates and accounting rules are both taken into account, Germany has the stiffest taxes on capital investment of any country in Europe. Sluggish Britain has the lowest! Germany also levies a small tax on net corporate wealth.

With heavy payroll taxes and taxes on consumption, German blue-collar workers pay tax at a higher rate than their American counterparts. But when all the provisions are added up, after-tax income is distributed more equally in Germany than in the U.S. And this doesn't seem to retard Germany's economic growth, or make Germany's capitalists give up their labors to clip coupons or play golf.

There are, however, other crucial differences between the political economies of West Germany and the United States. Germans consume less and save more. Whether this is a result of consumption taxes or national character, can never be proven. The German economy is far less hooked on consumer credit as the engine of aggregate demand. Social welfare spending, which the American trickle-downers consider such a waste, is itself a balance wheel that keeps German output steady.

Finally, German economic growth makes use of another source of capital investment which the U.S. trickle-down lobby disdains—capital formation in the public sector. For U.S. business conservatives, this idea is a contradiction in terms. Money "absorbed" by government is, by definition, draining money that would otherwise be used by private industry. But for most industrialized countries, the public sector is a prime source of investment capital. In social democratic West Germany, fully 22 percent of nonresidential capital formation takes place in the public sector, not counting nationalized industries and other public corporations.

Japan is the other favorite example of a free-enterprise, high-growth economy. Japan's total tax load is lighter than America's, for two main reasons. Japan spends far less of its national income on the military, and many social benefits provided through the public sector in the U.S. are paid as corporate fringe benefits in Japan.

But Japan refutes the argument that higher taxes on consumption and lower taxation of high-income investment are the key to prosperity. Japan is the only industrialized country that gets more of its revenues from taxes on capital than the U.S. Like Germany, Japan does exempt capital gains from long-term stock sales from taxation, but taxes other capital gains at higher, ordinary-income rates. According to a staff study by Congress's Joint Tax Committee, Japan has the world's heaviest reliance on taxation of capital as a percentage of total receipts, 43.5 percent, compared with 39.25 percent in the U.S.

In Japan, the effective corporate income tax rate is 52.61 percent, and 40.88 percent on profits earmarked to be paid out as dividends. This compares to a statutory rate of 46 percent but an effective rate of under 35 percent in the U.S. Moreover, Japan's maximum statutory personal income tax rate is 75 percent, somewhat higher than in the U.S.*

Japan also has the lowest reliance on regressive payroll and consumption taxes of any industrial country; yet it enjoys the world's highest savings rate. When the conservative government in 1979 proposed adding a value-added tax, the government suffered an unexpected and humiliating reverse at the polls.

Although Japan, like France, does exempt interest on household savings accounts from taxation, the effective interest rate on small savings is traditionally quite low. Japanese savings habits seems to have more to do with Japanese customs than the tax code. For example, as much as 30 percent of Japanese wages are paid in the form of lump-sum bonuses, which are traditionally plowed into household savings.

* The U.S. maximum rate is 70 percent for investment income and 50 percent on wage and salary income.

One country with very liberal capital investment incentives is Britain, which has the weakest economy in Europe. Three countries that leave capital gains almost entirely untaxed are Australia, Italy, and Holland, with widely different patterns of economic growth.

There are some aspects of the tax system that do retard investment—but they are not those embraced most dearly by the capital formation lobbyists.

Clearly, the U.S. tax code promotes borrowing. Expansions financed by debt produce a tax deduction for interest paid; expansions financed by selling stock do not. To a corporate money manager, it is far cheaper to use debt financing—doubly so in times of high inflation, since the debt will be paid off in cheaper dollars. The approximately $1.5 trillion in outstanding corporate debt produces a real savings to corporations, thanks to inflation, which almost offsets inflation's perverse effect on corporate accounting systems. (The bank does pay taxes on its profits in current dollars, but with the myriad of tax shelters available to banks, the real tax rate paid by banks seldom exceeds 10 percent.) Debt financing is all the more attractive to corporate managers because it avoids the need to dilute the dividend value of existing shares.

How to rectify the clear advantage of debt over equity financing? The obvious way would be to remove the tax deduction for interest payments, but this is not likely to win much support in capital formation circles. Indexation would probably help, too, since it would lower the effective capital gains rate on stock sales. But to be fair a system that indexed stock purchase prices would also have to index loans, and nobody wants to pay off loans in dollars adjusted upward for inflation.

The tax code also discourages pay-outs of corporate dividends, by taxing them twice. At present, corporations pay a tax on their profits, and when a portion of these dollars are paid out to shareholders as dividends, they are taxed a second time. (One's worry about this iniquitous double taxation must be tempered by the realization that double taxation is common throughout the economy. A worker is taxed on his income, and then is taxed again when he spends the income on household items subject to a sales tax, or when he buys a house subject to property taxes, or a car that incurs an excise tax. Similarly, when he pays a mechanic to fix his car, the mechanic pays income tax on the wage.)

Nonetheless, the double taxation of dividends combined with the tax deductions available for borrowing money have effectively killed any meaningful "capital market" in the U.S. Today, the capital market exists mainly in the economics textbooks. Housing, the biggest single consumer of capital, has its own protected capital market in the form of savings institutions and a federally assisted secondary mortgage market. By and large, household savings finance housing.

For corporate investment, the main source of capital is retained corporate earnings. By plowing their own profits back into investment, corporate managers don't have to compete in capital markets. Most business-oriented economists would brand this as highly inefficient, but corporate managers don't complain about it. Since retained earnings are taxed only once, they are "cheaper" than other forms of capital, which must be coaxed from the market.

The second biggest source of corporate capital is borrowed money. Far down on the list is new stock sales, which contributed only 4.1 percent of corporate capital in 1978, down from more than 20 percent in the early seventies. Retained earnings accounted for more than 60 percent. Borrowings provided the other 35 percent.

The history of the double taxation issue is quite revealing. Some years ago, it was a favorite hobby horse of the business trade associations. In recent years, many tax reformers have come to the conclusion that elimination of double taxation of corporate dividends might be a good thing, because it would allocate capital more efficiently. So-called full integration of corporate and personal income taxes would eliminate the corporate income tax and tax individuals at their personal rate on their share of corporate earnings, whether or not dividends were actually paid. This would force corporations to pay most of their profits out as dividends, and to compete in the capital markets to get their investment funds.

Interestingly, when tax reformers began taking this proposal seriously, most of the business groups backed off almost immediately. It's not hard to see why. Elimination of double taxation would increase the power of owners of capital (shareholders) at the expense of corporate managers and corporate boards. It would increase pressure to pay out dividends. Not surprisingly, the double taxation issue is far down on the capital formation lobby's hit list.

Finally, the tax code retards capital formation by steering dollars away from productive investment and into real estate. Investor-owned rental housing and owner-occupied housing get enormous tax breaks. Mortgage interest is deductible, no matter how expensive the house. The capital gain on a house is not taxable as long as you keep trading it in for a more expensive house. An investor can use rental real estate to show a paper tax-loss, while the property is actually appreciating in value. Small wonder that capital has poured into real estate, bidding up the value of housing, which only attracted more capital. During the last decade, approximately half a trillion dollars went into real estate mainly because real estate was appreciating faster than other capital goods.

A capital formation purist—as opposed to a self-interested businessman—might be concerned about this trend. Yet the capital formation lobby fought mightily in 1976 against Congress's efforts to remove some of the special tax benefits for rental property. It applauded when Congress enacted a temporary $2,000 tax credit to help home builders unload a temporary overstock, a tax credit that studies later showed to be almost pure windfall to purchasers who planned to buy anyway. And the capital formation lobby wrapped itself around the plight of the retired homeowner in pressing for a liberalization of the capital gains tax. The new $100,000 exclusion on capital gains produced by the sale of a house, will only make housing a more attractive investment, and absorb still more capital from other productive uses.

U.S. TAXES AND CAPITAL INVESTMENT

Business conservatives have been sounding alarms about a capital shortage for several decades. In the palmy Eisenhower years, which are held up as a period of freer enterprise and higher growth, corporate income taxes contributed about 28 percent of the federal budget, compared with about 12 percent today. Ah, responds the capital formation theorist, corporate profits haven't kept up because we're killing the golden goose. Not so. In 1957, corporations paid taxes of $20.4 billion on adjusted profits of $42.1 billion, an effective rate of 48 percent. By 1972 they paid taxes of $36.6 billion on adjusted profits of 92.1 billion, a rate of only 39 percent. The rate in 1978 was about 44 percent, still well below the average during the fifties.

During the Eisenhower era, statutory corporate tax rates were at their all-time high of 52 percent, compared with 46 percent today; capital gains were taxed at 50 percent of ordinary income rates (which were higher too); today they are taxed at 40 percent of lower rates. Yet the economy managed to grow faster.

There were those, of course, who thought that the economy wasn't growing fast enough, and one was John Kennedy. It took a Democratic President with Keynesian advisors to think up a new tax incentive to promote capital investment—the investment tax credit. This was part of

Kennedy's package of tax cuts intended to stimulate demand and "get the economy moving again."

The investment tax credit was a clever two-in-one play. It was designed to give the Keynesian technicians a new tool for fine-tuning the economy, in the form of a temporary tax subsidy to stimulate investment during slack times. Conservative businessmen would forgive the idea's Keynesian parentage—because the subsidy went to them. By giving a company seven, and later ten cents in reduced taxes for every dollar the company invests, the investment tax credit is at least a pure subsidy to capital investment. But it is arguable how much is gained by the subsidy. In the nature of things, corporations constantly buy new equipment as old equipment wears out. It is very difficult to determine how much investment would have taken place without the tax subsidy.

One survey by conservative economist Pierre Rinfret revealed that 75 percent of major corporations said they would not change their previous investment plans in response to the reinstatement of the tax credit in 1971; yet they all got the credit just the same, against every dollar they invested. As Professor Samantha Sanchez has quipped, "The investment tax credit is the shirt that is always on sale."

Moreover, since the credit is available automatically through the tax code, it is a scatter-shot subsidy to *all* investment. It may be that older industries need all the subsidy they can get, while hot new industries like minicomputers get more than enough incentives from the marketplace. But the investment tax credit treats all machinery and equipment equally, with no targeting for needs.

In another sense, however, the investment tax credit is very highly targeted—to the very biggest companies. While the credit was originally billed as a boon to small firms, of the $13 billion in taxes saved through this tax subsidy, nearly $10 billion went to corporations worth more than $250 million. These are the companies that consume the most capital, and as such they automatically get the biggest subsidy. AT&T alone gets a subsidy of close to a billion dollars a year from the tax system through this one credit. For many big corporations, the credit equals more than one-fourth of their annual after-tax profits.

Kennedy's Keynesian advisors originally assumed, in their naivete, that this tax credit could be turned on and off as necessary. But in 1966, when the economists turned the credit off for two years as an anti-inflation measure, they were not prepared for the result. Businessmen, seeing that a subsidy would be available if they simply deferred plans for two years, sharply reduced purchases of new machinery, depressing the economy far more than intended.

At worst, the investment tax credit does have the virtue of actually promoting some investment. The reduction in the capital gains tax, on the other hand, was almost pure windfall with very little detectable benefit for the general economy.

During the great 1978 debate over capital gains reduction, econometric studies were trotted out to show that the stock market slump was due to higher capital gains rates. In reality, the 1969 and 1976 tax reforms increased the average capital gains rate only from about 14 percent to about 16 percent—hardly enough to frighten away investors. And in fact, the stock market rose steadily after the 1969 reform took effect, reaching its all-time high in 1972. The 1973–74 slump, and the 1975–76 recovery, cannot be traced to anything in the capital gains tax, which was not changed again until 1976.

In a sharp criticism of Martin Feldstein's finding that the higher capital gains rates introduced in 1969 had reduced realization of capital gains by two-thirds, the late Arthur Okun, former chairman of the Council of Economic Advisors, pointed out that "the changes in capital gains taxes legislated in 1969 added roughly a nickel on a dollar to the average effective tax rate on potentially realizable capital gains. It is utterly implausible to me that offering the taxpayer roughly 75 cents after tax on the dollar —rather than 80 cents—could have reduced the realization of net gains by fully two-thirds, as Dr. Feldstein concluded."

Despite the rosy predictions that the 1978 capital gains tax cut would work miracles on the stock market, in fact the Dow Jones remained mired in the gloomy realities of the underlying economy. In a a revealing *New York Times* survey of Wall Street economists six months after the tax cut, the chief economist of the Securities Industry Association (a key member of the capital formation coalition) shrugged and said, "With inflation and high interest rates, the capital gains tax cut was not really strong enough to attract people back into the equity market."

Nor was there any evidence of the heralded "unlocking effect." Investors did not rush to cash in capital gains at a faster rate or otherwise increase their trades. *The Times* concluded: "The only clear winners from the tax cut appear to be the people who are actually taking capital gains, and paying less in taxes."

When the total numbers are put into perspective, it is hardly surprising that the capital gains cut was weak tea for the ailing stock market. The cut applied to *all* capital gains—real estate, gold, fine art, bonds, as well as common stock, which represents less than 25 percent of all taxable capital gains. For the stock market to do what Chase Econometrics predicted—boost values 40 percent—it would have been necessary for a tax savings of less than a billion to increase stock values by $300 billion. That would have been some leverage.

The capital formation lobby also tried to take credit for a small boom in venture capital—new issues of stock by small, high-risk, and potentially high-growth companies. In late 1979, Charls Walker's current press kit was filled with rosy press accounts of sizzling venture capital markets, many of the stories seeded by Walker himself, crediting the capital gains cut for setting off the boom.

But many Wall Street specialists in venture capital issues say privately that this is nonsense. In reality, small issues of stock by companies valued at under $5 million began growing in 1976 and 1977, for several reasons. Many small companies did far better than their bigger brethren, and portfolio managers and other institutional investors gradually have been getting in on the action. The Securities and Exchange Commission in recent years has liberalized disclosure and registration rules, making it easier to market small stock issues. The Labor Department in 1977 liberalized its pension fund regulations, permitting pension funds to invest in equity ventures. By early 1978, long before the capital gains cut, capital was pouring into the small stock issues.

And there is evidence that the venture capital boom actually leveled off in 1979, *after* the capital gains cut was passed. During 1978, small companies sold $129 million worth of publicly traded shares, but only $56 million in the first six months of 1979.

In addition, the Federal Reserve Board's tight money policies took the steam out of any capital investment boom. By late 1979, with interest rates in excess of 15 percent and a recession predicted, many companies were shelving expansion plans. This, of course, only confirms that investment decisions are made largely in response to general economic conditions; if interest rates are high and the public isn't buying, lowering capital gains rates to stimulate investment is like pushing on a string.

The failure of the stock market generally to perform as advertised did not daunt the capital formation lobby. At the annual meeting of the American Council for Capital Formation in November 1979, a genial Charlie Walker assured his audience that but for the capital gains tax cut, the market would have sunk even lower.

By late 1979, Walker was still riding the capital formation wave to promote the most audacious proposal of all, called the Capital Cost Recovery Act. While the capital gains cut saved wealthy investors a few billion dollars a year, this new bill would cut corporate income taxes by more than $50 billion a year.

The 1978 tax bill liberalized capital gains, made the investment tax credit permanent, and lowered rates on the corporate income tax. This left one obvious target—depreciation.

This latest panacea, sponsored by Democratic Representative Jim Jones, of Oklahoma, architect of the 1978 compromise capital gains cut, and Republican Barber Conable of Upstate New York, proposed to permit businesses to write off new investments over a far shorter time period than current law permits, producing bigger tax deductions each year. (Interestingly, the world's undisputed champion for liberal depreciation allowances is Great Britain, the current sick man of Europe; British companies are permitted to deduct the *entire* cost of an investment in the first year.)

The sponsors of the 1979–80 drive to liberalize depreciation frankly and gleefully proposed to abolish even the idea that business plant and machinery should be depreciated over a reasonably accurate "useful life," in favor of a fictitious depreciation formula—ten year write-offs for buildings, five years for machinery, and three years for light equipment such as automobiles, known as 10-5-3. This seemingly technical change would so increase tax shelters against corporate profits that corporate taxes would be cut almost in half.

Even accepting the premise that the higher after-tax profits would boost the economy, the net annual loss of revenues from corporate income taxes would soon rise to $50 billion. And, of course, the same amount of overall economic stimulus could be achieved by rebating the taxes to low-income taxpayers, rather than to the biggest businesses.

In theory the 1979–80 session of Congress was entirely the wrong season for promoting yet another tax cut for big business. Supposedly, thanks to the tax revolt itself, President Carter and the Congress were under great pressure to balance the federal budget. And a balanced budget requires cuts in spending with no cuts in taxes.

But Walker and the business groups suspected, not without reason, that the practical political value of an election year tax cut would far outweigh the more symbolic appeal of a balanced budget. And if a tax cut was to be, the business groups were determined to get a big piece of it for themselves.

The capital formation lobby essentially repeated its successful 1978 strategy: a coalition of all major business and financial groups behind one bill; a careful seeding of the friendly business press; and quiet personal buttonholing of legislators by businessmen back home. By the time hearing began in October 1979, an impressive majority of both houses of Congress had enlisted as cosponsors of the Jones-Conable Capital Cost Recovery Act.

The big business architects shrewdly called in an IOU with one of the small business trade associations, which came out for the bill. This was a coup, because accelerated depreciation is even more biased in favor of big business than the investment tax credit and is traditionally opposed by small business. An estimated 80 percent of the tax breaks under the new bill would go to the biggest one-tenth of U.S. corporations. Almost half would go to corporations valued at a billion dollars and over. This would occur because tax planning for accelerated depreciation is very complex; it requires matching capital investment dollars to offset current profits. Most small businesses are not positioned to program their investments with such precision. In effect, this subsidizes big business at the expense of small business, and enables the very largest corporations to operate with "cheaper" after-tax dollars than their smaller competitors.

The support of the National Federation of Independent Business for the Jones-Conable bill particularly annoyed other small business groups, but it was a coup for Walker. Once again, he had found an issue with a one-sided appeal. Depreciation gimmickry is a fairly arcane, accountants' sort of issue. It appeals mainly to companies with enough earnings to make use of it. Except during those rare periods when the general public gets worked up about tax equity, depreciation is quite esoteric to ordinary voters. And the congressman who resists business importuning to liberalize depreciation formulas, when there is no offsetting praise from his consumer or labor constituents, either has a stout heart or a safe seat.

Even Treasury Secretary William Miller, testifying in strenuous opposition to the bill, deferentially accepted Walker's premises—"Accelerated deductions reduce the 'tax wedge,' " Miller said. "The reduction in the 'tax wedge' reduces the cost of capital and thereby increases the amount of capital that can be profitably employed. . . ."

Outside corporate boardrooms and Washington corridors of influence, the name most closely associated with tax revolt is Howard Jarvis. But if Jarvis helped to launch a public mood demanding tax rollbacks, it was Charlie Walker and his clients—America's very biggest businesses—who made the most effective use of what Jarvis wrought. "At the rate we're winning," Walker said after 10-5-3 began to make headway, "I'm worried about working us out of business."

On October 22, 1979, testifying on his latest loophole, Walker reflected on how radically the game had changed in barely a year. Beaming as he instructed the members of the Senate Finance Committee on the new version of the old economics, Walker observed with the disarming candor of a man who has the votes:

> Mr. Chairman, nothing demonstrates more vividly just how far the country and Congress have come in the capital formation movement than to cast our minds back to the early 1970's and ask: How would the proposal for 10-5-3 have been received at that time? In all probability, it would have been subjected to extreme criticism and even ridicule. Tax purists would have attacked the scuttling of the useful-life concept with respect to capital cost recovery as heresy. The static revenue cost would have brought forth forecasts of huge increases in the Federal deficit. And the whole exercise would have been castigated as a "Fat Cat" plot to provide a "bonanza" for business by further "stacking" the Federal tax system in favor of the rich and against the poor. The fact that only a few voices are now raised in objection to 10-5-3 testifies to the great progress that has been made. And the fact that such progress has been made where it really counts, in Congress, is emphasized by the number of co-sponsors of 10-5-3 legislation—a clear majority of Members in both Houses.

PART IV

As
Goes
California

16

THE IMITATIONS

THE YEAR 1978 was especially sweet for political conservatives. After decades of unsuccessfully fighting government by opposing the enactment of programs, the tax revolt suddenly revealed a way to slice through the entire knot. What conservatives failed to achieve through the front door of opposition to spending, they might accomplish via the back door by limiting taxes. The public proved to be quite schizophrenic. Convinced that the government had layers of fat to spare, constituents who depended on expensive government programs could also support across-the-board tax limitation. The voters, it seemed, had picked up Congress's old saw: "Vote to increase programs and cut taxes."

Proposition 13 supercharged limitation ballot propositions that were already underway in Michigan, Idaho, Nevada, Massachusetts, and Arizona. Elsewhere, it helped home-grown tax rebels who were previously unknown get their propositions onto the ballot. At the July 1978 meeting of the National Conference of State Legislators, talk of Jarvis-Gann dominated the sessions. "That was a bullet from a loaded gun that went off in California and is now going through a few other states," said Oregon legislator Jason Boe, the president-elect of the conference. "But it's still on its way to its ultimate target—high level of Federal spending."

Midway through the meeting, word quickly spread that a ballot drive led by a perennial loser had qualified a Jarvis type of initiative in Boe's eminently rational home state of Oregon.

After Jarvis, the political landscape was quickly filled with a chaotic array of grass-roots tax revolt organizations—many of them fringe groups that had taken on political respectability for the first time, thanks to Proposition 13. "We used to be the kooks," marveled Yvonne Chicoine, the American Conservative Union's young director of tax issues, "now we're the moderates." At the ACU's annual convention, meeting in Washington's Hyatt Regency Hotel, the heroes of the hour were the grass-roots tax rebels—Dave Copeland, author of the Tennessee constitutional tax limitation; Dick Headlee, sponsor of the successful Michigan tax limitation initiative; and countless others. From the podium, Headlee warmly thanked his hosts, praising the members of the Michigan Conservative Union for supplying the troops to stuff envelopes and get his campaign going. "I only asked one thing," Headlee added. "Don't tell anyone you're supporting it until we get a broad-based coalition going, because we don't want the press labeling this a right-wing thing."

The press did not label it as a right-wing thing, but as a populist uprising.

Yet the clones of Proposition 13, which were rushed onto the November 1978 ballots in other states, produced a surprisingly mixed bag of results. Only one state, Idaho, enacted a direct copy of Proposition 13, largely because the Idaho property tax burden had shifted disastrously to homeowners in the preceding few years, just as it had in California. (See Chapter 9.)

Nevada voters, by a margin of better than 3 to 1, also adopted a 1 percent property tax limitation modeled on Proposition 13, but under the Nevada constitution the amendment had to be ratified again in 1980, before it could take effect. In the meantime, the 1979 session of the Nevada legislature passed a more moderate program of tax relief that replaced property tax revenues with other money, hoping to satisfy public tax-reduction sentiment in time to kill the 1 percent limit. The legislative package, promoted by Nevada Governor Robert List, took advantage of a $168 million state surplus to enact an unprecedented $224 million tax relief package. The bill reduces property taxes an average of 27 percent, replaces most of the loss to local government by giving cities and counties a share of gaming taxes, which previously had gone directly to the state. It limits the future growth of local government spending to the growth of personal income, along the lines of the NTLC formula, and repeals the sales tax on food.

In the November 1978 election, voters in Hawaii and Texas passed initiatives limiting the future growth of public spending to the growth of the state economy. Arizona voters overwhelmingly passed their initiative limiting state spending to a flat 7 percent of state personal income. But a similar statutory measure failed in Nebraska, and Colorado voters rejected a constitutional limitation on state spending. In Colorado a Jarvis-type property tax limit failed even to qualify for the ballot. In North Dakota, voters approved an initiative raising taxes on corporations and lowering them for individuals.

In two key states, Michigan and Oregon, voters rejected Jarvis imitations, while Michigan voters narrowly approved a very complex measure heavily lobbied by the NTLC and Michigan business limiting increases in the growth of public spending. In Massachusetts, voters approved an initiative backed by a liberal-labor-urban coalition, shifting taxes from homeowners to business.

It was not quite the uniform national sweep that had been widely predicted in the first flush of Jarvis' triumph.

THE NATIONAL TAX LIMITATION COMMITTEE

Of the several networks of tax protest groups to emerge in Jarvis' wake, the National Tax Limitation Committee quickly emerged as the most formidable. Most of the tax revolt leaders in the states today are part of the NTLC's network, the notable exception being Howard Jarvis.

Whereas Jarvis and his imitators promoted fairly radical ad-hoc remedies aimed mainly at long-standing grievances against the property tax, the NTLC stands for a more systematic conservatism and constitutional restraints on total government taxation and outlay, at all levels of government.

NTLC Chairman Lewis Uhler has a highly refined theory of the inevitability of fiscal ruin in a democratic society, and a highly refined remedy to prevent it: constitutional limitation on public expenditures as a share of total personal income. To Uhler, constitutional tax limitation is the twentieth-century equivalent of the restraints on popular passion that informed the original Constitution of 1787.

Given the natural alliance between special interest groups and their bureaucratic patrons, Uhler has written: "It is only natural that the prime motivating force and incentive is towards increasing the power and size of government. Measure by measure, more pressure can be brought to bear in favor of a particular proposal than the general interest, diffused as it is, can generate in opposition."

To anyone who has observed government at close range, this observa tion contains the ring of truth.

For Uhler, just as the original checks and balances restrained political passions from destroying liberties, only constitutional restraints can prevent democratic pressures for economic ruin today.

The theory, the remedy, and the political movement for tax limitation have been gradually refined over nearly a decade, having originated (where else?) in California.

Uhler is a onetime John Birch Society activist, and former aide to Representative John Rousselot, the first Bircher elected to the U.S. Congress. In 1971 he joined the Reagan Administration as the state antipoverty director and soon was under attack as a hatchet man for his hostility to many of the programs he was administering. Subsequently, Uhler was appointed to chair Reagan's Tax Reduction task force in 1972. Out of the task force came a ballot proposition of Byzantine complexity, Reagan's Proposition 1, which proposed to roll back state spending at the rate of one-tenth of one percent a year, until it reached 7 percent of personal income. It amended the constitution, on the theory that the legislature couldn't be trusted.

Uhler, a careful lawyer, included so many safeguards and formulas that the eventual proposition was virtually unintelligible. Reagan's sponsorship, at a time when the Governor's own popularity was waning, became a liability. Even so, Proposition 1 lost by only a slight margin, 56 to 44.

"The germ of an idea was born out of that failure," Uhler says. After Reagan stepped down, Uhler returned to his law practice, developing real estate as a profitable sideline. But the idea of constitutional tax limitation stuck with him. He spent over a year conferring with the conservative economists and businessmen who had helped devise Proposition 1. In 1975 they incorporated the National Tax Limitation Committee, with William Rickenbacker of the *National Review* as chairman and Uhler as president. Reagan's Proposition 1 would serve as the model of an idea that possessed wide appeal by the end of the decade. Many of the same men from the Reagan task force moved onto the board of the new committee—W. Craig Stubblebine, a conservative economics professor from Claremont College, William Niskanen, of the University of California at Berkeley and later chief economist for Ford Motor Company; and Milton Friedman, the country's best-known free market economist. Prior to Howard Jarvis' success in 1978, the NTLC remained a quite marginal operation, yet it was a latent network that was uniquely positioned to run with Jarvis' success and provide tactical and political support to the dozens of grass-roots groups that mushroomed after Jarvis' triumph.

Uhler quickly gave up the idea of trying to qualify another version of Proposition 1 for California's 1974 election. Governor Reagan was fairly unpopular by then, and he was not running again. Instead, Uhler turned to Michigan, where the same general idea already had some local enthusiasm.

In Michigan a young industrial engineer with the Dow Chemical company named William Shaker had come up with the same idea independently. Shaker had helped draft a report for the local Chamber of Commerce, fixing government spending as a percentage of personal income. In 1973, after he got wind of the Reagan proposal, Shaker flew to California, where he spent three weeks helping Uhler with the campaign. "After the defeat," Shaker recalls, "I spent another week or so poking through the ashes. I got back to Michigan with about three boxes of material. In 1973 I tried to sell our legislature on the idea. I was quite naive then."

Having failed to interest the Legislature, Shaker drafted a ballot proposition for the 1974 Michigan general election and organized a small group called Michigan Citizens United for Tax Limitation. His canvassers were mostly college students whom Shaker paid a dime for each signature they collected. The drive fell far short, with about 100,000 signatures, of which more than 10,000 were collected by one enterprising sophomore who was subcontracting the job to friends in his dorm for a nickel a signature.

In 1976, with Uhler working as his campaign coordinator, Shaker tried again. Bill Niskanen, who had moved to Michigan to become Ford Motor Company's chief economist, also helped out. This time, a revised and better-drafted Proposition C qualified for the ballot, with the support of the state Chamber of Commerce. It lost, but garnered a quite respectable 43 percent of the vote. By 1978, after Jarvis' victory, Shaker would finally have the right product at the right time.

The Tax Limitation network's first success, however, was the Tennessee spending limit, proposed by constitutional convention and ratified in March 1978, three months before Jarvis' triumph. Other successes would follow after Proposition 13.

Uhler and the National Tax Limitation Committee, interestingly, sat out Proposition 13. Jarvis was a little too nutty. Proposition 13 was too radical, and more seriously it was too *unsystematic*, Uhler thought. It rolled back one tax; it didn't really restrain government. He voted for it, of course, and today Uhler is happily coasting on the jet stream Jarvis created, to promote his own brand of tax cutting.

A month after Proposition 13 passed, Uhler and the National Tax Limitation Committee shifted into high gear. In July at a Washington press conference, Uhler introduced a prestigious drafting committee, to work on a proposed amendment to the U.S. Constitution. Unlike Jarvis' effort, which remained an amateur, antipolitics crusade, the NTLC assembled a quite respectable roster of mainstream conservatives: former U.S. Solicitor General Robert Bork, Nixon economic advisor Robert McCracken, Berkeley political scientist Aaron Wildavsky, tax scholar C. Lowell Harriss, as well as tax rebels Copeland, Headlee, Niskanen, and the ubiquitous Charls Walker. Howard Jarvis was notably absent.

In January 1979 the NTLC unveiled its amendment; a variation of Reagan's Proposition 1, the amendment proposed to limit any future increase in federal outlays to the increase in gross national product, with the proviso that in any year when inflation exceeded 3 percent, federal spending could increase only three-quarters as fast as economic growth. Assuming that inflation continues at a rate in excess of 3 percent, this would reduce spending from 21.3 percent of GNP to 19.3 percent of GNP by 1990.

The timing could not have been better, because within a month the Republican leadership in Congress seized on the NTLC amendment as a more responsible alternative to yet another conservative idea that seemed to be sweeping the country: the proposal for a new U.S. constitutional convention to require a balanced federal budget.

NATIONAL TAXPAYERS UNION

Like the NTLC, the National Taxpayers Union was on the scene well before Proposition 13, and took renewed strength from Jarvis' success. Paid membership doubled during 1978, to some 96,000. The National Taxpayers Union began with support mainly from the far right, but it soon became more freewheeling in its style and more libertarian in its outlook. Its national office in a rickety Capitol Hill townhouse could be mistaken for an environmentalist or an antiwar headquarters. Since its founding in 1969, the NTU has been breezily antitax and antigovernment, and its present board includes left-of-center intellectuals of vaguely anarchist sympathies such as Robert Sherrill, Washington correspondent for *The Nation* magazine, as well as more-conventional conservatives.

The NTU's chairman is an intense libertarian intellectual named James Dale Davidson, fond of quoting eighteenth-century philosophers and twitting twentieth-century opportunism. Davidson is a romantic conservative of considerable charm, who thoroughly enjoys directing his iconoclastic wit at the entire political spectrum. In Davidson's view, Adam Smith's free market doesn't really work anymore because reliance on big government has perverted incentives, making hypocrites of conservatives as well as liberals and blunting the force of personal heroism. "The American Revolution was really the work of about twenty people," says Davidson. "Today, everybody is so focused on avoiding risks, that we've emptied life of decisive meaning. When you have high taxes, it is very hard for new enterprise to compete. High taxes reward monopoly privilege. High taxes prevent people from changing their pattern of discretionary income. Institutional egoism gets substituted for personal egoism. The liberal ideal was really defeated in this century." One cannot engage in even casual conversation with Davidson without encountering Tocqueville, Lord Halifax, Von Hayek, Marx, Bentham, and Adolf Wagner, the nineteenth-century German economist who predicted that as the masses got the franchise, government would be under growing pressure to increase its own powers to redistribute wealth, to the point where much of the wealth would be appropriated by government itself.

Davidson accuses orthodox conservatives of "harshness and lack of compassion. They're also guilty of gross oversights, like their failure to criticize the Pentagon."

Where Uhler and the NTLC step lightly in criticizing the NTU's balanced budget drive, Davidson does not spare the NTLC. "Uhler is irrelevant," Davidson says. "They hire professional conservatives like [fundraiser Richard] Vigurie. He hasn't done the hard work necessary to create a grass-roots movement. Uhler's group is mainly a media event."

This is not entirely fair; although the NTLC itself is not a grass-roots organization, many of the state and local groups assisted by the NTLC are. And several state groups are listed as affiliates of both the NTLC and the NTU. Davidson is far more laudatory of Jarvis, whom he regards as an authentic, heroic figure, symbolizing rugged individualism. The NTU worked hard on Proposition 13. "The problem is that Jarvis isn't really a movement at all," according to Davidson. "He really doesn't tie into any network. He's surrounded by a group of people not of his caliber. Jarvis is a one-man band. If he fell under a truck tomorrow, his movement would be over."

The NTU's lively newspaper, *Dollars and Sense,* goes after Pentagon waste and corporate bail-outs with the same ferocity that it attacks Amtrak, the Post Office, tax-supported municipal trash collection, and other socialistic ventures. Davidson's ideological consistency makes him untrustworthy to many business conservatives.

NTU's best-known project is, of course, the constitutional amendment to require a balanced federal budget. The unusual wrinkle is that the NTU amendment uses a mechanism authorized by the Constitution but never before tried—a constitutional convention. Under Article V, the Constitution provides that upon petition of two-thirds of the state legislatures, Congress must convene a constitutional convention. The convention approach appeals to Davidson, because it circumvents the Congress entirely. "From the point of view of Congress," Davidson says, "the true danger is not that the convention would do something preposterous but that it is a repudiation of the current way of doing business. Beyond everything else, most congressmen wish to be reelected. As a matter of pure logic, they improve their chances by resorting to deficit spending."

The balanced-budget amendment was a classic sleeper. It was first introduced into the Maryland legislature by James Clark, in 1975. Promoted by the National Taxpayers Union and its affiliates, the amendment attracted virtually no national notice. Many state legislatures willingly approved a balanced budget resolution as a god and motherhood sort of declaration, with no hearing, no debate, and no opposition. Demanding that the federal government balance its budget cost nothing and provided a good vote for fiscal responsibility to show the voters. By March 1978, Colorado had become the twenty-second state, out of a required thirty-four, to memorialize Congress calling for a balanced-budget convention.

In early January 1979, the National Taxpayers Union got an unexpected phone call from California Governor Jerry Brown's chief of staff, Gray Davis, asking for information about the balanced-budget drive. The following week, in his second inaugural address, Brown out-Jarvised Jarvis with a surprise endorsement of the constitutional convention.

For the National Taxpayers Union, Brown's support was a very mixed blessing. Coming from Brown, the endorsement tainted the balanced-budget campaign with the flavor of opportunism and gimmickry. It also brought unwanted reams of press attention. Until then, the campaign had been doing just fine without publicity. "Jerry Brown blew our cover," Jim Davidson compained, only half-kidding.

More seriously, Brown's endorsement awakened potent political opposition. By the end of January 1979, Arkansas, North Carolina, South Dakota, and Utah had passed the required resolution, bringing the total to twenty-six. With a constitutional convention suddenly a very serious prospect, formidable opposition began mobilizing for the first time. Members of the congressional budget committees began suggesting that if Congress was forced to balance its budget, the best place to begin trimming might be with the $85 billion in annual federal aid to the states.

"If Congress must suddenly chop the deficit, it will land in the laps of the states. This is not a threat. It's a matter of arithmetic," warned Senator Edmund Muskie, chairman of the Senate Budget Committee.

"During its 1975–76 session, the Pennsylvania Legislature passed its call for a balanced federal budget. That was Resolution 236," Muskie added indignantly. Resolution 235 demanded a renewal of revenue sharing."

With state budgets showing a balance of $5 billion, the $6.8 billion a year in general revenue-sharing became a useful bargaining counter. The revenue-sharing program was set to expire in 1980. Funds for state government struck Congress as the lowest priority, and the nations' governors had to fight hard to get Congress to fund the program in 1979. The Washington *Post*'s cartoonist, Herblock, captured the congressional annoyance quite precisely in a cartoon showing a scruffy youth in a State sweatshirt writing a letter to his old Uncle Sam. "Dear Uncle," went the letter, "I've run into some extra expenses and need an increase in my allowance so I won't have to use my own money. Please hurry. By the way—when are you going to show some responsibility and balance your damn budget?" The political establishment of both parties began closing ranks against a constitutional convention.

In early February, Republican leaders meeting at their annual legislative conference in Easton, Maryland, passed a resolution supporting an NTLC–style constitutional limitation on federal spending, as an alternative to the more radically populist constitutional convention. Party Chairman William Brock told reporters that the Constitution, "the most fundamental document of our land," should not be subjected to a second constitutional convention. And Senator Paul Laxalt of Utah, a Reagan ally, warned that a convention might lose control and upset basic protections.

The sponsors of the convention idea challenge this. A study by the American Bar Association in 1973 concluded that a convention could be limited to a single topic, and in any event its product would have to be ratified by thirty-eight states.

In the debate that ensued, opponents carefully pointed out that in one key respect, the federal budget was already balanced: if the federal government separated current outlays from capital spending, which is the way states and local governments keep their books, the federal budget actually would run a slight surplus. Once a balanced-budget amendment did pass, Congress could easily change its bookkeeping to comply nominally.

From the other side, the NTLC and its supporters attacked the balanced budget as a misplaced remedy. A balanced budget doesn't necessarily cut spending or lower taxes. In fact, if the special interest groups that benefit from federal outlays (who are ten feet tall in the tax-revolt literature) marshal their forces against program cuts, then a balanced-budget requirement could actually lead to *higher* taxes.

But the debate was soon overtaken by political realities. Not only was the Republican leadership rallying against the constitutional convention; Jerry Brown's endorsement made the campaign a lightning rod for attacks by the Carter Administration and its allies. In Jerry Brown's home ground, California Assembly Speaker Leo McCarthy saw to it that the resolution was killed in committee, less than a month after Brown's endorsement.

In late January, 1979, Massachusetts Lieutenant Governor Tommy O'Neill, son of House Speaker Tip O'Neill, announced formation of a new national committee, called Citizens for the Constitution, to oppose the balanced-budget drive. Helping O'Neill were several trade unions and Carter Administration White House staffers led by Dick Moe, Vice President Mondale's chief of staff.

The first major test of strength came in Montana, where backers of the balanced-budget amendment won Montana House passage in mid-February by a vote of 70 to 30. But the new coalition in a last-minute telephone blitz by the White House and national trade unions persuaded the Montana Senate to defeat the resolution 31 to 18. This was followed by a second defeat in the Massachusetts House on April 2, leaving the balanced-budget campaign stalled at twenty-nine states out of the necessary thirty-four.

Now the next big battleground would be New Hampshire, which was doubly significant because it pitted Jerry Brown against Jimmy Carter in a preliminary, proxy version of the 1980 Democratic primary, with Brown siding with most of the state's Republicans in supporting the amendment, and Carter opposed.

In mid-March, the New Hampshire House speaker, Republican George Roberts, invited Brown to address a joint session of the legislature on the balanced-budget amendment. This infuriated leading Democrats in the state, who warned Brown not to come in as a guest of the Republicans. Roberts modified the format to a joint hearing, inviting opponents as well as supporters. Brown impulsively decided to come, taking with him for his first foray into the Granite State an entourage of seventeen reporters and not a single aide.

Having snagged Brown over the protests of the California Governor's fellow Democrats, Speaker Roberts decided to get even cuter. His witness list, unveiled the day of the hearing, put on all the supporters first, leaving opponents to cool their heels far into the night. And the leading opponent was New Hampshire's Democratic governor, Hugh Gallen, a strong supporter of Jimmy Carter. At this snub, the Democrats on the committee angrily walked out.

Before he got a chance to testify, Governor Brown found himself ushered into a private meeting with Governor Gallen, who asked Brown, Governor to Governor, not to attend the session. The press was then called in to hear Brown dutifully explain that he would not be a party to this snub.

"The Republican leadership has used this occasion as some kind of ploy to not show proper respect to the Democratic party and its outstanding governor," said Brown manfully. "I will not be a party to anything that will diminish the Democratic party in this state."

"Don't you find this a little embarrassing?" a reporter asked rhetorically.

Brown never got to testify; instead, he met privately with Democratic legislators and then repaired to Concord's premier political saloon, Osgood's Tavern. There he held forth for several hours, on the decline of the U.S. as a world power, space exploration, his favorite authors, and the new austerity.

Carrying the message of austerity to frugal New Hampshire was a bit like importing oil to Kuwait.

The state's Democrats were virtually united in opposition to the amendment. "We're a fiscally conservative state, Governor," said Harry Spanos, who was trounced as the Democratic candidate for governor in 1974 when he proposed a tax hike to pay for better public services. "We have no sales tax, no income tax, and you should understand something: the people are hurting."

Then the talk turned to Presidential politics. "Do you think the far right is gaining strength?" someone asked.

"Absolutely," Brown responded. "Look at Connally and Reagan. People are scared, they want simple solutions—nukes, invade Saudi Arabia, balance the budget . . ."

It did not seem an auspicious evening either for Brown or for the balanced-budget amendment. Two of Tommy O'Neill's operatives returned to Boston convinced that they had skewered both Brown and the balanced-budget amendment then and there.

But as it turned out, supporters of the amendment had a few countermoves left to make. Although many of the moderate Republicans in the New Hampshire legislature opposed the amendment, Speaker Roberts put substantial heat on his fellow Republicans to support the resolution. Until a day before the vote, opponents thought they could defeat the resolution by 30 votes. But Roberts had been working hard. One feminist legislator was warned that Roberts might bring up the Equal Rights Amendment for a recision vote unless she voted aye. Roberts threatened the chairwoman of the environmental committee to block passage of her coastal zone bill; and the chairman of the committee on banks was told he might not be reappointed unless he ducked the vote. In the end, the amendment passed by 17 votes on a party-line vote. And New Hampshire became the thirtieth state to call for a constitutional convention.

But there the movement stalled. The libertarian purists might support a balanced-budget resolution, but the big-money conservatives were betting on capital gains cuts and a NTLC-style tax limitation. The powerful Business Roundtable put out a statement advising against a constitutional convention. Even Milton Friedman, who had supported Jarvis and most other tax limitation plans that came along, said he thought a constitutional convention was a bad idea. This turn of events delighted Uhler. "Jerry Brown made moderates out of us all," he quipped.

Of the various forces promoting tax limitation, the National Tax Limitation Committee clearly had the upper hand by decade's end. With a paid membership of over 300,000, the NTLC had the right wing's fundraising wizard, Richard Vigurie, running a direct mail operation that sent out over a million pieces a month. In January 1980, the NTLC opened a Washington office, headed by Bill Shaker, architect of the successful Michigan initiative.

Howard Jarvis also attempted to go national, but with scant success. With the aid of his media advisors, Butcher-Forde, Jarvis produced a television extravaganza to raise funds and announce the formation of a new mass membership group, the American Tax Reduction Movement, to promote a new federal constitutional amendment to cut federal income taxes by $25 million a year spread over four years. The TV special raised $700,000 and cost $600,000 to produce.

Despite Jarvis' symbolic stature in the tax limitation movement, his new organization is widely considered to be little more than one man, a public relations firm, and a mailing list. His own constitutional amendment, introduced by Representative Robert Dornan, made virtually no headway in Congress.

In a wonderfully blunt appeal to buy votes for his new amendment, Jarvis sent telegrams to candidates for Congress, reading: "If you support the plan, my office will contact you with respect to possible financial assistance in your campaign, as well as direct mail, radio, TV and newspaper endorsements which will be available to our supporters. In addition, I will make selected personal appearances on behalf of candidates pledged to our plan."

There were few takers.

THE TAX FOUNDATION

The new wave of tax protest organizations overshadows a far more influential force for fiscal conservatism which has been part of the landscape since 1937—the Tax Foundation and its numerous affiliates at the state level.

Although a tax-exempt, nonprofit organization, the Tax Foundation makes no secret of its hostility to high taxes. According to a brochure put out by the foundation, "Many corporation executives consider Tax Foundation an extension of their own staffs. It provides services valuable to top level economists, government relations people, speech writers. . . . The Tax Foundation staff also answers many requests for specific information to meet research needs in key areas of business life which are affected by tax and related policies."

The members of the Tax Foundation are primarily corporation people. The board of trustees is made up almost entirely of business representatives, from such corporations as Exxon, General Motors, AT&T, Olin, G.E., Tenneco, U.S. Steel, Rockwell International, ALCOA, and a small sprinkling of college professors. Nationally, the Tax Foundation publishes its monthly *Tax Review* and its annual, authoritative *Facts and Figures on Government Finance*. Although the tone is far more restrained than that of the more strident tax revolt groups, the message is unmistakable: Taxes are too damned high.

It is at the state level that the several tax foundations exercise their greatest influence. There is no organic connection between the state groups and the national foundation, but there is an informal network of like-minded people. Like the national group, the state foundations are largely creatures of big business. Unlike Washington, in which dozens of public interest lobbies act to offset business influence, the tax foundations in the state capitals are usually considered *the* source of reliable data on tax matters.

To my knowledge, only one state (ironically California) has a permanent tax reform lobby. But business-organized and -financed tax foundations operate in thirty-three state capitals. They often provide the only nongovernmental fiscal analyses used by state officials and legislators, as well as key witnesses with expert testimony. In researching this book, I was struck how in state after state I was referred by public officials to the local tax foundation as the best unbiased source of information on fiscal matters. In California the California Taxpayers Association (CAL-TAX) has a sophisticated legislative staff and a comprehensive newsletter whose analyses are often more current than those of the state government. In Idaho the Associated Taxpayers group is extremely influential. And in Massachusetts even government officials use the Massachusetts Taxpayers Foundation's handbooks as the basic source of information on public finance.

The Massachusetts Taxpayers Foundation is financed by the big Boston banking and insurance interests, which are fiscally conservative but prudently unwilling to dismantle the state lest business confidence be shaken. As a consequence, the Taxpayers Foundation manages to insinuate itself into the center of most debates about tax policy in Massachusetts because it is an indispensable partner for any centrist coalition. In the jockeying over Proposition 2½, the Massachusetts equivalent of Proposition 13, MTF representatives were negotiating with both the No and the Yes forces, to try to bring about a compromise plan to slow down big government which would be less extreme than Proposition 2½. Like their feckless brethren in the original No-On-13 campaign, tax reformers in Massachusetts found themselves trying to argue against Proposition 2½ as a business-inspired tax shift while their supposed allies included Prudential Insurance and State Street Bank.

FEDERAL TAX LIMITATION

In Congress, Proposition 13 gave the budget cutters a great psychological lift but little else in 1978 and 1979. The most prominent of the congressional tax rebels was yet another conservative with roots in the Reagan Administration, Congressman Jack Kemp. Kemp, a former quarterback for the Buffalo Bills, got to know Reagan while he played for San Diego earlier in his football career. He is also a close ideological comrade of Arthur Laffer, Jude Wanniski, and the other prophets of "supply-side incentives" to stimulate the economy through more efficient trickledown.

Kemp is one of the Republican party's most attractive new faces, a quite serious intellectual, and a conservative who, like Jarvis, appeals to a blue-collar constituency. Kemp's legislative proposal, with Senator William Roth of Delaware, would cut federal income taxes about 30 percent, phased in over a three-year period, on the Lafferesque theory that the resultant incentive to get rich would so stimulate economic growth that federal revenues would not decrease.

Kemp's personal style is old-fashioned boosterism. His hero is John Kennedy, the last President in Kemp's view to inspire progress by appealing to national consensus rather than mobilizing factions. "The greatest obstacle to opportunity and advancement," according to Kemp is "static thinking: the idea that life is a zero-sum-game." Kemp argues that economic redistribution is wrong-headed because it presumes a fixed economic pie. "The football fan knows," he says, "that there aren't a fixed number of touchdowns to go around. The only limits are time and the potential of each player . . ."

Unfortunately for Kemp, the Republican party's embrace of the Kemp-Roth bill was so loving and so total that the bill soon became a different sort of football, which the vast majority of congressional Democrats refused to touch under any circumstances. In the 1978 session, after Kemp-Roth was badly defeated in both houses, Senate Democrats did approve a rather cynical bipartisan imitation sponsored by Senator Sam Nunn of Georgia, which would cut taxes by about 25 percent over five years if Congress balanced the federal budget. The Nunn amendment was such an election-year ploy that Republican leaders dubbed it "Son of Kemp-Roth," calling a press conference to claim parentage and pass out cigars. As expected, the Nunn amendment was watered down so far as to be rendered almost meaningless by the House-Senate conference committee that wrote the final 1978 tax bill.

In 1979, despite the strong national sentiment favoring a balanced budget as a political idea, strong resistance continued to the cutting of particular programs. The Kemp-Roth bill remained stuck at about 100 House sponsors and little prospect of enactment. In the spring of 1979, committees of the House and Senate began hearings on congressionally initiated constitutional amendments to require a balanced federal budget, but these were widely regarded as nothing more than moves to relieve some of the pressure from the state balanced-budget resolutions.

As recession loomed, the pressure for a balanced budget collided head-on with the pressure for a tax cut. Unless Congress was willing to make draconian cuts in public outlays—something unthinkable in a recession —you could not have a tax cut *and* a balanced budget.

Completing action on the fiscal 1980 budget, House and Senate conferees resolved their impasse in the time-honored fashion. Senators gave in to spending requests dear to the House, and House conferees accepted programs demanded by the Senate. The House conferees reluctantly agreed to higher military spending; in return, the Senate went along with higher spending for job training, education, and welfare. The final bill projected a federal deficit of just under $30 billion and exceeded the joint budget resolution by about $2.5 billion.

Nineteen eighty was another story. With inflation worsening, the Carter Administration vied with Republican conservatives to bring in a balanced budget in an election year. Until it was overtaken by the recession, a federal balanced budget suddenly took on a life of its own as a political totem—even though no politician seriously expected it to do much to reduce inflation. On the basis of economic assumptions projected in March 1980 when the looming recession seemed far milder than it turned out to be, both Carter and the Congress readily agreed to legislate a balanced budget. The only fight loomed over what measures of guns and butter to cut. But by late spring, when the budget was made final, the economic assumptions of March were preposterously out of date. The recession was coming on with such force that the Treasury would almost surely take in far less revenue than the March projections assumed, and the government also would have to pay out far more in unemployment compensation. Though the budget appeared nominally in balance, all the players in the game knew that when the final figures were in, it would be in deficit again. But the ritual was played out nonetheless.

Moreover, as the recession worsened, pressures increased for a tax cut, which of course would only increase the deficit. Even at the height of the balanced-budget fever, the Administration's economists and the congressional conservatives both knew that the "balanced budget" they were casting election-year votes for would not be balanced at all.

As a final irony, the balanced-budget fad was the only thing that kept Charls Walker and his capital formation crusade from completing their raid on the Treasury with their latest tax-cut gimmick, 10-5-3. Despite the overwhelming business pressure for the bill, a cut on federal revenues of $50 billion was plainly unthinkable in a year when most politicians were demanding a balanced budget.

Under the congressional budget review process begun in 1974, Congress attempts to set an overall spending limit, which it must live within as it makes outlay decisions on specific programs. A preliminary budget resolution is adopted in the spring of each year, and a final figure is agreed upon by September 15, two weeks before the start of the new fiscal year. While conservative groups would like the cuts to be far steeper, most will admit that the budget process has helped slow down the growth of federal spending to about the general rate of inflation. But since many of the biggest programs are in effect indexed to rise with inflation, their outlays are considered "uncontrollable," leaving very little leeway for Congress to enact new programs without cutting back old ones or busting the budget.

In this frustrating political climate, the National Tax Limitation Committee won a significant convert when the House Budget Committee chairman, Representative Robert Giaimo, a liberal Democrat from Connecticut, introduced his own bill restricting federal spending as a percentage of gross national product. As chairman of the House Budget Committee, Giaimo had grown weary of fighting for the budget resolution holding down spending to an agreed-upon figure, only to see it exceeded time after time by pressure from this or that special-interest group.

Special-interest politics frustrate the budget process in a variety of ways. While conservatives point to pressure for spending as the main culprit, in fact it was the defeat of a liberal proposal for hospital cost containment that was the final straw for Giaimo in 1979. The compromise budget resolution, which Giaimo defended over the opposition of many of his liberal-spending friends, was predicated on enactment of President Carter's hospital cost containment bill, which was intended to save the federal government some $600 million in 1980 by holding down Medicare reimbursements. But pressure from the hospital industry defeated the bill —and increased the federal deficit by $600 million.

Ironically, another prime reason why Congress often fails to stay within its budget goal is the ease with which the tax committees give away revenue through tax preferences. By reducing revenues, tax expenditures bust the budget as surely as program expenditures. Taking the House floor on December 5, 1979, Representative Giaimo explained that in the past he had always opposed an across-the-board limit on government outlays. But, said Giaimo, "I have become convinced that unless we devise stricter controls, we will not get a grip on federal spending." Here, Giaimo threw the tax limitation movement a curve. His bill proposed to limit both federal program outlays *and* tax expenditures to 28.5 percent of GNP for fiscal year 1981. This would drop to 27.5 percent by 1983.

Given Giaimo's restriction of tax expenditures as well as direct outlays, nobody in the tax limitation movement was turning cartwheels—yet. But the embrace of tax limitation by a key liberal Democrat was one more step toward broad national acceptance of the idea.

The ballot propositions voted in 1978 and 1979 suggested that Uhler's group had consolidated their dominance of tax protest at the state level, too. In many respects, the Michigan election of November 1978 summed up the national mood and pointed toward the future direction of the tax revolt.

MICHIGAN

Michigan voters faced three rival ballot propositions in 1978.

The Jarvis imitation was sponsored by Robert Tisch, a largely unknown figure, whose main previous political experience was as the Drain Commissioner of rural Shiawassee County. Like the Jarvis amendment, Tisch's proposition proposed to cut property taxes about in half by reducing the taxable value of a property from 50 to 25 percent. Tisch also limited increases in assessments to 2.5 percent per year, but left localities free to increase rates. On balance, this would produce a 43 percent cut in property tax revenues.

As Tisch explained it, he got riled up about property taxes when his daughter and son-in-law found that they had to sell a cabin they had built with their own hands because they couldn't afford the property taxes. The Tisch initiative qualified for the Michigan ballot, coasting on Jarvis' momentum, and like Proposition 13, it was opposed by most of the state's mainstream political figures.

A second even more controversial ballot proposition proposed to introduce a school voucher plan to Michigan and divorce local school finance from the property tax altogether. The voucher amendment would require the state to issue a tuition voucher to the parents of all primary- and secondary-school children, financed by a general program of state taxation. The voucher could be used to pay for the child's education, whether in a public or private school. The proposition was silent on costs, standards, or administrative details of the plan.

If the public school lobby was not already at the barricades to block the Tisch amendment, the voucher proposal drew out every last teacher, school administrator, and PTA in the state.

The most moderate of the three initiatives was William Shaker's third try to pass a general tax limitation amendment. This time, Shaker's Michigan Taxpayers United for Tax Limitation came extremely well financed, with strong backing from the state's leading corporations, the Realtors, the Farm Bureau, the retailers, and the Michigan Chamber of Commerce; and behind the scenes help from the American Conservative Union and the National Tax Limitation Committee. Taxpayers United also had an engaging new spokesman in the person of Richard Headlee, the president of the Alexander Hamilton Life Insurance Company and a onetime head of the state Jaycees. Headlee, a former assistant to Michigan Governor George Romney, and a bishop in the Mormon Church, took a leave from his job to run the campaign.

The Headlee amendment, Proposition E, was not simple. It comprised eight separate parts. The key provision limited total state revenues to their proportion of state personal income in 1977—9.4 percent. Government tax collections could grow only in this fixed ratio to the growth of personal income. Any revenues that exceeded this ratio would have to be refunded to taxpayers.* The Headlee amendment also reined in local government so that no new taxes could be imposed by local government, except by a popular vote. If assessed property values increase faster than the consumer price index, then rates must be reduced so that the total revenues equal last year's revenues corrected for inflation. Revenues needed to pay off existing bonds were outside the limit.

In short, the Headlee amendment began with the premise that state and local government had grown to a maximum tolerable cost. Accordingly, it systematically froze government spending at its current level. The amendment was complicated, but not arbitrary. Unlike so many of the tax limitation initiatives promoted in the wake of Jarvis, it contained no booby traps. Even its critics could predict no catastrophic effects if the amendment passed. And the Headlee amendment was more moderate than Reagan's Proposition 1 and many of the other initiatives promoted by the National Tax Limitation Committee, in that it did not attempt to roll back the ratio of government spending, but only to limit it to the status quo.

Still, Michigan was not an ideal state in which to promote even this idea, because, unlike in California, there was little cause for the average voter to be mad as hell about his tax burden. To begin with, property taxes had not gone berserk in Michigan. Housing inflation was far less severe than in California, even in the affluent suburbs, and Michigan

---

* If the excess was one percent it could be kept in a budget stabilization fund. State spending would be limited to the revenue ceiling plus federal aid. The state would be prohibited from reducing the current share of state outlays earmarked for local aid, and any new programs mandated by the state would be paid for by the state.

provided the most generous state program of local property tax relief in the country under its circuit-breaker law, granting $275 million in annual state-financed property tax relief in 1977. Individual taxpayers receive a state credit against their income tax, which can be as high as $1,200 if their local property tax bill exceeds 3.5 percent of their income. Largely as a result of this circuit-breaker program, the trends that produced a shift in tax burdens onto homeowners in many other states were largely neutralized in Michigan. The homeowner share of the total property tax load had increased only slightly between 1969 and 1978, from 48 percent of the total to 51.3 percent. Property taxes had increased sharply in relation to personal income between 1967 and 1972, the year before the circuit breaker was enacted, rising from 4.3 to 5.3 percent, but by 1977 they had dropped back to 4.9 percent.

Total taxes did increase faster than personal income during the seventies, but only slightly, from 9.02 percent in 1971–72 to 9.48 percent in 1978–79. Michigan's growth of government was far slower than the average state's. According to census figures, Michigan ranked thirty-ninth in the rate of growth of state spending.

Thus, Michigan was no California. Yet the climate created in California would have substantial influence even here. With two far more extreme tax limitation proposals on the ballot, and most state officials up for reelection, Michigan's politicians wanted to be recorded in favor of some tax relief plan. With the influence of Proposition 13, the early polls showed massive support for the Headlee initiative. Quickly, a "lesser evil" psychology took hold. Michigan's popular Governor William Milliken, a moderate Republican, had strongly opposed the Shaker initiative in 1976. Now, in a very different political climate, facing reelection himself, he reluctantly supported Headlee, as less dangerous than the other two.

While civic groups such as the League of Women Voters, the education lobby, and Michigan's influential trade unions sought to lump all three propositions together, as unacceptable, the "lesser evil" psychology proved insurmountable. Even Michigan's liberal House speaker, Bobby Crim, the state's leading Democrat, said he could live with the Headlee amendment, and a week before the election it was endorsed by the Democratic candidate for governor.

Unlike in California, where big business found Howard Jarvis personally distasteful and his Proposition 13 too unsettling, the Headlee amendment was just the sort of proposal Michigan business liked. It provided an orderly restraint on the growth of government, without seeding the risk of a backlash against business. Dick Headlee was a reassuring figure, and he had highly skilled lieutenants in Niskanen and Shaker. The Amway Corporation, a maker of household goods sold door to door and owner of subsidiaries including the Mutual Broadcasting System, heavily supported the Headlee amendment. Through a free enterprise academy, Amway uses its door-to-door merchants as salesmen for free enterprise as well as cosmetics, and also provides highly polished free enterprise curricula for public schools. Amway poured tens of thousands of dollars into the Headlee campaign. The Michigan Chamber of Commerce made the Headlee amendment its top priority for 1978.

Headlee was able to run a highly professionalized campaign, whose centerpiece was a smooth, moderate-sounding slide show narrated by Headlee, which was shown in countless Rotary clubs, Grange halls, and living rooms throughout the state. For his part, Tisch ran a far cruder campaign, featuring two guest appearances by Howard Jarvis. As in California, the legislature belatedly attempted to head off all the initiatives with a legislative package, but time proved too short.

Ironically, the rival ballot propositions had the effect of making Headlee run scared. He raised close to a million dollars, far more than he had originally intended. Ironically too, but for the competition of the more radical Tisch initiative and the bandwagon effect it created for Headlee, no tax limitation initiative might have passed. In the end, despite the massive business support and the "lesser evil" mentality among most Michigan politicians, Headlee squeaked through with a bare 52 percent.

"Proposition 13 put the fear of God into the politicians; many people who philosophically opposed Headlee supported it anyway," observed Robert Queller, the director of Michigan's Citizen's Research Council, a business-oriented nonpartisan group that studies fiscal questions. "Probably, if the political leadership had opposed Headlee, they could have beaten it." And well they might have.

But by 1980, several other states would follow the script written in Michigan. A Jarvis type of revolt, led by a kooky figure and proposing a crude, meat-axe remedy, would be rejected as too extreme. Business would appropriate the tax revolt fever, tame it, and promote a cap on public expenditures. And most politicians would hold their nose and support the measure, relieved that it wasn't worse.

OREGON

The Oregon vote in 1968 also suggested that in the absence of genuine voter anger, the electorate remained skeptical of extremist leaders and extreme proposals. The leader of Oregon's instant tax protest was an even more bizarre figure than Howard Jarvis. Jimmy Dale Whittenburg, a pharmacist by trade, was not even particularly identified with tax protest. He was well known by Oregon political figures as a perennial hanger-on. He attached himself to Presidential campaigns, liberal more often than conservative, including those of George McGovern and Republican maverick Paul McCloskey. Whittenburg ran a one-man organization called The Lobby for Social Concerns and Demands. Regarded by many Oregon politicians as personally erratic, Whittenburg achieved notoriety when he was subdued by the Secret Service after screaming at Nelson Rockefeller at a rally in 1972. He was also well known for circulating letters describing his personal problems, including one to Senator Sam Ervin in 1973 asking the Senator to "help me gain my credibility," and another ten-page letter sent to at least forty individuals and newspapers describing his woes since 1968 when he had lost most of his possessions through a divorce, was robbed, and had a series of financial altercations with attorneys and physicians.

Whittenburg was also well known for leaving a trail of bad checks up and down Oregon. He was sued in 1976 by a local credit bureau for thirty-two worthless checks spanning a period of several years. Midway through the tax limitation campaign, Whittenburg was arrested, and criminal charges were filed against him for more bad checks. Shortly after the campaign concluded, he began serving a forty-five day sentence in the Lane County Jail.

In 1978, Whittenburg dumped several ballot propositions into the hopper. One of them was a measure to prohibit prosecution of people who pass bad checks. Another was a copy of California's Proposition 13. For once, Whittenburg got lucky. A few weeks after Jarvis' success, Whittenburg and his hastily assembled followers collected nearly 200,000 signatures to put a copy of Proposition 13 on the Oregon ballot. Whittenburg's Proposition 6, in fact, was quite literally a copy of the Jarvis-Gann amendment, with Oregon penciled in over California, and the 1 percent limit raised to a slightly more moderate 1½ percent.

Like Michigan, Oregon was not fertile territory for taxpayer revolt.

The state has a long tradition of good government and independent voting. Oregon's tax system is one of the nation's fairest, and one of the few that taxes higher incomes at higher effective rates. Oregon's state circuit-breaker program rivals Michigan's in its coverage. In the Census Bureau's rankings of assessment disparities within a state, Oregon consistently is ranked as a state with extremely accurate assessments and a scant degree of discrepancy from true value. Since 1913, Oregon has also had a "levy limit" restricting the annual increase in local taxes to 6 percent unless the voters approve an override. Total state taxes grew only slightly faster than in Michigan during the seventies, placing Oregon thirty-fifth in rank in the growth of state spending.

The rapid inflation in housing values did produce a distinct shift in property taxes onto homeowners, who were paying 44 percent of the load in 1978, up sharply from 33 percent in 1974.

The tax shift was blunted somewhat by the circuit-breaker program, but the legislature had failed to increase circuit-breaker relief substantially as the tax shift accelerated. Thus, there was some voter anger, but far less aggravated than California's.

After Jim Whittenburg qualified his initiative, the Governor and panicky leigslators called the Oregon legislature into special session. The legislature quickly placed on the ballot its own tax relief package as an alternative to Whittenburg's.

The legislature's rival constitutional amendment, Proposition 11, was slapped together in a frenetic week. It proposed to earmark most of the state's half-billion-dollar revenue surplus to local property tax relief, limit the growth of assessments to 5 percent a year, and through a complex formula reduce the growth of future spending. "It was a hurry-up kind of a deal," according to Roger Martin, one of the legislators who put through the proposal, "not really the kind of program that thinking people would support once they understood it, but we felt the voters had to have an alternative or they would support Whittenburg's ballot Measure 6."

In late June, three weeks after the passage of Proposition 13, polls in Oregon showed Whittenburg's initiative far out in front, by a margin of 63 to 22. But like Proposition 13 itself, before L.A.'s assessments went haywire, Proposition 6 began losing support. "Everytime we polled it, Proposition 6 dropped," said Tim Hibbits, who heads a statewide polling company called Oregon Attitudes. "I've never seen anything trend downward so dramatically."

At several points during the campaign, Whittenburg was openly at odds with the Proposition 6 campaign's other supporters, who regarded him as unstable and helpful to the opposition. But as author of the initiative, Whittenburg had the sole responsibility for filing financial disclosures of the campaign's expenses. If he failed to do so, the law provided that the initiative could be declared invalid. At one point, Whittenburg was threatening to withhold the filings and kill his own initiative unless his presumed allies reimbursed him for trips to California and other campaign expenses. (After the election, the legislature passed a bill known as the Whittenburg amendment, making it impossible for any one individual to control a ballot initiative in the future.)

Most politicians in the state assumed that one measure or the other would pass. But in the end, both lost. Roger Martin, the legislator who headed the No-on-6 committee regularly made television appearances with Greg McLeod, the treasurer of the Yes-on-6 committee, along with a moderator from the bar association. "I did a pretty good job of shooting holes in 6, and he did a pretty good job of shooting holes in 11," recalls Martin. "By the time it was over, all three of us were ready to recommend that people vote against both of them."

People did. Whittenburg's Proposition 6 went down by about 30,000 votes, a margin of 51 to 49. The legislature's rival package lost by about 55 to 45. Historically, Oregon's voters have been wary of ballot propositions that tinker with the tax system. It doesn't seem to matter whether they propose to raise taxes or lower them; a one percent limit on the property tax first appeared on the ballot in 1968; it was defeated almost 2 to 1. A year later, voters overwhelmingly rejected a tax reform package sponsored by Governor Tom McCall, probably the most respected governor in Oregon history.

Oregonians like to believe that their state is different, and it is probably one of the few states in the country where emulating California is no recipe for success.

Despite the unexpected result of the 1978 election, most members of the Oregon legislature recognized that their electorate was demanding major tax relief. Thankful that the voters rejected both an ill-conceived, extremist remedy, as well as the legislature's own rather slapdash counterproposal, the legislators spent several months drafting a complete overhaul of Oregon's tax system.

The final bill, enacted in June 1979, and still subject to popular ratification, combines a liberal approach, preferential taxation of owner-occupied property, with a conservative limitation on future state outlays. The main property tax reforms include a classified property tax, with the reimbursing of homeowners for about 30 percent of their local property tax bills (renters also get a tax credit equal to 4.7% of their rent); a 5 percent limit on the annual increase on local property assessments; and increased circuit-breaker relief. The tax program also indexes the state income tax, requires the refund of state surpluses in excess of 2 percent, and limits the growth of state outlays to the growth in state personal income during the previous two years. Finally, the bill requires voter approval for any local tax increases in excess of local limits. This both remedies the tax shift, by relieving homeowner and rental burdens, and addresses the widespread feeling that the growth of public spending should be restrained.

DADE COUNTY

Probably the most extreme ballot proposition of the post-13 period was a Dade County (Miami), Florida, measure, which voters rejected in the autumn of 1979. Because of a misuse of terminology, discovered after the petitions were certified, the initiative offered voters an opportunity to cut county property taxes from about $8 per thousand to less than a penny, a cut of over 99.9 percent.

Voters' overwhelming rejection of a Proposition 13 style of tax initiative in Dade County, Florida, could be taken to prove almost anything. Indisputably, it proved that tax terminology is often confusing. Harry L. Wilson, who describes himself as a retired pet-supplies salesman, circulated petitions to put the tax reduction proposition on the ballot. Wilson thought he was proposing to reduce Dade County's tax rate from $8.096 per thousand to $4 per thousand, cutting the effective tax in half. But Wilson, wishing to sound fluent in the lingo, wrote on his petitions that the rate would be "4 mills per thousand."

A mill being one-tenth of one cent, a tax described as four mills is indeed four dollars per thousand, but a tax described as "four mills per thousand" means, literally, four-tenths of a penny per thousand. None of the voters who signed Wilson's petition noticed this. On a $50,000 house, the annual tax would be a cool twenty cents, which makes even Howard Jarvis look like a big spender. Unfortunately, for Wilson, the courts subsequently ruled that he meant what he wrote. Consequently, Dade County voters got an unusual opportunity to vote themselves a 99 percent cut in their county taxes. But, since the county gets only a fraction of the total levy, the actual tax reduction on a homeowner's total property tax bill worked out to about 25 percent.

Undaunted, Wilson pressed on, claiming that "they don't have to cut back on anything. They've got money buried all over the place." In fact, Dade County pays for such services as fire, hospitals, jails, day care, and nursing homes, and subsidizes public transit, and gets about 80 percent of its revenue from the property tax.

Opponents organized into a group called "Concerned Citizens Against Chaos," warning against massive cuts. They also pointed out that big reductions would accrue to business property. The Fontainebleau Hotel, for instance, would enjoy a cut in its property tax from $183,937, to $97 a year, while a typical homeowner would save perhaps $360.

Most significantly, the Miami tax revolt was mainly a California import that failed to take root, because the grievance just wasn't severe. Dade County residents, with per capita income some 10 percent higher than the national average, have a very low tax burden. With no sales tax, no income tax, and a moderate property tax, state and local taxes in Dade County total about 4 percent of personal income—far lower than most metropolitan areas. The real tax burden per capita increased only about 10 percent in the last decade.

In the end, the Dade initiative was rejected, by a vote of 165,140 to 89,200. In one sense this was a reassuring margin; in another it meant that more than a third of the voters were sufficiently alienated to vote for a drafting error which would have wiped out the Dade County government.

The use of the popular initiative was clearly an indispensable ingredient to the tax revolt. Despite popular feelings for tax reduction, some legislatures proved quite balky, even after Proposition 13.

In Maine, the maverick conservative governor, James Longley put great pressure on the state legislature to enact a tax limitation proposal tying the growth of public outlays to the growth in the cost of living. The proposal was backed by the NTLC and lobbied hard by the state's biggest businesses.

Failing to get the measure during the regular session, Governor Longley called the legislature back into special session just before the November election, taking advantage of Jarvis fever. In the end, the legislature adjourned the session without passing the Governor's bill.

In Illinois, which does not have a California-style initiative, both a liberal and a conservative tax relief measure narrowly missed becoming law during the 1978 session, and taxpayers vented their feelings by overwhelmingly passing an "advisory" (nonbinding) initiative measure urging the legislature to cut property taxes.

Illinois was one of the first states targeted by the National Tax Limitation Committee. State Representative Don Totten, head of the Illinois Tax Limitation Committee, proposed a "Taxpayers' Rights Amendment," with eighty legislative cosponsors. Totten's amendment, much like the other tax limitation proposals, limited state revenues to 8 percent of personal income and provided that local property tax bills could not increase more than 3 percent per year.

The Totten amendment was strenuously lobbied by conservative groups, and opposed with equal force by local officials, consumer and education groups, and public employee unions. With the Republican governor, James Thompson, quietly opposing the bill, it passed the House but died in the Senate. Governor Thompson, however, was equally opposed to a measure strongly supported by liberal groups in Illinois, which would have capped property taxes, and made up the revenues through a more progressive state income tax. This bill did win passage in both houses of the legislature, only to be vetoed by the Governor. In the end, Illinois had only the advisory referendum.

Other legislatures, however, did enact fairly moderate tax limitation measures, mostly limiting the taxing authority of local government. These measures, enacted in Florida, Iowa, Kentucky, and Nebraska, were quite similar to the time-honored revenue limits in force elsewhere for many decades, and were not the invention of the recent taxpayer revolt. In Louisiana, the legislature did pass an NTLC-style law limiting the growth of state tax revenues to the growth of personal income.

WASHINGTON STATE

If Michigan was the metaphor for post-Jarvis tax limitation politics in November 1978, Washington State framed the issue in 1979.

There, another of the National Tax Limitation Committee's seemingly moderate tax limitation proposals swept to victory by better than a 2-to-1 margin; the proposal, ballot Initiative 62, was backed by Washington State's most influential businesses. The list of biggest contributors tells the story: Boeing, $8,500; Seattle First National Bank, $8,000; Rainier National Bank, $4,000; Weyerhaeuser, $3,500; Safeco Insurance, $3,000; Pacific Northwest Bell, $3,000. . . . There was no Howard Jarvis figure associated with Initiative 62, and not even a Dick Headlee. By 1979 the tax revolt had become quietly institutional, and corporate.

Opposing the measure were the state's liberal, labor, and consumer groups: the League of Women Voters, the AFL-CIO, the Urban League, major public education groups, the social workers, the librarians, and the state Democratic party. This formidable coalition proved surprisingly impotent, and liberal groups nationally worried that this outcome portended worse things to come.

Washington State's constitution permits the voters to petition the legislature with popular initiatives. If the lawmakers fail to enact the proposal, it goes directly before the electorate. Supporters of Initiative 62 began their efforts in 1977. They went public with the proposal the same week Proposition 13 passed in California. By December 1978 they had obtained 125,000 signatures, 40,000 more than the minimum necessary to qualify for consideration by the legislature.

Initiative 62 limits the growth of state revenues to the growth in state personal income. It prohibits the state from mandating new programs to local government, unless the state pays the cost. The measure did not deal with local government taxation, because Washington already had a stringent limit on local property tax growth.

Based on the record, Washington was another place where a taxpayer revolt seemed unjustified. Washington state ranked forty-ninth out of fifty in its rate of growth in state spending between 1970 and 1976. Taking the longer period 1965-77, state and local tax revenue, as a portion of personal income, grew at an average of 0.8 percent a year, or half of the U.S. average. Between 1975 and 1977, Washington's rate of increase dropped to only one-third of the U.S. average. Since property taxes were already capped, there was no significant voter anger stimulated by skyrocketing hikes in residential assessment. Local taxation grew far more slowly then personal income. Between 1965 and 1976, state personal income rose by 203 percent; taken together, state and local taxes increased only slightly faster, by 211%.

Yet, Initiative 62 won handily. It won despite a well-organized opposition, which included financial assistance from a national group organized by the American Federation of State, County, and Municipal Employees (AFSCME) to fight right-wing attacks on the public sector. The group, called the Coalition of American Public Employees (CAPE), helped the No-on-62 committee do public opinion polling and generally assisted with election strategy.

Joe Dear, the No-on-62 statewide director, believes that although the No campaign might have made some tactical errors, the initiative was virtually invincible. The No campaign's main pitch was that the initiative left all the inequities in the Washington State tax system intact; businesses and wealthy individuals continued to avoid bearing their fair share of the load. The No campaign's main advertising piece read: "Initiative 62 is great if you're a millionaire (Vote No if you're not)."

The statistics bear out the contention that little people bear an inequitable portion of Washington State's tax load. According to the Advisory Committee on Intergovernmental Relations, the state and local tax system in Washington is highly regressive. A family of four living in Seattle in 1976 paid 8.1 percent of its income in state and local taxes if its income was $7,500; but only 6.8 percent at $10,000, 5.3 percent at $15,000, 4.0 percent at $25,000, and only 2.8 percent at $50,000.

But the tax equity theme of the No campaign fell on deaf ears. Such issues as loophole closing and tax progressivity were simply out of fashion for most voters. The issue with voter appeal was tax limitation.

In addition, Initiative 62 accidentally turned out to be even more moderate than its sponsors had intended. Because a base year was picked in which the highly cyclical Washington State economy was booming (1978–79), the tax limitation formula rested on a fairly high base and was unlikely to be exceeded in any event. Opponents tried to turn this argument against the sponsors, pointing out that Initiative 62 would permit taxes to increase at 13.5 percent a year, and that this ceiling could well turn into a floor, but this argument, too, cut little ice.

As in Michigan, Initiative 62 preempted the political center, even though it was promoted by the political right. Opposition leader Joe Dear observed afterwards, "Initiative 62 was described as a moderate, sensible approach. If it failed, hot-headed hardliners could be expected to come back with something even worse than Proposition 13. This pitch seemed to work well with opinion leaders."

Because of the bandwagon psychology and the politicians' fear of voters' wrath, no statewide elected official, Republican or Democrat, was willing to identify with the opposition, let alone lead it. Even the labor and public-interest groups that did organize the No campaign through a statewide coalition called People for Fair Taxes had a difficult time mobilizing their own rank and file.

Based on the dismal failure of the anti-Proposition 13 campaign and the findings of their own polls, the anti-62 campaign did not even try to use the threat of service cuts as an issue. This would have been useless, because unlike Proposition 13, the Washington Initiative did not cut government spending but only limited its future growth. Instead, the No campaign tried to exploit the latent public sentiment that the corporations who were behind the Initiative did not pay their fair share of taxes and

that the Initiative would do nothing for tax equity. But this feeling, however evident in the public opinion polls, did not equal votes. "Big business is probably not even a close second to big government as a perceived
threat to the voting public," Dear admitted ruefully after the campaign
ended. "The finger is pointing to government as the source of all economic problems. Business has worked, successfully, to absolve itself of
responsibility."

. . . SO GOES CALIFORNIA?

The spectacular success of Paul Gann's "Spirit of 13" initiative in
November 1979 ended any wishful thinking that the taxpayer revolt might
be an act of voter caprice limited to one political season.

As the junior half of the Propositon 13 team, Gann was never comfortable with either Jarvis or his approach. As soon as Proposition 13 was
approved in the June 1978 primary election, Gann laid plans for his own
follow-up initiative, which he hoped to qualify in a single day, by having
canvassers collect signatures outside polling places on the day of the
general election, November 7, 1978. It took Gann a bit longer, but by
mid-March 1979 he had qualified his initiative with more than 900,000
signatures.

Gann's Spirit of 13 initiative (also called "Proposition 4") was another
of the measures based on the recipe of Reagan's Proposition 1 and the
National Tax Limitation Committee, Gann being the national treasurer of
that organization. The Gann initiative limits the annual increase in both
state and local spending, adjusted for population changes, to the increase
in the consumer price index. Thus, if the rate of inflation is 10 percent,
the 1981 limit may not exceed the 1980 limit plus the 10% adjustment,
with the final limit adjusted to take population growth into account. This
is more stringent than other state measures, according to the NTLC's
Shaker, because it "denies the state government a share of real economic
growth."

As the numbers work out, the Gann amendment also turns out to be
somewhat more liberal than its sponsors had intended. The base year,
1978–79, in California as in Oregon, was a year of high inflation. Proposition 13 limited the actual growth of state and local spending in 1978–79
to less than the rate of inflation. Under the wording of the Gann amendment, next year's limit equals this year's *limit* plus the rate of inflation,
rather than this year's actual spending plus inflation. The state can

"bank" unspent dollars for future years. Many California politicians expect that the limit will far exceed what they will actually spend, and some conservatives fear that the Gann initiative will actually increase spending by encouraging officials to spend up to the limit. "The Spirit of Thirteen measure," warned *Tax Revolt Digest*, a Sacramento newsletter sympathetic to tax limitation, "will provide a test of an old Parkinson's Law which states that government will find ways to use all the money it is allowed to spend."

Apparently, the main hardship worked by the Gann amendment will be on older cities like San Francisco that have lost population; for them, spending must be reduced in tandem with population loss.

As in Washington State, no major political figure in California was willing to oppose the Gann initiative. Governor Jerry Brown, the butt of numerous "Jerry Jarvis" jokes, had the last laugh when his arch rival in the Democratic party and principal foe of Proposition 13, House Speaker Leo McCarthy, not only endorsed Gann's Proposition 4 but actually was listed on the ballot as one of its principal sponsors. McCarthy said privately that he thought Proposition 4 was meaningless, but after the Gann campaign, no Democratic politician in California could reasonably chide Jerry Brown for opportunism.

California's big businesses had suffered great humiliation when they made doomsday predictions about Proposition 13, only to see it become law over their opposition. Proposition 4 gave them a chance to resume leadership of the tax revolt. Paul Gann, unlike Jarvis, was quite a reasonable fellow. The influential California Taxpayers Association, representing the state's biggest businesses, enthusiastically joined with Gann to promote Proposition 4. The trade associations that had either sat out Proposition 13 or helped the opposition all supported Gann—the Realtors, the California Chamber of Commerce, the Federation of Independent Businessmen, the big banks and insurance companies.

The only well-known California conservative missing from the Gann coalition was, of course, Howard Jarvis, who agreed with Leo McCarthy's private view that the amendment was all but meaningless. After carping at Gann throughout the initiative drive, Jarvis finally said that he would vote for the measure, but only because "it doesn't do any harm."

Jarvis was saving his fire for his own new initiative, dubbed "Jarvis II," an initiative to cut the state income tax in half. And most of the potential opposition was saving its own credibility for that far more serious encounter in 1980. The state AFL-CIO, led by the public employee unions, major education groups, many local officials, and the California

Tax Reform Association, all opposed the measure, but spent little effort or money on the campaign. On Election Day 1979, the voters approved the Gann amendment a shade under 3 to 1. Gann had finally outdone even Jarvis.

For Lew Uhler, who had helped draft Proposition 4, the California win marked the end of a very satisfying eighteen months, which had begun when Tennessee ratified the nation's first constitutional tax limit in March 1978. Though temporarily eclipsed by Jarvis, and later by the National Taxpayers Union's balanced budget crusade, Uhler's Tax Limitation Committee had racked up the big wins—Texas, Michigan, Arizona, and Hawaii in 1978, and Washington and California in 1979. Constitutional tax limitation was voted down in a voter referendum only in Colorado, and that state already had a more stringent statutory limit. Several other constitutional tax-limitation initiatives or legislative amendments were being readied for state ballots in 1980—in Florida, Ohio, Nevada, Massachusetts, Montana, South Dakota, Maryland, and Pennsylvania. And in an election year, they made excellent sense to jittery incumbents.

The California win, Uhler remarked afterward, was "another notch in the handle of the pistol aimed at Washington D.C."

17

THE COUNTERATTACK

IN THE AUTUMN OF 1978, after President Carter, the first tax reform President, had signed the Tax Reform Act of 1978, reversing a decade's progress toward greater tax equity, Bob Brandon decided it was time to change careers. As director of Ralph Nader's Tax Reform Research Group for more than five years, Brandon was widely considered to be one of the two or three most effective public interest lobbyists in Washington. The thirty-one-year-old Brandon moved on to a job as director of a new lobbying group, the Citizen-Labor Energy Coalition.

Almost the same week, Thomas Reese, the highly skilled legislative director of the other major tax reform lobby, Taxation with Representation, decided to accept an offer to become Washington editor of the Jesuit magazine *America*.

"The time just wasn't right to advance tax reform," sighed Brandon. "The whole game has changed. The special interest groups have grown far more sophisticated in providing justifications for their tax breaks. There's nobody out there demanding consistency. And after a while slogans like 'capital formation' just go unchallenged, so that the entire political spectrum has to be for capital formation. The liberals who think it's a lot of crap start saying, 'Well, I'm for capital formation, too, but there's a better way of doing it.'

"It used to be that business would hire a tax counsel to get a special tax break. Maybe we made that more difficult. Now they don't get special tax breaks; they change the whole system."

Tax reform had been a lonely issue, even when the liberals were winning. Now that conservatives were defining the issue as tax limitation, the other members of the liberal coalition started paying a lot more attention. Labor, in particular, which had provided lobbying support in Washington, but no money and no energetic grass-roots constituency, began to realize that the tax revolt could unravel the entire welfare state. Not surprisingly, the public employee unions were the most vigorous, pulling along the leadership of other trade unions, many of whose rank and file like lower taxes.

In 1978 the big American Federation of State, County, and Municipal Employees (AFSCME) created a new lobbying group, the Coalition of American Public Employees (CAPE), to monitor tax revolt activity in the states and press other trade unions for old-fashioned labor solidarity in the face of a common threat.

And in late 1979 another major public-employee union, the Service Employees International Union, launched a broader national coalition called Citizens for Tax Justice, which eventually was expanded to include most of the major trade unions, most of the statewide citizen-action groups such as Massachusetts Fair Share, as well as such venerable civic organizations as the N.A.A.C.P. and the League of Women Voters.

The strategy of these new groups was based partly on self-interest and partly on the very real sense that the tax revolt was not primarily an ideological movement but a pure pocketbook protest that conservatives were articulating more effectively for the moment than liberals. Polls seemed to show that the public did not really want services cut. And thus far, because of a time lag between the cause and the effect, no tax limitation proposal had yet forced the public to choose directly between tax cuts and services. As long as this was the case, conservatives would probably continue to win. But the California rent control movement, and the success of an unusual ballot proposition in Massachusetts, seemed to show that economic hardship, not ideology, was the main motivating force behind taxpayer protest, and under the right circumstances it could be mobilized behind populist remedies.

That, at least, was the hope. If the story could be told that the regressive distribution of the tax burden rather than the profligacy of government was to blame for high taxes, then perhaps voter unrest could be converted into support for tax reform rather than tax limitation.

A new wave of statewide citizen action organizations provided the backbone of the constituency for this strategy. They included a group called ACORN (Arkansas Community Organizations for Reform Now) in

Arkansas with affiliates growing in several other states, the Illinois Public Action Council, Citizens Action League (CAL) in California, the Ohio Public Interest Campaign, and Massachusetts Fair Share. These groups had a core of dues-paying members, nowhere near a majority of the electorate, but they represented the one new, grass-roots populist force to emerge in the seventies. They were rooted in blue-collar neighborhoods. Often, they worked closely with progressive trade unions. On the tax issue, they represented a far more credible spokesman than the other natural opponent to the tax revolt, the public employee unions, whose opposition seemed so self-serving.

By 1980 the counterattack had only begun. The tide was still running with the tax revolt, but events in a few states, notably Massachusetts and Ohio, suggested that pocketbook protest was not yet the exclusive property of the right wing.

MASSACHUSETTS

"I'm Mad as Hell and I'm Not Gonna Take It Any More," screamed the full-page ad in the Boston *Globe,* repeating the tag line from the film *Network* which had been widely appropriated as the slogan of the tax revolt. But in this case the ad was sponsored by a formidable coalition of liberal trade unions, mayors, consumer groups, senior citizens organizations, and even the Archdiocese of Boston. The ad was promoting a ballot proposition to classify the property tax, which would provide some homeowner relief at the expense of business property.

Massachusetts was the one state, in 1978 at least, where the Left articulated tax revolt more authentically than the Right, and the tax equity theme had some meaning for voters. This was the result of several fortuitous accidents, peculiar to this one state—but the same could be said of Proposition 13. And the success of the Massachusetts classification initiative greatly encouraged progressive groups throughout the country, in a year that otherwise brought unremitting catastrophe for the cause of tax equity.

The Massachusetts public was indeed mad as hell—at chronically high property taxes and at the State Supreme Court's *Sudbury* decision which threatened to shift another $265 million a year of business property taxes onto homeowners. In response to this threat, the statewide coalition was promoting a ballot initiative to classify the Massachusetts property tax into four categories, with a homestead exemption and preferential assessment ratios for homeowners. Admittedly, this would not cut property taxes very much, but without the amendment, things would get far worse.

In many respects, the Massachusetts tax system was the polar opposite of California's. Taxes were high in both states, but there the similarity ended. California had a fairly progressive distribution of its tax load, thanks to a steeply graduated income tax, and fairly high corporate taxes. In Massachusetts, with a flat 5 percent income tax and heavy dependence on the property tax, the tax load fell most steeply on the working poor. In Boston an average family of four with $7,500 income paid state and local taxes at a rate of 17.5 percent, the highest in the country. At $15,000 a year the rate dropped to 14.2 percent; at $50,000 it dropped to 11.4 percent. For blue-collar homeowners the disparity was far worse. Many working homeowners were paying as much as 15 percent of their total income just in property taxes. For the $50,000-a-year family, the average rate was only about 4 percent.

Secondly, California had reformed its property tax system, to require uniform, periodic reassessments, which had caused so much voter anger when housing prices rose. Massachusetts had not. While Boston's nominal property tax rate was an astronomical $252.90 per thousand dollars, in practice, homes remained assessed far below their actual market value; this gave homeowners some protection, but produced gross inequities among different neighborhoods.

When the town of Sudbury sued the tax commissioners in 1974, charging that its reformist move to full-value assessment unjustly deprived the town of state aid, the court responded with the sweeping *Sudbury* decision (see Chapter 9) requiring the entire state to assess all properties at 100 percent of their market value. Given the tax shift and the political turmoil that this would produce, Boston Mayor Kevin White, whose city had the worst assessment disparities, orchestrated a campaign to amend the state constitution to legalize a classified property tax.

While all of this was set in motion long before Proposition 13, it happened that the classification initiative, Question 1, came before the voters in November of 1978.

It also happened that Massachusetts was the home of a highly effective statewide citizen action group, Massachusetts Fair Share, which was seeking to organize working-class neighborhoods throughout the state around issues of economic equity.

Fair Share began with a small neighborhood organization in the city of Chelsea, Massachusetts, in 1973, which called itself Chelsea Fair Share. Its director is a skilled organizer, Michael Ansara, a veteran of the early

Students for a Democratic Society, who took seriously the S.D.S. gospel to go out and build grass-roots advocacy organizations in blue-collar communities. By 1978, Fair Share had a constituency of some 12,000 dues-paying members in local chapters throughout Massachusetts.

One local Fair Share stalwart, Mrs. Agnes Tomaszycki of Dorchester, pays about $1,500 in property taxes on her modest frame house, or nearly one-sixth of the total family income. She is precisely the sort of person who might be mobilized by a Jarvis-style crusade were it not for Fair Share. Instead, she became a local Fair Share activist and one of the leaders of the classification drive. Without classification, her own taxes would at least double. "We'd lose the house," Mrs. Tomaszycki said. "We couldn't even sell it. Who's going to buy a $30,000 house with a $3,000 tax bill?"

By the time of the classification initiative, Fair Share was already organizing heavily around tax issues; it was also working on utility rates, rent control, auto insurance reform, redlining and other bread-and-butter issues of concern to the poor, stressing an anticorporate rather than antigovernment theme, but staying independent of any elected officials.

In 1976, when the Boston tax rate was increased by more than 20 percent, Fair Share launched a highly successful campaign against assessment inequities and tax abatements for downtown developers; a second campaign attacked tax delinquencies. Long hours of research revealed that several locally prominent businesses and individuals owed back property taxes, including Eastern Airlines on its property at Logan Airport. Eastern countered with the absurd threat to close down its highly profitable shuttle service, but eventually paid up. With a flair for the dramatic, Fair Share staged marches, sending citizens' tax bills to the staid New England Life Insurance Company, which was deeply embarrassed by the publicity and paid its back taxes of over $110,000 within a week. Demonstrators held brown-bag lunches outside Jimmy's Harborside Restaurant, a fancy eatery frequented by politicians, and forced prompt payment of the restaurant's taxes.

The protests made great copy, and soon Mayor White picked up the theme. Under pressure of a lawsuit, Boston made public its list of tax delinquencies. They included one state senator, a state representative, the first assistant D.A., a former member of the Boston Finance Commission, the prestigious Boston Skating Club, the Roman Catholic Archbishop, and even the Boston Stock Exchange. The city treasurer estimated that $50 million in back property taxes were collectible, plus another $10–15 million unpaid auto excise taxes.

Fair Share also successfully lobbied the Massachusetts legislature to enact a circuit-breaker program of tax relief, only to see it vetoed by Governor Dukakis.

Thus, when the classification initiative came along, it was a natural for Fair Share. While Fair Share often goes after local mayors and avoids endorsing electoral campaigns, tax classification gave the mayors and Fair Share a common purpose. It was an excellent political match: the mayors gave the campaign some big money and professionalism; Fair Share gave the mayors some authentic, angry foot soldiers. For once, the hated big-spending politicians could lead the charge for tax relief.

Kevin White, with the political gall of a good Boston Mayor, rammed through the Boston City Council a measure appropriating up to a million dollars of public funds to promote the classification initiative. To stunned critics of this blatantly political expenditure of public funds, White responded that the classification initiative was indispensable to the fiscal base of the city. It was, of course, also indispensable to White's own reelection in 1979, but not even his opponents were prepared to argue that Boston should simply accept full-value assessment and suffer the fiscal (and political) consequences. A million dollars meant that the tax reform side, for once, could match the big contributions of the corporations opposing classification, dollar for dollar. It meant a professionally run campaign, with funds for careful public-opinion polling, and highly effective media. After the money was spent and the campaign won, the Supreme Court ruled that public money could not be properly spent to promote ballot initiatives, after all. Kevin White did not return the million dollars.

Even with classification, the Left did not monopolize tax protest in Massachusetts. A far-right group called Citizens for Limited Taxation was founded in 1977; its executive director, Don Feder, was given to statements contending that the only proper function of government was public safety, and that all other functions such as schools, sanitation, fire, water and sewers, should be sold off to free enterprise.

Citizens for Limited Taxation was promoting a version of the Jarvis amendment popularly called "Proposition 2½"; so heavily dependent was Massachusetts on the property tax that a one percent ceiling was unthinkable. But the CLT initiative limiting the property tax to 2½ percent of property value was kept off the ballot on a technicality, leaving the classification initiative as the only tax relief measure before the voters. One purely advisory measure was also on the ballot, but it attracted very little attention.

Legislative efforts promoting tax limitation, by Citizens for Limited Taxation and the state's mainstream business-oriented tax group, Massachusetts Taxpayers Foundation, bore no fruit. The legislature did approve standby legislation implementing the classification initiative in the event that it was approved by the voters.

THE CLASSIFICATION CAMPAIGN

Just as the vagaries of the California property tax produced a popular protest that took on an ideological life of its own, circumstances in Massachusetts worked to lend credence to the view that taxes were oppressive for the little people with a heavy dependence on the property tax and a flat income tax, because the privileged were getting off too lightly. Massachusetts taxes were already fairly regressive. Now the courts had handed business an unintended windfall, and business characteristically was resisting a measure that would do little more than preserve the status quo.

The coalition backing Question 1 was impressive: mayors, consumer groups, senior citizens, minorities, trade unions, teachers, and even the American Legion. It was almost reminiscent of the anti–Proposition 13 coalition—with one crucial difference. In Massachusetts the liberal coalition included small homeowners, and big business was the opposition. In California, business bankrolled the opposition, and Jarvis had the homeowners.

The opposition to Question 1 set up shop as the Committee Against Property Tax Discrimination, headed by a Waltham industrialist named Herbert Roth and financed by the state's biggest businesses: Raytheon, New England Telephone, State Street Bank, Boston Edison, Gillette, John Hancock, and a score of others, all standing to enjoy windfall property tax cuts if classification failed to pass. For Fair Share it was the perfect opposition.

"This is the classic populist campaign," exulted the director of Boston Fair Share, an organizer named Miles Rapoport. "They have the core of Boston's business elite. We have everybody else. They don't even have bumper stickers."

It was true. "We don't have ground troops," conceded the spokesman for the No-on-1 committee, Peter Harrington. "This is a public information effort. We have not tried to build a mass organization."

"If they win this one," Rapoport contended, "it will only prove that enough money can buy anything." But in reality, the Yes campaign far outspent the No committee, thanks to Kevin White's audacious million dollars.

The opposition attempted to make the subtle appeal that voters should oppose classification because it really wouldn't roll back taxes and because with classification "they" were simply playing games with the people's tax dollars. The argument was far too subtle. The supporters of classification, with greater skill, built their campaign against another "they"—big business. One memorable two-page ad showed a monstrous Chaplinesque machine menacing a modest little house, with the headline: "These people . . . want to shift $265 million taxes onto . . . these people."

The $265 million figure was computed by Mayor White's fiscal affairs consultant, University of Massachusetts economist Ray Torto. The so-called Torto report, though it used assumptions that later turned out to overstate the shift slightly, was the best-documented piece of research in the campaign, and it was widely accepted as factual by both sides and by the media. Torto's calculations projected the degree of tax shift in each of the Commonwealth's 351 cities and towns, pointing to a very angry electorate in most communities unless classification was enacted.

Armed with these figures, Kevin White appealed to the Massachusetts Mayors Association, March 10, to take a central role in the campaign.

There was little rapport between White and the other Massachusetts mayors. White had seldom taken an interest in the affairs of the statewide Mayors Association. But now he needed them badly to make classification seem like more than just a device to bail out Boston homeowners and White's own political future. Many of the mayors started out quite suspicious of White's motives. "They didn't wonder *if* White would screw them, but *how*," according to one observer. But the statistics presented at the meeting persuaded the state's other key mayors that full-value assessment spelled real political trouble for them, too, and the mayors agreed to form a statewide committee to back classification and lobby the legislature to pass the enabling legislation in advance of Election Day.

The other mayors, many of them quite popular in their home communities, helped the classification initiative roll up big majorities outside Boston. Several wrote mass mailings to their local residents, warning of the effect of full-value assessment on homeowner taxes and appealing for votes and contributions. One such letter, by Antonio Marino, the popular mayor of Lynn, Massachusetts, began: "Dear Homeowner: I want to alert you to a serious threat facing Lynn taxpayers; the threat is 100%

valuation.'' The letter went on to explain what the court's ruling could do to taxes in Lynn, how classification would block the tax increase, and it ended with an appeal for funds. Marino's letter produced an astounding return of 8 percent, using a technique in which a one percent response is considered excellent.

Although classification at first seemed far too complicated an issue to explain to the voters, the Question 1 campaign began to have impact. Fair Share distributed thousands of bright red "For Sale" signs to be posted in front yards, reading: "For Sale," and in smaller print: "unless we stop 100%. Vote Yes on Question 1."

Two weeks before the election, a genuine taxpayers' rebellion broke out in the city of New Bedford, which had previously decided to comply with the *Sudbury* decision that year, raising its assessments one step closer toward 100 percent valuation. After the notices of assessment increases went out, a local disc jockey opened up his phone lines to take listener complaints, casually suggesting that callers complain to their mayor. The next day, in a scene quite reminiscent of the film *Network*, 4,000 voters did, wrecking the mayor's car and temporarily closing down City Hall.

In their next ad, supporters of Question 1 picked up *Network's* rallying cry: "I'm Mad as Hell . . ." The ad continued: "You've heard it in New Bedford. They want you to take a quarter of a billion dollar tax hike. Why not tell *them* to take a hike? Vote Yes on Question One."

In the campaign's last days White was out at neighborhood meetings four and five nights a week, sounding the alarms about 100 percent valuation. Critics charged Mayor White with using city employees to tune up his campaign apparatus for his 1979 reelection race. This was widely acknowledged by the White camp, but it didn't detract from the essential message: Unless Question 1 passed, taxes would go up. This was far more important to voters than White's ultimate motives. Addressing an emotional final rally at Boston's historic Faneuil Hall, White evoked the role of taxes in the American Revolution. "Their slogan was 'No Taxation Without Representation,' " he cried. "Ours is 'No Taxation Without Classification.' "

It all worked as planned. Question 1 passed by nearly 2 to 1, winning by better than 10 to 1 in the city of Boston.

MASSACHUSETTS' FISCAL FUTURE

The success of the classification initiative did not mean that the Left had permanently taken over the tax revolt, even in Massachusetts. Question 1 avoided a tax increase; it did not reduce taxes, and the property tax burden remained one of the highest. That same Election Day, Massachusetts voters elected an extreme conservative as their governor, Edward King, who had campaigned on a platform of stringent tax cuts.

King turned out to be an almost ludicrously inept governor. During his first months in office, one high appointee of his after another turned out to have a criminal record, or forged credentials, or other hidden skeletons that King should have known about. The parade of revelations and resignations was tagged the "Thug of the Month Club." Also, King's campaign pledge to increase state aid by $500 million to reduce local property taxes was considered a statistical impossibility by virtually every other politician in the state. They turned out to be right.

But King did carry out his pledge to ask the legislature to enact a spending cap, prohibiting city and town governments from increasing either taxes or expenditures over last year's amount. This "zero cap," if enacted in a period when inflation was running at an annual rate of 13 percent, would have been the nation's most stringent. In the end, the legislature approved a compromise cap law, allowing local governments to increase taxes and outlays no more than 4 percent. However, the cap excluded public schools, whose budgets are approved and taxes levied by local, autonomous school committees, and it permitted cities and towns to override the cap law by a two-thirds vote. Given Massachusetts' strong appetite for public services, it is not surprising that many cities and towns did override the cap; others used state aid funds to lower the property tax rate. In general, however, taxpayers still awaited tax relief.

But how to cut taxes without cutting services? Even with the strong momentum of the classification initiative and the political coalition that favored greater tax equity, Fair Share and its allies were hard pressed to come up with a politically marketable formula that would cut property taxes and replace the lost revenues with a more equitable taxing system.

The most obvious source of new revenue for Massachusetts would be a graduated income tax. But this would require a constitutional amendment. Good-government groups have tried and failed four times in recent years to persuade Massachusetts voters to authorize a graduated income tax. The last time, in 1976, it was rejected by about 3 to 1. Business groups are strenuously opposed, and the public opinion polls show that Massachusetts voters simply don't believe that the additional proceeds of a graduated income tax would go to cut other taxes. Thus, the conventional wisdom in Massachusetts political circles is that the state will never go for what Bay State politicians call "the grad tax."

Another possible source of new revenue might be a broader sales tax; Massachusetts' sales tax exempts food and clothing, making its incidence less regressive than most sales taxes. A broadened sales tax is the pet project of the Massachusetts Taxpayers Association, which represents the state's blueblood business and banking establishment. But adding clothing or food to the sales tax would be strenuously resisted by liberal and labor groups and shunned by politicians.

Fair Share eventually devised a plan called the "Taxbraker," which could cut property taxes by between 10 and 20 percent and replace the lost revenues with a new excise tax on services such as legal and accounting fees, insurance and real estate brokerage, data processing, stock transfers, and other such professional transactions that currently are not taxed.

Leaders of Fair Share saw this proposal as a magnificent organizing device for their blue-collar constituency, since it proposed to tax transactions that almost exclusively serve the rich and powerful. But other members of the classification coalition argued that the Taxbraker amounted to a tactical disaster that would bring down the wrath of every powerful interest group in the state, beginning with—of all people—the lawyers.

"Half of the legislature is lawyers," scoffed one of the political consultants who worked closely with Fair Share to mastermind the classification initiative, "and the other half sell insurance."

Stymied by resistance to their Taxbraker plan in the legislature, Fair Share rewrote the proposal as a ballot initiative, renamed "The Tax Justice Act." Petitions were circulated in October and November 1979, to qualify for the 1980 ballot. In theory, the new initiative was supported by most of the coalition that had successfully promoted classification in 1978.

But in the end, Fair Share was left all alone, holding the bag. The mayors never bought the approach. Many trade unions, though nominally supporting the proposal, privately had deep doubts. The biggest public employee union, the State, County, and Municipal Employees, promised to provide Fair Share 20,000–30,000 signatures from their membership and families, but in the end produced barely 1,500, leaving the initiative 5,000 signatures short, Fair Share bitter, and the classification coalition in tatters. At the same time, the right-wing group, Citizens for Limited Taxation qualified its own alternative, Proposition 2½. Fair Share was also grousing that Boston Mayor Kevin White had sold out the classification initiative by going along with an amendment giving each locality the right to set its own classification ratio. This would probably help Boston, but in smaller cities it would enable business property owners and developers to play off one city against another to win favorable tax treatment.

"Proposition 2½" would limit the property tax to 2½ percent of a property's market value, cut the stiff auto excise tax in half, and limit the total growth of property tax levies to 2½ percent per year.

In a year, the scene had changed radically. Where the Left coalition had seized voter grievances in 1978 and made big business the target of popular anger, now the most right-wing of the tax protest groups had the only tax initiative on the ballot. Faced with no other alternative, even the Fair Share rank and file and trade unionists looking for tax relief might well vote for Proposition 2½.

Moreover, Citizens for Limited Taxation, basically a Jarvis type of fringe group, suddenly enjoyed powerful allies. Both the Associated Industries of Massachusetts (the manufacturers trade association), as well as the High Technology Council, representing Massachusetts' fast-growing electronics and computer industry, were backing Proposition 2½.

Like Proposition 13, Proposition 2½ rolled back property taxes, but did not indicate how government should make up the money. Unlike Proposition 13, there was no prospect of a state bail-out; Massachusetts' state budget was expected to be in deficit in 1980, with a governor in office who had no intention of proposing new taxes. Unlike the benign tax limitation formulas slowing down the *growth* of public spending, Proposition 2½ would drastically squeeze municipal public service. In Boston, where property taxes average upward of 6 percent of true value, Proposition 2½, once fully effective, would cut Boston's property tax revenues by two-thirds.

This turn of events left the moderate and liberal groups in the state divided and confused. Fair Share was licking its wounds. Mayor White was toying with trying to have the state legislature devise a more moderate rival ballot proposition. Around Boston's City Hall and in the gold-domed state house on Beacon Hill, the most cynical politicians—those with a taste for truly big risks—thought that it just might be salutary if 2½ passed. The cities would be out half of their budgets. The fickle electorate, which wants tax cuts *and* public services, would then demand that the revenues be replaced. The legislature would have to come up with some other tax system—and almost anything would be better than the present property tax.

OHIO

As 1980 dawned, Ohio offered the brightest opportunity to address taxpayer grievances with a populist remedy. Like Massachusetts, Ohio has a highly dynamic citizens' organization, the Ohio Public Interest Campaign (OPIC), with a paid staff of about 20, almost 100,000 contributors, and close working ties with labor, consumer, religious, and neighborhood groups throughout the state. OPIC has concentrated its campaign on two issues: job losses caused by plant closings, and tax abatements. On both, it has taken on Ohio's biggest businesses, with surprising success.

Fiscally, Ohio is entirely different from high-tax states like Massachusetts and California. Ohioans have a deep streak of conservatism and a long-standing reluctance to tax themselves heavily. Ohio's tax burden is the second or third lowest of any state, and far lower than that of comparable industrial states. It was Ohio that invented the 1 percent property tax limit, back in 1910.

Local governments, and especially local school systems, remain heavily dependent on the property tax. The tax burden as a whole is regressive, with a Cleveland family of four paying 9.4 percent of income at $7,500, but only 7.7 percent at $15,000 and 7 percent at $50,000.

The Governor, James Rhodes, is a conservative Republican now in his fourth term, who has built the state's fiscal policy around cutting taxes on business. (See Chapter 10.) Gubernatorial politics in Ohio follow a pattern. Republicans (or very conservative Democrats) normally hold the office of governor. Once in a generation some cataclysmic event unexpectedly sweeps a liberal Democrat into office; he discovers how broke the state really is and cajoles the reluctant legislature to raise taxes. For this public service, he is thrown out of office after one term by the voters. Then the Republicans come back in and cut taxes, beginning the cycle again. That happened to Governor Mike Disalle in the sixties and John Gilligan in the seventies.

In Ohio, there is no effective urban liberal mayor playing the role of a Kevin White. Dennis Kucinich, as the avenging populist mayor of Cleveland, was far too crude personally, and eventually alienated many of his own supporters before he was defeated for reelection in 1979 by a Republican campaigning on a platform of rapprochement with business.

Kucinich did accomplish one durable tax reform before leaving office. He effectively put an end to tax abatements for big developers in Cleveland. In early 1978, when the abatement issue was still hot, developers argued that property tax abatement was necessary to reduce the effective rent level on new Cleveland office buildings from $11.57 to $11.00 in order to make them competitive. Today with no tax abatement, prime office space rents for $14.00–$16.00 when you can find it, and there is a building boom.

The abatement campaign marked the first big victory for the Ohio Public Interest Campaign. "You don't learn what works abstractly," says Ira Arlook, the thirty-six-year-old founder and executive director of OPIC. "You learn by going up against the business groups, in a campaign; it enriches your concrete ability to move people. You're following up the abstractions with something vivid that corresponds to people's gut sense that the corporations are getting away with murder." In the abatement fight, OPIC's weapon was ridicule—of the fact that a law designed to prevent "blight" was being used to help Cleveland's biggest bank to develop a prime piece of downtown property it had owned for years; of the fact that abatements at public expense merely induced companies to move from one Ohio site to another.

"We learned from the abatement fight that you can expect to lose the first round in the legislature. But in the process we created a public issue and built a field organization, and eventually many politicians stopped being willing to carry the tax-abatement banner," Arlook adds.

Under Ohio's version of state aid to localities, the state provides funds based on a complicated formula to make up for a locality's inability to raise revenues locally. Thus, when a local tax base goes up, state aid goes down. In practice, localities aren't able to increase their revenues even if they choose to tax themselves at higher rates.

Most of the tax limitation devices under discussion nationally have already been tried in Ohio—rate limits, levy limits, rollback formulas. In a sense they have been all too effective. "Our problem here," says Professor Frederick Stocker, a public finance scholar at Ohio State University, "isn't tax relief. It's scraping together enough revenue to keep our schools open."

If you wonder what a state will look like *after* the tax revolt, consider Ohio. Because of the heavy dependence of public schools on the property tax and the relatively low revenues produced by other taxes, Ohio voters regularly vote down supplemental school levies. And every time Governor Rhodes reduces business property taxes or makes it easier for businesses to win property tax abatements from local governments, the money comes out of the public schools, leaving Ohio homeowners paying more tax dollars for lower-quality services. Both Cleveland and Cincinnati temporarily shut down their public schools in 1979.

In a 1974 report commissioned, ironically, by the state development department, Professor William Oakland, then a fellow of Columbus' determinedly centerist Academy for Contemporary Problems, warned that the state's fiscal strategy of inducing development by reducing services was backward. "Since Ohio lacks many of the natural resources of the sunbelt," he wrote, "public services may be the only vehicle for offsetting this deficiency. Some of the fastest-growing states outside the South are among the highest tax states."

In this fiscal climate, OPIC calculated that decent services were as important to the voters as tax relief. In late 1978, OPIC devised its "Fair Tax initiative," using the appealing slogan "We Can Have Tax Relief And Keep Our Schools Open Too."

The initiative has three parts. Property tax relief is provided through a classic circuit-breaker that requires the state to reimburse property tax payments that exceed 2.5 percent of income, with such reimbursement limited to households with less than $30,000 a year. This would provide about $150 million a year in tax relief. Second, the initiative closes a variety of business tax exemptions; it repeals the phase-out of the tax on business equipment; it repeals Ohio's tax abatement laws. Banks would be subjected to the corporate franchise tax for the first time. These provisions would provide additional revenues to Ohio local governments. Finally, the initiative increases income tax rates on incomes over $30,000 a year, including a substantial hike—from 3.5 to 6 percent for incomes over $50,000. It also creates a graduated corporate income tax, lowering the current tax rate on small businesses with profits under $25,000, and raising it on profits in excess of $50,000, from 8 to 10 percent.

The money raised by the initiative would improve services in two ways. The additional taxes generated by loophole closings on business property taxes would flow directly to hard-pressed local governments. And the increased revenues from the more progressive income tax would go into the state general fund, about half of which goes for aid to public schools and local government.

In all, the initiative would raise about half a billion dollars in new taxes. About $150 million would go to finance property tax relief; the rest would help local government improve public services. Although OPIC has a fairly impressive coalition of forces behind its initiative, the powerful public school lobby hung back, because the initiative did not directly earmark the new state revenues for education, but left their distribution up to the legislature. However, the Ohio Education Association is quite sympathetic to the general approach, and public opinion polls commissioned by the OEA indicate that if taxes are to be raised to pay for services, the public prefers an increase in business taxes by a margin of about 2 to 1.

This initiative deliberately draws class battle lines as clearly as possible. It lowers taxes on those with incomes of less than $30,000—the vast majority of voters—and raises taxes on corporations and on the well-to-do. Depending on your point of view, it either improves tax equity or soaks the rich. ''Soak,'' is not quite accurate, because Ohio's tax levels are currently so far below those of comparable states.

OPIC could well have the only proposition on the 1980 Ohio ballot that actually provides tax relief. There is a Jarvis-style tax protest group headed by a Republican state legislator, Jackson Betts, but the group is quite weak, without a real mass base, and may not qualify its own petition. The Betts initiative would limit the growth of future taxation and increase state aid to localities, but would not provide any direct tax relief. Ohio's state budget is already so bare that it is hard to imagine what could be cut to provide tax relief without increasing other taxes. In this respect, the Ohio situation is the opposite of that in Massachusetts and most other states: the Left coalition has the proposal that actually lowers taxes, while the Right is offering only theoretical tax limitation.

As a consequence, OPIC has seized the initiative as the one group effectively articulating tax revolt. One OPIC member, a retired industrial planning engineer named Jim Shaffer, was interviewed by his local paper in Parma, Ohio, as he stood outside a local Bingo parlor soliciting signatures for the Fair Tax initiative. Shaffer seemed to be the classic little guy who had gotten mad as hell about high taxes, and finally took some direct action. ''Most people were instantly willing to sign as soon as they heard 'tax relief,' '' Shaffer told the reporter, adding that only one man refused to sign. ''I wanted to know why and the guy said he wouldn't because he made over $30,000 and there was no break in it for him. Well, my answer is: if you're making over $30,000, you already have your breaks."

This sort of publicity delights OPIC and tax reform groups nationally, because it suggests that public grievances over taxes are indeed fluid and ideologically up for grabs. Government doesn't have to be the scapegoat.

Understandably, the prospect of a populist group defining tax revolt as tax reductions for small homeowners at the expense of big business terrifies Ohio's corporate elite. Business groups have said the initiative could destroy "Ohio's future as an industrial state," though in reality it would bring Ohio's business taxes into a range competitive with Pennsylvania, New York, California, Wisconsin, and other major industrial states. But the prophesies have been quite dire. A bulletin of the Ohio Chamber of Commerce warns: "If successful the OPIC effort would negate every positive step taken in recent years by state government to half Ohio's steady economic decline and loss of manufacturing jobs. Ohio's business climate and tax climate would become one of the worst in the nation."

Another newsletter by the Ohio Manufacturers Association, proclaimed grandly: "To paraphrase Cato 2,100 years ago. OPIC must be destroyed if Ohio is to survive."

The Ohio Manufacturers Association has been quite candid in its appraisal of the Fair Tax initiative, and willing to do almost anything to kill it. The association waged a lengthy court battle to throw out OPIC's petitions on a technicality, in the hope of avoiding a more direct fight on the ballot.

"The people of Ohio read the papers," says Douglas Trail, the Manufacturers' tax counsel. "They see people in other states voting themselves tax cuts. If the OPIC proposal gets on to the ballot and it were the only game in town, it would take a substantial effort by the business community to defeat it."

So the manufacturers went from county courthouse to county courthouse, challenging the validity of OPIC's signatures before local judges. "So far, they've filed suits in thirteen counties," sighs OPIC's chief lobbyist, Mary Lynn Cappelletti. "They keep losing the suits, but they're winning their aim of keeping us off the ballot. And the OMA can certainly afford to file ten more."

OPIC originally planned to qualify for the November 1979 ballot, but the legal challenge has delayed the campaign a full year. "Actually," OPIC Executive Director Arlook commented in late 1979, "we'll do a lot better in 1980, with the legislature up for reelection."

In Ohio, a legislative petition must qualify for the ballot in several steps. First, it requires the signatures of 3 percent of the voters in the last gubernatorial election, or about 85,300. OPIC collected some 94,000 signatures in just six weeks, which were filed in December 1978. At that point the manufacturers filed separate suits challenging the signatures in several counties and succeeded in getting a Franklin County judge to issue an order restraining the secretary of state from proceeding to the next step, the collection of additional signatures in a ten-day period, to make up for invalid ones in the first batch. When this legal hurdle was finally overcome in mid-1979, OPIC collected more than 34,000 additional signatures, starting on just two day's notice.

As of this writing, the court delays have stalled the third and fourth steps of legislative consideration of the initiative, followed by collection of signatures of another 3 percent of the voters if the legislature rejects the measure, which is likely.

The manufacturers have opened up a second legal front, contending that the circuit breaker was an indirect way of enacting a preferential property tax rate for homeowners, which would be a violation of Ohio's uniformity clause. This theory was rejected by a lower court and an appellate court. By all indications, the initiative will eventually get on the ballot one way or another, because OPIC has the troops to collect the signatures.

OPIC's Arlook doesn't mind these preliminary skirmishes, because they warm up his troops—about 1,000 volunteer field workers—and paint business in the worst possible obstructionist light.

The campaign has also rejuvenated OPIC's alliance with Ohio organized labor. Organizers at the big Chevy plant in Parma were able to catch workers leaving the plant gate and collect 2,000 signatures in a few hours.

If the OPIC initiative does qualify for the ballot, the manufacturers might well ask the legislature to put some rival proposition on the ballot providing property tax relief, but financing it with other taxes such as sales taxes, rather than raising income taxes on corporations and the well-to-do. And that would give Ohio voters a direct choice between a tax relief plan that provided additional funding for services by raising taxes on the wealthy, and one that just put money into one pocket of moderate-income families and took it out of the other.

Either way. Ohio gives the populist coalition a fighting chance to make tax revolt its own issue.

JARVIS II

For the beleaguered tax reformers, the decisive defeat of Howard Jarvis' Proposition 9 in June 1980 was the sweetest victory of all. With Proposition 13 enjoying wide popularity and the tax revolt current seemingly still running strong with the passage of the Gann amendment in 1979, Jarvis had moved to qualify his income tax amendment for the 1980 ballot.

Jarvis II, as it was dubbed, proposed to cut state income taxes by 54 percent, or an estimated $4.9 billion. The script, Jarvis hoped, would be much the same as the successful campaign for Proposition 13—a chance for voters to vote themselves some money during difficult times, Cassandra warnings by not terribly credible politicians, a big state surplus, and another blow against big government. Again, Jarvis used the direct-mail talents of Butcher-Forde to raise money. As it turned out, because of the absence of a popular ground swell, more than $2 million went to a direct-mail campaign to collect signatures for Proposition 9, an omen that hinted early in the game that this would be a very different campaign.

Until well into the spring, Proposition 9 seemed unbeatable. Early surveys by California pollster Mervin Field found the initiative favored by margins of about 2 to 1. *The Wall Street Journal,* an eager editorial supporter of Jarvis II, ran a story in late January with the incautious headline "California Voters Appear Sure to Approve Proposition to Slash Personal Income Tax."

And then small clouds began to appear. Careful polls conducted for the new No coalition by Washington, D.C., pollster Vic Fingerhut detected several soft spots. First, the fiscal mood of most California voters was now profoundly conservative—in a sense that helped the opposition: they had gotten away with a steep tax cut once and services had suffered only slightly, but there was a good deal of hesitancy about screwing up a good thing.

Moreover, because of the formula Jarvis chose for cutting the steeply graduated state income tax, the biggest benefits by far would go to the wealthy. Of the estimated $4.9 billion in tax cuts, more than $2 billion would go to the richest 5 percent of Californians; 30 percent of the cuts would go to just 3 percent—those with taxable incomes exceeding $50,000. At the other end of the scale, the savings were minimal. A family of four earning $12,500 stood to save $63. Even at $17,500, the same family would save only $131. But at $75,000, a family would save $1,992.

For the new No coalition, an obvious argument was that people in moderate-income brackets were being asked to vote to scrap vital government services in order to provide windfall savings to the rich. Polls showed that these arguments had credibility. Unlike 1978, when a cumbersome grand coalition ran a campaign fearful of offending anybody (even Jarvis), the 1980 No campaign did not have big business underwriting it. The powerful business tax lobby, California Taxpayers Association, stayed carefully neutral. Consequently, the No campaign was far bolder than it had been in 1978, and its appeal was frankly to class interests. Proposition 9 was simply a windfall for the well-off and would do little for working people except to deny them services.

The No campaign also hit hard the idea that Proposition 9 should not be confused with Proposition 13. A series of well-done very brief TV spots featured ordinary-looking Californians saying some variation of the line "I voted for 13, but I'm not voting for 9," and expressing concern for some vital service (schools, police, assistance for the elderly, etc.).

One of these was an unlikely recruit to the No cause, a thirty-four-year-old financial adviser named Roland Vincent. A sort of populist conservative, Vincent had been a leader in the California Presidential campaign of George Wallace and a campaign director for Jarvis. He signed on to the No-On-9 coalition as its cochairman, explaining that Proposition 9 gave too much relief to the rich.

In March, Governor Jerry Brown, the man who Made Proposition 13 Work, came out against Proposition 9, calling it a boon for the rich. Another important symbolic defection came when economist Milton Friedman, one of the first to lend broader respectably to Proposition 13, deserted Proposition 9, expressing concern that the legislature might try to make up the revenue loss by raising business taxes. This, Friedman warned, could make California "a less attractive place for business enterprise." Friedman was not convinced by fellow conservative economist Arthur Laffer's characteristic predictions that the $4.9 billion cut would so stimulate business that revenues would actually increase.

Gradually, these doubts began seeping into broader public opinion. Between January and March, the gap narrowed in public support for Proposition 9, from 55 and 25 to 44.6 in favor and 42.6 opposed. By April, voters said they opposed the measure by a plurality of 48 to 43. And by late May, voters opposed Proposition 9 by an astounding margin of 27 points. Interestingly, polls showed that voters felt by wide margins that the rich would benefit the most.

In the last weeks of the campaign, Jarvis' crusty irreverence, which had seemed charming in the Proposition 13 battle, soured into mean rancor. San Francisco, he said, was a "shithole," with "too many assholes." According to the San Francisco *Examiner,* he termed a leader of the No campaign, Los Angeles City Controller Ira Reiner, a "God-damned lying kike lawyer from Brooklyn." Asked whether schools might suffer from Proposition 9, Jarvis responded, "I want money cut out of the schools. . . . I want a hell of a lot of money cut out of the schools. Because the schools manufacture permanent welfare recipients."

His own campaign grew increasingly desperate. One appeal was tagged "Save Proposition 9," which failed to be very persuasive to a majority of voters who had never accepted its rationale in the first place. Jarvis even managed to insult one block of voters unintentionally when he compared his opposition to the "Japs" at Pearl Harbor, provoking an angry denunciation by a Japanese-American group. Very late in the campaign, Jarvis sought to present Proposition 9 as the answer to school-busing fears, on the ground that it would make school systems too broke to bus.

None of it worked. California voters rejected Proposition 9 by a vote of 61 to 39.

Interestingly, the voters also failed to provide enough signatures to qualify the Left's proposed initiative, called the Tax Simplicity Act, which was being circulated for the November 1980 ballot. This proposal would have eliminated income taxes on people with earnings of less than $20,000, producing tax savings for 92 percent of Californians, make indexing permanent, and raise business taxes.

Evidently, Californians were in no mood to tinker with the status quo. Two other initiatives went down to defeat, one sponsored by landlords to restrict local rent control laws, and another backed by a coalition of environmentalists and liberals to increase taxes on oil companies.

For his part, an undaunted Howard Jarvis immediately announced plans to circulate yet another initiative to cut public employee pensions. For both the Left and the Right, the defeat of Proposition 9 signaled only failure of the electorate to buy a particular remedy—not the end of taxpayer unrest. "People want tax reform, they want tax relief," said Mickey Kantor, the cochairman of the No campaign. "But they want it to be fair."

18

CONCLUSION

A LEANER POPULISM

The scene was a conference room at the AFL–CIO's national head-quarters across Lafayette Park from the White House, one morning in late 1979. Attending the strategy meeting were about twenty-five people, representing most of the major trade unions, consumer groups, minorities, senior citizens' organizations, and even the venerable League of Women Voters. They were talking tax politics.

These were the groups that still believed in an activist government, with enough revenue for decent social programs. Against the simple demands for across-the-board tax cuts, they hoped to articulate a progressive version of the taxpayer revolt and channel voter discontent against the unfair distribution of tax burdens, rather than the size of the public sector. As this review of tax burdens suggests, tax reform partisans make a convincing case. But selling tax reform politically is another matter altogether.

The news from the front was not good that November day. In Washington State, despite the absence of widespread tax grievances, a right-wing big-business coalition had just decisively won its tax limitation initiative campaign. The Gann tax limitation initiative had sailed to victory in California, with even liberal politicians afraid to oppose it publicly. In Massachusetts the left tax-reform coalition had temporarily broken down over what tax relief formula to sponsor and had failed to collect enough signatures to qualify its initiative for the 1980 ballot, opening the way for a right-wing initiative. Even in Ohio, where prospects looked especially good, OPIC's Fair Tax initiative was sidetracked in a costly court fight.

The talk turned from strategy to the financing of tax reform contests. Several trade unions had kicked in a few thousand dollars each. Now there would have to be a direct mail campaign and perhaps a drive for individual contributions. Whom to solicit?

"How about using the McGovern list?" someone suggested, meaning the well-worn list of ideological liberals who had given money to Senator McGovern's disastrous 1972 Presidential campaign.

"No!" several voices groaned in chorus. The McGovern donors were ideological allies, but they tended to be professionals and businessmen earning $35,000 a year and up. It was the last place to look for elements of a new blue-collar tax reform coalition.

"My God, the McGovern list," one of the assembled labor leaders exclaimed afterward. "We have the limousine liberals who would lose money in any meaningful tax reform. And Howard Jarvis has *our rank and file!*"

It was not the first meeting of the late seventies where perplexed leaders of the old New Deal coalition gathered to ponder why they were so badly at odds with their supposed constituency. In late 1978, the UAW president, Douglas Fraser, organized a new "Progressive Alliance" of no fewer than 106 national groups to keep the pressure on Jimmy Carter from his left, and to try to redefine a progressive agenda fit for a period of fiscal austerity. "Not only is the right-wing out-working us," Fraser admitted to the group. "But for the first time in my memory they're out-thinking us."

And every year, from 1974 on, another group called the National Conference on Alternative State and Local Public Policies had held a convention to consider what progressive policies might command majority support at the state and local level. Many of the participants here were former student protest leaders and alumni of the antiwar movement, who had gravitated to positions in state or local government, or, like Mike Ansara of Mass Fair Share or Ira Arlook of OPIC, had dug in to organize local citizen action groups.

In one sense, these annual conventions represented a periodic reunion of the sixties' New Left. But the sessions also presented serious discussions of public policy issues. And interestingly, it was state and local government that held out the most promise for these no-longer-quite-so-young progressives and radicals.

Like much of the country, even the organized Left was voting—with its feet—against Washington. With a few exceptions serious young progressives, often the natural or spiritual children of New Dealers, did not see the federal government as the natural instrument of social progress. More revealingly, few of them saw it as a congenial place to spend their own careers. Bureaucracy was deadening, not just for the program recipients but for the people who had to work in it. In local government, at least, you got your fingers into real problems.

Well before Proposition 13 gave the issue urgency, state and local tax reform was a popular topic at these sessions. In most states, local taxes fell very unfairly on the poor. There was no great mystery about what needed to be done. The staid Advisory Commission on Intergovernmental Relations had written the basic cookbooks a decade before:

Strive for a balanced public finance system. Remove excessive dependence on the property tax by adding sales taxes and broad-based income taxes. Increase state aid to assist fiscally strapped cities and assure basic public services at reasonable local tax rates. Modernize assessment systems, but use circuit breakers or homestead exemptions to keep the tax load from shifting to homeowners. Make sure the state aid actually translates into local property tax relief. When the state mandates a program for local government, the state should pay for it. Look for new revenue sources, like taxes on minerals. Share the growth in the tax base among metropolitan areas.

Only a handful of states with notable good-government traditions followed the recipes. And when tax revolt struck, such progressive bastions as Minnesota, Oregon, and Wisconsin found themselves nicely battened down against the storm. But in most states during the late sixties and early seventies, when state treasuries had ample funds to balance the tax load and liberals had the votes, tax reform as a state issue lacked a sense of urgency. And now, with the stakes far higher, liberals knew all the moves. But it was no longer their turn at bat.

There were other meetings. During the federal budget season in the spring of 1979, representatives of some fifty national groups met every Monday morning in the Washington office of the U.S. Conference of Mayors. It was the same old coalition Doug Fraser wanted to forge into a new progressive alliance—representing housing, civil rights, the elderly, the poor, the constituencies for day care, health care, welfare, food stamps, and of course the backbone of the institutionalized liberal presence in Washington, organized labor. These groups had in common an ideological liberalism and a commitment to federal action to better the lot of the downtrodden. More immediately, they represented the recipients of the social pork barrel.

In the spring of 1979, Washington's ears were still ringing with the message of Proposition 13. President Carter was trying to outflank his Republican critics by sounding a note of fiscal conservatism. And even Carter was willing to spend somewhat more than the average member of Congress, who feared Jarvis-style retribution from his constituents.

Carter's own State of the Union speech in 1979 spoke of "New Foundations," sounding a frank theme of retrenchment. Carter's emissary to the liberal camp, Stuart Eizenstat, put the issue even more bluntly in a speech to the Women's National Democratic Club, warning Democrats that they now lived in an era of constraints. "Washington does not have all the answers or possess all the resources or have the power to solve every problem plaguing society," Eizenstat said, using almost the same language of Richard Nixon's first inaugural precisely a decade earlier.

Coming from a Democratic administration, this sort of rhetoric infuriated the liberals as they met those Monday mornings planning a strategy to limit the damage. Carter was sounding like a Republican, but after one of the strategy meetings, Kenny Young, the AFL–CIO's chief lobbyist, mused, "The real fight is going to be against even deeper cuts than Carter's proposing. We have to keep the pressure on, but I don't expect any political benefits."

He was right. The old liberal coalition found itself painted into a political corner. The public was demanding fiscal responsibility, and the liberals were trying to hold the line against program cuts but still look reasonable. Like the respectable antiwar protestor of Jules Feiffer's 1966 cartoon who carried a sign calling for A Little Less Bombing, the cautious liberals of the late seventies were for a little less cutting. It was not a slogan likely to bring anybody to the barricades.

During the seventies, basic political assumptions changed. Government spending ceased to be a viable strategy for achieving broader social justice. The Left no longer could count on economic grievances to rally political support. Pocketbook distress was acute, but events conspired to direct these frustrations, not against economic injustice, but against government. And the liberal leadership looked at their constituencies—the poor, minorities, jobless youth, the sick, the old—and saw in their economic frustrations the seeds of a new militancy, but no apparent way to turn the frustrations into a political program.

Turning tax revolt fever into a reasoned drive for tax reform was a formidable task; harder still would it be to redefine the liberals' own attitude toward big government.

After all, *what* was so worth defending even at the high cost of political isolation? HUD? HEW? The Department of Energy? In private, the liberal lobbyists who knew Washington best were bitterly critical and cynical about the big bureaucracies. Yet in public, and in Congress, the programs had to be defended down to the last expensive failure.

Why?

Part of the reason was reflexive. Since the New Deal, liberal has equaled government program. And old habits die hard.

Much of the reason was more practical. As wasteful, inefficient, and ineptly designed as many of the programs are, compassion for the needy remains the test of a good liberal. Those who depend most on the admittedly flawed welfare state are still the poor, the black, the old, and the sick. Go down the list: medicaid is a rathole, but who suffers when we cut the benefits? CETA—the big make-work program—is a mess, but it does provide jobs. Public housing is demeaning and scandal-ridden; yet there are waiting lists. Food stamps are out of control, but at least people don't starve. Cities are hopeless federal-aid junkies, but what else is there?

Retrenchment will hurt these people. It is too early to tell with any certitude just what will be cut as the public sector retrenches, but California, Newark, Cleveland, and New York City provide clues. Hospitals close, free libraries cut back hours, parks deteriorate, welfare benefits drop, home services for shut-ins disappear, low-level employees are laid off, free recreation starts charging fees, municipal services slip.

Cuts in government spending hurt the poor. Politically, armchair theorists of a new populism cannot get away with sacrificing the very real interests of the needy on the altar of a better long-term strategy of government. But events, and shifting public tolerance for government outlays, may do the job just as surely.

Thanks to the tax revolt and the popular disaffection with big government and the resulting political realignments, it has become at least permissible in progressive circles to acknowledge that many programs are failures. There is finally the beginning of a serious Left critique of the American welfare state, which the tax revolt is helping to draw out of the closet.

Why, after all, don't these programs work? Why must government be so wasteful and inept? Special interest politics may explain why government keeps growing, but it doesn't explain the program failures. Presumably, the special interests are interested in programs serving them.

Bureaucratic institutions suffer from some of the same deficiencies worldwide, but there are some peculiarities of the American system of government that predispose us to special inefficiencies in the American version of the welfare state.

First, American subsidies tend to be broadly diffused, because of the nature of our representative democracy. It is very difficult to persuade congressional majorities to target subsidies to the truly needy. With the Senate apportioned according to geography rather than population and with the absence of party discipline in both houses of Congress, relatively small minorities can block enactment of legislation, or demand enactment on their terms.

In dealing with ideological opponents of legislation, Congress's frequent strategy is to sweeten the pot, so that most members can claim something for their districts. Often, the sugar coating proves more costly than the pill; small wonder that the eventual medicine is often as expensive as it is inadequate. My former colleague, Howard Shuman, recalls hearing Senator Chavez, then the floor manager of a public works pork barrel bill, address Senator Paul Douglas' opposition to the bill with the words: "I don't understand why the Senator from Illinois is against this bill. There is something in it for everybody."

The habit of sugar-coating social legislation has worsened in recent years as money has gotten tighter. During the Depression, President Roosevelt could persuade Congress to devote a major program to the needs of a single depressed region, the Tennessee Valley. Such sectoral altruism would be very unlikely today.

The congressional devotion to My District First has increased with the advent of the computer and formula revenue-sharing. When President Nixon assumed office in 1969 by the narrowest of electoral margins, the recipients of federal aid were almost naturally Democratic voters, with farmers as the one general exception. Nixon used the concept of revenue sharing to steer federal grants-in-aid to a more Republican, middle-class, and suburban constituency. Under revenue sharing, tens of billions of dollars go every year to state and municipal governments, regardless of fiscal need. The formulas do give extra money to jurisdictions with large numbers of poor people and other signs of special distress; but as a general rule under this system, before more money can go to Newark, additional sums must also be found for Phoenix.

Also, in the name of cutting red tape and restoring local autonomy, Nixon persuaded Congress to replace many specific social programs with "special revenue sharing" grants that could be used for any legal purpose within a broad category, such as community development or social services. These were called "block grants." This approach indeed removed federal strings, and like general revenue sharing, it dilutes the impact of the subsidy and increases the public cost of pumping money to the true hardship cases. Most municipalities get community development money regardless of need; and within communities, the money has been spent on tennis courts, swimming pools, civic auditoriums, and downtown luxury hotels, as well as on projects that directly benefit the poor.

In 1977, an urban-liberal-minority coalition in Congress with the strong backing of the Carter Administration narrowly won an epic battle to change the formulas to target more community development money to seriously distressed cities. But that year, HUD Secretary Patricia Harris also lost her battle to require that 75 percent of these funds be spent directly on the poor. And since 1977 the tide in Congress has generally run in the direction of more diffusion of funds and more latitude for their expenditure.

Thanks to computers, a congressman can instantly determine how much his district will get in comparison with other districts, under any proposed aid formula. This has been called politics by printout. In recent fights over the allocation of grants in aid, coalitions of legislators representing suburban and sunbelt districts have been quite successful in keeping the money spread around.

No other central government spreads around its assistance to local government quite so blithely without regard to need. In parliamentary systems, where the government has the votes to govern, there is less need for logrolling.

Secondly, government spending in the U.S. tends to be more wasteful simply because the American system has more layers of government. In dozens of programs, money flows from federal to state, and then from state to municipality, and then from municipality to private "providers" of services, before it finally reaches the intended beneficiary. Each level of government must devote manpower to the supervision of how the money is spent by the subordinate level. Adding to the confusion are counties, special service districts, autonomous port authorities, and even regional councils of government to keep track of one another's doings.

In most agencies, the federal government itself has three layers—national, regional, and local offices, which overlap and duplicate state and municipal authorities.

The basic elements of this system are written into our federal Constitution. This may seem like a digression into high school civics, but one not-so-obvious result is that in the United States it takes more bureaucrats per capita than in other nations to spend the same amount of public money. According to the OECD, the U.S. has more of its work force employed by some level of government than do Western European countries that spend far more of their national income through the public sector. Almost 20 percent of the American labor force works for government. Germany, which spends nearly a third more of its national income through government, manages to do it with only 15 percent of the work force. For example, the West German housing bureaucracy, with a far more ambitious housing program than ours, operates with fewer than 1,000 employees. In the U.S., with about four times West Germany's population, HUD has more than 25 times the number of employees. Even France and Italy, with supposed armies of comic opera *petits fonctionnaires* and redundant *dottores* rubber-stamping documents in quintuplicate, the welfare state manages to operate with a smaller work force— about 14 percent.

There is a third and far more potent reason why social programs in America are often costly failures. To reach the needy under our political system, government usually has not only to buy off other layers of government and congressmen from well-off districts; government also has to deal-in private business. Far from providing greater efficiency, this approach often increases the cost. More insidiously, it tends to reinforce and bloat systems of production and distribution which should have been revised rather than subsidized.

In other advanced industrialized countries with less ideological opposition to anything smacking of socialism or of national planning, when government decides to run a program for example in health or housing or transport or public works, it simply runs the program. In the United States, government must first accommodate private interest groups. In fashioning our version of the modern welfare state, we have evolved a curious mixed system of public-private partnerships that often manages to take the worst features from each sector. Instead of marrying the efficiency of private enterprise with the public purpose of government, these partnerships combine the greed of business with the sloth of bureaucracy.

Typically, such programs offer lucrative inducements to private producers of services for the needy. The profit is often made whether or not the product succeeds. In place of the marketplace incentive, risk, to assure efficiency, this approach requires bureaucratic policing; and there never seem to be enough police. But this is the price of a system that attempts to serve social objectives without altering modes of production and distribution.

To be more specific, consider health care and housing:

HEALTH

In 1965, after more than twenty years of futile effort, the heavily Democratic Eighty-ninth Congress jubilantly enacted a program of medical and hospital insurance for the aged (Medicare) and for the poor (Medicaid). The Medicare bill directly affected the pocketbook and ideological interests of five immensely powerful private groups: doctors, hospitals, insurance companies, Blue Cross–Blue Shield, and the pharmaceutical industry. Despite the heavy liberal majority in Congress, Lyndon Johnson was able to get his health insurance bill only by designing a program that built on to the existing structure and accommodated the private groups. This also suited Johnson's own style of consensus politics.

Crucial concessions that would later grossly inflate health costs were made to each of the interest groups: there would be no limitation on doctors' fees or procedures; hospitals would be reimbursed for their charges on a cost-plus basis; private insurance companies would be hired to process claims for the government; and no cost controls would be placed on drugs.

In effect, the government was giving a blank check to expand the existing health industry, in exchange for a broadening of the industry's clientele. It turned out to be a very bad bargain.

Government had already been subsidizing the health industry's basic capacity, through grants for hospital construction, medical education, and basic research. Unlike the health care systems in most other Western countries, ours is poorly positioned to provide broader services at reasonable costs. Under the system that has evolved during the postwar period, most doctors and hospitals bill on a fee-for-service basis, and most bills are actually paid, not by patients, but by "third parties," insurance companies, Blue Cross–Blue Shield, or the government. In this system, nobody has the power or the incentive to seriously control costs. Rising charges are simply passed along in the form of increased premiums or taxes.

Organized medicine in the United States favors a high-technology, high-specialization approach, over the provision of basic public health.

As long as third-party insurance companies or the government was paying the bill, individual patients understandably demanded the highest-quality, most sophisticated care available. And the doctors and hospitals happily complied.

Given this setting, it was inevitable that the marriage of laissez-faire health care with government dollars would produce runaway costs. Between 1965 and 1978, hospital room charges increased at twice the general level of inflation. Hospital expenditures quintupled. The share of GNP spent on health rose from 7.1 percent to 9.6 percent.

A middle-income family with a private health insurance plan may have to fill out an insurance form every time a family member visits the doctor, only to find that many of the charges are excluded and others are not covered until an annual deductible is satisfied. A family of four can easily spend a thousand dollars a year on premiums, and several hundred more out of pocket on medical bills before the insurance policy becomes of much use. Under a system of "deductibles," though the intent is to discourage frivolous doctor visits, the effect is often to promote the use of treatments expensive enough to soak up the deductible so the insurance takes over. This system wastes billions of dollars by forcing every doctor and hospital to double as a claims-processing bureaucracy, whose costs are passed on to the consumer.

There ought to be better systems to provide health care. Today, Americans are debating whether the country can "afford" a national health insurance system. Liberals generally favor government insurance; conservatives want to expand private coverage. But it should be obvious that we cannot afford a national health program that merely grafts further subsidy onto the present, highly inefficient private health system.

In advocating more dollars for health, liberals are once again painted into a politically isolated corner. Liberals are paying the price for having failed to secure structural changes earlier in the game. A national health system that fails to alter radically the way health care is delivered is probably not worth having, and politically moot because taxpayers won't buy it.

The next government intervention into health care ought not further bloat the present private system, but change the form of the system. Without belaboring a well-known point, there are several available models. Prepaid "health maintenance organizations" pay doctors a flat salary according to their patient load or their workday; the British national health services use the same basic approach, but it is operated directly by government, whereas HMOs are local and private. Canadian provincial health plans control costs through advance budgeting; individual fees are paid directly from the health plan to the provider, without the need for a patient to file claim after claim. In the U.S., Congress gave the private insurance industry a big piece of the action. In Quebec, government resisted this pressure and decided to eliminate the middleman. Instead, the patient simply "pays" his doctor with a plastic card resembling a credit card, and the bill is sent directly to the provincial health plan. In Canada, under this approach, the public's health has improved while the fraction of GNP spent on health has actually diminished.

In other countries, governments have responded to rising prices by directly controlling costs. In the U.S., authorities have responded to medical inflation by limiting eligibility, rather than confronting established medicine to change the system of delivery. For example, Medicaid was originally designed to serve large numbers of working poor who could not afford private health insurance. Eligibility ceilings have been repeatedly lowered, to the point where Medicaid is mainly for people on welfare, leaving a whole class of people with neither private insurance nor Medicaid.

Neoconservative critics have excoriated the way America subsidizes health care. For example, Martin Feldstein argues that health costs have inflated because Americans are "overinsured," either through Medicare or through tax-deductible private health insurance. This, says Feldstein, encourages us to "overconsume." But surely this critique puts the cart before the horse. Most Americans carry health insurance, not for the tax advantage (it's deductible only for the 25 percent of taxpayers who still itemize), but because without insurance they could not afford serious illness. The problem is not the amount of insurance, but the lethal combination of third-party payments reimbursing uncontrolled fees and hospital charges. Study after study has shown that doctors and hospitals use simpler and less-costly procedures when their fees are not tied directly to the services. And the record of HMO's and foreign medical-care systems show that the standard of health need not suffer.

The general failure of the American welfare state fills the pages of magazines like *The Public Interest* and *The Washington Monthly*. Much of the critique describes program failures with accuracy and wit. But like Feldstein's attack on health insurance, the conservative explanation for the failure tends to miss the deeper cause. In sifting through the failure of Medicare and Medicaid, one should look for the fingerprints of AMA, the hospital lobby, and the insurance industry far more than the fingerprints of clumsy bureaucrats or the greedy needy. Unfortunately, the critique of American society found in Left journals tends to be far more theoretical, properly criticizing corporate power as a generalized nemesis, but largely failing to dissect just how corporate accommodation in the design of programs blunts and bloats government attempts to serve social needs.

HOUSING

Housing policies provide an even more vivid illustration. Most subsidized low-income housing today involves a government subsidy paid to a private developer or landlord supposedly on behalf of a low-income tenant. The costs are astronomical, and a large proportion of these subsidized projects go broke, requiring government to spend additional billions to compensate the mortgage lender and salvage the structure.

While the government spends billions to induce developers to build and manage gold-plated new housing projects for the poor, half a million potentially sound housing units are abandoned and torn down every year for want of effective demand to keep them rented and in good repair. In New York City, the worst case, the U.S. Department of Housing and Urban Development pays private developers as much as $600 *per month per unit* to build low-income towers on some of the most expensive real estate in America, while in other parts of the city thousands of low-cost apartments are abandoned yearly. The total cost of the subsidy can run as high as $300,000 per apartment unit. Why not just take the money and buy each poor family a small estate in Westchester?

This money goes to private developers for supposedly providing a service to the poor. To add insult to injury, these are the statistics that ultimately show up in the tallies of overly generous subsidies to the *needy*, and enable conservative critics to demonstrate that America already suffers from "too much equality."

In fact, fewer than one poor family in ten lives in subsidized housing. The problem is not the amount of the subsidy, but the form. There is too little money to go around because the mechanism is so wasteful. This is readily understandable because the program is designed for the primary benefit and convenience of the private interest groups—the developer, the landlord, and the lender. The interests of the tenant and the public purse are decidedly secondary.

It was not always this way, and a history of the evolution of housing policy is quite instructive. The federal government first got involved in providing low-rent housing during the Depression, when millions were out of work and thousands lived in "Hoovervilles." The approach then was quite direct; through Roosevelt's Public Works Administration, the government paid workers to build housing. But that soon proved too socialistic, even for the New Deal era. Under the Housing Act of 1937, which institutionalized a permanent public-housing program, local autonomous housing authorities were established; they could sell federally guaranteed bonds to finance the construction of low-rent housing; they managed and maintained the housing, charging modest rents; the federal government paid an annual operating subsidy. Later, private contractors were hired to build the housing, but the local public authority continued to manage it.

That remained the government's basic housing program for the poor for thirty years. It built about a million units. Some of the architecture was criticized as too institutional, but much of it was an improvement over the tenants' previous accommodations, and most cities still have long waiting lists. There were few scandals, and costs were kept reasonable.

A second, little-remembered approach to low-rent housing was attempted after World War II. This program, called Section 608, contained the seeds of the disastrous public-private partnerships of the sixties and seventies. Under Section 608, private developers were offered subsidized, government-guaranteed loans to build housing projects for returning veterans. As a further inducement, the government allowed developers to borrow more than 100 percent of the project's actual cost. Thus, even before a brick was laid, the developer had his profit. Windfalls could be made, not from managing the housing, but from taking out the loan, which supposedly would be eventually repaid by the project's rental income. Not surprisingly, many of these Section 608 projects were poorly built, and few developers showed an interest in staying around to manage them. Most had to be torn down long before their mortgages were paid off, leaving the government, rather than the entrepreneur, holding the bag for the debt. There was a lesson here somewhere, but it was ignored by the next generation of program designers.

A second key element of today's failed public-private housing system was added in 1954, when Congress amended the Internal Revenue Code to liberalize depreciation formulas. Depreciation is not even mentioned in the government's labyrinthine handbook of housing programs, but it is the most important single influence on what gets built.

After 1954, developers could take deductions against other income for the depreciation of apartment buildings, far faster than the property's economic worth actually depreciated. This tax gimmick perverted normal entrepreneurial incentives. After 1954 the tax advantages of a housing deal became more crucial than its real economic viability. Housing that was otherwise uneconomic could be profitably built, for the tax breaks. Poorly maintained housing could continue to provide profits through the tax write-offs. It became economically logical to run good housing into the ground after the depreciation breaks were used up, because the tax gimmickry was often more important to the landlord than his rent roll. Later, developers figured out how to collect all this tax bonanza in the first year by selling off shares of the tax shelter to syndicates of absentee investors.

For middle-class and luxury rental housing, where steady profits can also be made from rental income, this extra tax subsidy was merely an added benefit for the landlord. But for low-income housing, it proved catastrophic. When the tax gimmickry was combined with new public subsidies to private developers after 1968, the last piece was put in place.

In 1968, prodded by President Johnson's Kaiser Committee, a blue ribbon Presidential advisory panel dominated by businessmen, Congress enacted a new program not unlike the Section 608 program of the early postwar years. The Kaiser Committee's theme was that the private sector and the profit motive had to be harnessed to the task of providing enough housing for the bumper baby crop that would come of age in the seventies. The report called for the construction of 26 million new housing units in a decade. The program passed by Congress closely followed the committee's recommendations. Public housing was played down. The government's secondary mortgage financing agency was sold off to Wall Street. The centerpiece of the legislation created a new subsidy program, which was combined in practice with the supercharged tax artistry. The results recalled the Section 608 program: a lot of housing got built; a lot of developers got rich; and a lot of the housing quickly went broke, leaving tenants bitter and government stuck with the debt.

Under this 1968 program, called "Section 236,"* developers could borrow up to 99 percent of a project's costs; with a little discreet padding,

---

* Unlike more imaginative agencies, HUD identifies its housing programs with numbers. The numbers aren't even chronological. The newest rent-subsidy program is Section 8, which used to describe a discharge from the U.S. Army for military inaptitude or undesirable character traits.

they could borrow all their costs, at interest rates as low as one percent. And the big money was made on the tax write-offs.

Where a normal entrepreneur has incentives to cut costs and maximize returns, the tax gimmickry introduces a whole new set of incentives. The economics of these projects encouraged their owners to pad costs and show a paper loss, to maximize tax write-offs and justify rent hikes. Thousands of pages of congressional testimony are filled with the story of projects whose true costs were understated at the beginning to qualify the developer for the deal, and then subsequently padded.

Within four years, almost a quarter of these projects went broke; the liability to the government, which had insured the loans, became so great that in early 1973, President Nixon issued an order shutting the whole program down. An entire division of HUD is still bogged down keeping the remaining projects afloat, restructuring loans on more-favorable terms, finding new managers, piling rent subsidies on top of mortgage subsidies.

In 1974, Congress once again rewrote low-income-housing legislation, hoping to rescue private enterprise with a further dose of private enterprise. The interest subsidy was changed to a rent subsidy; regulations were liberalized; in some cases, the subsidy was paid as a housing allowance to the tenant, who was encouraged to "shop around" for the landlord of his choice. But in its essentials the system remains the same. For new housing, the government still pays a developer a huge subsidy to build and operate housing for the poor; the developer makes most of his money from the tax write-offs; the net capital contributed by the developer is close to zero, and his net risk of loss is nearly zero. And the cost is more exorbitant than ever.

The obvious question is: Why bother with the private entrepreneur? Theoretically, there are two main advantages of using the private sector rather than the public sector. The private investor contributes capital; and with his own money at stake, the risk of loss makes him manage the venture more efficiently and prudently than a bureaucrat; secondly, the prospect of economic gain stimulates the entrepreneur to greater ingenuity and efficiency.

But housing programs, despite the presence of the entrepreneur, demonstrably eliminate all these supposed benefits and substitute costs. The profit is virtually automatic, thanks to the tax shelter. It is not dependent on the economic efficiency of the venture. The tax subsidy more than cancels the investment nominally contributed by the developer. There is no real capital contributed by the private investor. Instead, there is a net contribution of capital by the government *to* the developer. Thanks to the syndication of tax shelter, most of the profit is made before the venture begins. There is no liability to the developer for the debt, which is federally guaranteed. Only in very special circumstances, if excess depreciation is taken and the mortgage is foreclosed, are the absentee partners liable to repay tax write-offs. Moreover, HUD imposes so many rules and procedures that entrepreneurial ingenuity suffocates.

Thus, here is a public-private partnership that virtually divorces entrepreneurship from its most redeeming virtue, risk. Here, the government takes all the risk, and the entrepreneur all the profit. Without the element of risk, the value of entrepreneurship and the justification for subsidizing the profit disappear.

This system is a terribly inefficient way to build low-rent housing; not just because of the high initial subsidy cost, which is serious enough. More seriously, the absence of risk produces a very high failure rate, which costs the taxpayers additional billions for the high bureaucratic cost of supervising these ventures to keep them minimally honest, bailing out the ones that go totally broke, assisting the ones that stay barely afloat, and paying to dispose of the wreckage.

Why, then, do we build housing this way?

The answer is not economic, but political: The housing industry wants it that way. The forces that influence housing policy in Washington are, in descending order of influence: home builders, mortgage lenders, and realtors first; HUD, itself, second; the AFL–CIO building trades, professional housing administrators, and local officials third; and a very poor fourth, a loose coalition of neighborhood and community groups. There is no national lobby representing tenants at all, save for ad-hoc efforts by legal services lawyers, and something called the Ad Hoc Low Income Housing Coalition (a national tenant organization began in May 1980), which is essentially one indefatigable woman named Cushing Dolbeare.

Significantly, Ms. Dolbeare uses her very limited influence not to challenge the form of the subsidy, but to press for increased dollars. Thus, apart from the very general pressure of the taxpayer revolt rumbling dimly in the background, there is no effective pressure group whatsoever screaming that the entire system is designed backward, for the benefit of providers rather than consumers.

In early 1980, after his budget officials had recommended cuts in housing subsidies, President Carter overruled them and called for an election-year increase. This happened after a stormy meeting between Vice President Mondale and a group of "housing advocates." The meeting was arranged and the delegation led by a vigorous man named Leon Weiner, who is president of the National Housing Conference. Mr. Weiner is, among other things, an early Carter campaign contributor and—a builder. It was not pressure from tenants that produced the increased appropriations.

WHOSE WELFARE STATE?

The approach to housing subsidy is a metaphor for the American mixed welfare state. It appears to serve the common interest both of low-income tenants and of the people in the business of building and financing housing and trading real estate. But like the health system, it serves providers first and consumers badly, at an exorbitant price to taxpayers.

To advance the welfare state during the sixties and seventies, American liberals made a Faustian bargain with established economic interests. Ironically, when the price finally provoked voter resistance, conservative opponents of the welfare state reaped the political benefit. The tax revolt was the demand for repayment of the due bill.

Two other aspects of American housing policy are also revealing. The government does not spend subsidy dollars only on low-income apartments. Even more money goes to the middle class, through the tax deduction for mortgage interest and the deferral of capital gains from the sale of a home. This makes housing even more attractive as an investment than it would otherwise be during a period of inflation, allocates additional capital from other uses to housing, and bids up prices. It is a regressive subsidy, because its value increases with the value of the house.

The other great instrument of American housing policy is the FHA mortgage, which brought homeownership to a broad middle and working class. The singular achievement of FHA was to invent the low-down-payment, long-term, self-amortizing mortgage. Until FHA, mortgage loans were seldom made for periods longer than ten years, down payments were typically 50 percent, and the loan was written to require periodic payment of interest only, with the lump sum repayment due at the end of the term. The heroine of the melodramas who was losing the family farmstead for want of money to pay the mortgage was not skipping a monthly payment, but failing to come up with the entire outstanding debt.

FHA not only introduced a new kind of mortgage; it changed the entire system. FHA demonstrated to a skeptical financial community that people of modest means, with very little of their own money invested, could slowly retire a mortgage debt over a period as long as thirty years. FHA did this, not by making loans, but by insuring against default loans made by banks and savings associations. By the sixties, few lenders were even bothering with FHA insurance, so safe was the home mortgage loan as an investment.

But FHA did not go out of the business of insuring single-family loans. The same 1968 housing legislation put FHA into the business of insuring subsidized loans for low-income home buyers. The intent was laudable, but once again, a misconceived public-private partnership wrecked the program and destroyed countless neighborhoods. The FHA loan essentially turned into a second-class home-financing instrument, reserved for risky neighborhoods and marginal buyers. This often meant a code word for minorities.

With banks and savings associations largely out of the FHA business, by 1970 most FHA loans were being made through mortgage companies, an unregulated, far-less-ethical, and notoriously undercapitalized industry. Mortgage companies, which prefer to be called mortgage bankers, are essentially loan brokers, who make their own profits largely on loan organization fees. Unlike a bank or savings association, which often keeps a mortgage for its own investment portfolio, mortgage companies are not depository institutions with their own supply of funds; instead, they sell the mortgages to other investors like insurance companies or pension funds. Thanks to the FHA loan insurance, there is no risk when a mortgage company makes an FHA loan, either to the mortgage company or to the ultimate investor who buys the paper.

In the late sixties, when FHA aggressively began promoting loans to low-income buyers, FHA, working with fast-buck mortgage companies, unwittingly fueled an epidemic of racial blockbusting. The failure of established lenders to lend to minorities or to whites living in older neighborhoods ("redlining") left a vacuum for sleazy real estate brokers, dishonest mortgage companies armed with FHA insurance, and blockbusters. An "FHA neighborhood" quickly became a code word for a racially changing neighborhood.

Blockbusters working these neighborhoods played on the fears of white homeowners, to promote panic selling at bargain prices. Housing-starved minority buyers, often with insufficient income to afford homeownership, were recruited by blockbusters working hand in glove with the mortgage companies to provide the financing. Thanks to the no-risk FHA loan insurance, the mortgage companies willingly made loans to almost any applicant. There was no attempt to introduce racial integration in a manner that stabilized the existing community. Instead, spurred by this profit motive, integration was introduced in the most threatening manner possible. Because many of the new buyers were steered into houses beyond their means, many defaulted on their low-down-payment loans and simply walked away from the houses, leaving a trail of partially abandoned neighborhoods.

In early 1975, when I was about two weeks into my new job as chief investigator for the U.S. Senate Banking Committee, I was visited by a remarkable Chicago housewife and community leader named Gale Cincotta, representing angry black and white homeowners from dozens of cities whose neighborhoods had been redlined and blockbusted. Mrs. Cincotta's argument was that the wholesale use of risk-free FHA loans promoted by fast-buck mortgage companies coupled with widespread redlining by more-responsible lenders was wrecking entire neighborhoods and making stable integration impossible.

One's first reaction was simply to dismiss Mrs. Cincotta as a bigot resisting neighborhood racial change. But her group was racially mixed, and their goal was to preserve racially and ethnically diverse neighborhoods that blockbusters were turning into half-abandoned ghettos. At Mrs. Cincotta's instigation, Congress passed laws against redlining and insisted that the FHA crack down on mortgage company abuses.

A decade earlier, liberals might have addressed the red-lining controversy by pressing for additional subsidies. But Mrs. Cincotta's sense of where the system really broke down was far surer than Washington's. She had grasped something that had eluded the program planners. The problem was not a lack of subsidy. The problem was the form of the existing subsidy: a flawed, public-private mechanism that perverted the profit motive to one in which maximum profits were made by orchestrating racial turmoil, resegregation, and the wreckage of otherwise quite viable old communities.

Even more significantly, here was a blue-collar, quintessentially New Deal constituency demanding not more federal dollars, but two inexpensive structural interventions: a law requiring disclosure of banks' mortgage-lending patterns to enable community groups and bank examiners to tell which banks were redlining; this in turn helped restore a normal real estate market to older neighborhoods; and better supervision by HUD of mortgage companies dealing in FHA loans. Both of these interventions produced far more effective results than additional subsidy.

Until Mrs. Cincotta moved Congress to investigate, FHA had three separate divisions—one to rubber-stamp loan insurance applications; another to manage the growing stock of houses whose owners had defaulted on their FHA–insured mortgages; and a third to sell off these surplus houses—often to the same blockbusters who had initiated the process. Officials of these three divisions did not exchange information or grasp that they were all part of a common, failing system.

There is a moral here. Government may be far better at promoting structural innovation than at running bureaucratic programs. And government's habit of serving social objectives by writing blank checks to business interests may be the most lethal combination of all. Sociologists Paul Starr and Gosta Esping-Andersen call the American habit of addressing social needs by buying off and dealing in private interests "passive intervention." In a classic discussion of the failure of the American welfare state, they observe:

> Policies of passive intervention—or accommodation policies— take private institutions as they are and attempt to work with them and around them. When there are inefficient forms of production, as there are in housing and health care, accommodation policies reinforce them and reduce the incentive to reorganize on a more rational basis. The alternative to accommodation is structural reform. Such reform need not involve centralized state control; instead, it may mean reorganizing the structure of private interests . . . Policies of structural reorganization require more political effort than accommodation policies because of the opposition they arouse. But by eliminating the expensive practice of providing incentives and subsidies to the dominant private interests, they may actually cost less.

The redlining matter is a good illustration of successful, low-cost structural reform. A disclosure law induced banks to shift their lending policies, to stabilize rather than weaken older neighborhoods. Another example is the alternative form of health delivery, the prepaid HMO, although thus far, organized medicine has succeeded in blocking attempts by public policy to widely favor HMOs.

Again: in 1979, Congress created a national bank to promote co-ops, not to subsidize them but to provide technical support and businesslike financing to stimulate producer and consumer co-ops of all kinds as a decentralized alternative to both public- and private-sector giantism. The bill was a fluke. It was pushed mainly by existing co-ops and by Ralph Nader and was largely ignored by both the Carter Administration and mainstream liberal groups.

Another illustration: since 1970 a very small program called Neighborhood Housing Services initially financed by the Ford Foundation and later adopted by the Federal Home Loan Bank Board has worked systematically on a very small scale to help blue-collar homeowners in older neighborhoods improve their houses and make sure that houses that become vacant are occupied by committed new homeowners rather than speculators. Unlike the megapartnerships between FHA and the mortgage-banking industry or between HUD and developers, where the stock in trade is tax write-offs or wholesale mortgage paper, NHS creates a real partnership at the local level where partners have some accountability to each other, and bring mutual strengths rather than weaknesses to the partnership. The program now operates in about 150 neighborhoods and has had enormous broader influence on the betterment of urban real estate markets, lending practices, and rehabilitation techniques. In ten years the entire cost of NHS to the U.S. Treasury has been less than the cost of one medium-sized FHA foreclosure.

The concept of structural intervention as an alternative to big-program spending may strike some readers as just another euphemism for "regulation," which is almost as out-of-fashion as big spending. But the interventions need not be directly regulatory. The tax preference for owner-occupied housing is a form of structural intervention; the market responds to the inducement and goes on uninterrupted; it requires no extra red tape. Whether the inducement is a desirable one is another issue, but it certainly operates efficiently. Government could just as easily create structural inducements to stimulate housing co-ops. At present, landlord-owned apartments get far more favorable tax treatment than co-ops.

Economist Charles Schultze has coined the term "the public use of private interest," a concept that sounds like an idea straight from *The Federalist Papers*. Schultze argues that rather than influencing private behavior by direct regulatory or programmatic intervention, government should create rewards and punishments that help steer market forces in desired directions, and then let the market go its own way. The favorite example is the use of fines or emission charges rather than regulations to deter pollution. When it becomes too costly to pollute, industry will invent antipollution technology. I would add that where government can do something more efficiently directly, it should resist the political temptation to give business a piece of the action.

The tax revolt and the scarcity of government resources may at last force government to become more resourceful. The broad public disaffection from centralized institutions of all kinds could encourage a new kind of locally controlled, smaller institution, like co-ops or HMOs. It still remains for public policy to create the context in which these can flourish.

Structural reform of the private economy is, after all, an American tradition older than the New Deal. Its heyday was the progressive era around the turn of the last century, when reformers turned to government to restrain private excess, not by operating programs but by setting ground rules. Though some elements of the progressive program were far more radically egalitarian than anything proposed today, their instrument was not the expenditure of more public dollars. Rather, progressive legislation sought to temper the abuses of capitalism by regulating wages, hours, and working conditions, restricting economic concentration through antitrust laws, occasionally creating alternative institutions like workingmen's savings banks or even state-owned banks and co-ops, protecting consumers against unsafe or unclean products, and opening up the political process with municipal reform, women's suffrage, direct election of senators, and much more. The greatest achievements of the populist/ progressive era occurred at the state, not the federal, level.

It was not until the New Deal that federal spending became the chosen instrument of the liberal coalition. The use of government's power to make structural reforms has continued to coexist uneasily as a muted counterpoint to the dominant liberal chorus in recent years calling for more spending. But a strong case can be made that the most far-reaching egalitarian measures of the twentieth century were based on government's power to make rules, not operate programs. These include the progressive income tax, the Wagner Act, antitrust, most consumer protection laws, and perhaps most importantly, the civil rights acts.

One problem remains: where is the constituency today for a new structural reform? By reason of habit and self-interest, as well as ideology, most liberals are still pork-barrel liberals.

Had the money held out, liberals might never have abandoned the spending paradigm. But today that paradigm is evaporating, and from both sides of the balance sheet. On the revenue side, even the New Deal constituency is rebelling against higher taxes; and on the outlay side, many of the programs are really not worth defending.

In addition, real scarcity is likely to produce political realignments. For thirty years, economists have had the rare pleasure of presiding over an uninterrupted boom. Now, political economy is again the dismal science of allocating *scarce* resources, not expanding resources. Before the Great Depression, government was not held directly accountable for how the chips fell during periodic hard times. Before Keynes, scarcity was allocated by seemingly random and uncontrollable forces.

Today, as government presides over a period of scarcity, government will be held accountable for how that scarcity is distributed. It is not a question of whether "we" must lower our living standards, as Paul Volcker, the Federal Reserve Board chairman asserted, but of *who* must lower his standards.

The distribution of sacrifice is, of course, determined by public policy. Government decides to what extent the cost of the Chrysler bail-out is borne by bankers, Chrysler workers, executives, or taxpayers; the government determines whether the painful costs of retrenchment in New York are paid by public employees, pensioners, welfare mothers, or Wall Street. Whether oil company customers or oil investors make the greater sacrifice. And in an atmosphere of tax revolt, government also awards the tax cuts.

Right now, as public policy decides whose belt is to be tightened, the corporate sector is defending its interests brilliantly. As the UAW's Douglas Fraser has said of the early eighties, "perhaps this just isn't the liberal hour."

But the new, almost un-American phenomenon of a limited pie and the painful experience of retrenchment—something unknown to most Americans under the age of fifty—could usher in a far nastier sort of class conflict than anything since the Great Depression, and a very different brand of government and politics.

NOTES

Introduction

p. 21 Lile study: Steven E. Lile, "Interstate Comparisons of Family Tax Burdens," by Steven E. Lile. Kentucky Department of Revenue, 1978. See also: Advisory Commission on Intergovernmental Relations, "Significant Features of Fiscal Federalism," 1978–79 ed. p. 32, Washington, D.C.: Government Printing Office, 1979.

p. 21 Phares study: Donald Phares, "Who Pays State and Local Taxes," unpublished paper, Pt. II, p. 82. St. Louis: University of Missouri, 1980.

p. 22 Social security expenditures: cited in Joseph Pechman, ed., *Setting National Priorities: The 1980 Budget,* Washington, D.C.: The Brookings Institution, 1980, p. 104.

p. 24 Public opinion polls: see Everett Carll Ladd, "What the Voters Really Want," *Fortune*. Dec. 18, 1978. See also: "Public Opinion Index," Mar. 1979, Princeton, N.J.: Opinion Research Center, Also: Daniel Yankelovich and Larry Kaagan, "One Year Later: What It Is and What It Isn't," *Social Policy*, May–June 1979; Also: S.M. Lipset and Earl Raab, "The Message of Proposition 13," *Commentary*, Sept., 1978.

p. 25 Fat in government: "Poll Discloses Property Tax Cuts Are Widely Backed Around Nation," *The New York Times,* June 28, 1978.

p. 25 Barney Frank quote: interview.

PART I—MR. JARVIS AND HIS REVOLT
INTRODUCTORY NOTE ON SOURCES

In reconstructing the causes and effects of Proposition 13, I have relied on several sources of printed material that recur too frequently to cite, except where they document statistical data. These include: the Los Angeles *Times; California Journal;* a subsidiary of *California Journal* called *Tax Revolt Digest,* which helpfully was published between November 1978 and October 1979; the newsletters of the business-oriented California Taxpayers Association, and its rival, the populist California Tax Reform Association, as well as numerous official documents. Most prolific in issuing current documents analyzing the fiscal impact of Proposition 13 were the Office of the Legislative Analyst, and the state assembly Committee on Revenue and Taxation. Other official and academic papers are collected and inventoried by the Institute of Governmental Studies at the University of California (Berkeley). For readers interested in an exhaustive academic bibliography of the hundreds of scholarly papers written on Proposition 13, one is available from that institute. An additional primary source of interest to public finance scholars is the series of 57 task reports prepared for the Commission on Governmental Reform, which was appointed by Governor Brown to recommend a new fiscal structure for the state of California. (The commission failed to do so.) Several dozen scholarly papers are also available from two conferences held on Proposition 13; one sponsored by the Lincoln Land Institute in Cambridge, Massachusetts, a property tax research center; the other sponsored by the U.S. Department of Housing and Urban Development. The papers from the latter conference, most of which are extremely technical, were published in a special June 1979 supplement to the *National Tax Journal*. A very useful general compendium of papers was collected by the U.S. House of Representatives Subcommittee on the City, titled "Local Distress, State Surpluses and Proposition 13," Washington, D.C.: Government Printing Office, 1978.

Much of the material is based on interviews. Both the pro-13 and anti-13 camps were extremely cooperative in granting interviews and sharing materials. Except where confidentiality was requested, I shall cite sources for anecdotes and interpretations.

Chapter 1   THE CROOKED ASSESSOR

p. 31   Bumper sticker: interview with John Shannon of the Advisory Commission on Intergovernmental Relations (ACIR).

p. 32   Wolden: the story of Wolden's downfall is told in Diane Paul, *The Politics of the Property Tax*, Lexington, Mass: D.C. Heath & Co. 1975. Also, interviews with San Francisco *Chronicle* reporter Michael Harris and Ronald Welch, formerly of the California State Board of Equalization. Also, several press stories from the *Chronicle* and the San Francisco *Examiner*.

p. 33   Wolden quote: Michael Harris.

p. 34   Board of Equalization politics: from State Board of Equalization annual reports, Sacramento, Cal., and Welch interview.

p. 35   Tax shift in San Francisco: Paul, *op. cit.*, p. 96.

p. 35   Long-term tax shift: William H. Oakland, "Proposition 13—Genesis and Consequences," Federal Reserve Bank of San Francisco *Economic Review*, winter 1979.

p. 35   Legislative history of A.B. 80: interviews with Sen. Petris, Dean Tipps, Ronald Welch; Paul, *op. cit.*

p. 36   Watson: interviews with Watson, Howard Jarvis, Alexander Pope. The best chronology of earlier California property tax initiatives is in Frank Levy and Paul Zamolo, "The Preconditions of Proposition 13," Washington, D.C.: The Urban Institute, 1979. An abbreviated version is Levy's "On Understanding Proposition 13," *The Public Interest*, summer 1979. Also, various Los Angeles *Times* articles on earlier tax initiatives.

p. 38   Tax protests in Southern California during the sixties: interviews with Jarvis, Doris Crown, James Earle Christo, Amy Justice, Fred Kimball. Also: Howard Jarvis, with Robert Pack, *I'm Mad as Hell*, New York: Times Books, 1979.

p. 39   Memo: by Joe Roos, Los Angeles Community Relations Committee, May 24, 1966.

p. 39   Jarvis fund-raising episodes: Jack Anderson column, Washington *Post*, Aug. 29, 1978.

p. 40   Jarvis biography: interviews, and Jarvis, *op. cit.*

p. 43   Reagan initiative: *California Journal*, various issues; Los Angeles *Times*, various articles; interview with Uhler.

p. 43   Watson controversy: interviews with Watson and Pope; also: articles in Los Angeles *Times*, Jan. 8, Feb. 10, Mar. 19, Aug. 22, 1977.

Chapter 2   HAM AND EGGS

p. 47   History of initiatives: a good history of the early California ballot initiative is Winston W. Crouch, *The Initiative and Referendum in California*, Los Angeles: The Haynes Foundation, 1950.

p. 48   On special districts: see John C. Bollens, *Special District Government in the United States*, Los Angeles: University of California Press, 1957. Also, ACIR Report A-22, "The Problem of Special Districts in American Government," Washington: Government Printing Office, 1964. Also, for a passionately pro-special-district view, Robert B. Hawkins, Jr., *Self Government By District*, Stanford, Cal.: Hoover Institution Press, 1976.

p. 50   Tax shift data: William H. Oakland, "Proposition 13—Genesis and Consequences," Federal Reserve Bank of San Francisco *Economic Review*, winter 1979, and California Legislative Analyst, "An Analysis of Proposition 13," May 1978, and data supplied by the California Board of Equalization. See also: Dean Tipps, "California's Great Property Tax Revolt: The Origins and Impact of Proposition 13," in *State and Local Tax Revolt: The Progressive Challenge*, Washington, D.C.: National Conference on Alternative State and Local Policies, 1980.

p. 51   California housing boom: Los Angeles *Times*, Nov. 19, 1978. Also, Federal Home Loan Bank Board data; the Irvine Ranch anecdote is from Martin Mayer, *The Builders*, New York: W.W. Norton, 1978.

p. 52   Decline in percentage of property taxes: A.C.I.R. "Significant Features of Fiscal Federalism 1978–79," p. 61.

p. 54   Growth of the California economy: from press release, "Governor's Budget for the 1979–80 Fiscal Year," California Department of Finance, Jan. 9, 1979; see also: Frank Levy and Paul Zamolo, "The Preconditions of Proposition 13," *The Public Interest*, summer 1979, pp. 32ff.

p. 54   Revenue projections: "Governor's Budget Summary, 1979–80," p. A-99; and staff analysis by California State Assembly Revenue and Taxation Committee provided to the author; also, interviews with Revenue and Taxation Committee staff, Kirk West of the California Taxpayers Association, and Dean Tipps.

p. 56   TUFF protest: Los Angeles *Times*, Oct. 25,1976.

p. 56   Jarvis calls for tax strike: paid ad in Los Angeles *Times;* Dec. 6, 1976; failure of strike: Los Angeles *Times*, Dec. 16, 1976

Chapter 3   POLITICIANS

p. 57   Tax reform efforts: interviews with Gov. Brown, Sen. Petris, Speaker McCarthy, legislative staff, lobbyists for various organizations. See also Dean Tipps, "California's Great Property Tax Revolt: The Origins and Impact of Proposition 13," in *State and Local Tax Revolt: the Progressive Challenge*, Washington, D.C.: National Conference on Alternative State and Local Policies, 1980.

p. 59   Brown quote: interview with the author.

p. 60   Business tax enforcement: interviews with Martin Huff, formerly executive officer of the California Franchise Tax Board, and Jonathan Rowe, formerly

Washington representative of the Multi-State Tax Commission. Also, Rowe's article "Tax Dodging at the State Level," *The Nation*, Apr. 15, 1978.

p. 61 Huff anecdote: San Francisco *Chronicle*, Oct. 1, 1979; Sacramento *Union*, Oct.1, 1979; interview with Huff; copy of Brown telegram.

p. 62 Christo's role: interviews with Christo and Jarvis.

p. 62 1977 assessments: reported in numerous California press accounts; see for example, Los Angeles *Times*, July 19, 1977.

p. 63 Legislative jockeying: Dean Tipps and Kirk West, lobbyists for rival tax lobbies, were the best sources on tax politics during the 1977 session. Tipps and Petris quotes are from interviews with the author.

p. 63 Oakland Labor Day picnic: eyewitnesses heard Brown make the remark.

p. 64 McCarthy strategy: recounted by legislative staff.

p. 64 Steirn's remarks: Los Angeles *Times*, Sept. 16, 1977.

p. 64 Defeat of the bill: various legislators and lobbyists provided accounts of the defeat. The *Bee* cartoon was reprinted in the California Tax Reform Association's "Tax Back Talk," Oct. 1977.

p. 65 One percent limit: in fact, Jarvis did permit the exclusion of property taxes earmarked to pay off past general obligation bonds. Because of this exclusion, the actual average property tax rate in California the first year after Proposition 13 was 1.2 percent, rather than one percent.

p. 66 Distribution of tax savings: see California Legislative Analyst, "An Analysis of Proposition 13," 1978; State Assembly Revenue and Taxation Committee, "Facts About Proposition 13," 1978, and California Commission on Governmental Reform, "Final Report," 1979. Since Proposition 13 permitted new buildings to be assessed at full market value, and also newly purchased buildings, the eventual savings turned out to be slightly less than predicted: less than $6 billion rather than the $7.1 billion projected.

p. 67 Business's opposition: Kirk West, the influential lobbyist for the business-oriented California Taxpayers Association, was instrumental in persuading key corporate leaders that Proposition 13 was too radical to support.

Chapter 4 THE CAMPAIGN

p. 69 Benefits under Proposition 8 versus Proposition 13: Los Angeles *Times*, Mar. 3, 1978.

p. 69 Business's leadership of coalition: Los Angeles *Times*, Feb. 28, 1978; also, interviews with several leaders of the No-on-13 coalition.

p. 70 No-coalition stalemate: interviews with Chuck Winner and his associate, Scott Fitz-Randolph.

p. 70 Campaign contributions: Los Angeles *Times*, May 3, 1978.

p. 71 Pro-13 campaign: interviews with Jarvis, Butcher, and Harvey Englander; also, internal materials from the campaign prepared by Butcher-Forde associates.

p. 71 Butcher quotes: from interview with the author.

p. 71 Polls: provided by No-on-13 campaign.

p. 72 Tipps quote: interview with the author.

p. 73 Shift in polls: from Los Angeles *Times*, Apr. 12 and May 18, 1978.

p. 73 Jarvis commercial and mailing: supplied by Yes-on-13 campaign.

p. 74 Butcher-Forde conversation: interview with Butcher.

p. 74 L.A. assessments: material provided by assessor's office.

p. 74 Pope's dilemma: reconstructed from several interviews.

p. 75 Pope quote: from interview with the author.

p. 75 Marjorie Jordan: Los Angeles *Times*, May 18, 1978.

p. 76 Assessments on Pope's own house: unpublished paper, Alexander Pope, "The Assessor's Perspective," presented to conference on Proposition 13, Lincoln Land Institute, Cambridge, Mass., June 1979.

p. 76 Los Angeles politics in late May 1978: several interviews and press accounts. See Los Angeles *Times*, May 25, 26, and 27, 1978. Pope's attempt to freeze assessments is described in his press release of May 26, 1978.

p. 77 Jarvis' habits: from author's interviews with officials of the Yes-on-13 campaign.

p. 77 Butcher quote: interview with the author.

p. 78 Pat Brown quote: Los Angeles *Times*, Mar. 11, 1978.

p. 78 Control room anecdote: from press accounts.

p. 78 Jarvis ancecdotes: from the Yes-on-13 campaign staff. Drunk-driving episode: Howard Jarvis with Robert Pack, *I'm Mad as Hell*, New York: Times Books, 1979, pp. 78ff; also various press accounts.

p. 78 Forest Lawn quote: cited in Arthur Blaustein, "The Big Message from California," unpublished paper. A shorter version of Blaustein's paper appeared as "Proposition 13 = Catch-22," *Harper's*, Nov. 1978.

p. 79 Sugar in the bottom of the cup: quoted in Phil Tracy's prescient profile of Jarvis, "Rallying 'Round an Old Man's Obsession," *New West*, May 22, 1978. Jarvis loves that line, which he uses repeatedly in speeches and interviews.

Chapter 5 THE MORNING AFTER

p. 80 Jerry Brown quote: Los Angeles *Times*, Apr. 27, 1978.

p. 80 Hufford's budget: from his office; he is chief administrative officer of Los Angeles County. "Doomsday budget" was released by Hufford May 2, 1978.

p. 81 $4.4 billion loss: June 1978 estimate by U.S. Office of Management and Budget. See also "Will Federal Assistance to California be Affected by Proposition 13?," General Accounting Office report, Washington, D.C., 1978.

p. 81 San Francisco runs on libraries. Washington *Post*, June 7, 1978.

p. 82 Brown reaction and address to legislature: various press accounts.

p. 82 State bail-out: see "Summary of Legislation Implementing Proposition 13 for Fiscal Year 1978–79," Assembly Revenue and Tax Committee, Oct. 2, 1978; and California Commission on Governmental Finance Final Report, Jan. 1979.

p. 83 Fees: see *Tax Revolt Digest*, Nov. 1978 and Feb. 1979. Also, various press accounts. See *The Wall Street Journal* survey, July 1, 1979.

p. 83 Corporate tax savings: Assembly Revenue and Taxation Committee, "Facts About Proposition 13," Sacramento, Cal., Feb. 15, 1978, p. 34.

p. 86 *The Wall Street Journal*. Nov. 27, 1979, and Ann Robinson McWaters, "Financing Capital Formulation For Local Governments," Berkeley, Cal.: Institute of Governmental Studies, 1979.

p. 86 Welfare and public school funding: see "Summary of Legislation Implementing Proposition 13," also, materials presented at Gov. Brown's press conference Jan. 10, 1979.

p. 86 California education-aid rank: "Tax Reform and School Finance," California Tax Reform Association policy reader, Feb. 1979. p. 24.

p. 87 Metropolitan Hospital: author's interview with assemblyman Tom Bates.

p. 87   Lackner quote: Washington *Post,* Apr. 16, 1979.

p. 87   Developmental disabilities: source is a report by Harold Meyerson to the Coalition of American Public Employees (CAPE), Apr. 1979.

p. 88   Alameda County impact: several interviews with human services workers.

p. 88   Oakland layoffs: interview with Roger Kemp, city official. See also Kemp's "Proposition 13: A Case Study," *Western Cities Magazine,* Aug. 1978.

p. 89   Effects on education: numerous interviews and press articles. See especially "Tax Reform and School Finance" reader, *op. cit.*

p. 89   Rossi quote: interview with the author.

p. 90   Joseph Young: interview with the author.

p. 90   Cut in arts funding: *The Wall Street Journal,* July 14, 1978.

p. 91   Jarvis's campaign for conservatives: author's interview with Harvey Englander of Jarvis' staff;

p. 91   Brown speech: official text.

p. 91   Brown exchange with press: from Governor's press briefing, Jan. 9, 1979.

Chapter 6   SYMBOL AND REALITY

p. 92   *Newsweek* quote: June 19, 1978, issue.

p. 92   Evans and Novak quote: from their syndicated column, June 5, 1978.

p. 93   Jarvis visit to Washington: from several press accounts and author's interview.

p. 94   Lipset and Raab: *Commentary,* Sept. 1978.

p. 94   Tipps quote: interview with the author.

p. 95   Growth of state expenditures: see Levy's "On Understanding Proposition 13," *The Public Interest,* summer, 1979; other calculations from 1979–80 California Budget, p. A-11.

p. 96   Blaustein: in his unpublished paper "The Big Message from California."

p. 96   McGovern speech supplied by his office, given June 17, 1978.

p. 96   Kraft: syndicated column, June 12, 1978.

p. 96   Lewis quote: interview with the author.

p. 97   Distribution of vote: Los Angeles *Times,* June 11, 1978.

p. 97   Heckathorn quote: Washington *Post,* June 16, 1978.

p. 97   Mrs. Peabody: interviewed by the author.

p. 97   Springer quote: Washington *Post,* June 16, 1978.

p. 97   Schneider: in Los Angeles *Times,* June 11, 1978.

p. 98   Farmer: testimony before the U.S. House Subcommittee on the City, July 25, 1978; in "Local Distress, State Surpluses and Proposition 13," Washington, D.C.: Government Printing Office, p. 599.

p. 99   Toigo quote: interview with the author.

p. 99   Toigo-Keyser conversation: in author's presence.

p. 101   CBIA study: internal document dated Sept. 11, 1978; and interviews; See also "Savior of the Cities—Would You Believe, Howard Jarvis?," *California Journal,* Apr. 1979.

p. 101   Development costs: "New Housing: Paying its Way?," report by California Office of Planning and Research, Sacramento, Cal., May 1979. Also, materials presented at Lincoln Institute Conference, "Proposition 13: A First Anniversary Assessment," June 19–20, 1979, Cambridge, Mass.

p. 102   Press: quoted in *California Journal, loc. cit.* Apr. 1979.

p. 102   Leveling up: author's interview with Riles.

p. 103   Beverly Hills–Baldwin Park: *Tax Revolt Digest*, special issue, "Proposition 13 and the Schools," Dec. 1978. The *Serrano* case was originally decided in 1971 (*Serrano v. Priest* 487 P.2d 1241 [1971]); subsequently the U.S. Supreme Court ruled that the Texas school finance system did not violate the equal protection guarantees of the U.S. Constitution (*San Antonio v. Rodriguez*), but the California Supreme Court upheld the original *Serrano* doctrine under the California state constitution (*Serrano v. Priest* 18 C3d 728 [1976]). School finance, as a distinct issue, is largely outside the scope of this book.

p. 104   Rent control: various press accounts; interview with Hayden.

p. 104   McCarthy hotline and quote; author's interview with McCarthy and his staff.

p. 105   Post commission: California Commission on Governmental Reform: "Final Report," Sacramento, Jan. 1979. See also, Maureen S. Fitzgerald, "What Went Wrong with the Post Commission," *California Journal*, Mar. 1979

PART II—A SHORT COURSE ON THE PROPERTY TAX
INTRODUCTORY NOTE ON SOURCES

The classic works on the property tax and on state and local finance generally include E.R.A. Seligman, *Essays in Taxation*, New York: Macmillan & Co., 1895 and 1913; Richard T. Ely, *Taxation in American States and Cities*, New York: Thomas Y. Crowell & Co., 1888; and Jens Peter Jensen, *Property Taxation in the United States*, Chicago: University of Chicago Press, 1931. All three are in the great tradition of progressive era scholarship. They are at once meticulously academic and passionately reformist, and they are entertaining to read. A more recent work in this tradition is Diane Paul, *The Politics of the Property Tax*, Lexington, Mass.: D.C. Heath & Co., 1975. For insights into the frustrating history of property tax reform, the annual proceedings of the National Tax Association beginning in 1907 and the *National Tax Journal* are excellent sources.

A very good but more technical book on the property tax is Dick Netzer, *The Economics of the Property Tax*, Washington, D.C.: Brookings Institution, 1966. A good basic public finance text is James A. Maxwell and J. Richard Aronson, *Financing State and Local Government*, Washington, D.C.: Brookings, Institution, 1977. A very valuable case book of documents and articles is Oliver Oldman and Ferdinand P. Schoettle, *State and Local Taxes and Finance*, Mineola, N.Y.: The Foundation Press, 1974. The Advisory Commission on Intergovernmental Relations, created by Congress in 1959 to monitor the fiscal aspects of the American federal system, has published scores of very useful materials on state and local tax burdens.

In recent years, several local groups have revived the tradition of pamphleteering for property tax reform. These include several statewide citizen action groups, such as Massachusetts Fair Share, the Ohio Public Interest Campaign, the Illinois Political Action Campaign, the Arkansas Community Organizations for Reform Now, and numerous Nader-affiliates, usually called the Public Interest Research Group. Nader's national tax reform organization has published an excellent book, which includes material on the property tax, Robert M. Brandon *et al., Tax Politics*, New York: Pantheon Books, 1976.

I have also relied heavily on interviews and material from numerous professional and trade associations concerned with property tax issues. These include the International Association of Assessing Officers, based in Chicago, and its local affiliates; the Municipal Finance Officers' Association, in Washington; the National Conference of State Legislatures, based in Denver; the National Conference on Alternative State and Local Public Policy, in Washington, among others. The latter group publishes a series of readers on state and local issues, including several on fiscal issues. The Urban Institute in Washington also has a public finance project, which has published numerous useful studies and reports. Another very good compendium of materials on property tax protest as it developed in the early 1970s is the two-volume series *Property Taxes,* and *Property Tax Relief and Reform Act of 1973* from hearings before the Senate Subcommittee on Intergovernmental Relations, Washington, D.C.: Government Printing Office, 1972 and 1973.

Most states in recent years have had blue-ribbon commissions to make recommendations to overhaul their public finance systems. Two of the best reports are "Financing An Urban Government," by the District of Columbia Tax Commission, Washington, D.C., 1977; and the six-volume *Report of the New Jersey Tax Policy Committee,* Trenton, 1972.

Three basic statistical reference works on public finance are *Facts and Figures of Government Finance,* published annually by the Tax Foundation in Washington, D.C.; the annual *Economic Report of the President,* Washington, D.C.: Government Printing Office; and the annual *Significant Features of Fiscal Federalism,* published by the ACIR. Far more extensive data on property taxes can be found in the Census of Governments series published by the U.S. Bureau of the Census, especially the volume entitled *Taxable Property Values and Assessment/Sales Ratios,* Washington, D.C.: Government Printing Office, 1977.

Chapter 7 THE CROOKED ASSESSOR REVISITED

p. 109 Seligman quote: E.R.A. Seligman, *Essays in Taxation,* New York: Macmillan, 1913 ed., p. 62.

p. 110 Jensen: Jens Peter Jensen, *Property Taxation in the United States,* Chicago: University of Chicago Press, 1931, p. 479.

p. 110 Dependence on property tax: *Facts and Figures of Government Finance,* Washington, D.C.: The Tax Foundation, 1979, p. 242.

p. 111 Early exemptions: Jensen, *op. cit.* p. 34ff.

p. 112 Sheep, swine, etc.: Jensen, *op. cit.,* p. 28, quoting M.H. Robinson, *A History of Taxation in New Hampshire.*

p. 112 Brewers' exemption: Bennett Harrison and Sandra Kanter, "The Great State Robbery," *Working Papers for a New Society,* spring 1976.

p. 113 Equalization: Jensen, *op. cit.,* p. 361.

p. 113 Quote: report of the California Commission on Revenue and Taxation (1906), p. 70.

p. 114 Illinois law: Jensen, *op. cit.,* p. 387.

p. 115 Sims quote: National Tax Association *Proceedings* of 1916, pp. 88–89.

p. 115 Austin watches: NTA *Proceedings,* 1917, p. 372.

p. 116 Jensen quote: Jensen, *op. cit.,* p. 268–70.

p. 117 Seattle salmon: NTA *Proceedings,* 1909, p. 334.

p. 118 Assessment inequities and courts: see Oliver Oldman and Ferdinand P. Schoettle, *State and Local Taxes and Finance,* Mineola, N.Y.: The Foundation Press, 1974, especially ch. 3. A comprehensive review of court cases dealing with assessment inequalities is "In the Wake of *Hellerstein:* Whither New York?," a study by the New York State Division of Equalization and Assessment, Albany, *p. 118*   Massachusetts case: *City of Lowell v. County Commissioners of Middlesex,* 152 Mass. 372, 25 N.E. at 469 (1890), pp. 168, 169.

p. 118   "Loosing of a stitch": *Appeal of Kliks,* 153 Or. 669, 76 P2d 974 (1938).

p. 118   Nashville, Chattanooga and St. Louis railroad: *Nashville, Chattanooga and St. Louis Railway v. Browning,* 310 U.S. 362, 60 S.Ct 968, 84 L.Ed 1254 (1940).

p. 119   Thurow: see his "How the Rich Get Rich and How They Can Be Taxed," *Working Papers for a New Society,* winter 1976.

p. 119   Hagman: cited in Robert M. Brandon *et al., Tax Politics,* New York: Pantheon Books, 1976, p. 148.

p. 120   Henry George: George's master work is *Progress and Poverty.*

p. 121   Inequities getting worse: U.S. Bureau of the Census, *1977 Census of Governments,* vol. 2, Washington, D.C.: Government Printing Office, p. 21

p. 122   Diane Paul, *The Politics of the Property Tax,* Lexington, Mass.: D.C. Heath & Co., 1975, p. 39.

p. 123   CLT controversy: See U.S. Senate Subcommittee on Intergovernmental Relations, Washington, D.C.: Government Printing Office, 1972 and 1973 especially Tax Reform Research Group materials, and testimony by CLT representatives.

p. 125   Gary episode and Faddell testimony: *ibid.* pp. 129ff.

p. 126   Washington, D.C., assessments: Washington *Post,* May 11, 1977.

p. 126   Watson quote: author's interview.

p. 126   Albany: "Assessment Politics," N.Y. Public Interest Research Group, Albany, 1979.

p. 126   For illustrations of studies showing how less-valuable houses tend to be assessed at higher fractions of value, see Jensen, *op. cit.,* NTA *Proceedings* for 1919, Paul, *op. cit.* See also George Peterson, Arthur Solomon, William C. Apgar, Jr., and Hadi Madjid, *Property Taxes, Housing and the Cities,* Lexington, Mass.: D.C. Heath & Co., 1973.

p. 127   Boston: see Oliver Oldman and Henry Aaron, "Assessment-Sales Ratios Under the Boston Property Tax," *National Tax Journal,* Mar. 1965.

p. 127   Chicago: *The New York Times,* Apr. 16, 1979.

p. 127   Peterson: in George Peterson *et. al., Property Tax Reform,* Washington, D.C.: The Urban Institute, p. 111.

p. 128   Detroit: computed by George Peterson in testimony before the House Subcommittee on the City hearings, in "Local Distress," July 25, 1978, p. 79.

p. 129   Swartz quote: interview with the author.

p. 130   Schroeder quote: interview with the author.

Chapter 8   LIMITING TAXES

p. 131   Ohio's Smith Law: see Ernest Ludlow Bogart, *Financial History of Ohio,* Urbana: University of Illinois Press, 1912. Also, Jens Peter Jensen, *Property Taxation in the United States,* Chicago: University of Chicago Press, 1931, p. 473.

p. 132   Early tax and debt limitations: a good summary is "State Limitations on Local Taxes and Expenditures," ACIR document A-64, Washington, D.C.: Government Printing Office, 1977.

p. 133   Most prominent legal textbook: see Oliver Oldman and Ferdinand P. Schoettle, *State and Local Taxes and Finance,* Mineola, N.Y.: The Foundation Press, 1974, p. 753, quoting the U.S. Congress Joint Economic Committee.

p. 134   Petersen: author's interview.

p. 134   Washington case: State ex. rel. *Washington Building Financing Authority v. Yelle*, 47 Wash2d 705, 289 P.2d 355. See Oldman and Schoettle, *op. cit.*, pp. 727ff.

p. 135   Arizona: see *The Wall Street Journal*, Nov. 3, 1978.

p. 135   Kansas: see Jensen, *op. cit.*, p. 469.

p. 135   On modern limits: see ACIR Document A-64, *loc. cit.*

p. 135   Idaho: Isadore Loeb, "Constitutional Limitations Affecting Taxation" NTA *Proceedings*, 1907, p. 79.

p. 136   Dukakis anecdote: press accounts and author's interview with Dukakis.

p. 138   ACIR reports: ACIR Document A-64, *loc. cit.*, Marquis of Queensbury quote at p. 10; also ACIR, *State Constitutional and Statutory Restrictions on Local Taxing Powers*, A-14, Washington, D.C: Government Printing Office, 1962.

p. 140   New Jersey: See: "New Jersey's Limits on State and Local Spending —Model for the Nation?" *New Jersey Municipalities*, Nov. 1978; also, "Capping New Jersey's Taxes," *The Wall Street Journal*, Oct. 31, 1978; also, Margaret E. Goertz and Jay H. Moskowitz, "Caps and Kids: The Impact of New Jersey's Education Budget Caps," paper presented to annual conference of the American Education Finance Association, Jan. 15, 1979. Also, author's interviews with New Jersey public officials.

p. 141   Newark data: provided by Tom Banker; Banker quotes from interview with the author.

p. 143   Shapiro: interview with the author.

p. 143   Copeland: interview with the author.

p. 144   Tennessee Fiscal Review Committee: interview with the author. See also Barbara S. Haskew, "Implementing the Tennessee Spending Limit," Conference Papers Series #51, Murfreesboro, Tenn.: Middle Tennessee State University, June 1979.

p. 145   Colorado: interviews with several state officials; Kadlacek strategy: author's interview with Kadlacek.

Chapter 9   SHIFTING TAXES

p. 147   Decreasing business share: ACIR, *Significant Features of Fiscal Federalism*, 1978–79 ed., Washington, D.C.: Government Printing Office, 1979. p. 49.

p. 148   Idaho: data provided by Idaho Education Association.

p. 148   Idaho tax shift: calculated from data provided by Idaho State Board of Equalization.

p. 149   Eardley quote: interview with the author.

p. 150   Value of farmland: author's interview with Ada County assessor Bill Schroeder.

p. 150   Don Chance: interview with the author.

p. 150   Schroeder and Chance quotes: author's interviews.

p. 152   Oldman quote: interview with the author.

p. 152   Idaho case: *Idaho Telephone v. Board*, 423 P2d 337, 91 Idaho 425 (1967).

p. 152   Hellerstein: *Matter of Hellerstein v. Assessor, Town of Islip*, 37 N.Y.2d 1, 332 N.E.2d 279, 371 N.Y.S.2d 388 (1975).

p. 153   Sioux City Bridge: *Sioux City Bridge Co. v. Dakota County*, 260 U.S. 441, 43 S.Ct. 190, 67L Ed. 340 (1923).

p. 153 A good summary of these full valuation cases is in Robert L. Beebe and Richard J. Sinnott, "In the Wake of Hellerstein: Whither New York?," New York State Department of Equalization and Assessment, Albany, 1977.

p. 154 Hellerstein quote: *Matter of Hellerstein v. Assessor, loc. cit.*

p. 155 On tax classification: see "An Evaluation of the Split Assessment Roll in the United States," Sacramento: California Taxpayers Association, 1977; also, Steven Gold, *Property Tax Relief,* forthcoming.

p. 155 South Carolina: interviews with the author.

p. 155 Circuit breakers and homestead exemptions: see Gold, *op. cit.;* see also ACIR's "Property Tax Circuit Breakers: Current Status and Policy Issues," ACIR Document M-87, Washington, D.C.: Government Printing Office, 1975; also: George Peterson, ed., *Property Tax Reform,* Washington, D.C., The Urban Institute, p. 111. For several journalistic accounts of tax reform politics in individual states, see the *Reader* on tax reform and revolt published by the National Conference on Alternative State and Local Policy, Washington, D.C., 1980.

p. 156 Wisconsin: data supplied to the author by the state department of revenue.

p. 157 Oregon: state data provided to the author.

p. 157 New York: interviews by the author with several officials, including New York City Finance Administrator Harry Tishelman and City Tax Commission Chairman Mary Mann.

p. 158 Guth: *Guth Realty v. Gingold,* 34 N.Y.2d 440, 358 N.Y.S. 2d 367, 315 N.E.2d 441.

p. 159 Kaplan quote: interview with the author.

p. 159 Mann quote: interview with the author.

p. 159 Fischoff quote: interview with the author.

p. 160 Probable tax increases: "The Legislative Response to the Property Tax Crisis," New York State Assembly Task Force on School Finance and Real Property Taxation, Albany, Sept. 1979, p. 28.

p. 162 Sudbury case: *Town of Sudbury v. Commissioner of Corporations and Taxation,* 321 N.E. 2d 641 (Mass. 1974).

p. 162 Probable tax shift: source, Raymond G. Torto, "Estimating the Impact of 100% Valuation and Taxation by Classification in Massachusetts: Part I," Mass. Mayors Association, Boston, June 14, 1978.

p. 163 Tregor case: *Norman Tregor, Trustee, v. Board of Assessors of the City of Boston,* 1979 Mass. Advance Sheets, p. 770. See also "The Tregor Windfall," Massachusetts Fair Share, Boston, 1979.

p. 164 Spending as a percentage of GNP: *Facts and Figures of Government Finance,* Washington, D.C.: The Tax Foundation, 1979 ed., p. 33

p. 165 Shift in property tax burdens: ACIR: "Significant Features of Fiscal Federalism," 1978–79 ed., *loc. cit.,* p. 61.

p. 165 Corporate and individual income taxes: *Facts and Figures of Government Finance, loc. cit.,* pp. 99, 151.

p. 166 Muller: *Growing and Declining Urban Areas: A Fiscal Comparison,* Washington, D.C.: Urban Institute, 1975. p. 24.

p. 166 Federal aid to cities: Roy Bahl, ed., *The Fiscal Outlook for Cities,* Syracuse, N.Y.: Syracuse University Press, 1978. p. 32.

p. 166 Petersen: John Petersen and Robert Rafuse, "Big City Finances in 1982: Will Closing Budget Gaps Cause Financial Strain?", unpublished paper, 1979.

p. 167 Tax Foundation: *Tax Review,* Mar. 1980, p. 11.

Chapter 10 THE ABATEMENT GAME

p. 168 Quote: from New York State Department of Commerce advertisement, *The Wall Street Journal*, Mar. 22, 1979.

p. 169 Gaskell: interview with the author.

p. 170 Solomon: interview with the author.

p. 170 Data on NYC incentives: provided by Solomon.

p. 171 Goldin audit: "Performance Audit of the Industrial and Commercial Incentive Board," New York City Office of the Comptroller, Mar. 12, 1979.

p. 171 "City Delays": *The New York Times*, May 31, 1979.

p. 171 Solomon quote: interview with the author.

p. 172 J-51 program: state audit of New York City housing programs, New York State Department of Audit and Control, May 16, 1979; also, analysis of J-51 program by New York City Councilwoman Ruth Messinger, Aug. 15, 1979.

p. 172 Solomon: interview with the author.

p. 173 Dorgan: interview, *People and Taxes*, Sept. 1978.

p. 173 Nader study: "Bidding for Business," Washington, D.C.: Public Interest Research Group, Aug. 1979.

p. 173 "Candy-store": *The Wall Street Journal*, June 30, 1978.

p. 174 Shelby: this anecdote and other background information on Ohio are from reporter Fred McGunagle's excellent series in the Cleveland *Press*, Apr. 24–28, 1978.

p. 174 Krumholz quote: interview with the author.

p. 175 Sewer quote: Jay Westbrook, now a Cleveland City councilman, interview with the author.

p. 175 Parma anecdote: several interviews and press accounts.

p. 175 Nichol quote: interview with the author. Nichol is no longer in office, following Kucinich's defeat in November 1979.

p. 176 U.S. Shoe: several interviews and press accounts. See Cincinnati *Enquirer*, Jan. 4, 1979.

p. 176 Nationwide: interviews and press accounts.

p. 176 Capitol South: interviews and press accounts.

p. 177 Meysenburg quote: interview with the author.

p. 178 L. Schuler company: Columbus *Dispatch*, Sept. 7, 1978.

p. 178 Ford: see *Ohio AFL–CIO News*, Mar. 1978. Also, McGunagle series, *loc. cit.;* also interview with Merrill Goozner of the Ohio Public Interest Campaign (OPIC) and several issues of OPIC's *Public Interest Report*.

p. 179 Stocker: interview with the author.

p. 180 Cuyahoga County increase in residential share of property tax: press release by Cuyahoga County Auditor Vincent Campanella and County Treasurer Francis Gaul, June 22, 1978.

p. 181 Eastgate Mall episide: several interviews and press accounts.

p. 181 Universal Grinding: Medina *Gazette*, Jan. 19, Jan. 30, Mar. 6, 1979.

p. 181 Toledo: interviews.

p. 181 A good summary of Ohio's business incentive laws is "Review of Industrial Development Legislation Enacted by the General Assembly," Ohio Legislative Budget Office Memo No. 71, Mar. 19, 1979.

p. 182 For the history of the Missouri program, I have drawn on research by the National Commission on Neighborhoods, material collected by St. Louis Alderman Bruce Sommer, a critic of the program, and two academic studies: Paul F. Cretin, "Perspective on Missouri's Urban Redevelopment Corporations

Law," School of Administration, University of Missouri at Kansas City, Sept. 1976; and Robert Eugene Olson, "A Critical Analysis of the Missouri Urban Redevelopment Corporations Law . . ." (master's thesis), St. Louis: Washington University School of Architecture, Sept. 1975.

p. 182   "What a wonderful gesture . . ." Olson, *op. cit.,* p. 17.

p. 183   Mansion House: investigation by the author.

p. 184   St. Louis data: provided by Alderman Sommer.

p. 185   Neighborhoods Commission anecdote: author was executive director of the commission.

p. 185   Marziotti quote: from his testimony before the commission.

p. 186   "Nice kicker": *The Wall Street Journal,* June 30, 1978.

p. 186   Birch study: David Birch, "The Job Generation Process," Cambridge, Mass.: M.I.T. Program on Neighborhood and Regional Change," 1979.

p. 186   Other classic studies on tax incentives and job development are the Nader study "Bidding for Business," *loc. cit.;* Roger Vaughan's "State Taxation and Economic Development," Washington, D.C.: Council of State Planning Agencies, Feb. 1979; and Bennett Harrison and Sandra Kanter, "The Political Economy of States' Job-Creation Business Incentives," *AIP Journal,* Oct. 1978.

p. 187   Massachusetts program: Harrison and Kanter, *loc. cit.*

p. 187   Harrison calculation: Harrison and Kanter, "The Great State Robbery," *Working Papers,* spring 1976. p. 63.

p. 187   Pollak: interview with the author.

p. 188   North Carolina: cited in *The Wall Street Journal,* June 30, 1978.

p. 188   Business motivations: see Vaughan, *loc. cit.*

p. 188   Increases in inducements to business: "Bidding for Business."

p. 189   Springfield case and Boston abatement bar: Diane Paul, *The Politics of the Property Tax,* Lexington, Mass.: D.C. Heath & Co., 1975. Also, author's interviews with Oliver Oldman and Raymond Torto.

p. 189ff.   New York abatement bar: interviews with Fischoff, Brandt, Tax Commissioner Mary Mann, and former Commissioner Kaplan.

p. 190   Assessment reductions: *New York City Tax Commission Annual Report,* 1979.

p. 190   Reductions to big landlords: data from New York City Tax Commission public records. See also *The New York Times,* Aug. 24, 1975. Also *Public Employee Press,* June 20, 1975; also, *Public Employee Press,* July 21, 1978. Also, author's interview with Martin Rosenblatt.

p. 191   Kaplan and Fischoff quotes: interviews with the author.

p. 192   Mann quote: interview with the author.

p. 193   Kaplan: interview with the author.

p. 193   Fischoff: interview with the author.

Chapter 11   WHO REALLY PAYS THE PROPERTY TAX?

p. 195   Mieszkowski: "On the Theory of Tax Incidence," *Journal of Political Economy,* June 1967; and "The Property Tax: An Excise Tax or a Profits Tax," *Journal of Public Economics,* Apr. 1972.

p. 195   Henry Aaron: *Who Pays the Property Tax?,* Washington D.C.: The Brookings Institution, 1975.

p. 195   Incidence: An excellent summary of the scholarly debate on incidence is in Diane Paul, *The Politics of the Property Tax,* Lexington, Mass.: D.C. Heath & Co., 1975, pp. 13ff.

p. 195 Mason Gaffney: "The Property Tax Is a Progressive Tax," *NTA Proceedings,* 1971. Also, Gaffney's "An Agenda for Strengthening the Property Tax," in George Peterson, ed., *Property Tax Reform,* Washington, D.C., The Urban Institute, p. 5. The quote is from Joseph Nocera, "Surprise: The Property Tax Could Be Good for You," *Washington Monthly,* May 1978, p. 12.

p. 196 Dick Netzer: "The Incidence of the Property Tax Revisited," *National Tax Journal,* Dec. 1973.

p. 198 Netzer quote: *Ibid.,* p. 531.

PART III—HAVES AND HAVE-NOTS
Introductory Note on Sources

A variety of books are available on the failure of the economy and the economists to perform as directed. One of the best is Robert Lekachman's *Economists at Bay,* New York: McGraw-Hill Book Co., 1976. A good reader on inflation is Gardiner C. Means *et al., The Roots of Inflation,* New York: Burt Franklin & Co., 1975. On who bears the costs of inflation, the work of the Exploratory Project on Economic Alternatives in Washington has documented that inflation falls more heavily on the poor if one looks at the rising cost of "necessities;" however, other economists contend that the typical purchases of the rich have risen in price just as fast. The debate has raged in the useful pages of *Challenge* magazine. On the questions of inflation and the distribution of income and wealth, Lester Thurow of M.I.T. is the best source. For a summary of the conservative view of stagflation, see Jude Wanniski's *The Way the World Works: How Economies Succeed and Fail,* New York: Basic Books, 1978; or Jack Kemp's *An American Renaissance: A Strategy for the 1980's,* New York: Harper & Row, 1979. The Kemp book was a collaboration with leading neoconservative economists and pamphleteers.

On productivity and its relation to taxes, the best source is the body of work by Edward Denison of The Brookings Institution. Surprisingly, there is no basic comparative public finance text that describes in detail tax systems in different countries. The best substitute is the down-to-earth series of pamphlets published by Price Waterhouse for business executives, entitled "Doing Business in ———." The Organization for Economic Cooperation and Development (OECD), based in Paris, is the source of basic comparative statistics on taxation and economic performance.

On the history of tax reform, see *People and Taxes,* published monthly by Ralph Nader's Tax Reform Research Group, and *Tax Notes,* published by Tax Analysts and Advocates. Two literate, scholarly works are George Break & Joseph Pechman, *Federal Tax Reform: The Impossible Dream?,* Washington: The Brookings Institution, 1975; and Stanley Surrey, *Pathways to Tax Reform,* Cambridge: Harvard University Press, 1974.

Chapter 12 The Shattered Keynesian Contract

p. 201 Jeremiah: the quote is from *Jeremiah 8:20,* which is also the title of Carol Hill's excellent novel.

p. 203 Thurow: Interview with the author. See also his "Stagflation and the Distribution of Real Economic Resources," *Data Resources U.S. Review,* Dec. 1978, and his *The Zero-Sum Society,* New York: Basic Books, 1980.

p. 204 Growth of the federal budget: *Facts and Figures of Government Finance,* Washington, D.C.: The Tax Foundation, 1979 ed., p. 34.

p. 205   Growth of per capita income: *Economic Report of the President, 1979,* Washington, D.C.: Government Printing Office, p. 209.

p. 205   Decline of poverty: Henry Aaron, *Politics and the Professors,* Washington: The Brookings Institution, 1978, p. 38.

p. 205   World Commodity prices: IMF, *International Monetary Statistics,* various issues.

p. 206   Import costs: *International Economic Report of the President, 1977,* Washington, D.C.: Government Printing Office, p. 143. I am indebted to Carol Greenwald for this insight.

p. 208   Budget office: *The New York Times,* Feb. 25, 1979.

p. 209   Conservative analysis: For example, see Jack Kemp's *An American Renaissance: A Strategy for the 1980's,* New York: Harper & Row, 1979.

p. 210   Slowdown in real growth: *Per capita* income increased during the seventies only slightly less than during the sixties. But the real income of *wage earners,* as calculated by the Bureau of Labor Statistics, was slightly less in 1979 than in the late sixties.

p. 210   U.S. rank in tax levels: "Public Expenditure Trends," Paris: OECD, 1978, p. 42

p. 211   Rate of growth of tax burden: *ibid.,* pp. 16, 43.

p. 211   Rate of growth of real incomes: *ibid.* p. 53

p. 212   Tax levels on different incomes: ACIR, "Significant Features of Fiscal Federalism," 1978–79 ed. p. 31.

p. 212   Joseph A. Pechman and Benjamin A. Okner, *Who Bears the Tax Burden?,* Washington, D.C.: The Brookings Institution, 1974. A more recent book published by the conservative American Enterprise Institute uses different incidence assumptions to argue that the tax burden is in fact highly graduated. See Edgar K. Browning and William R. Johnson, *The Distribution of the Tax Burden,* Washington, D.C.: AEI, 1979.

p. 212   Social security: See Martha Derthick's excellent history, *Policymaking for Social Security,* Washington, D.C.: The Brookings Institution, 1979.

p. 213   Payroll taxes: "Facts and Figures of Government Finance," 1979, pp. 75, 95. See also Robert M. Brandon, *et al., Tax Politics,* New York: Pantheon Books, 1976, p. 20.

p. 213   Ratio of benefits to wages: Derthick, *op. cit.,* p. 277.

p. 214   U.S. benefits compared with other countries: *Social Security in a Changing World,* U.S. Department of Health, Education and Welfare, Washington, D.C., Sept. 1979, pp. 6, 7. On comparative income maintenance programs, see also OECD: "Public Expenditure on Income Maintenance Programmes," Paris, July, 1976.

p. 215   Edgar Browning: "How Much More Equality Can We Afford?" *The Public Interest,* spring 1976, p. 92.

p. 216   Simon ad: *The Wall Street Journal,* Mar. 22, 1979.

p. 216   Henry Aaron: *Politics and the Professors,* particularly Ch. 1. Statistic is at p. 6.

p. 216   Income distribution: U.S. Bureau of the Census, *Current Population Reports,* Series P-60, various issues.

p. 217   Income inequality: Malcolm Sawyer, "Income Distribution in OECD Countries, *OECD Economic Outlook,* Occasional Studies, July 1976

p. 217   Calculations by Professor Mattsson provided to the author.

p. 217   Comparison of high-income families: Peter Wiles, *Distribution of Income East and West,* Amsterdam (Holland): Elsevier Publishing Co., 1974.

p. 218   Nulty statistic: see Leslie Ellen Nulty, "Understanding the New

Inflation," Washington, D.C.: Exploratory Project for Economic Alternatives, 1977.

p. 219　Data on working wives: source: Lester Thurow, "Lessening Inequality in the Distribution of Income and Wealth," Princeton, N.J.: Institute for Advanced Study, 1975.

p. 219　John Kenneth Galbraith, *The Affluent Society*, London: Penguin Books, 1958.

p. 220　Brie and the revolution: The author was, unfortunately, present.

p. 220　Retailers: *The New York Times*, Jan. 22, 1979.

p. 220　Snug sacks: *Business Week*, Dec. 18, 1978.

p. 220　Furniture: *The Wall Street Journal*, Dec. 12, 1978.

p. 221　Value of housing: Washington *Post*, Nov. 18, 1979.

p. 222　Housing squeeze: Federal Home Loan Bank Board data, Nov. 1979.

Chapter 13　INFLATION AND TAXES

p. 223　Keynes quote: in *The New York Times*, Dec. 2, 1979.

p. 224　Higher inflation effect on low-income taxpayers: Source, U.S. Congress Joint Tax Committee, cited in Donald J. Senese, "Indexing the Inflation Impact of Taxes: The Necessary Reform," Washington, D.C.: Heritage Foundation, 1979.

p. 225　Long quote: widely repeated. Author confirmed it with Long's staff.

p. 225　Increase in real income tax rate: Henry Aaron, *Inflation and the Income Tax*, Washington, D.C.: The Brookings Institution, 1976, p. 21.

p. 225　Okner: interview with the author; also Benjamin Okner, "Distributional Aspects of Tax Reform During the Past Fifteen Years," *National Tax Journal*, Mar. 1979, pp. 11ff.

p. 226　Increasing tax rates: U.S. Treasury compilations provided to the author.

p. 226　Chart: Source, U.S. Treasury Dept. data and author's computations.

p. 227　Brookings Conference: Aaron, *Inflation and the Income Tax, op. cit.*

p. 228　General Motors and AT&T: *ibid.*, p. 92.

p. 228　Aaron quote: *ibid.*, p. 4.

Chapter 14　THE LIGHT TAXES OF THE RICH

p. 230　Mellon quote: Andrew Mellon and Gerrard B. Winston: *Taxation: The People's Business*, New York, 1924; Pechman quote: to the author.

p. 231　Louis B. Mayer: The Louis Mayer story has been widely retold; see Philip Stern's *The Rape of the Taxpayer*, New York: Random House, 1973, or Robert M. Brandon *et al., Tax Politics*, New York: Pantheon Books, 1976.

p. 232　Surrey: see Surrey's *Pathways to Tax Reform*, Cambridge, Mass.: Harvard University Press, 1973.

p. 233　History of tax reform in the seventies: numerous interviews with the author and published accounts.

p. 234　Public reaction to 1976 tax legislation: interviews with staff of the Joint Tax Committee.

p. 236　Number of returns with capital gains: source, Joint Tax Committee.

p. 236　Seven percent of taxpayers paid more than 25 percent: *People and Taxes*, Aug. 1978.

p. 237　Wriston quote: Washington *Post*, July 14, 1975, cited in "Tax Policy and Capital Formation," Washington, D.C.: House Ways and Means Committee, 1977.

p. 238 Walker: interviews with the author and materials published by the council. Also, see Elizabeth Drew's devastating profile "Charlie," in *The New Yorker*, Jan. 9, 1978.

p. 239 Quote: interview with the author.

p. 240 Securities Industry Association study: "Tax Policy, Investment and Economic Growth," Mar. 1978. Chase study: "The Economic Effects of Reducing Capital Gains taxes," Apr. 1978.

p. 240 Feldstein study: Feldstein *et al.*, "The Effects of Taxation on the Selling of Corporate Stock and the Realization of Capital Gains," National Bureau of Economic Research working paper No. 250, Cambridge, Mass., June 1978.

p. 240 Laffer curve: see Jude Wanniski, "Taxes, Revenues and the 'Laffer Curve,'" *The Public Interest*, winter, 1978.

p. 241 "Test" of Laffer's calculations: see Michael Kinsley, "Alms for the Rich," *New Republic*, Aug. 19, 1978.

p. 242 Wanniski: *The Way the World Works: How Economies Fail and Succeed*, New York: Basic Books, 1978.

p. 242 Stein quote: *The Wall Street Journal*, Mar. 19, 1980.

p. 243 Zschau anecdote: interviews and published accounts. His poem was quoted in Walker's literature (American Council for Capital Formation *Newswatch* [monthly] and occasional press kits), and in *Fortune*, July 17, 1978.

p. 244 Bloomfield quote: to the author.

p. 244 Mikva quote: interview with the author.

p. 245 Ullman quote: Rahn to the author. The substance of the anecdote was confirmed by other sources.

p. 245 "Stupendous Steiger": *The Wall Street Journal*, Apr. 26, 1978.

p. 246 Walker quote: in Charls Walker and Mark Bloomfield, "How the Capital Gains Tax Fight Was Won," *The Wharton Magazine*, winter 1979, p. 38.

p. 246 Evolution of the tax bill: author's interviews with members of Congress, lobbyists, and staff; and published accounts.

p. 247 Rahn quote: to the author.

p. 248 Merrill Lynch: "Economic Impact of a Capital Gains Tax Rate Reduction," Aug. 22, 1978.

p. 248 Okner quote: to the author.

p. 249 Walker testimony: Senate Finance Committee hearings on tax legislation, at p. 186.

p. 249 Distribution of tax cuts: calculation by Joint Tax Committee.

Chapter 15 THE CAPITAL FORMATION THEOLOGY

p. 252 Capital investment data: *Economic Report of the President, 1979*, p. 128. Also, Richard Musgrave: "Tax Policy and Capital Formation," *National Tax Journal*, Sept. 1979.

p. 253 Joint Economic Committee quote: "U.S. Long-Term Economic Growth Prospects: Entering a New Era," U.S. Congress Joint Economic Committee staff study, Jan. 25, 1978, p. 55.

p. 254 On international comparisons of productivity and productivity growth, the outstanding authority is Edward Denison. See his *Accounting for United States Economic Growth, 1929–1969*, and Denison and William K. Chung, *How*

Japan's Economy Grew So Fast, both published by The Brookings Institution, Washington, D.C. See also Denison's "Some Factors Influencing Productivity Growth," in *The Future of Productivity*, Washington, D.C.: National Center for Productivity and the Quality of Working Life, 1977.

p. 255   Statistics: Denison, "Some Factors Influencing Productivity Growth," *op. cit.*

p. 256   Table: *Economic Outlook*, Paris: OECD, July 1979, p. 29.

p. 257   Productivity statistics: Testimony by Dr. Rudy Oswald before the Senate Finance Committee, using Bureau of Labor Statistics data, November 18, 1979.

p. 257   Savings rates: *Economic Outlook, op. cit.*, p. 152.

p. 257   Debt statistics, *The Wall Street Journal*, Feb. 26, 1980.

p. 258   Feldstein: Martin Feldstein, "National Saving in the United States," in Eli Shapiro and William L. White, *Capital for Productivity and Jobs*, New York: American Assembly, 1977. Quote at p. 133.

p. 259   Sweden: "Social Security in a Changing World," U.S. Department of Health, Education and Welfare, Washington, D.C.: GPO, Sept. 1979, pp. 64ff.

p. 261   West Germany: see "Doing Business in Germany," Price-Waterhouse information guide, New York, Sept. 1978, pp. 174–5. Also, "The Taxation of New Wealth, Capital Transfers and Capital Gains of Individuals," Paris: OECD, 1979.

p. 262   German taxes on capital investment: see Bernard Snoy, *Taxes on Direct Investment in the European Economic Community: A Legal and Economic Analysis*, New York: Praeger, 1975.

p. 262   German capital formation: *Economic Outlook*, Paris: OECD, July 1979, p. 101.

p. 262   Japan's tax burden on capital: "Tax Policy and Capital Formation," House Ways and Means Committee Task Force on Capital Formation, Apr. 1977, Washington, D.C.: Government Printing Office, p. 42.

p. 262   Japanese tax rates: See "Doing Business in Japan," Price-Waterhouse information guide, New York, Oct. 1975. Also, Denison and Chung, *op. cit.*

p. 263   Britain: Britain permits the entire amount of an investment to be deducted in one year. See, *Effects of Tax Policy on Capital*, New York: Financial Executives' Institute, 1976.

p. 264   Source of corporate capital: Washington *Post*, Nov. 18, 1979, citing data compiled by Salomon Brothers.

p. 265   Half a trillion dollars: author's calculation based on the difference between the inflation in real estate values and the appreciation on other types of capital investment.

p. 265   Corporate taxes: source, *Economic Report of the President, 1979*, several tables. Author's calculations.

p. 266   Ten cents. The Kennedy investment tax credit was 7 percent; it was later raised to 10 percent and made permanent. An excellent capsule history of investment tax politics is provided by Robert McIntyre in *People and Taxes*, May 1978.

p. 266   Rinfret: cited in Robert M. Brandon et al., *Tax Politics*, New York, Pantheon Books, 1976, p. 44.

p. 266   Distribution of investment tax credit: *People and Taxes*, May 1978, p. 8.

p. 267   Okun: in a letter to Sen. Russell Long, Sept. 6, 1978.

p. 267   *New York Times* quote: Apr. 30, 1979.

p. 267   Influence of capital gains cut on stock market. Author's interviews.

p. 268　New small issues: Washington *Post,* Nov. 18, 1979, citing Salomon Brothers data.

p. 269　Revenue impact of 10-5-3: William Miller testimony before Senate Finance Committee, Oct. 22, 1979.

p. 269　Small business politicking: several interviews with lobbyists.

p. 270　Miller on "tax wedge": Miller's testimony before Senate Finance Committee, Oct. 22, 1979.

p. 271　Walker testimony: Senate Finance Committee, Oct. 22, 1979.

PART IV—AS GOES CALIFORNIA
INTRODUCTORY NOTE ON SOURCES

This section of the book is, of course, very recent. Here, I have relied almost exclusively on interviews and, for background, on press accounts.

Chapter 16　THE IMITATIONS

p. 275　Boe: from press accounts. See also his testimony before House Subcommittee on the City, July 25, 1978, p. 20.

p. 276　Chicoine quote: to the author.

p. 276　Headlee quote: author was present.

p. 276　Nevada data: *Tax Revolt Digest,* July, 1979.

p. 277　Uhler on special interests: "A Constitutional Limitation on Taxes," paper presented to the National Tax Association, Sept. 12, 1973.

p. 278　Uhler quote: to the author.

p. 278　National Tax Limitation Committee (NTLC): from NTLC literature.

p. 279　Shaker material and quote: Shaker interview with the author.

p. 280　NTLC amendment: from NTLC materials; see NTLC press release, Jan. 30, 1979.

p. 281　National Taxpayers Union. Interviews with NTU officials and NTU literature.

p. 281　Davidson quote: interviews with the author.

p. 282　Davidson quote: to the author.

p. 283　Muskie quote: from press accounts

p. 283　Herblock cartoon: from Washington *Post,* Feb. 1979.

p. 283　Republican reaction: from press accounts.

p. 283　ABA Study: "Amendment of the Constitution by the Convention Method Under Article V," American Bar Association Special Constitutional Convention Study Committee, Washington, D.C., 1974.

p. 284　Citizens for the Constitution: interviews with O'Neill staff.

p. 284　New Hampshire episode: author was present.

p. 285　Brown and Spanos quotes: author was present.

p. 286　Roberts: author's interviews with New Hampshire legislators.

p. 286　Uhler: *Cal-Tax News,* Nov. 15, 1979.

p. 286　NTLC membership: figure provided by NTLC.

p. 287　Jarvis fund raising: source, Jarvis staff and press accounts.

p. 287　Jarvis telegram: copy obtained by the author.

p. 289　Kemp quote: from his article "Let's Not Become a Nation of Losers," *Industry Week,* Oct. 29, 1979, adapted from his *An American Renaissance: A Strategy for the 1980's,* New York: Harper & Row, 1979.

p. 291　Giaimo: speech to the House, Dec. 5, 1979, and interviews with Giaimo's staff.

p. 292 Michigan ballot initiatives: "Tax Proposals on the 1978 Ballot in Michigan," Senate Fiscal Agency, Lansing, Sept. 1978.

p. 294 Shift onto homeowners: calculated from state tax data. See Robert Kuttner and David Kelston, "The Shifting Property Tax Burden," Conference on Alternative State and Local Policies, Washington, D.C., Dec. 1979.

p. 294 Michigan circuit-breaker relief: ACIR, "Significant Features of Fiscal Federalism, 1978–79 ed.," p. 63.

p. 294 Michigan growth in revenues: Senate Fiscal Agency "Redbook," Lansing, Mich., 1979, p. 15.

p. 294 Property tax drop in relation to income: ACIR, *op. cit.*, p. 61

p. 294 Michigan rank in the rate of growth of spending: Census data, cited in *National Journal*, Nov. 4, 1978, p. 1783.

p. 295 Michigan campaign: author's interviews and press accounts.

p. 295 Queller: to the author.

p. 296 Whittenburg: *Oregon Journal*, July 8, 1978 and Jan. 1, 1979.

p. 297 Oregon's tax system: see Kuttner and Kelston, *loc. cit.*

p. 297 Oregon tax shift: *ibid.*

p. 297 Martin quote: to the author.

p. 297 Polls and Hibbits quote: Hibbits to the author.

p. 297 Martin quote: to the author.

p. 298 Oregon tax relief program: *Your Taxes*, Portland: Oregon Tax Research, May–June 1979.

p. 300 Wilson quote: Miami *Herald*, Sept. 9, 1979.

p. 300 Tax reductions for big properties: Miami *Herald*, Sept. 16, 1969.

p. 300 Dade County tax burden: Miami *Herald*, Sept. 9, 1979.

p. 301 Illinois defeat: from interviews and press accounts.

p. 301 Washington State contributions: from press accounts of official campaign filings.

p. 302 Washington rank in state spending: *National Journal*, Nov. 4, 1978, p. 1783.

p. 302 Growth of taxation in Washington: source, "A Legislator's Guide to Tax and Spending Limits," National Conference of State Legislatures, Denver, Col., 1979, p. 75.

p. 302 Joe Dear: see his paper, coauthored with Russell M. Lidman, "Initiative 62: Washington State's Formula Tax Limit—An Analysis of the Campaign," Nov. 1979, unpublished; also, author's interview with Dear.

p. 303 Regressivity of Washington's tax structure: ACIR, *op. cit.*, p. 32.

p. 303 Dear quote: from his paper, *loc. cit.*

p. 304 Gann initiative: several issues of *Tax Revolt Digest* and *Cal-Tax News*.

p. 304 Shaker quote: to the author.

p. 305 *Tax Revolt Digest* warning: July 1979, p. 2

p. 305 Jarvis quote: to the author.

p. 306 Uhler quote: *Cal-Tax News*, Nov. 15, 1979, p. 2.

Chapter 17 THE COUNTERATTACK

p. 307 Brandon quote: to the author.

p. 309 Boston *Globe* ad: several editions in Oct. and Nov. 1978.

p. 310 Distribution of Massachusetts taxes: ACIR, "Significant Features of Fiscal Federalism," 1978–79 ed., p. 32.

p. 310 History of Fair Share: interviews, and materials provided by Fair Share.

p. 311 Mrs. Tomaszycki quote: interview with the author.

p. 311 Tax delinquencies: Boston *Herald-Examiner,* May 21, 1977.

p. 312 The campaign: author's interviews with both sides.

p. 313 Rapoport: to the author.

p. 313 Harrington: to the author.

p. 314 Torto Report: Raymond Torto, "Estimating the Impact of 100% Valuation and Taxation by Classification in Massachusetts," Massachusetts Mayor's Association, June 14, 1978.

p. 315 Marino letter: author obtained copy; also, interviews with leaders of the campaign.

p. 315 New Bedford: press accounts and interviews.

p. 316 White quote: author was present.

p. 317 Political consultant quote: to the author.

p. 318 Ohio Tax burden: ACIR: *op. cit.,* p. 32.

p. 320 Cleveland abatements: see Ch. 10.

p. 320 Arlook quote: interview with the author.

p. 320 Stocker quote: interview with the author.

p. 321 Oakland report: "Ohio's Economic and Population Trends," quoted in Cleveland *Press,* Apr. 27, 1978.

p. 321 OPIC initiative: provided by OPIC.

p. 322 Betts: interview with the author.

p. 322 Polls: cited in *Saturday Review,* Apr. 28, 1979.

p. 322 Shaffer: *Parma Post,* January 4, 1979.

p. 323 Cato: quoted in *Saturday Review,* Apr. 28, 1979.

p. 323 Trail: interview with the author.

p. 323 Cappelletti: interview with the author.

p. 323 Arlook: interview with the author.

p. 325 *The Wall Street Journal:* Jan. 30, 1980.

p. 325 Fingerhut: author's interview.

p. 325 Proposition 9 savings: Source: William G. Hamm, California Legislative Analyst.

p. 326 No campaign commercials: provided by the No campaign.

p. 326 Friedman: Los Angeles *Times,* Mar. 2, 1980.

p. 326 Polls: Various polls by Mervin Field, L.A. *Times,* Vic Fingerhut.

p. 327 Jarvis quotes: Reiner description: San Francisco *Examiner,* May 29, 1980.

p. 327 Schools: KNXT, Los Angeles, Feb. 2, 1980.

p. 327 Kantor quote: L.A. *Times,* June 5, 1980.

Chapter 18 CONCLUSION

p. 329 Meeting: accounts by several persons present.

p. 329 Fraser quote: to the author. Fraser has used the line on several occasions.

p. 330 ACIR: The first of the "cookbooks" was "The Role of the States in Strengthening the Property Tax," Document A-17, June 1963., Washington, D.C. Government Printing Office.

p. 331 Eizenstat speech: January 4, 1979. Copy provided by Eizenstat.

p. 331 Kenny Young: to the author.

p. 333 Shuman: from his provocative paper "Congress, the President and Urban Policy," presented to the 1978 Annual Meeting of the American Political Science Association, Sept. 3, 1978, New York, N.Y.

p. 334 Harris' battle: the author was a participant while on the staff of the Senate Banking Committee.

p. 335 U.S. government employee data: *Economic Outlook*, Paris: OECD, July, 1979, p. 32–33.

p. 335 German-American housing comparison: from Morton Kondracke's excellent article "The German Challenge to American Conservatives," *New Republic*, Sept. 29, 1979.

p. 336 The definitive book on health industry lobbying against Medicare is Richard Harris, *A Sacred Trust*, New York: New American Library, 1966.

p. 337 An excellent discussion of how the influence of the health industry inflates costs is Paul Starr and Gosta Esping-Anderson, "Passive Intervention," *Working Papers*, July/Aug. 1979.

p. 339 Cost of housing subsidy: author's computation from official figures provided by U.S. Department of Housing and Urban Development.

p. 340 History of housing programs: *Housing Development Reporter* provides a complete legislative history. For a critical analysis, see Leonard Downie, *Mortgage on America*, New York: Praeger, 1974o or Lawrence Friedman, *Government and Slum Housing*, Chicago: Rand McNally, 1968. A superb, irreverent primer on how landowners pyramid tax deductions to the detriment of the property is "People Before Property," Cambridge, Mass.: Urban Planning Aid, 1972.

p. 341 Housing failures: author's work as chief investigator for the U.S. Senate Committee on Banking, Housing and Urban Affairs.

p. 344 Weiner: information supplied by sources familiar with the meeting.

p. 345 Mortgage banking and FHA: see "Housing Management, Foreclosures and Abandonments," hearing before the Senate Banking Committee, July 14, 1975. On mortgage banking, see "Opportunities for Abuse: Private Profits, Public Losses and the Mortgage Banking Industry," Washington, D.C.: Center for Community Change, Oct. 1977.

p. 346 Gale Cincotta and redlining: see Mrs. Cincotta's testimony before the Senate Banking Committee, May 5, 1975. See also Committee hearings on redlining generally, published as "Home Mortgage Disclosure Act," Hearings May 5, 6, 7, and 8, 1975, Washington, D.C.: Government Printing Office.

p. 347 Starr and Esping-Anderson: in *Working Papers*, July/August, 1979, p. 16.

p. 348 Schultze: See his book *The Public Use of Private Interest*, Washington: The Brookings Institution, 1977.

p. 350 Fraser: to the author.

INDEX